J. H. (Joseph Henry) Dubbs

Historic Manual of the reformed Church in the United States

J. H. (Joseph Henry) Dubbs

Historic Manual of the reformed Church in the United States

ISBN/EAN: 9783337162221

Printed in Europe, USA, Canada, Australia, Japan

Cover: Foto ©Lupo / pixelio.de

More available books at **www.hansebooks.com**

HISTORIC MANUAL

OF THE

Reformed Church

IN THE

UNITED STATES.

BY

JOSEPH HENRY DUBBS, D. D

LANCASTER, PA.
1888.

PREFACE.

THE General Synod of the "Reformed Church in the United States" (formerly known as the "German Reformed Church"), at its triennial meeting in Tiffin, Ohio, in 1881, requested the author to prepare a "Manual of the Reformed Church," containing an historical sketch of the denomination, with such additional information as its ministers and members might naturally desire to possess in a compact form. Such a book, it was believed, would be valuable, both as furnishing information to members of the church, and as conveying to others proper views of its origin and history.

In accordance with this request of the General Synod a manuscript was prepared, and when almost completed was presented to the same body, in 1884, at its meeting in Baltimore, Maryland. On this occasion the Synod was pleased to declare its approval of the general plan of the book, and to express a desire for its speedy publication. In consequence of this action the present volume appears; but it is necessary to state, for the purpose of guarding against misapprehension, that it is purely an individual publication, and that the Synod is in no way to be held responsible for its contents.

As the author had not been favored with specific instructions, he was at first inclined to believe that he would perform his task most acceptably by preparing a small volume, for reference only, containing, besides a brief historical sketch the Catechism and Constitution of the

Church, together with statistical information and the forms most generally employed in the transaction of ecclesiastical business. It was found, however, that at least one publication of this order was already in existence, and upon reflection and consultation he was induced to change his plan, and to prepare a volume consisting mainly of historical sketches illustrative of the history of the Reformed Church from the days of the Reformation down to the present time. Some of these sketches were, at the time of their composition, printed in "The Guardian," a monthly magazine of which the author is editor, and though not strictly consecutive they are inserted in deference to the wishes of partial friends.

In its present form the book is intended to serve a double purpose. While it furnishes reading for the family, it also claims to be useful as a book of reference by enabling the reader to trace the career of individual ministers and the chronological order of the meetings of ecclesiastical bodies.

In the preparation of Book I., which relates to the Church in Europe, the writer has by preference consulted works whose authors have been members of the Reformed Church. Among these may be mentioned: "Leben der Väter und Begründer der Reformirten Kirche," 10 vols., Elberfeld, 1857; Max Goebel's "Geschichte des Christlichen Lebens in der rheinisch-westphälischen evangelischen Kirche," 4 vols., Coblenz, 1849; Heppe's "Protestantismus," 2 vols., Marburg, 1852; and Cuno's "Gedächtnissbuch deutscher Fürsten und Fürstinnen reformirten Bekenntnisses," Barmen, 1884. The author has also frequently referred to the writings of Herzog, Ebrard, and Lange, as well as to the more usual German and English authorities on the history of the Reformation.

The materials composing Book II., which more immediately concerns the Reformed Church in the United States, have to a considerable extent been derived from original documents. Besides using his private collection of autograph letters and personally examining the records of many churches, the author has enjoyed the privilege of consulting a volume of manuscripts collected by Dr. H. Harbaugh, and the transcripts of the colonial correspondence with Holland made by Dr. Lewis Mayer. He is also in possession of the original Minute-book of the "Free Synod." Among the volumes which have been frequently consulted are, besides the Minutes of Coetus and Synod, Harbaugh's "Life of Michael Schlatter," "The Fathers of the Reformed Church," 5 vols., begun by Dr. H. Harbaugh and continued by Dr. D. Y. Heisler; Löher's "Deutschen in America," Seidensticker's "Ephrata," Russell's "Creed and Customs," "The Tercentenary Monument," "History of the Westmoreland Classis," Demarest's "History of the Reformed Protestant Dutch Church," Corwin's "Manual of the Reformed Church in America," and the monographs, memorial-sermons, or local histories of the Rev. Drs. L. Mayer, E. Heiner, D. Zacharias, J. W. Nevin, J. Berg, E. V. Gerhart, J. H. A. Bomberger, C. Z. Weiser, T. G. Apple, A. H. Kremer, G. W. Williard, D. Van Horne, the Rev. D. W. Gerhard, the Rev. D. C. Tobias, and others.

Special thanks for assistance rendered in various ways are due to the Rev. Drs. I. H. Reiter, D. Y. Heisler, E. V. Gerhart, H. J. Ruetenik, J. H. Good, T. G. Apple, J. S. Stahr, E. T. Corwin, the Rev. Messrs. C. G. Fisher, H. J. Stern, N. S. Strassburger, L. Praikschatis, T. A. Fenstermaker, Prof. A. W. Drury, and Messrs. H. S. Dotterer and D. McN. Stauffer. The author is also under many obligations to the Rev. G. D. Mathews, D. D., of Quebec, Canada, for information concerning the Reformed Church in foreign countries. The above list by no means indicates the extent of his obligations, but the author assures his friends that their kindness is fully appreciated and will be gratefully remembered. He especially regrets that he has been compelled by the limits of his volume to exclude much valuable information which was kindly contributed by his correspondents.

The Appendix is by no means the least valuable portion of this book. As it is intended for reference only, the author has ventured to employ many abbreviations, which are, however, fully explained. Some doubtful names which appeared in earlier lists have been omitted, but their place has been supplied by others which have hitherto escaped attention, and it will be found that this section contains much new material. A few names of pretenders, who at an early date imposed upon the churches, have been retained, not because they deserve to be remembered, but because they appear in congregational records, and it is sometimes desirable to identify them. There are no doubt many inaccuracies and omissions, and the author will be grateful for such information as may hereafter enable him to complete the record.

The collection of the materials for this volume has been a fascinating employment, and though conscious that his work is in many respects incomplete and unsatisfactory, the author is encouraged in its publication by the fact that his researches in certain periods of the American history of the Reformed Church have not proved unsuccessful. The book is now sent forth, with all its imperfections, in the hope that it may help to awaken the Reformed people to a consciousness of their precious historical inheritance.

CONTENTS.

BOOK FIRST.
THE REFORMED CHURCH IN EUROPE.

CHAPTER I.
Introduction—The Reformed Name—The Origin of the Reformed Church—The Reformation in Zurich—Ulric Zwingli—Zwingli's Relation to Luther—The Death of Zwingli 9

CHAPTER II.
After Zwingli's Death—Leo Juda—Henry Bullinger—The Great Synod of Berne—Beneficiary Education in Zurich—The Anabaptists 25

CHAPTER III.
The Genevan Reformation—John Calvin 35

CHAPTER IV.
The Palatinate—Frederick the Pious—The Heidelberg Catechism—Casper Olevianus—Zacharias Ursinus 48

CHAPTER V.
The Defense of the Catechism—The Second Helvetic Confession—The Diet of Augsburg—Frederick's Later Years—After Frederick's Death 61

CHAPTER VI.
The Martyrs—The Waldenses—Spain and Portugal—The Huguenots—The Massacre of St. Bartholomew 73

CHAPTER VII.
Holland—The First Martyrs—Spanish Tyranny—"The League of the Beggars"—The Revolt of the Netherlands 84

CHAPTER VIII.
England—Cranmer and Bullinger—Peter Martyr—John De Lasky—Martin Bucer. 97

CHAPTER IX.
Scotland—Before the Reformation—The Great Reformer, John Knox—Mary, Queen of Scots—The Conclusion of the Work 106

CHAPTER X.
Women of the Reformed Church: Anna Reinhard—Idelette De Bures—Jeanne D'Albret—Charlotte De Bourbon—Catharine Belgica of Hanau—Gertrude von Bentheim—Louisa Henrietta of Brandenburg 115

CHAPTER XI.
The Great Theologians—Gomarists and Arminians—The Scholastics—Coccejans or Federalists 128

CHAPTER XII.
The Great Revival—Jean De Labadie—Jodocus Van Lodenstein—The Pietists—Philip Jacob Spener—The Great Hymnologists—Joachim Neander—Gerhard Tersteegen 135

CHAPTER XIII.
After the Thirty-Years' War—The Treaty—The People—The Invasion of the Palatinate and its Consequences—Present State of the Reformed Church in Europe . 143

BOOK SECOND.
THE REFORMED CHURCH IN THE UNITED STATES.

CHAPTER I.
The Reformed Church in America—A German Reformed Pioneer—William Penn's Mother—Earliest German Reformed Ministers in America 157

CHAPTER II.
Pennsylvania Pioneers—John Philip Boehm—George Michael Weis—John Henry Goetschius—John Bartholomew Rieger—Peter Henry Dorstius 164

CHAPTER III.
John Peter Miller—Tulpehocken—The Dunkers—Conrad Beissel and "The Ephrata Brethren"—Beissel's Visit to Tulpehocken—Miller as a Monk 175

CHAPTER IV.
"The Congregation of God in the Spirit"—Antes—Bechtel—Brandmiller—Rauch—Lischy 188

CHAPTER V.
Michael Schlatter—Birth and Education—Sent to America by the Synods of Holland—Pastor in Philadelphia—Missionary Journeys—The Organization of the Coetus—The Rival Congregation in Philadelphia—Schlatter's Mission to Europe—The Charity Schools—Later Years—The Character of his Work 196

CHAPTER VI.
The Decline—The Lost Churches—Streaks of Daylight 206

CHAPTER VII.
The Church in Maryland—The Rev. William Otterbein and the "United Ministers". 214

CHAPTER VIII.
The Reformed Church in the Revolution—Baron Steuben—Patriotic Ministers—The Loyalists 225

CHAPTER IX.
After the Revolution—Rev. John William Weber—Educational Movements—Franklin College—The Last Years of the Coetus 239

CHAPTER X.
The Synod of the German Reformed Church—"Die Synodalordnung"—The First Hymn-book—The Conflict of Languages—Correspondence with other Denominations—Condition of the Church—Unionistic Tendencies—Signs of Progress—The Classes 253

CHAPTER XI.
The Theological Seminary—Popular Opposition—"The Free Synod"—Repeated Failures—The Seminary Founded at Carlisle—Removed to York, Pa.—The Seminary and College at Mercersburg 269

CHAPTER XII.
The Synod of Ohio—Western Theological Seminary—Literary Institutions in the East and West 297

CHAPTER XIII.
The Widows' Fund—Home Missions—The German Church in the West—Foreign Missions—Beneficiary Education 313

CHAPTER XIV.
Publications—Parochial and Sunday-schools—Orphan Homes 332

CHAPTER XV.
Doctrine—Discipline—Cultus 346

CHAPTER XVI.
Tercentenary Celebration—General Synod—Conclusion 362

APPENDIX.
Necrology—Meetings of Synods—Comparative Statistics 382

BOOK I.
THE REFORMED CHURCH IN EUROPE.

CHAPTER I.

Introduction—The Reformed Name—The Origin of the Reformed Church—The Reformation in Zurich—Ulric Zwingli—Zwingli's Relation to Luther—The Death of Zwingli.

THE ancient Israelites were solemnly commanded to relate to their children what God had done for His people in the days of old. This duty we believe to be incumbent, not only upon the church at large, but on every community of Christians. The Reformed Church has, for instance, enjoyed many marks of Divine favor, and has experienced many signal deliverances which one generation should relate to the other, "that we may know the hand of the Lord that it is mighty: that we may fear the Lord our God forever."

It is with this impression that we venture to offer our readers an account of the beginnings of the Reformed Church. We have no ambition to write a history, and hope to avoid controversial statements. No doubt, in our brief sketches, we shall be compelled to omit some things which certain learned scholars regard as of great importance; but it will, we trust, be remembered that this book is intended for the general reader, and that we have no room to consider minute particulars.

THE REFORMED NAME.

The Reformed Church is older than its name. Its

early leaders, as is well known, strenuously objected to being called after any individual teacher. In fact, they had no idea that they were about to establish a separate Christian denomination. They did not imagine that their work could in any way break the succession of the ancient church, any more than a thorough scouring could be supposed to destroy the buildings in which they worshiped. As they insisted on the preaching of the pure Gospel they preferred to be called "Evangelical Christians;" but different names were given them in various places. Finally, when a more distinctive name became necessary, some one in France, it is said, called the church "Reformed," and this name was generally adopted. It was felt to be appropriate, for the body of Christians which was called by this name claimed to be the old Catholic church *reformed*. For this reason, some of its strictest members, until a comparatively recent period, objected to the use of a capital letter in writing the name of the church. They wished to be known as the "reformed church," or more comprehensively as "the church reformed according to God's word"—and objected to any other title as savoring of sectarianism. "On the continent of Europe," says Dr. Mayer, "Reformed is the distinctive title of those Protestant communities which are not Lutheran, exclusive of Socinians and Anabaptists." These communities, as will be seen hereafter, differed from the beginning in minor matters, but held in a general way to the same religious system, and were evidently pervaded by a common life. In a certain sense the English and Scotch reformers may be regarded as belonging to the Reformed type; but, as Dr. Hagenbach says, "whoever is familiar with the peculiarities of the churches which they founded will find it natural that their names should not prominently appear" in a sketch of the history of the Reformed church.

THE ORIGIN OF THE REFORMED CHURCH.

In its history the Reformed church has sometimes been supposed to bear a certain analogy to the river Rhine, on whose banks so many of its children have made their home. Like that beautiful river it has its source among the mountains of Switzerland, derives its tributaries from France and Germany, and flows on to fertilize the plains of Holland. As has already been indicated, the Reformed Church does not derive its origin from a single individual, but there are in its history certain plainly marked stages of development, which enable us to form a correct idea of its growth and advancement. These must be studied separately, as the geographer would separately examine three streams which unite to form a mighty river. Zurich, Geneva, and the Palatinate were the places where these developments occurred, and from them the latter may respectively be regarded as taking their names. Besides these great movements, it must not be forgotten that the Reformed Church gained strength, in Switzerland, by absorbing the Waldenses, an ancient mediæval body of Christians, the majority of whom, as will be seen hereafter, formally joined the Reformed church, though a minority has kept up its organization to the present day. The Polish branch of the Hussites, as we are informed by Bishop E. De Schweinitz, in his "Moravian Manual" was, in 1627, also "grafted upon the Reformed church of Poland, and in the next decade grew to be one with it."

THE REFORMATION IN ZURICH.

The Swiss Reformation was the result of a process whose beginnings may be discovered far back in the Middle Ages. The movement, like that of an Alpine glacier, was at first almost imperceptible, but it gradually became more rapid, until its progress could no longer be restrained.

Switzerland, at the beginning of the sixteenth century, it will be remembered, consisted of thirteen cantons, which were, in fact, independent states, though united by a league for common defence. Since the beginning of the thirteenth century they had been, in part, at least, in possession of civil liberty, and these Swiss republics were naturally a thorn in the side of the kings of Europe. For nearly two hundred years the Swiss were involved in almost constant conflicts with the house of Austria; but their mountains constituted an impregnable fortress, and all the power of the empire was unable to dislodge them. The wants of the people were few. On their high Alpine pastures flocks could safely feed, and the numerous lakes furnished an abundance of fish. Switzerland might be blockaded, but the people cared but little for communication with other countries, and every attempt to penetrate their valleys with hostile armies was sure to prove a failure. The Swiss were a warlike people, and if their battle-axes and cross-bows failed, they could roll down rocks on the head of the invader.

It was but natural that Switzerland should become a place of refuge for the oppressed and persecuted. Not only political offenders, but those who had exposed themselves to ecclesiastical censures, were glad to escape to the valleys of the Alps. The church of Rome, it is true, appeared to be nowhere more firmly established than in Switzerland; but it is also true that, on account of the political condition of the country, the church rarely attempted to press her authority to the utmost extent. Except in the cities, the poverty of the people was regarded as an excuse for simplicity of worship, and there were many priests who sympathized with the sufferings of the refugees, if they did not venture to accept their doctrine.

It is not to be supposed that the kings and nobles of surrounding nations could favorably regard a country in which their authority was so thoroughly defied. The very existence of the Swiss league was a constant menace to royalty, and the rulers hated it with perfect hatred. Indeed, it is not too much to say, that the influence of the nobles had caused a wide-spread dislike for the Swiss, even among the lower classes: and this feeling will in part account for the evident unwillingness of the Germans to coöperate with the Swiss at the beginning of the Reformation. Without this prejudice, we feel assured, the doctrinal differences might have been more easily reconciled.

ZWINGLI.

Ulric Zwingli, the most prominent of the Swiss Reformers, was born in the Alpine village of Wildhaus on the first of January, 1484. His father was an "Amman," or district judge, and the family, though unpretentious, was comparatively wealthy and eminently respectable. Each of his parents had a brother who was eminent in the church, and they naturally desired that at least one of their children should choose the same vocation,

Ulric was the youngest of ten children. At an early age it became evident that he was gifted with extraordinary talents. When stories of Swiss heroism were related in his father's house, they fell like sparks upon his spirit and left it glowing with patriotic enthusiasm. Even more profound was the impression made upon his mind by the magnificent scenery that surrounded his birthplace. At an early age he accompanied his brothers to the Alpine pastures, where the grandeur of the mountains on which he gazed kindled his imagination and awakened his devotion. "I have often thought in my simplicity," wrote his friend, Oswald Myconius, at a later period, "that on these heights, so near to heaven, he (Zwingli) assumed something heavenly and divine. When the thunder rolls along the mountains and the deep abysses are filled with its reverberations, we seem to hear anew the voice of God, saying, 'I am the Almighty God, walk in my presence with reverence and fear.' When with the dawn of morning the glaciers glow with rosy light, so that an ocean of fire rolls over the mountain tops, the Lord of hosts appears to stand upon the high places of the earth; as though the hem of His garment glorified the mountains, while we hear the words that were spoken to the prophet Isaiah: 'Holy, holy, holy, Lord God of Sabaoth! All the earth is full of Thy glory!'"

When Ulric had reached his ninth year, his father resolved to place him in the care of his brother, Bartholomew, who was dean of the church of Wesen. It seems to have been understood that the boy should study for the priesthood, and for this purpose educational advantages were abundantly provided. He was a natural musician and learned to play all the instruments which were then known. Under the care of the celebrated scholar Lupulus he learned to speak Latin, to use his own expression, better than he spoke his mother tongue. The study of Greek he pursued in later years with great enthusiasm, not only because it introduced him to the grandest literature in the world, but especially as a means of becoming familiar with the sacred Scriptures. After taking a full course at the University of Vienna, Zwingli became a teacher in the Latin school of Basel, and at the same time attended lectures in the University. Here there was a celebrated teacher named Thomas Wyttenbach, who gathered around him a company of young men whom he delighted to lead away from the arid wastes of scholasticism to the green pastures of the Word of God. In one of his lectures he said: "The time is at hand when the ancient faith shall be restored according to the Word of God. Indulgences are a Roman delusion, and the death of Christ is the only ransom for our sins." Among his students, besides Zwingli, were Leo Juda, Capito, and others, who subsequently took a prominent part in the Reformation.

Having been ordained to the priesthood, Zwingli, in 1506, assumed charge of the church at Glarus, in which relation he continued until 1516. During this period he was twice required to accompany the Swiss troops on expeditions to Italy. There he received impressions which greatly influenced his subsequent career. In those days the Swiss cantons furnished armies of mercenaries, which fought for the side paying the highest wages. By visiting distant countries and becoming familiar with rapine and slaughter, these soldiers acquired vices of which they never would have even heard in their native valleys. Zwingli became convinced that the mercenary system was the curse of Switzerland and determined to contend against it with all his might. Much of the opposition which he subsequently endured was owing to the enmity of the mercenaries who through his influence had been deprived of their employment, and this was also indirectly the cause of his early death.

In Italy the attention of Zwingli was directed to the corruption of the papal court, and he resolved to pray and labor for its reformation. He also lost confidence in the Roman mass by discovering in an ancient liturgy that in former times both bread and wine were distributed to communicants, and not bread alone, as had become usual in the church. Strangely enough the significance of the doctrine seems not at this time to have occupied his attention. Neither he nor any of his Swiss friends had ever believed in the Roman doctrine of Transubstantiation.[1]

Zwingli always acknowledged Erasmus as his great master and teacher, and it was from the time of reading one of the books of the latter that he dated his conversion.

One of the ablest men in Switzerland at this time was Cardinal Matthias Schinner. He had been a poor shepherd boy who with no aid but genius, had risen to be a prince of the church and entertained hopes of being elected to the papal chair. This man observed the youthful priest of Glarus, and determined to gain his support by

---
[1] Max Goebel's "Geschichte des Christlichen Lebens," I., p. 277.

2

securing for him a pension from the Pope, "so that he might purchase books to pursue his studies." The cardinal was, however, mistaken in his man if he supposed that he could in this way purchase his silence. At this time Zwingli wrote: "I will be true towards God and man in all the relations of life. Hypocrisy and lying are worse than stealing. It is only through truth that man can come to resemble his Maker."

In 1516 Zwingli became parish priest of the convent of Einsiedlen, and there began to preach the doctrines of the Reformation. This convent was then, as it is now, the centre of Romanism in Switzerland. Thousands of Pilgrims came thither to worship an image which was supposed to be miraculous and to receive the benefit of certain papal indulgences. These pilgrims Zwingli addressed with extraordinary eloquence, exhorting them to put their trust in Christ alone and not in the saints whose relics were preserved in the convent. The effect of these discourses was wonderful. Hundreds, perhaps thousands, accepted the truth and declared it wherever they went. Soon afterwards the monks began to leave their cloister, and for some time it was entirely deserted.

When Zwingli was called in 1518, to be pastor of the Cathedral Church of Zurich, it was with the full understanding that he would labor to advance the cause of the Reformation. He entered upon the duties of his pastorate on the first of January, 1519; this, however, was not the beginning of his work, but rather its full recognition. From this time forward his labors were unremitting.

When the monk Samson came to sell indulgences, as Tetzel had done in Germany, it was his eloquence that drove him back beyond the mountains. Except during a season when he suffered from a serious illness, he preached almost every day, wrote many volumes, and was forced by his position to take a profound interest in affairs of state. He also kept up an extensive correspondence, labored to perfect the organization of the churches, and was the first to convene Protestant synods. Under such circumstances it was hardly to be expected that he should elaborate a theological system; and indeed he owed his prominence in the Church more to the extraordinary eloquence with which he popularized evangelical doctrine than to his profundity as a theologian. His view of the Lord's Supper was perhaps incomplete, and it was left for Calvin to formulate the faith of the Reformed Church concerning that great mystery. This fact is, however, no excuse for the manner in which he was treated at the conference at Marburg, in 1529, where Luther refused to take his hand in Christian fellowship, though he pleaded with tears. Certain it is, that in that conference Zwingli appeared to no disadvantage. He at least kept his temper, which is more than can be said of his great antagonist.

ZWINGLI'S RELATION TO LUTHER.

When Luther had been excommunicated by the Pope, the enemies of Zwingli insisted that he was included in the same condemnation as a friend and admirer of Luther.

Then he published a declaration of which the following is an extract.

"I began to preach the Gospel of Christ," said Zwingli, "in the year 1516, before any one in this region had heard the name of Luther. Who called me a Lutheran then? When Luther's book on the Lord's Prayer appeared, concerning which prayer I had recently preached, many good people finding in it the same thoughts as mine, could hardly be convinced that I was not the author of the book, supposing that I was too fearful to own my work, and had therefore put the name 'Luther' on the title-page. Who could at that time have called me a Lutheran? How does it happen that the cardinals and legates, who at that time dwelt in the city of Zurich, did not call me a Lutheran until after they had declared Luther a heretic, though of course they could not really make him one? Then they cried out that I too was a Lutheran, though I did not know Luther's name for two years after I had made the word of God my only guide. It is only a Papist trick to give me and others such names. If they say, 'you must be a Lutheran: you preach as Luther writes,' this is my answer: I preach as Paul writes—why do you not call me a 'Paulist?' I preach the Gospel of Christ—why do you not rather call me 'Christian?' In my opinion Luther is a noble champion of the Lord, who searches the Scriptures with a degree of earnestness that has not been equalled in a thousand years. What care I that the Papists call both of us heretics? With such an earnest, manly spirit as that of Luther, no one has ever attacked the papacy during all the years of its existence. But whose work is it? Is it God's work or Luther's? Ask Luther himself and he will surely tell you, 'It is the work of God' . . . Therefore, dear Christians, do not suffer the name of Christ to be exchanged for that of Luther; for Luther has not died for us, though he teaches us to know Him from whom our whole salvation flows. If Luther preaches Christ he does precisely what I do; though, thank God! an innumerable multitude is led through him to Christ—far more than through me and others, to whom God gives a greater or smaller measure of success, as pleases Him. I will bear no other name than that of my captain, Jesus Christ, whose soldier I am. No man can regard Luther more highly than I do. Nevertheless, I testify before God and man, that in all my life, I have never written a line to him nor he to me, nor have I caused it to be done. I declined to do it, not because I was afraid of anybody, but rather because I desired to show all men the uniformity of the working of the Spirit—how Luther and I dwell so far apart and yet are so harmonious; but I do not pretend to be his equal, for every man must do that to which God has called him."

The fact is that Zwingli advanced through the study of the classic authors to the contemplation of the Scriptures, while Luther dwelt with especial pleasure on the writings of the pious mystics of the Middle Ages. In this way they reached the same point from opposite directions, without being aware of each other's existence, and almost simultaneously protested against the corruptions of Rome.

According to Zwingli's own statement his chief conflict was not with Luther, but with the Anabaptists. It is almost impossible for us to form a proper conception of the conduct of these fanatical extremists, and it is not surprising that several of them should have rendered themselves amenable to the Swiss laws against treason; but there is plenty of evidence that Zwingli did not approve the violent means employed by the government. He always declared that he would attack them with no weapons, but the word of God.[1]

THE DEATH OF ZWINGLI.

Zwingli was cut down in the prime of his manhood, and much of his work was left unfinished. In 1531, war broke out between the Catholic and Protestant cantons of Switzerland, and an army of eight thousand Catholics crossed the frontier of Zurich. It was a complete surprise, and the army of defence numbered not more than nineteen hundred men. At the command of the Great Council of Zurich, Zwingli accompanied the army as a chaplain. It is not true that he incited the war, and there is abundant proof that he fully appreciated the almost hopeless nature of the conflict; but religion and patriotism alike urged him to accompany his people to encourage and comfort those who were about to die for their country and their faith.

---
[1] Christoffel's "Life of Zwingli," p. 251.

THE DEATH OF ZWINGLI.

The Zurichers fought bravely at Cappel, on the 11th of October, 1531, but they were overpowered and Zwingli was mortally wounded. His last words were: "What does it matter? They may kill the body but they cannot kill the soul!"

After the battle Zwingli was found by the enemy lying on the field, but was not at first recognized. He was still conscious but unable to speak. To a question whether he desired the services of a priest he replied by a negative gesture. Then a soldier recognized him and an officer killed him with his sword. Next day his body was mutilated under the most revolting circumstances, and then burned to ashes. It was a shameful act of brutality on the part of his enemies; but to him it did not matter, for they could not " kill the soul."

To a noble soul like that of Zwingli the accident of death was a small thing. "No Christian is afraid of death; he can only dread dying." He trusts his Master's word, and knows that he is about to receive a crown of everlasting glory.

The dying words of Zwingli have been wonderfully illustrated in the history of the great religious movement in which he was so prominently engaged. Its enemies have always been threatening its destruction. At an early period its chosen emblem was "the burning bush," because, though constantly enveloped by the flames of persecution, it was never consumed. Almost everywhere it has been attacked with fire and sword, yet it is still green and flourishing. Even in this country it has suffered persecutions which were not less dangerous because they were more refined, but it still bears its full measure of flowers and fruit.

Sometimes, in seasons of persecution, the best men are in danger of yielding to despair. Yet the peril is in appearance only. The enemies of the truth can never destroy God's people. "They may kill the body, but they cannot kill the soul."

The death of the leader of the Swiss Reformation was, of course, a great catastrophe, and for a time it seemed as though the work must fail.

It did not, however, depend upon a single man, and there was a multitude of laborers ready to carry on the work. The most eminent of these were, in Zurich, Henry Bullinger and Leo Juda; in Basel, John Œcolampadius and Oswald Myconius; in Berne, Berthold Haller; in Strasburg and Southern Germany, Wolfgang Capito and Martin Bucer. Concerning some of these eminent men and their coadjutors we shall have more to say hereafter.

CHAPTER II.

After Zwingli's Death—Leo Juda—Henry Bullinger—The Great Synod of Berne—Beneficiary Education—The Anabaptists.

IN the library of the Theological Seminary at Lancaster there is a large German Bible which was printed by Christoffel Froschauer of Zurich, 1531. It contains all the canonical books, as well as the Apocrypha, and is an excellent specimen of early printing. In it there are many illustrations, colored by hand, which give us an excellent idea of the primitive condition of art in the earlier part of the sixteenth century. Some of these are quaint and almost amusing. Thus, for instance, the serpent in the temptation is represented as having the head of a man and wearing a golden crown. Jacob is depicted as sleeping on the shore of a lake, with a castle near at hand, and an Alpine scene in the distance. Pharaoh wears a crown ornamented by the three lilies of France.

This Bible, it will be observed, was published in the very year of Zwingli's death; but it was not the earliest German Bible that had been printed at Zurich. The New Testament had issued from Froschauer's press in 1524; the first part of the Old Testament in 1525, and the concluding portion in 1529. In the latter year an edition of the entire Scriptures was also printed in Latin characters. Luther, it will be remembered, had published his translation of the New Testament as early as 1522, but his first complete German Bible was printed by Hans Lufft, in Wittenberg, in 1534. Indeed, no less than six editions of the Swiss version had been published before the appearance of Luther's Bible; but they had one defect which prevented their general use. The translators had rendered the Scriptures as nearly as possible into the language of the common people, without exactly adopting any one of the Swiss dialects; while Luther had carefully chosen the refined language of the upper classes, thus producing a work that was both permanent and beautiful. The Swiss version was naturally almost confined to Switzerland and Southern Germany, while that of Luther was used everywhere else, and is still regarded as one of the noblest productions of German literature.

Leo Juda (born 1482—died 1542) was the chief of the Swiss translators. His curious name has induced some writers to suppose him to have been a convert from Judaism, but this is incorrect. He himself supposed that he must be descended from some remote ancestor who had been a convert, but the fact could not be established. Like Bullinger, he was the son of a priest, who had privately married, notwithstanding the prohibition of the Roman church. At the university he formed an intimate friendship with Zwingli, and subsequently became his assistant in Zurich. After Zwingli's death Leo was offered his position, but he declined it, feeling that he was not suited for an office of such great responsibility. He was a great Biblical scholar, and delighted in preaching; but it was necessary that the head of the church of Zurich should be more than an ordinary preacher or pastor. In a certain sense he must have "the care of all the churches." Leo Juda knew that he was physically too weak for such a position, and preferred to remain an assistant. He was, however, unwearied in his labors, not only translating the Scriptures, but composing hymns and catechisms, and assisting in the preparation of the Swiss confessions of faith. His last great work was a translation of the Scriptures from Hebrew and Greek into Latin, which was regarded by theologians as an achievement of the very highest order.

After Leo Juda had declined the position of chief pastor, or "antistes," of the church of Zurich, it was offered to Œcolampadius, who declined it, prefering to remain in Basel. Then a call was extended to Bullinger, who accepted it, and was afterwards for many years regarded as the chief religious leader of the German Reformed Church.

Henry Bullinger (1504–1575) was the best man who could possibly have been chosen, for this prominent position, and we may even venture to affirm that he was the chief instrument in the preservation and completion of Zwingli's work. He came to Zurich at a time of great depression. "The ship," says Pestalozzi, "had lost its main-mast, and appeared about to go down." There was danger everywhere. In consequence of the victory of

Cappel the Catholic party had become greatly encouraged, and in outlying districts the Protestants were bitterly persecuted. At this time King Ferdinand wrote to his his brother, the emperor, Charles V.: " We have won the first of the battles of faith. Remember that you are the head of Christendom, and will never have a better opportunity of covering yourself with glory. The German sects will be lost when they cease to be sustained by heretic Switzerland." The German Protestants, however, failed to appreciate this community of interest, and continued to denounce the Swiss in the most unsparing terms. Besides doctrinal differences, the princes and nobility blamed them with sympathizing with the peasants in their unfortunate rebellion, which was known as the " Peasants' War." No wonder that Bullinger said: " Even if we were wrong they ought not treat us so." Worst of all, Switzerland was full of Anabaptists, who claimed to be divinely inspired, and who, therefore, pretended to be superior to the laws of the Church and State.

In these dark and gloomy days Bullinger was recognized as the father of all who were desolate and depressed. His house was always open, and at his table there were plenty of hungry guests. He adopted Zwingli's children, and provided for his widow as long as she lived. Fortunately he possessed some private property which enabled him to meet the expenses which were thus incurred. His eloquent sermons had an extraordinary effect, and the Church was soon so thoroughly reorganized that Ambrosius Blaarer, of Constance, wrote to him : "All hail! Under the heavy cross the church of Zurich has grown stronger, and the strength of the Lord has become perfected in your weakness."

THE GREAT SYNOD OF BERNE.

The canton of Berne had long halted between two opinions, but had finally, in 1528, decided in favor of the Reformation. On the 9th of January, 1532, a synod of the clergy of the canton, 230 in number, was held at Berne, and adopted a series of decrees which were of great importance in the future development of the Church. Though the synod was primarily intended for the canton of Berne, there were also delegates who came from a distance, and it is generally regarded as the first of the great Reformed Synods. On this occasion Capito, of Strasburg, secured the adoption of the famous article entitled, "*Christ is the substance of all doctrine;*" in which it is said that "Christ is the sum of the teaching of the Scriptures, and that whatever is contrary hereto is also adverse to our salvation, and that even God Himself must be held forth as He is in Christ." This utterance had a great effect on the subsequent teachings of the Church, and its influence may be plainly traced in the Heidelberg Catechism.

The article concerning the Lord's Supper declares that "the breaking of bread is not an empty ceremony, but a sacrament which conveys to the believer the body and blood of Christ, by the Holy Ghost, as really as bread taken into the mouth feeds the perishable body."

The results of the Synod of Berne were very encouraging to the Reformed churches, and did much to promote their organic unity.

BENEFICIARY EDUCATION.

Before the Reformation it was hardly necessary to provide means for the education of young men for the service of the church. The priesthood offered wealth, comfort and a brilliant career, and there was no lack of applicants for its dignities. Now all this was changed. The Reformed Church could offer its ministers nothing but poverty and persecution, and it was soon observed that wealthy parents were disinclined to submit their children to such privations. Even before the death of Zwingli a small fund had been gathered for the support of worthy young men who desired to devote themselves to the work of the Gospel ministry; but it was Bullinger who made the work a great success. Through his influence a deserted convent was set apart for the work, and there upwards of twenty students gratuitously received their food and sometimes even their clothing. Some of the most promising students were allowed to study at foreign universities, and received a suitable stipend. Every year several young ministers were sent to preach the Gospel in other countries, and in this way the Church simultaneously inaugurated Beneficiary Education and the work of Missions.

We shall have to speak hereafter of Bullinger's restless activity, his valuable service in the preparation of the Helvetic Confessions, and his influence in promoting the Reformation in foreign countries, particularly in England. He has, however, been accused of having treated the Anabaptists with extraordinary rigor. Let us see what these people were like, according to the testimony of their cotemporaries.

THE ANABAPTISTS.

The sects which were known by this general title sprang up almost simultaneously in Germany and Switzerland, at the beginning of the Reformation. It is difficult to describe them in general terms, and it must not be forgotten that though some of their least objectionable peculiarities are found in certain more modern denominations, the latter have no direct historical connection with them.

Thomas Münzer (1490-1525) was the most prominent leader of the early Anabaptists. He was a man of learning, and for a time was an earnest adherent of Luther. Having joined the fanatical sect known as the "Zwickau Prophets," he came to regard himself as divinely inspired to preach a dispensation of the Spirit, and suceeeded in gaining many adherents. He was instrumental in introducing the Anabaptist movement into Switzerland, where under his influence hundreds of people began to "see visions and dream dreams." Münzer subsequently became involved in the "Peasant War," and was finally executed as a rebel.

The Anabaptists soon divided among themselves; and

Schwenkfeld, the contemporary of the Reformers, when he lived in Suabia, counted no less than forty-four different sects. Bullinger knew of thirteen sects of Anabaptists, and found it difficult to say what doctrines they held in common. They all agreed in rejecting infant baptism, but this was not regarded as their chief peculiarity. Most of them believed that present "inspirations of the Spirit" are to be ranked higher than the written word of God. According to Bullinger: "They insisted that the true Church must be formed by the withdrawal of the righteous from all existing church organizations; they had little faith in the Old Testament, and denied justification by faith; they approved of community of goods, though this was not obligatory, and they absolutely refused to appear before courts of justice or swear to a judicial oath." Elsewhere the same writer says: "Some of the Anabaptists are very good people, and really live separate from the world. But, like a new order of monks, they make rules about clothing, what garments people shall wear, and of what cut, and how long their coats must be. They reject all ornaments, and call those heathen who wear them. They also prescribe rules about eating, drinking, sleeping, standing, and walking. They often sigh deeply, and when they see any one laughing they cry, 'Woe unto you, that laugh now!' In some places they oppose the bearing of arms and weapons."

If all the Anabaptists had been of the character which is here described, there would probably have been but little political trouble; but there was unfortunately a warlike as well as a peaceful party. The warlike faction insisted that all existing governments must be subverted so as to make room for the celestial kingdom that was about to be established. In 1533 they proclaimed that the time for the establishment of the millennium had come and it seemed likely that they would attempt to set it up in Switzerland. The leaders were, however, expelled from the country, and this is said to have been done at Bullinger's suggestion. No doubt some innocent people had to suffer, and Bullinger has been harshly blamed for being concerned in the matter.

After they had been driven out of Switzerland the Anabaptists gathered at Strasburg, and insisted on making it "the celestial Jerusalem." Here, too, they were repulsed. Then they went to Münster, in Westphalia, where they seized the civic government, and declared their prophet, John of Leyden, "king of Zion and of the whole world." The new king was publicly crowned, and established a brilliant court, "after the example of David and Solomon." Soon afterwards he had a "revelation" which commanded him to introduce polygamy, and he married sixteen wives, though only one of these was recognized as "queen of Zion." It was announced "that baptism was regeneration, and that the regenerate could commit no sin." This opened the door to every kind of excess, and for nearly a year there was a reign of terror. Those who opposed the will of the king were barbarously executed. At last, on the 25th of June,

1535, the city of Münster was taken by an army in the service of the Bishops of Cologne and Paderborn, and the retribution was dreadful. The victors behaved more like cannibals than like civilized human beings, not to say Christians. Not only were the "king" and his immediate followers condemned to a barbarous death, but the whole conquest was little better than a massacre. From this time forth the Anabaptists were everywhere persecuted as rebellious fanatics, though many of them were the most peaceful of men. As some one has said: "The ghost of John of Leyden could not be laid."

"What a blessing," says Pestalozzi, "it was for the Reformed Church that all this evil did not happen in Switzerland. How easy it would otherwise have been to ascribe its cause to the republicanism of the Swiss government, or to the teachings of Zwingli. That it did not happen there we owe, in so far as human wisdom could accomplish anything, to the prudence and unceasing vigilance of Bullinger."

According to the historian Goebel, the whole Reformed Church of Switzerland was at this period seriously tainted with Anabaptism, and its future appeared exceedingly gloomy. It was surrounded by enemies who constantly threatened its destruction. At this time, however, a young man appeared on the scene, who is recognized as the greatest theologian of his age, and who was instrumental in transmitting the Reformed faith to distant nations. Who he was will become evident when in our next chapter we consider *The Genevan Reformation.*

CHAPTER III.

The Genevan Reformation—John Calvin.

IN the south-western corner of Switzerland, where the Rhone emerges from Lake Leman, stands the ancient city of Geneva. Situated on both sides of the river, and within sight of the snow-clad summit of Mont Blanc, its location is unsurpassed in Europe. Here the peculiar civilization of France was brought into close contact with that of Germany; and Geneva was therefore especially well suited to be the center of a religious movement embracing many nations. It is here that we must look for the second great historical source of the Reformed church.

To understand the Genevan reformation it must be remembered that its earliest leaders were exiles from France. At the beginning of the sixteenth century the French had been regarded as far less under the influence of Rome than the people of Germany. Classical studies were prosecuted with great enthusiasm, and as the priests were generally opposed to secular learning, they were unsparingly lashed by all the authors in the land. The King's sister, Margaret of Navarre, was herself a brilliant authoress, and took part in this general attack. Though she never formally accepted Protestantism, her works prove that she believed many of its teachings; and the early French reformers found in her a constant and faith ful friend. Many of the leading French ecclesiastics felt the necessity of a reformation, and sought in their own way to bring it about. Briconnet, Bishop of Meaux, gathered around him such men as Farel, Lefevre, and other enthusiastic evangelical teachers, and sought to reform his diocese. In this way the cause of the Reformation and of the revival of letters were closely allied, and the foremost people of France sympathized with the Protestant movement. Even to this day many of the leading French families are Protestant, though the vast majority of the population belongs to the Roman Catholic Church.

Protestantism appeared to be working it's way through all ranks of society when suddenly it received a blow from an unexpected quarter. In 1521 the Sorbonne, the chief theological school of France, declared Luther a heretic, and the government consequently forbade Protestant worship under the severest penalties. Then there came a time of persecution. Farel and most of the other reformers, fled for their lives, and some of them found a refuge in Geneva. The few who remained in France met in secret places, and subsequently organized congregations under the guise of literary societies, calling them by such fanciful titles as the Rose, the Lily, the Vine, or the Olive.

John Calvin was born July 10, 1509, at Noyon, near Paris. His mother, whose maiden name was Francke (or Le Franc), is said to have been of German descent. His parents were in comfortable circumstances, and gave him an excellent education. Having studied successively at Paris and Bourges, he acquired a brilliant reputation. It was observed that he had no fondness for poetry, but his fellow students declared him to be "all Logic and Latin." Sometimes, in the absence of one of the professors, he was requested to teach his class, and every one wondered at his extraordinary ability.

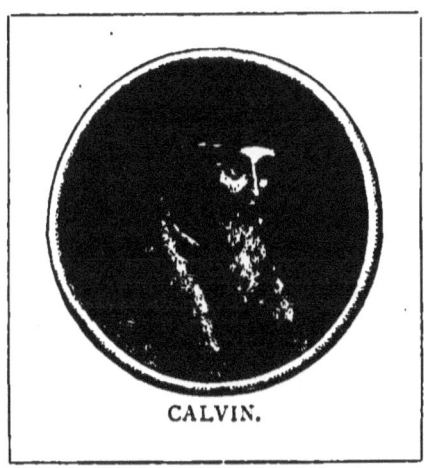

CALVIN.

At the request of his parents Calvin studied law, and soon became familiar with the principles of that science. He was, however, especially attracted to the study of theology, and it was afterwards said that he had studied law by day and theology at night. His legal studies had an immense effect in shaping his mind, and in subsequent years he proved himself a statesman of the highest order.

It was in the midst of a period of the deepest gloom that the infant church was electrified by the news that Calvin had been converted to the truth. He had been under the instruction of a celebrated German teacher, Melchior Wolmar, who is believed to have been the first to teach him not only to read but to understand the word of God; but he always spoke of his conversion as sudden and wonderful, though he never related its particulars.

It could not be otherwise than that such a man should immediately become a leader in the cause which he had espoused. At Paris and elsewhere he secretly gathered the scattered believers and preached the word of God. Then he published a learned commentary on some of the writings of the heathen philosopher Seneca, which was intended to influence the king to treat the Protestants less harshly. Having published one of his sermons he was compelled to flee, and found a temporary refuge at the court of Margaret of Navarre. He now began to write against the Anabaptists, in the hope of preventing the Reformation from running into fanatical extremes.

For about a year Calvin lived in retirement in Normandy, under the assumed name of Charles d'Espeville. During this period he is said to have preached to a select company, in a cave which was long afterwards called "the cave of Calvin." In this season of retirement he collected the materials for his great work "The Institutes of the Christian Religion."

The latter work was first published anonymously in 1535; but the first edition bearing Calvin's name was printed in Basel in 1536. It is recognized even by its enemies as the greatest literary achievement of the sixteenth century. No other Reformer produced anything that was so complete in the systematic exposition of Christian doctrine. Strangely too, though the author was hardly twenty-five years old at the time of its composition, he never afterwards altered a single one of his doctrinal positions. He added to it in every subsequent edition, but at the very beginning his system was complete, and he never afterwards found occasion to change it.

Calvin's "Institutes" are a development of the ruling principle of his thinking and of his life, which was, as he expressed it, the utter destruction of all human glory that God might be all in all. This principle, together with his strictly logical and literal interpretation of St. Paul's epistles, gave rise to his doctrine of predestination, which has been especially known as "Calvinism." It must, however, be remembered that on this subject there was no difference between him and the older Reformers. Luther and Zwingli would both in these days be called extreme predestinarians. They all acknowledged themselves disciples of St. Augustine.

With regard to the doctrine of the Lord's Supper, Calvin taught that the believer partakes of the body and blood of Christ in the Sacrament, but he did not bind this effect to the visible elements, but rather believed it to be conveyed by the power of the Holy Ghost. This is, in fact, the view which, more fully developed, is found in the Heidelberg Catechism, and in all the other symbols of the Reformed Church. It is wrong to imagine that Calvin denied the real presence by regarding it as spiritual in its nature. It is the spiritual alone which is real and permanent; the material is always changeable and evanescent.

When Calvin returned to Paris after his season of retirement, he found the affairs of the Church in a very depressed condition. The king was persecuting the Protestants with fire and sword, and had burned at the stake seven men and women, among whom was one of Calvin's most intimate friends. The Protestants in retaliation secretly affixed doctrinal placards to the walls of public buildings, and one of them was even found fastened to the wall of the king's bed-chamber. It was deemed unsafe for Calvin to remain in France, and he consequently went first to Strasburg and then to Basel, hoping to devote his life to the quiet study of God's word. Next year (1536) he came to Geneva. He had been on a visit to the pious Duchess of Ferrara, and only intended to remain a short time; but Farel, who had been principally instrumental in bringing Geneva to Protestantism, insisted that he must assume the direction of the church. When Calvin declined this proposition, Farel, recognizing in him the man for the hour, exclaimed with a degree of earnestness like that of the ancient prophets: "I announce to you in the name of Almighty God that if you do not remain to assist me in the holy work to which I am called, He will dreadfully punish you for preferring your own pleasure to His service."

Such an appeal was irresistible, and Calvin accepted the call.

Geneva was at that time in a dreadful condition. There had been a long struggle between the city and the Duke of Savoy, who had sought to deprive it of its independence. Berne and Fribourg had interfered in behalf of liberty, and thus Geneva had been brought into close alliance with German Switzerland. Farel and Viretus preached the Gospel with extraordinary effect, and on the 27th of August 1535 the council declared that the city had passed over to the Reformed Church. For some time Geneva was in a state of anarchy. Farel had gone to extremes, not only destroying pictures and images in the churches, but even requiring the removal of organs. All who would not accept Protestantism were required to sell their property and leave the country. Among those who called themselves Protestants there were some who seemed to think that evangelical freedom must allow them to indulge in the wildest excesses. There was confusion everywhere. Farel felt himself unable to allay the storm, and was glad to become subordinate to a stronger man.

Calvin was called upon to build up a social order which had been utterly broken down. It was an immense work, but he proved himself equal to the occasion. In conjunction with the other pastors he preached powerfully against existing abuses, and sought to establish church-discipline, but for a time it seemed as though every effort in this direction must be in vain. The wickedness of the people became so great that Calvin and his co-adjutors refused to administer the Lord's Supper until there were signs of moral improvement. They persisted in their refusal, though threatened with death, and finally Calvin and Farel left the city, saying, "It is better to obey God than man." Calvin remained two years in Strasburg, ministering to a congregation of fifteen hundred French refugees, and taking part in the general affairs of the Church. In the meantime the state of affairs in Geneva had grown worse and worse. At last there came a reaction. It was felt that the city had need of Calvin, and the council vainly urged him to return. Finally, in 1541, when the authorities of a number of Reformed cities had solicited him to come to the rescue, he returned to Geneva, with the full understanding that his plans of discipline were to be carried out.

From this time to the end of his life no king in Europe exercised such power as did John Calvin. His salary was only 250 francs, with a 'plain house,' which is still standing near the old church, and to this the council occasionally added a gift of cloth for a new coat. He cared nothing for money or display, but soon bent everything to his iron will. He arranged the laws of the state, and Ancillon says that his "labors for civil law give him a higher title to renown than his theological works." His views with regard to the character and functions of the Church were much higher than those of his cotemporaries. The Church he regarded as standing higher than the State, whose main object it is to aid her in the preservation of truth and order. "Man," he said, "cannot enter into life unless he be born of her womb, nourished at her breast, and kept under her fostering care." In accordance with these views he insisted on the independence of the Church from the control of the State. It is to him that the Reformed Church owes its classes, or presbyteries, and its consistories. He also was the first to define the four offices of the church: Minister of the Word, Teacher of Theology, Elder, and Deacon. Thus in many ways, he influenced the organization of the Reformed Church. He had no trust in princes, and taught the churches self-reliance and independence. As may well be supposed, this course did not remove the suspicion with which the defenders of absolute government regarded the Swiss churches.

The discipline which Calvin introduced into the Church of Geneva was exceedingly strict and stern, and could hardly have been carried out in a larger state. The Church, indeed, decreed no greater punishment than ex-communication, but the government generally declared the excommunicated persons deprived of all civil rights. When those who were disciplined by the Church appealed to the State for redress, the punishment was apt to be increased, and sometimes even Calvin's intercession could not secure a milder sentence.

Though Calvin's discipline appears to have been extremely harsh, it was probably the only thing that was suited to the exigencies of the case. Its success was wonderful. Perfect order was established, and the city became exceedingly prosperous. Geneva became the most quiet and orderly city in Europe, and men of the most diverse religious views were unanimous in declaring their astonishment at the great change which Calvin's system had effected. By the power of church-discipline Calvin produced an effect which in these days would require a standing army and a multitude of police.

This close union of Church and State sometimes led to great excesses. The most flagrant of these was the burning of Servetus for heresy. Servetus was a Spanish physician who had written a book against the Trinity in which he uttered the most dreadful blasphemies. He came to Geneva with the intention of leading a party known as the Libertines, in their opposition to the existing order. He was arrested, and after a long trial was condemned to be burnt at the stake. Calvin vainly interfered to have his punishment changed to decapitation. The indignation of the people was so intense that nothing short of the execution of the ancient law would satisfy them, and the dreadful decree was carried out. On this subject we can only quote the words of the "American Cyclopedia:" "The execution was in accordance with the laws of all the European states of the time. It was the inherited spirit of the times, and not the power of Calvin that burnt Servetus. The penalty was cruel; it is indefensible; it was even at that time impolitic. Neither civil nor religious liberty was yet understood; still less was there any sharp distinction made between them. That analysis was the fruit of time, and of the seed which Calvin was then sowing in Geneva." It should also be remembered that in that period of convulsion such events were happening, among the Catholics and Protestants, all over Europe. Even as late as 1601 the Protestant authorities of Saxony executed Dr. Nicholas Krell because he sought to introduce "the peculiar doctrines of Calvin."

After long discussion, the churches of Zurich and Berne united with Geneva, in 1549, in a common confession of faith concerning the Lord's Supper. There were still many local differences, but the Swiss churches were practically united. Calvin's fame and influence now rapidly increased. He established a Theological institution at Geneva which opened with six hundred students. Theodore Beza, his ardent friend, biographer, and successor, was the first rector. Calvin taught theology, though he refused the title of professor, and the brightest young men of many nations gathered around him. The most celebrated of these was John Knox, who was afterwards mainly instrumental in founding and organizing the Presbyterian Church of Scotland.

The amount of labor which Calvin performed at this period is almost incredible. Though he was in bad health, and, it was said, "looked like a ghost," he sometimes for long periods preached every day, taught theology, wrote books, and was actively engaged in directing the affairs of Church and State. His correspondence was enormous. Cranmer sought his advice with reference to the organization of the Church of England. In Holland his letters made men strong to battle for their rights. Far away in Poland, Bohemia, and Hungary, his advice was sought in respect to the organization of the Churches. Among the Protestants of France his influence was almost unlimited, and in Spain and Italy he secretly had many devoted adherents. Even in Germany his influence was extensive, but here his system was never fully received even by those who accepted his doctrine of the sacraments. It was said that "Calvin never slept," and it is true that "many a night he did not sleep, and many a day he had no time to look up to the light of the blessed sun." Utterly worn out, he died in his fifty-fifth year, on the 27th of May 1564. His whole estate amounted to about 250 dollars, and at his own request no monument was erected over his grave.

It is difficult to form a just estimate of such a person as John Calvin. He is generally represented as a hard, stern man, who disliked poetry and art, and had no room in his head for those tender affections which are the solace of life.[1] Yet Beza, who was a distinguished poet,

---

[1] As was to be expected, Calvin could not escape the tongue of slander; and his enemies repeated many calumnies concerning his private life, some of which are still occasionally brought forth from their hiding-places. These stories are mostly derived from Bolsec, a personal enemy of Calvin who was banished from Geneva, and who after returning to the Roman Catholic Church, took a mean revenge by writing a book full of the most outrageous calumnies. These have often been refuted; and even Catholic historians—such as Masson, De May, and Michelet—express their horror at the falsehoods of Bolsec.

with a keen appreciation of everything that is beautiful and sweet, loved that stern, cold theologian with more than filial affection. Melanchthon said of him "that he wished he could lay his weary head upon that faithful heart and die there." Farel, Viretus, Bullinger, and Bucer, confessed that they were devotedly attached to him. Calvin was no doubt a fierce controversialist, but a person who enjoyed the affection of such men as these can hardly be regarded as cold and unimpressive.

Calvin was probably the most eminent man in the history of the Reformed Church, but he is in no sense to be regarded as its founder. He was at best the most prominent director of one of the chief currents which entered into its life.

CHAPTER IV.

The Palatinate—Frederick the Pious—The Heidelberg Catechism —Caspar Olevianus—Zacharias Ursinus.

THE third great source of the Reformed Church must be sought in the Palatinate. There are, however, no doubt, many young geographers who would be puzzled to define the limits of that historic region, and even among older students there are probably not a few who would be inclined to say of it, as the historian Lambarde said of a certain undefined district in England, that "it would be easier to deny its existence altogether than to attempt to indicate its extent." The fact is, that the Palatinate has disappeared from the map of Europe, its territories having been absorbed by avaricious neighbors, but the name is so illustrious in history that it will probably never cease to be popularly applied to the region that was at one time included within its boundaries.

At the time of its greatest political importance the Palatinate consisted of two large provinces, which were not contiguous, with several outlying principalities. The Upper Palatinate (*Ober-Pfalz*) was situated in the eastern part of the present kingdom of Bavaria. Its principal town was Amberg. Though governed by the elector of the Palatinate, its people took but little part in the religious movements which claim our present attention. They had become Lutheran early in the Reformation, and most of them are even now members of the same church. The Lower Palatinate (*Unter-Pfalz* or *Rhein-Pfalz*) was by far the most important of the elector's possessions. It is often called " *Wein-Pfalz,*" on account of the abundance of wine which it produces. Situated on both sides of the Rhine, and extending upward along the banks of the beautiful Neckar, it has always been regarded as one of the most fertile countries in the world. It consisted of five principalities: Simmern, Zweibruecken, Sponheim, Veldenz, and the Palatinate Proper. The principal cities were Heidelberg, Manheim and Franckenthal.

FREDERICK THE PIOUS.

In 1559 the elector Otto Heinrich died without children, and the succession passed to Frederick III., a prince of the house of Simmern. Frederick was born at Simmern in 1515, and was educated a Catholic; but had been converted to Protestantism, mainly, it is believed, through the instrumentality of the celebrated John De Lasky. His conversion was thoroughly sincere, and he was always ready if needs be, to suffer and die for the cause of truth.

In his early manhood Frederick had distinguished himself in the wars against the Turks, and, having thus become very popular, there was great rejoicing when he attained to the electoral dignity. He was, indeed, a model prince. In his character gentleness and firmness were wonderfully blended. His reputation was beyond the reach of calumny, and the trust in God, which kept him safe in the midst of trials, was the constant wonder of his cotemporaries. It must, however, not be forgotten that Frederick believed himself to be the absolute ruler of his people in religious no less than in secular matters. It was at his court that the Swiss physician, Thomas Erastus, taught the doctrine, since known as Erastianism, that all ecclesiastical authority is subordinate to the civil power. Those who held to this view were in the habit of saying "*Cujus regio illius religio*," which has been rendered, "Who owns the region owns the religion."

On this subject, it will be observed, Frederick occupied a position as far distant as possible from that of Calvin. The latter advocated the independence of the Church in matters of discipline, and was even inclined to regard the State as the handmaid of the Church. Frederick, on the other hand, was a German prince, and, like others of his order, supposed himself to be, by virtue of his office, the head of the Church in the country over which he ruled. He firmly believed that he was responsible to God for the faith of his individual subjects, and therefore sought to be their religious guide no less than their temporal ruler. With this purpose he became a profound student of theology, and did not hesitate to use his secular power in enforcing the acceptance of what he believed to be the truth. He was, however, thoroughly sincere; and if any one had accused him of unnecessary rigor in the execution of his decrees, he might have replied in Scriptural language: "The zeal of thine house hath eaten me up."

PHILIPISM.

Philip Melanchthon (1497–1560) had been the ruling spirit in the reformation of the Palatinate. As Protestantism was not formally introduced there until 1546—the year of Luther's death—the whole work of organizing the church may be said to have been confided to his care. The order which he introduced closely resembled that of Würtemberg. It was Lutheran in its general characteristics; but was mild and conciliatory; and it seemed for a while as though under its influence, the old confessional differences would entirely disappear.

Melanchthon's history is so well known that it is not necessary that we should relate its details. He was the only one of the prominent reformers who was born in the Palatinate. As the foremost scholar of his age, the value of his services in the cause of the Reformation was inestimable; and in the inscription placed on his tomb at his burial he is justly termed "the most industrious and most faithful of the assistants of Dr. Martin Luther in explaining and sustaining the pure doctrine of the Word of God."

Melanchthon was at first greatly prejudiced against the Swiss Reformers; but when he came to know them better, he regarded many of them with tender affection. Calvin, Bucer and De Lasky became his most intimate friends and correspondents. Though he always maintained

Luther's doctrine of the Lord's Supper, he acknowledged that Calvin's view might at least be tolerated; and he therefore changed the tenth article of the Augsburg Confession, of which he was the author, so that it might be acceptable to the Reformed Church. In conjunction with Bucer, he, in 1536, drew up terms of union between the Lutheran and Reformed Churches. These articles were approved by Luther, and were formally adopted by the Reformed Churches of Switzerland, but eight years later, Luther unexpectedly repudiated them. It is believed that he was prompted to this act by a manifest tendency among his own immediate followers towards the acceptance of the Reformed doctrine. Melanchthon, however, remained faithful to the agreement to the end of his life.

Even before Luther's death, Melanchthon was regarded with suspicion by the extremists of his own church. The fact that he had changed the Augsburg Confession, to accommodate the Reformed Church, was considered by them an unpardonable act of treason. After the death of the great master, this feeling became intense. Melanchthon's disciples were contemptuously called Philipists, after the name of their teacher, who was familiarly known as "Master Philip." "Philipism" was declared to be as bad as Calvinism. Minor points of difference between Luther and Melanchthon were sought out and made the occasion of a series of bitter controversies. Melanchthon's friends were in many instances deposed and banished for trivial reasons, and the extremists did not hesitate to say that they would not rest until they had driven Melanchthon himself out of Germany. In this purpose they were foiled, for Melanchthon had powerful friends; but it is not surprising that he prayed to be delivered from "the wrath of the theologians," and that, a short time before his death, he even seriously proposed to go to Palestine to spend his remaining days in the cell once occupied by St. Jerome in Bethlehem.

In 1552, the old sacramental controversy broke out with renewed violence. Joachim Westphal, Lutheran pastor at Hamburg, sounded the trumpet for the onslaught against the Swiss churches, and he was powerfully seconded by Matthias Flacius, Tilemann Heshusius, and many others. The occasion for this assault was probably the formal union of the Zwinglians and Calvinists in the Zurich Consensus of 1549, which had rendered the Reformed Church more powerful than it had previously been. The attack was, however, most effective against the Philipists and secret Calvinists (Crypto-Calvinists) in the Lutheran Church, who were made to suffer intensely. When in the reigns of Philip and Mary, thousands of English and Dutch Protestants fled to escape persecution, they were refused a refuge in many parts of Germany, because they were regarded as belonging to the Reformed Church. In the Palatinate, however, more moderate counsels prevailed. The foreign fugitives were welcomed, and many of them settled in that country, especially in the town of Franckenthal, which by their industry and enterprise, they soon raised to a high degree of prosperity.

When Frederick III. assumed the government he had no idea of introducing the Reformed Church, but he soon found himself involved in the prevalent controversy. Heshusius, a strict Lutheran, and Klebitz, a disciple of Calvin, were engaged in a violent discussion, by which the minds of the people were greatly excited. Frederick, by the advice of Melanchthon, dismissed both the contestants from their charges, but peace did not ensue. It soon became impossible to hold the irenical position of Melanchthon. Frederick was forced to take sides in the conflict, and, in 1559, he formally passed over to the Reformed Church, though he always insisted that he had not in any way renounced his allegiance to the Augsburg Confession. It was a bold step, but its effects were extraordinary. Hitherto the existence of the Reformed Church had not been officially recognized in Germany, but now its position was secure, and it soon became the leading church along the whole course of the Rhine, from its source to the ocean.

THE HEIDELBERG CATECHISM.

After the Palatinate had passed over to the Reformed Church, a new Confession of Faith became absolutely necessary. The German people generally knew but little concerning the Reformed Church, and ascribed to it many errors which no one had ever dreamed of maintaining. Heshusius even hinted that Frederick was preparing his people to become Mohammedan, in anticipation of a Turkish invasion. The Elector, therefore, determined to prepare a catechism which would not only properly represent the faith of the Reformed Church, but might serve as a means of conveying its precious truths to subsequent generations. With this intention he selected two young men to engage in the work of its composition, and the result proved the wisdom of his choice. These were Olevianus and Ursinus, the first of whom was but twenty-six and the other twenty-eight years of age. Together they produced a work which has ever since been regarded as the crown and glory of the Reformed Church.

OLEVIANUS.

Caspar Olevianus (1535-1587) was a disciple of Calvin. He was a native of Treves, and belonged to a wealthy family whose name was properly Von der Olewig. Having passed through the schools of his native city, he went to Paris, and then to Bourges, to complete his education. Here he studied law, but secretly devoted much time to reading the Scriptures. One of the sons of Frederick III.—who was then only Count of Simmern—was also a student, and the two young men soon became intimate friends. One day they took a walk on the banks of the Oron river, in company with the private tutor of the prince. They were met by a party of young German noblemen, who proposed that they should all cross the river in a boat. Olevianus declined to accompany them, as some of the party had taken too much wine, but the prince and his tutor accepted the invitation. In the middle of the river they began playfully to rock the boat; it was thus upset, and the whole party was drowned. Olevianus sprang into the water and tried to rescue the prince, but it was in vain, and he himself almost lost his life. In his greatest peril he vowed that if God would save his life he would consecrate it entirely to the conversion of his native land. Having been wonderfully rescued, he remembered his vow, and the father of the young prince subsequently became his best friend and patron. Like Calvin, Olevianus now sought admission into one of the secret Reformed churches, and then successively visited Geneva and Zurich. Returning to his native city, he began to preach the Gospel, but was arrested and cast into prison. Delivered through the potent intercession of Frederick, he went to Heidelberg, where he was at first professor of theology, and subsequently pastor of the principal church of the city. He was a man of extraordinary eloquence, and was far more instrumental in the general work of organizing the church than the retiring and scholarly Ursinus. His part in the composition of the Heidelberg Catechism was by no means insignificant, as has sometimes been represented. Traces of his hand may be noticed almost everywhere, and Sudhoff insists that after Ursinus had composed the catechism in Latin, Olevianus prepared the German version. This is probable from a comparison of the style of the two men, as manifested by their separate compositions. It is also almost certain that what is said in the Catechism concerning the Office of the Keys and Christian Discipline was derived from Olevianus, as its substance may be found in his previous writings.

After the death of the Elector Frederick, Olevianus went to Herborn, where he spent his remaining years. He passed away from earth on the 15th of March, 1587. When he was evidently drawing near his end, some one asked him whether he was certain of salvation, and he replied, laying his hand on his heart: "*Certissimus*," that is, "Most certain." With this beautiful word his spirit winged its flight to heaven.

Zacharias Ursinus (1534–1583) was a faithful disciple of Melanchthon. He was a native of Breslau, in Silesia, where his family, whose name was Von Baer, were reckoned among the nobility. His father was a clergyman, who had Latinized the name, according to the fashion of the times.

Ursinus studied at Wittenberg, where he acquired

great distinction, and was declared by Melanchthon to be his most promising pupil. Subsequently he visited the universities of Switzerland and France, and made the acquaintance of Bullinger, Calvin and Peter Martyr. Accused of "Philipism," or possibly Calvinism, he at a later date, fled from Silesia and found a refuge in Switzerland. Peter Martyr had been requested by Frederick to assist in the organization of the Church of the Palati-

URSINUS.

nate, but feeling the weight of years, he recommended Ursinus to take his place. Concerning the latter Frederick subsequently said to a Silesian: "His fatherland was not worthy of such a man. Tell your countrymen to banish many such men, so that they may come to me."

Ursinus became Professor of Theology at Heidelberg. He was not gifted as a preacher, but was an excellent instructor. When he and Olevianus were directed to prepare a confession of faith, each of them submitted a plan. That of Ursinus was preferred by the Elector, and he thus became the main author of the Heidelberg Catechism. To him it owes its irenic character; for it is known that the polemic questions were inserted at the direct command of the elector. In its composition he used materials found in the catechisms of Calvin and De Lasky, but the originality of his work has never been questioned. "The Heidelberg Catechism," says Max Goebel, " may be regarded as the flower and fruit of the entire German and French Reformation; it has Lutheran sincerity, Melanchthonian clearness, Zwinglian simplicity, and Calvinistic fire. Whoever is not familiar with the Heidelberg Catechism, does not know the German Reformed Church, as it was and as it still remains; whoever is acquainted with all its particulars, its excellencies and imperfections, is alone able to appreciate the Christian spirit and Christian life of our Reformed Church in all its strength and weakness."

Ursinus was personally a man of retiring disposition, who made but few intimate friends, and took the greatest delight in profound study. He did not like to be disturbed in his work, and over the door of his study he had placed an inscription in Latin verses to the following effect: "Friend, whoever thou art, if thou comest to me, be brief. Either leave me soon, or aid me in my labors." In the opinion of his contemporaries, Ursinus lived a life of prayer, which seemed too pure and holy for this world. It was said that he never spoke an unnecessary word, and yet all who were brought into contact with him could not help loving him for the almost angelic sweetness of his character.

After the death of Frederick, the opponents of the Catechism enjoyed a temporary triumph, during the brief reign of his son Louis, and Ursinus left Heidelberg to become a Professor in a Reformed Theological Seminary which Frederick's second son, John Casimir, had just founded in Neustadt. Here, after five years of faithful labor, his noble life was brought to a close, on the 6th of March, 1583, in the forty-ninth year of his age. The inscription on his monument in the church at Neustadt justly calls him "a great theologian, a conqueror of heresies concerning the Person of Christ and the Lord's Supper, mighty with word and pen, an acute philosopher, a wise man, and a stern instructor of youth."

CHAPTER V.

The Defense of the Catechism—The Second Helvetic Confession—The Diet of Augsburg—Frederick's Later Years—After Frederick's Death.

THE Heidelberg Catechism is so mild and pacific in its general character that we can hardly realize how its publication, in 1563, could have given the signal for one of the most violent conflicts in the history of the Church. No doubt its authors did not expect their work to be received without question; but the fierceness of the attacks which it invoked must have far exceeded their anticipations. The Roman Catholics were of course its bitter enemies. The Council of Trent, which had been in session for many years, was just coming to a close. Though ostensibly called to restore peace to the Church, it had but served to intensify the existing bitterness. It had been entirely under Jesuit influence; the Protestants had not been heard, and the anathemas by which they were condemned were unexampled in their violence. It has been said that "nobody can curse like the pope," and the council certainly adequately expressed the papal sentiments.

It is not impossible that the publication of these anathemas may have had some influence on the Elector Frederick, in inducing him to insist on the insertion, in the second edition of the catechism, of the celebrated 80th question, in which the mass is declared to be "an accursed idolatry." Compared with the decrees of the council, this was a moderate statement. It did not curse individual opponents, as the Roman Catholics had done, but was at most a very emphatic assertion of the grounds which had induced Protestants to reject the mass. The fact, however, that the Heidelberg Catechism had, in unmistakable language, declared the universal sentiment of Protestants with reference to this subject, was enough to exasperate the Romanists to employ all possible means for its suppression.

The extreme Lutheran party was hardly less violent. Heshusius, the controversialist whom Frederick had expelled from Heidelberg, saw his opportunity, and at his instigation the pulpits of northern Germany rang with denunciations. The Catechism was charged with teaching doctrines contrary to the Augsburg Confession, especially with reference to the Person of Christ and the Lord's Supper, and the emperor and princes were adjured to employ the sword of secular power for the extinction of heresy.

In describing a storm, it is in vain to attempt to speak of every single blast. The elector's troubles rapidly accumulated. Even his household was divided, and his eldest son Louis, who ruled the Upper Palatinate as his father's representative, took sides with the extreme Lutheran party. All this opposition, however, only served to fortify Frederick in his position; he proceeded to remove pictures and crucifixes from the churches, and introduced the Calvinistic form of church government, which many of the German princes regarded as treason to the privileges of their order. In reply to the accusations brought against him, he calmly asserted his faithful adherence to the Augsburg Confession. With regard to the question of the real presence, his declarations were clear and decided. Thus he says in his reply to the princes who had accused him of Zwinglianism and Calvinism: "We would kindly inform you that we have never been greatly troubled to know what Zwingli and Calvin wrote, and have not read their books. . . . If it is Zwinglianism and Calvinism to suppose that the elements in the Lord's Supper are mere signs, and that the body and blood of Christ are not present, or received,[1] we beg to inform you that this is not our view of the subject and that we are unjustly suspected of holding it, inasmuch as the true and living presence of the body and blood of Christ in the Lord's Supper is in our

---

[1] Zwingli had emphasized the memorial character of the Lord's Supper, maintaining that the meaning of the words of institution is: "This signifies my body." It is, however, an error to suppose that according to his view, "the elements in the Lord's Supper are mere signs." In the confession which he sent to Francis I. a short time before his death, he wrote: "We believe that the true body of Christ is eaten in the Communion in a sacramental and spiritual manner by the religious, believing, and pious heart." "Calvin, indeed, emphasized the reality of the spiritual presence of Christ at the Supper; but had he been spared to see the time of Calvin, Zwingli would, without doubt, have adopted his more elaborate definition, for their views were not conflicting."—*Dr. Van Horne's Life of Zwingli, p. 171.*

churches preached, taught, and believed. That you may not suppose that our words and deeds do not agree, we would inform you that we require of our ministers and theologians to offer the following testimony concerning the Lord's Supper, namely:

"'That we do not therein receive bread and wine alone, as holy, divine signs and seals (as the Holy Scriptures as well as the Augsburg Confession and the Apology call them); nor that we receive only the merits of Jesus Christ alone, nor His Divinity alone, but the Lord Christ wholly and completely, true God and man, His real body and real blood which was broken and shed for us upon the cross—also all His merits, benefits, heavenly treasures, blessings, and eternal life—truly, without all deception and not in mere fancy, but substantially *re ipsa*, by the power and effect of the Holy Spirit; and all this is given and presented to us by the Lord himself, through faith, as the meat and drink of our souls; and also that we thereby have complete communion with Christ, becoming true members of His blessed body, so that He lives and remains in us and we in Him forever.'"

It might seem to the modern reader as though this strong confession ought to have satisfied Frederick's opponents that he believed in the doctrine of the real presence, but it was far from having this effect. "What is it after all," they inquired, "but a Calvinistic confession? Does it not represent the humanity of Christ as conveyed by the Holy Spirit, through faith, as the meat and drink of our souls?" The confession was objectionable to the extremists because it did not explicitly declare that Christ's humanity is present in the sacrament "under the form of bread and wine," being thus orally received by unbelievers as well as believers. On the other hand there was a more moderate Lutheran party which was willing to accept Frederick's confession as substantially in accordance with the Augsburg Confession, and it was owing in great measure to their silent influence and support that the Elector was able to sustain himself during these dark and trying hours.

THE SECOND HELVETIC CONFESSION.

Immediately after the publication of the Heidelberg Catechism, Olevianus had sent a copy of the book to Bullinger, accompanied by a letter in which he said: "If there is any good in this book we owe a great part of it to you and to other noble spirits in Switzerland." In reply, Bullinger said: "I regard this as the best Catechism that has ever been written. May God crown it with his blessing." These intimate relations between Switzerland and the Palatinate continued, and when Frederick found himself in trouble he wrote to Bullinger, requesting him to prepare a full Confession of the doctrines of the Reformed Church. This Confession, which was published by Frederick in 1566, was primarily intended to serve as a defense against those who said that the Reformed churches were at variance among themselves; but it actually became a bond which united the church of the Palatinate with those of Switzerland and France. In this way Henry Bullinger was not only instrumental in uniting the followers of Calvin with those of Zwingli, but succeeded in bringing the church of Frederick III. into the same communion.

THE DIET OF AUGSBURG.

The Emperor Maximilian II., who had ascended the throne in 1564, was a man of extraordinary ability. Though a Catholic, he was more liberal than any of his predecessors, and was even supposed to be secretly inclined to Protestantism. He had addressed a friendly warning to the Elector Frederick immediately after the publication of the Heidelberg Catechism, but seemed disinclined to carry matters further. The importunity of the German princes, however, finally induced him to call a meeting of the Diet, and Frederick was cited to appear.

This citation was a very serious matter. It was well known that the majority of the princes proposed to exclude the elector from the terms of the treaty of Augsburg, which would have deprived him of his government, and perhaps even have cost his life. His brother, Richard of Simmern, warned him of the danger of attending the Diet, but he exclaimed: "I believe that God who has brought me to a knowledge of His Gospel still reigns, and if it should cost my blood, I would regard martyrdom as an honor for which I could not sufficiently thank Him in time or eternity."

The Diet met in Augsburg on the 23d of March, 1566. The emperor and empress appeared with a magnificent retinue, and were welcomed with extraordinary festivities. At the beginning of the meeting the Protestant delegates held what might now be called a "caucus," in which they determined to prepare an address to the emperor, demanding greater religious liberty; but they at the same time resolved not to allow Frederick to sign the petition unless he should first satisfactorily explain his views concerning the Lord's Supper. Several princes even insisted that he must sign what was designed to be an "iron-clad" confession, to the effect that "the real body and blood are actually present in the sacrament under the form of bread and wine, and are offered and received with the visible elements; that the aforesaid true body and blood are not only spiritually but corporeally presented and received, so that through the communion of His flesh and blood Christ dwells in us corporeally; and also that Christ is not only in us spiritually through His love, but also by natural communion."[1]

A few days after these proceedings Frederick arrived, and it soon became evident that his presence was producing a reaction. Those who had never before seen him were impressed by his evident sincerity, and this favorable impression was heightened by several eloquent sermons preached by his chaplain.

The elector quietly but firmly declined to sign any new confessions. His danger was, however, by no means at an end; and at one time it was currently reported in Heidelberg that he had been arrested and executed.

---
[1] Heppe's "History of German Protestantism," 2, p. 120.

On the 14th of May the emperor proposed a decree commanding Frederick to abstain from introducing "Calvinistic novelties," and requiring him to restore to the Roman church the property of certain convents which had been alienated by the civil power. During the discussion of this measure the elector was required to absent himself from the assembly; but after its adoption he re-entered the hall followed by his favorite son John Casimir, whom he called his "spiritual armor-bearer," the latter carrying the Bible and the Augsburg Confession. On this occasion he offered his memorable defense of which the following is a brief extract: "I am still of the opinion that in matters of faith I have but a single master, who is King of kings and Lord of lords; therefore, I am not troubled about my head, but about my soul, which is in the hands of God who created it . . . I have never read Calvin's works, and therefore do not know whether you are right in calling me a Calvinist, but I confess that my catechism contains the substance of my faith; it is so fortified with proofs from the Scriptures that it cannot be refuted. Finally, I am comforted by the assurance that my Lord and Saviour Jesus Christ has given unto me and all believers this blessed promise, that all we lose here for His name's sake will be restored to us a hundred fold in the world to come."

The effect of the elector's defense was very great. At its conclusion Augustus of Saxony put his hand on his shoulder and said: "Fritz, thou art more pious than the whole of us!" The Margrave of Baden also said to the princes at the close of the session: "Why trouble ye the elector? He has more piety than all of us together." When the emperor finally inquired whether Frederick was to be regarded as standing under the Augsburg Confession it was resolved "that he was in full accordance with the confession in the article of justification by faith, which had caused the schism in the church, and in many other articles, but that he did not fully accept the article concerning the Lord's Supper. As, however, he had indicated his willingness to yield to proofs taken from the Word of God, they would in due time seek to convince him of his error. In the meantime the princes had no desire to oppress the Elector of the Palatinate, or others, in Germany or in foreign lands, who might vary from the confession in one or more articles, and thus to increase the sufferings of the confessors of Christ."

This action of the Diet had been unexpected. Frederick returned to Heidelberg and was received with great rejoicing, and was now permitted to proceed unmolested in his work of reformation. The sacramental controversy was, however, by no means concluded. In the Lutheran church, especially, it continued to rage with great violence, until finally a number of German princes followed the example of Frederick, and with many of their people formally entered the Reformed Church.[1]

---

[1] Among the most important of the German cities and principalities which passed over from the Lutheran to the Reformed Church, after the Palatinate had led the way, we may mention Nassau (1578), Bremen

FREDERICK'S LATER YEARS.

The Elector of the Palatinate was now known as Frederick the Pious, and well deserved his honorable title. In his efforts for the upbuilding of the church he was indefatigable. The university of Heidelberg flourished as it had never done before, and was withal prevaded by an earnest Christian spirit. The oppressed and persecuted Protestants of foreign countries found in him a friend and protector. After the dreadful massacre of St. Bartholomew he sent an army, under the command of his favorite son John Casimir, to aid the persecuted Huguenots. Another of his sons lost his life in battle in the Netherlands, but the father consoled himself with the thought that he had died on the field of honor in defense of God and of religion. Gradually the Elector came to occupy a sort of paternal position with reference to the whole Reformed Church, and his influence was felt in distant lands. Even Queen Elizabeth consulted him with reference to the affairs of the Church of England.

During Frederick's later years his chief source of sorrow was the continued alienation of his eldest son, Louis,

---

(1581,) Anhalt (1597), Baden (1599), Lippe (1600), and part of Hesse (1604). The Elector of Brandenburg, John Sigismund, from whom the present imperial family of Germany is descended, accepted the Reformed faith in 1613. Most of the people, however, remained Lutheran, and the Elector of Brandenburg was the first to proclaim the religious liberty of all his subjects. It was on this decree that King Frederick II, more than a century later, based the curious proclamation in which he expressed his desire that in Prussia "every one should go to Heaven after his own fashion."

who was still violent in his opposition to the Reformed Church, and even refused to see his father on his death-bed, though the latter earnestly requested it. The last days of the pious Elector were, however, exceedingly edifying. To the friends that gathered around his dying bed he said: "I have lived long enough for you and the Church; I am now called to a better life. I have done for the Church all I could, but my power was limited. God, who can do all things, and who cared for His Church before I was born, liveth and reigneth in Heaven still, and will not forsake us; nor will He suffer those prayers and tears which I have offered up in this chamber upon my knees, for my successor and the Church, to be without a blessing." Then addressing the court-preacher he said: "The Lord may call me hence whenever it pleaseth Him; my conscience is at peace with the Lord Jesus Christ, whom I have served with all my heart. I have been permitted to see that in all my churches and schools the people have been led away from men and directed to Christ alone." And again he exclaimed: "I have been detained here long enough through the prayers of God's people; it is now time that I should be gathered into the true rest with my Saviour." Then he requested his pastor to read the 31st Psalm and the 17th chapter of John, and after praying audibly and fervently he gently fell asleep in the Lord. His death occured on the 26th of October, 1576.

Louis VI. assumed the government immediately after his father's death. He dismissed the Reformed professors, and introduced a strictly Lutheran church-order. Pastors were required to subscribe to the new order or to leave the country. "Many of these," says Von Alpen, "submitted for the sake of their wives and children," but others found a refuge at the court of Prince John Casimir, who ruled over several provinces. This state of affairs continued for about seven years, when Louis suddenly died, leaving an infant son, in whose name John Casimir assumed the government. The young prince was brought up in the Reformed Church, and so it happened that the latter was for many years the established church in the Palatinate. The lines between the confessions had now been drawn, and the Reformed and Lutheran churches existed side by side. The struggle was not yet over, but there was a season of rest.

The books in explanation and in defense of the Heidelberg Catechism, written during this period and subsequently, are almost innumerable. The most celebrated of these is the commentary bearing the name of Ursinus, first printed at Heidelberg in 1591, of which an English version has been published in this country by the Rev. Dr. G. W. Williard.

The defense of the Heidelberg Catechism was everywhere conducted with self-sacrificing devotion. Though often attacked, it was so thoroughly grounded in the Word of God that it could never be refuted. The Reformed Church everywhere still regards it as a precious legacy, and it will, we trust, be venerated to the latest generation.

CHAPTER VI.

The Martyrs—The Waldenses—Spain and Portugal—The Huguenots—The Massacre of St. Bartholomew.

THE Reformed Church has often been called "the church of the martyrs." It certainly deserves this honorable title, for no other denomination of Christians has had so many members who have sealed their faith with their blood. Its history abounds with examples of the most sublime heroism; and its continued existence, notwithstanding all the persecutions which it has endured, is an evident proof of its divine mission.

The trials of the Reformed Church were, in great degree, owing to its geographical location. In Switzerland it was, almost from the beginning, strong enough to defend itself; and in Germany, though always in the minority, it was to some extent protected by the terms of the treaty of Augsburg; but its members were widely scattered through countries in which Roman Catholics held the reins of power, and they were therefore peculiarly exposed to the wrath of their enemies. In Italy, Spain, France, Holland, and other countries, the martyrs of the Reformed Church may perhaps be numbered by hundreds of thousands.

The names of most of these patient sufferers are now forgotten. They disappeared in the dungeons of the

Inquisition, and their friends hardly ventured to ask a question concerning their fate. It is enough for us to know that they were faithful unto death, and that their Saviour knows them all.

THE WALDENSES.

The Swiss Reformers had at an early date crossed the Alps for the purpose of preaching the Gospel in Italy. Here they were warmly seconded by a community of peasants, who, in the secluded valleys of Piedmont, had for ages cherished a faith very similar to their own. These people were known as the Waldenses, a name which simply signifies "the people of the valleys." Some writers, it is true, assert that they were named after a certain Peter Waldus, a merchant of Lyons, in the twelfth century; but others hold that Waldus was so called because he belonged to the sect, which is believed to have had a much more ancient origin.

From the valleys of Piedmont the Waldenses had gradually spread to the valley of the Rhone, and thence northward along the Rhine as far as Holland. Some of them even settled in Poland and Bohemia, while others sailed to England, where they principally engaged in commerce. Everywhere they were compelled to keep their religion a secret, so that their church organization came to resemble an extensive secret society. They had signs and passwords, and placed emblems on their houses which were recognized only by the initiated. At the beginning of the sixteenth century, it is said, there were so many Waldenses in Switzerland and Germany that a member of the society could leave Italy on foot and find lodging every night with a brother of the faith until he reached Holland, whence he might sail to England and be once more hospitably received.

Though there were certain minor differences, especially in church-government, the members of the Reformed Church from the beginning acknowledged the Waldenses as brethren. The latter, in 1532, held a synod at Angrogna, at which they formally accepted the doctrines of the Reformed Church, and thus thought to consummate the union of the two churches. Several prominent Waldenses were, however, absent from the synod; and these, with their brethren in Bohemia and Poland, subsequently protested against this action. Though the majority of the Waldenses, therefore, at this time formally united with the Reformed Church, a minority have kept up their church organization to the present day.

At this synod the Waldenses resolved to bear public testimony to the idolatry of the mass. This action roused the Roman Catholics to take active measures for the suppression of Protestantism. The Inquisition was put to work, and every one who was suspected of being disloyal to Rome was committed to its tender mercies. Soldiers penetrated into the valleys of the Waldenses, killing every one whom they could find, and it was only by hiding in the fastnesses of the Alps that a remnant was enabled to escape.

There were, at this time, thousands of people in Italy who sympathized with the Reformation, and Reformed churches had actually been established in many of the Italian cities; but now all who desired to save their lives were compelled to leave their native land. Refugees became so numerous in Switzerland that they were able to found Italian churches, and some of their earliest pastors —such as Peter Martyr and Bernard Ochino—were universally recognized as among the most prominent ministers in the Reformed Church. In the border region, now included in the canton of Ticino, the Romanists were, however, in the majority, and the refugees became the helpless victims of their wrath. No language can adequately describe the horrors of that persecution. The persecutors were not satisfied to take the lives of their victims, but first subjected them to unheard-of tortures. Finally, at a time of comparative quiet, the Catholics of a part of the Canton des Grisons suddenly rose and massacred almost the entire Protestant population. Altogether, the violent measures of the papacy were so successful that of all the Italian congregations founded in the days of the Reformation, only two are still in existence. These are situated in two little valleys in the Canton des Grisons, called Bregell and Puschlav, where a few people of Italian blood still listen to the preaching of the Gospel in the language of their ancestors. The Waldenses have, however, recently become much more active and prosperous, and many Protestant missions have been founded by them in Italy.

SPAIN AND PORTUGAL.

In spite of the dreadful Inquisition, Protestantism was quietly making its way through all classes of Spanish society, when Philip II. returned from the Netherlands to assume the government after the death of his father. Philip was a merciless fanatic. Under his auspices the agents of the Inquisition sought everywhere for victims, and even the archbishop of Toledo, the foremost ecclesiastic of Spain, was imprisoned on suspicion of favoring the new doctrines. Spaniards are proverbially fond of spectacular display, as is evident from their bull-fights, and Philip gratified this taste by burning Protestants. He was always present on such occasions, and when one of the victims asked him from the stake, how he could bear to see the sufferings of his innocent people, he replied: "I would gladly carry the wood to burn my own son, if he were as great a heretic as thou." In his insane wrath Philip even contemplated burning the remains of his father, the Emperor Charles V., because he had not succeeded in crushing Protestantism at its beginning, but was finally persuaded that such an act would recoil upon its perpetrator. The confessor of the late Emperor, the celebrated Carranza, was, however, imprisoned for seven years.

At this time Protestantism had to encounter a new enemy in the rapid rise of the order of Jesuits. This powerful body was founded in Spain, in 1534, by Ignatius Loyola, a young nobleman, and six companions, of whom the most eminent were Francis Xavier, and

James Laynez. In addition to the usual monastic vows, they promised unconditional obedience to the pope, and were directed to labor for the suppression of Protestantism. They are even now the most powerful secret order in the world.

In the face of such opposition, Spanish Protestantism could make no progress. It was, in fact, stamped out by the heel of tyranny, though at the same time the best part of the nation was ruthlessly sacrificed. At that time Spain, which had previously been the foremost nation in Europe, began to decline, and finally lost all political and ecclesiastical significance.

In Portugal, the course of affairs was very similar. Though there was a manifest disposition on the part of the most intelligent portion of the people to accept Protestantism, which had found decided advocates among the professors of the university of Coimbra, it was speedily suppressed by the strong hand of the government. From that day, Portugal has remained a thoroughly Roman Catholic country.

THE HUGUENOTS.

As we have already seen, the Protestants of France were regarded as the followers of John Calvin, and belonged to the Reformed branch of the Reformation. It is impossible to decide with certainty at what time and for what reason they came to be called Huguenots. Webster says the name was probably derived from a French conspirator, named Hugo, or Hugon, but no reason can be given why the name of such an obscure individual should have been applied to the whole body of French Protestants. It seems much more likely that the name Huguenot was formed by a mispronunciation of the word "Eidgenossen," or Confederates, a term which the Swiss Protestants applied to themselves. Strange as it may seem to English ears, the French would be likely to pronounce "Eidgenos" very much as they pronounce "Huguenot."

The French Protestants, it will be remembered, were cruelly persecuted during the reigns of Francis I. and Henry II., but they had rapidly increased in numbers until extensive districts, especially in Southern France, were almost exclusively occupied by them. The old nobility, were generally on the Huguenot side, and in their fortified castles could defy the power of the King. The city of Rochelle was thoroughly Protestant, and now ranked as one of the three most important cities of the Reformed Church.[1] The French court was therefore desirous of crushing Protestantism, not only for the purpose of aiding the Catholic Church, but to increase the King's power by humbling the great Huguenot nobles.

After the death of Henry II., the throne of France

---

[1] These three cities were Geneva, in Switzerland, Wesel, in Germany, and Rochelle, in France. They were not the largest Reformed cities, but the most influential. The Catholics had a rough saying which took the rounds of Europe:

"Geneva, Wesel, and Rochelle
Are the devil's second hell."

was held for a few years by each of his three sons, Francis II., Charles IX., and Henry III., but during all this period, the supreme power was held by their mother, the notorious Catherine de Medici. Unless she is greatly caluminated she was one of the most wicked women that ever lived, and it is believed that two, at least, of her royal sons, were murdered at her instigation, because they sought to free themselves from her domination. Closely allied with her was the great Catholic house of Guise, and a crowd of Italian retainers whom she had advanced to high positions, and who were enthusiastically devoted to the papal cause.

We have no room to describe the so-called religious wars which occupied this period. They culminated in the fearful act of treachery which is known as

THE MASSACRE OF ST. BARTHOLOMEW,

or "The Bloody Wedding." Queen Catherine had succeeded in arranging a marriage between her daughter, the beautiful but worthless Margaret of Valois, and the Huguenot leader, Henry of Navarre. The Protestants were thoroughly deceived by the prospect of approaching peace, and most of their leaders came to Paris to attend the wedding, which was celebrated with great pomp. Four days afterwards, an unsuccessful attempt was made to assassinate Coligni, Grand Admiral of France, who was the most distinguished of the Huguenots. Many historians believe that this attempted murder was instigated by Catharine de Medici, who had hoped to throw the blame on the Catholic leader, the Duke of Guise, whom she desired to destroy; but finding herself implicated, she succeeded in persuading the King that the Protestants were about to retaliate by murdering him, and wrung from him a reluctant consent to a general massacre. Catholics were warned to illuminate their houses, and not to appear on the streets without wearing the badge of the cross. The signal of the slaughter was the ringing of the great bell of the church of St. Germain l'Auxerrois, and as soon as it began to sound, the Catholics fell upon the Protestants and murdered them by the thousands.

This dreadful massacre began on St. Bartholomew's day, the 24th of August, 1572, and continued for several days. It extended to the provinces, and was no doubt horrible beyond description. During the prevailing excitement, enemies murdered each other without regard to religion. Innumerable stories of hair-breadth escapes are related, which vividly depict the horror of the times. In some places, however, the governors refused to execute the orders of the King; and the Roman Catholic bishop of Lisieux even opened his palace to the Huguenots, and protected them from the violence of the mob.

Historical authorities differ so widely that it seems impossible to determine whether or not the massacre of Bartholomew was premeditated. It is now, we believe, the prevailing opinion that it was hastily determined upon after the attempted murder of Coligni, and that it was due almost exclusively to the machinations of Catharine de

Medici. To what extent the court of Rome was involved in it, is also an open question; but it is certain that when the pope heard of it, he ordered a *Te Deum* to be sung, and had a medal struck with the inscription "*Hugonottorum Strages*," that is "the massacre of the Huguenots." Subsequently the Church of Rome saw fit to disavow all connection with the massacre, insisting that it was entirely political in its character; but the reproach has never been removed.

The effect of the massacre was very great. Queen Elizabeth made her court wear mourning, and received the French ambassador in a hall draped with black. Henry of Navarre was imprisoned in Paris for some time, but finally escaped and put himself at the head of the Protestant party. He had but one-tenth as many soldiers as the Catholics, but soon proved himself a great general; and after long wars, with varying success, he finally utterly defeated his enemies at the battle of Ivry, in 1590. This victory caused great rejoicing among the Huguenots. No wonder that Macaulay represents them as singing:

"Now glory to the Lord of hosts, from whom all glories are!
And glory to our sovereign liege, King Henry of Navarre!
Now let there be the merry sound of music and the dance,
Through thy cornfields green and sunny vales, O pleasant land of France!
And thou Rochelle, our own Rochelle, fair city of the waters,
Again let rapture light the eyes of all thy mourning daughters.
As thou wert constant in our ills, be joyous in our joy,
For cold, and stiff, and still, are they who wrought thy walls annoy.
Hurrah! hurrah! A single field has turned the chance of war!
Hurrah! Hurrah! For Ivry and Henry of Navarre!"

By the death of Henry III., Henry of Navarre had now become the heir to the crown of France, but it was not to be expected that the Catholic majority would permanently submit to be governed by a Protestant King. Influenced by his ambition he yielded to temptation and renounced Protestantism. It is certain that as King of France, he was able to protect the Huguenots as he had never done before, but his act cannot be defended on grounds of mere expediency. He reigned under the title of Henry IV., and became one of the greatest of French monarchs. On the 15th of April, 1598, he issued the celebrated Edict of Nantes, which secured the Protestants in the possession of their civil rights.[1] The strict Catholics, however, did not trust him, and in 1610 he was assassinated by a fanatic named Ravaillac. His death was regarded as a national calamity, but the effect of his victories remained, and for nearly a hundred years the Protestants of France enjoyed comparative security.

---

[1] Cardinal Richelieu inaugurated the policy which, after his death in 1642, was continued by his successor Mazarin, according to which Protestantism was discouraged by the government as a discordant element in the State. On the 22d of October, 1685, Louis XIV., at the instigation of the Jesuits, revoked the Edict of Nantes, and during the subsequent persecutions at least 500,000 Huguenots fled to foreign countries. Many of these refugees found their way to America, and some of them became prominent among the founders of the earliest congregations of the Reformed Church in the United States.

CHAPTER VII.

Holland—The First Martyrs—Spanish Tyranny—" The League of the Beggars"—The Revolt of the Netherlands.

The country called Holland, or originally Hollow-land, is one of the most interesting in the world. By the unremitting toil of centuries, fertile provinces have been rescued from the sea, and wealthy cities now stand where once the waters played. Here at one time the people, in their gigantic conflict for the preservation of the Reformed faith, made their dykes and sluices a means of defense, and thus employed their ancient enemy as an ally against the new.

At the beginning of the sixteenth century the seventeen provinces, known by the collective names of the Netherlands, Low Countries, or Holland, were regarded as the most precious possessions of the Spanish crown. They had formerly been attached to Burgundy, but had now by inheritance become a part of the enormous patrimony of Charles V., who was simultaneously emperor of Germany and king of Spain. The Dutch provinces, however, claimed to possess certain liberties and reserved rights, which the emperor generally permitted them to enjoy, and on the whole, Charles was more popular in Holland than in any other part of his dominions. "He was a native of the country, preferred their free manners to the reserve of the Spaniards, conferred office on natives, and was courteous in his intercourse with his subjects." The first serious trouble occurred in connection with his attempts to suppress Protestantism. He was not of a cruel disposition, but was thoroughly devoted to the pope, and deemed it his duty to labor with all his might for the extinction of what he regarded as a pestilent heresy. In Germany he could not accomplish this on account of the opposition of the Protestant princes; but in his hereditary dominions he was free to act, and here he issued edicts which threatened the most dreadful punishment to all who refused to submit to the Roman Catholic Church. These edicts were unrelentingly executed, and multitudes suffered death. In many places, however, the inquisitors were greatly impeded by local laws and the naturally independent character of the people.

THE FIRST MARTYRS.

On the 30th of June, 1523, two young men, Henry Voes and John Esch, were burned for their Protestant faith, in the great square of the city of Antwerp. When they stood bound at the stake their persecutors cried: "Be converted, or you will be lost forever." But they replied: "We will die as good Christians for the faith of the Gospel." When the flames rose around them heavenly joy filled their hearts, and one of them exclaimed: "These are surely beds of roses." When death came nearer they cried out: "Lord Jesus, thou son of David, have mercy upon us!" Then they alternately repeated the Apostles' Creed. When the flames had completely surrounded them they began to sing the *Te Deum*, and continued to sing until their voices were hushed in death.

The heroism of these early martyrs produced an effect directly contrary to that which was anticipated by the persecutors. It was an age which admired, above all things, self-sacrifice and patient endurance; and those who beheld such triumphant death-scenes were sure to be attracted to the faith that produced them. "The blood of the martyrs was the seed of the church."

"THE CHURCH UNDER THE CROSS."

Holland, like many other countries, had gradually become prepared for the doctrines of the Reformation. Long before the days of Luther and Calvin, John de Wesel, sometimes called the abbot Rupert, and John Wessel, otherwise known as Gansevoort, had contested the claims of the Roman hierarchy. The writings of the latter were republished by Luther, in order to show that the doctrines of the Reformation were not new. Erasmus and Agricola, distinguished scholars and forerunners of the Reformation, were also natives of the Netherlands.

During the earlier years of the Reformation, the Protestant Church of Holland was known as "the church under the cross." There was no formal confession of faith, and all forms of doctrinal opinion were represented.

The great body of Protestants was, however, from the beginning attached to the Reformed faith. Gradually the churches were organized according to the principles of Calvin and De Lasky, and in this way received an indelible character. The doctrines of election and predestination were consequently more prominent in the theological systems of the Dutch divines than in those of the Palatinate. In the great Arminian controversy of the succeeding century, these doctrines were still more distinctly intoned, and for a while it seemed as though the Divine Sovereignty was to be the exclusive object of study. The German churches were less affected by these controversies, and, it has been said, "did not thrive well in the theological atmosphere of Holland," but it would be a mistake to suppose that there ever was a lack of fraternal feeling between the various Reformed Churches of the continent. The Belgic confession, adopted in 1568, was specially intended for the Netherlands, so that there was no occasion for its formal acceptance by the churches of Germany, and the Heidelberg Catechism became the common standard of faith. So far as we know, it has never occurred to any one in Europe to regard the Dutch and German Reformed Churches as different denominations; and though the two American organizations which have borne these names still severally preserve certain national and theological peculiarities, it should be remembered that their separation was caused by local circumstances and differences of language, and not by theological or personal disagreement.

SPANISH TYRANNY.

In 1555 Charles V. voluntarily abdicated, and retired to the convent of Yuste to spend his declining years. It has been customary to represent him as a penitent, weary of the world and desirous of atoning for his sins by the mortification of the flesh; but the recent discovery of cotemporary documents has rendered it certain that his life in the convent by no means resembled that of an anchorite. On his abdication the Netherlands came under the rule of his son, Philip II., who is one of the most unpleasant characters in modern history. Educated exclusively by Spanish priests, he had none of his father's liking for the Netherlands. They had already become a great commercial rival of Spain, and it is not unlikely that even on this account he would have been glad to see them humbled.

When Philip assumed the government of the Netherlands, it was with the double purpose of eradicating Protestantism and of taking away the civil rights of the Dutch people. Far from being discouraged by the failure of the violent measures adopted by his father, he resolved to prosecute them more vigorously, like the foolish king who said to the Israelites on his accession to the throne: "My father made your yoke heavy, and I will add to your yoke; my father also chastised you with whips, but I will chastise you with scorpions" (1 Kings xii. 14).

At first Philip confided the government of the Low Countries to his sister Margaret of Parma, but as her disposition proved too mild for his purpose, she was superseded by the infamous Ferdinand of Toledo, Duke of Alva. This man appears to have been destitute of the ordinary feelings of humanity, and was for this reason a suitable instrument for the sanguinary purposes of the king. He introduced the Inquisition, and death was decreed against all who had been in any way connected with the Protestants; all who had heard a sermon, sung a psalm, or furnished lodging to an heretical preacher. It was his boast that during seven years he had given eighteen thousand Protestants into the hands of the executioner. One hundred thousand houses stood empty whose inmates had fled to other countries. The Reformed Church was, however, actually strengthened by these persecutions. Religious services were held at obscure places in the open country, and though thousands attended these meetings, it was but rarely that the authorities were informed in time to prevent them. In 1568, the year of most violent persecution, the ministers and elders, at the peril of their lives, secretly crossed the boundary of Germany and held an important synod in the city of Wesel. When the Inquisition burned its victims the people regarded them as martyrs. At the stake the sufferers began to sing, and the multitude, outside of the circle of Spanish guards, joined with them, until the whole city rang with the inspiring strains of the second psalm:

"Hoe rasen so die Heydenen te hoop,
End die volcken betrachten ydel dinghen?"

It might seem as though the persecutors ought to have become convinced of the futility of their undertaking, but Philip and the Duke of Alva showed no signs of weariness. Philip said he would "rather be a king without subjects than a ruler over heretics." Alva was entirely unmoved by the suffering around him. When his only son died, the cardinal of Trent attempted to comfort him; but he replied: "If my boy had been the only person that ever died, it might be worth while to speak words of consolation; but death is such a common accident that no sensible man will allow himself to be troubled by it."

"THE LEAGUE OF THE BEGGARS."

The southern part of the Netherlands—now constituting the kingdom of Belgium—had from the beginning remained prevailingly Roman Catholic. The people had, however, no sympathy with the tyranny of the Spaniards, and some of the leading noblemen joined in a petition for religious liberty. Alva took his revenge by treacherously arresting and executing Counts Egmont and Horn. This exasperated the Catholic provinces, and for a while, during the subsequent revolt, they contended bravely for civil liberty; but they finally submitted, and remained a dependency of Spain until a comparatively recent period.

On the occasion of the presentation of the famous petition, the Count of Barlaimont whispered in the ear of the regent, that the petitioners were "nothing but a crowd of beggars." This title, first given in derision, they applied to themselves, and the confederacy was subsequently known as "Les Gueux," or "The Beggars." In Germany the name was corrupted into "Guesen" or "Goesen," and it is said that in Juliers the term is still contemptuously used by the Roman Catholics.

The earliest naval forces of the Dutch Republic were known as the "beggars of the seas," and these beggars succeeded in sweeping the rich fleets of Spain so utterly from the ocean, that Spanish commercial supremacy was destroyed forever. Their first important success occurred in 1572, when William Van de Mark, with a fleet of twenty-four vessels, took possession of the harbor and town of Brill. The word "brill" in Dutch, as in German, signifies "spectacles," and this gave rise to the *jeu de mot:*

"De eerste dach van April
Verloor Duc d'Alva zynen Brill."

THE REVOLT OF THE NETHERLANDS.

In a brief sketch like the present it is impossible to enter into particulars concerning this gigantic struggle. We shall be glad if we succeed in directing some of our younger readers to the fascinating works of Prescott and Motley.

The conflict continued, with varying intensity, from 1568 to 1609, and witnessed scenes of heroism and self-sacrifice which are probably unequalled in the history of the world. During the earlier portion of the revolt the leading spirit and commander of the Dutch armies was

William, Prince of Orange. He was born at Dillenburg, in Germany, in 1533, and as he was the eldest son of the duke of Nassau-Dillenburg, is often called William of Nassau. His principality of Orange was a small district which had originally belonged to Burgundy, but was not yet swallowed up by France, though almost entirely surrounded by French territory. His private estates in the Netherlands, however, were worth far more than his little principality. He is called "the silent," not from his taciturnity, for he was pleasant and talkative, but because he showed extraordinary wisdom in keeping his own counsel.

At the beginning of the revolt William was a Catholic, but he had joined in the petition of the nobles, and would have been executed if he had not been wise enough to keep out of the way of the Duke of Alva. His conversion to Protestantism occurred several years later, and was, we think, thoroughly sincere. He hesitated long before accepting the leadership of the revolted provinces, but subsequently manifested the most extraordinary courage and endurance. After he became Stadtholder of Holland he called on England, France, and Germany, for assistance in the coming struggle, but these countries afforded little aid except in the way of money. Indeed, the attempt to resist the immense power of Spain appeared utterly hopeless, and the Hollanders at first did not expect to free their country from the yoke. In a petition addressed to the king they said: "Since they (the duke and his creatures) take pleasure in our death, and think it their interest to be our murderers, we will much rather die an honorable death for the liberties and welfare of our dear country than submit to be trampled under foot by insolent foreigners who have always hated or envied us. By so doing we shall at least transmit to our posterity this fame and reputation, that their ancestors scorned to be slaves to a Spanish Inquisition, and therefore made no scruple of redeeming a scandalous life by an honorable death. We contend for nothing less than freedom of conscience, our wives and children, our lives and fortunes. We do not desire to be discharged from our allegiance to your majesty, but only that our consciences may be preserved free before the Lord our God, that we may be permitted to hear His holy word, and walk in His commandments, so that we may be able to give an account of our souls to the Supreme Judge at the last day."

Many incidents of the war with Spain were exceedingly romantic. During the winter of 1572, the Dutch fleet was frozen up in the harbor of Amsterdam. The Spanish army undertook to march across the ice to attack it, but the Dutch soldiers put on skates, and hovered around the enemy "like flocks of birds," until they succeeded in repulsing them. At the siege of Haarlem several hundred high-born ladies enrolled themselves as soldiers, and fought like men. The town was, however, finally taken, and nearly three thousand citizens were put to death.

The siege of Leyden was regarded as one of the most

wonderful events of the century. The garrison was small, but the citizens joined in the defense with the utmost valor and constancy. The people suffered dreadfully from famine, but when at last some of them, maddened with hunger, came to the burgomaster, Peter Vanderwerf, and demanded that he should give them food or treat for the surrender of the city, he replied: "I have made an oath, which by the help of God I will keep, that I will never yield to the Spaniard. Bread, as you well know, I have none; but if my death can serve you, slay me, cut my body into morsels and divide it among you."

William of Orange was at Delft with his fleet, but could not approach without breaking the dykes that kept out the sea, and thus laying the whole country under water. The young grain was in the fields, but the States submitted to the sacrifice, and the dykes were cut. Anxiously the starving citizens of Leyden watched the rising of the flood that was to bear them deliverance. A fleet of two hundred vessels set sail from Delft, but twice the waters were driven back by an east wind, and the ships lay helplessly stranded. Finally a northwestern gale set in and the waters of the German ocean came pouring in over the ruined dykes. The Dutch and Spanish fleets had a singular midnight conflict amid the boughs of orchards and the chimneys of submerged houses. William was, however, finally successful in reaching Leyden, and sailed up the channel distributing loaves of bread to the famished people who crowded along the banks. As soon as the pangs of hunger were relieved, the whole population hastened to the principal church to return thanks for their great deliverance. The Prince of Orange, desirous of establishing some permanent memorial of this great event offered the people of Leyden, either the establishment of an annual fair, which would bring them commerce from all parts of Holland, or the foundation of a Reformed University. The people chose the latter; and the Prince was so well pleased with their decision that he not only founded the university, but also granted them the fair.

In July, 1584, William of Orange was assassinated by an emissary of the king of Spain. It was a sad day for the Reformed people of Holland when their leader was thus stricken down in the midst of his glory. His son Maurice was but seventeen years of age, but the people would have no other leader. Their confidence was not misplaced, for he soon proved himself a brilliant commander, who successively defeated a number of the most celebrated generals of the age.

The political independence of Holland was not acknowledged by Spain until 1648. Long before that time the conflict was practically ended, and Holland had become the foremost naval power in Europe. The conflict which had been waged against such fearful odds had been decided in favor of civil and religious liberty. The blood of the martyrs had not been shed in vain, and Holland became a refuge for the distressed and persecuted of all nations. The Mennonites, who in some other countries were persecuted with fire and sword, were tolerated in the Netherlands, and there became a wealthy and influential body. The "Pilgrim Fathers," who in America showed themselves so intolerant to the Baptists and Quakers, never had reason to complain of their treatment during the twelve years they had spent in Amsterdam.

When the persecuted exiles of the Palatinate fled to Holland, they were received as brethren of a common faith, and all classes united in relieving their necessities. Even after they had emigrated to America, they were followed by the generosity and fostering care of the Dutch churches, and many of our oldest congregations were in great measure founded and established by their beneficence. We should never forget the debt of gratitude which we owe to the Reformed Church of Holland.

CHAPTER VIII.

England—Cranmer and Bullinger—Peter Martyr—John De Lasky—Martin Bucer.

It is not our intention to give an account of the English Reformation. There are, however, some facts in connection with that great movement which, though frequently ignored, are sufficiently important to claim our attention. Though the Reformed Church of England differs widely from other Protestant bodies, especially in external organization, it is easy to show that at the beginning it stood in intimate relations with the churches of the Continent. Indeed, in its earlier history, it was generally recognized as one of the branches of the Reformed Church. "The Anglican, that is the English Church," says Stilling, "is only different from the rest of the Reformed Church in this, that it has an episcopal form of government. Are the Swedish and Danish Churches not Lutheran because they have bishops? Does the garment make the man?"[1]

At the beginning of the sixteenth century, the authority of the pope appeared to be as firmly established in England as in any other country in Europe.[2] Henry

---

[1] "Wahrheit in Liebe," p. 228.

[2] At an earlier date there had been earnest protests against the pretensions of the Church of Rome, but these had not succeeded in diminishing

VIII., who became king in 1509, was an enthusiastic defender of the Papacy; and when Luther, in 1521, published his book on "The Babylonish Captivity," Henry condescended to write a very violent reply, which he called, "The Defence of Seven Sacraments." In return for this service the pope gave Henry the title of "Defender of the Faith," but Luther read him such a lecture as had never been heard by a crowned head before. Afterwards, when Henry quarrelled with the pope, Luther was willing to become reconciled, but the king rejected his advances.

The circumstances which occasioned the alienation of Henry from the pope are well known, and need not be related in detail. It is a scandalous history, beginning with his divorce from Queen Katharine and his marriage with Anne Boleyn, and continuing through all his domestic relations. In 1534 the Church of England was, by Act of Parliament, declared independent of Rome, and Henry was acknowledged as the head of the Church; but to the end of his life the king maintained the Roman faith, while he remorselessly persecuted all, whether Catholics or Protestants, who refused to acknowledge his supreme authority in spiritual as well as temporal matters. It is wrong, therefore, to regard Henry as having

---

its power. *John Wycliffe* (1324-1384) was the most eminent of the English "Reformers before the Reformation." His disciples, who were termed "Lollards," were mercilessly persecuted. The five-hundredth anniversary of his death has recently been appropriately commemorated in England and America.

introduced the Reformation into England, but it is true that his alienation from Rome rendered the Reformation possible.

While the king occupied this schismatic position, Protestantism was quietly advancing throughout the kingdom. His third wife, Jane Seymour, was at heart a Protestant, and did all in her power to advance the cause. Thomas Cranmer, Archbishop of Canterbury, had been converted to Protestantism in Germany, and was privately married to a German lady, a niece of the celebrated Osiander. It was not, however, until after the death of Henry that Cranmer was able to take active measures for the organization of the Protestant Church of England.

CRANMER AND BULLINGER.

In 1536, just after the king of England's marriage to Jane Seymour, Cranmer was introduced to Henry Bullinger by Prof. Simon Grynæus, of Strasburg. In August of the same year Cranmer sent to Zurich three young Englishmen, John Butler, William Woodruff, and Nicholas Partridge, for the purpose of studying theology and becoming acquainted with the Swiss churches. They remained more than a year, and on their return to England were accompanied by Rudolph Gualter, who studied for some time at Oxford. Gualter was afterwards married to Zwingli's daughter Regula, and became the third antistes or chief-pastor of the church of Zurich.

From this time the relations of Cranmer and Bullinger

were very intimate. The works of the latter were translated into English, and a letter from Bishop John Hooper is still extant, in which he declares that he had been greatly profited by reading them. On the death of Henry VIII., in 1547, the succession devolved on his son, Edward VI., who was but ten years of age. The government was, however, really in the hands of the king's uncle, the Duke of Somerset, and a council of state of which Cranmer was a member. Every effort was now made to organize the Church of England on a Protestant basis. The king was a precocious boy, and soon took a profound interest in the movement. In 1550 he sent Christopher Mont to Zurich, with a letter to Bullinger, in which he desired a closer connection between the churches of England and Switzerland. During this period Bullinger corresponded with Warwick, Dorset, and other English statesmen, and constantly counselled moderation and mildness. He did not object to the Episcopal form of government as a matter of expediency, but advised that the services should be "clean and simple, and without pomp." When Hooper was, in 1550, appointed bishop of Gloucester, he objected to wearing the robes, but Bullinger advised him to accommodate himself in such minor matters to the policy of the Government.

The organization of the Church of England, in the reign of Edward VI., was to some extent of the nature of a compromise. There were two parties which it was deemed absolutely important to reconcile. One of these held the position of Henry VIII.; they desired to be separated from Rome, but insisted that every peculiarity of the ancient church should be scrupulously preserved. The other was thoroughly Protestant, and would gladly have assimilated the Church of England to the Reformed Churches of the continent. Neither of these parties was quite satisfied with the result of the compromise; but the influence of the former party was most felt in government and worship, and that of the latter in doctrine, as expressed in the confessions of the Church. Bullinger expressed his fears that the two parties would never become thoroughly united, and we need not say that his anticipations have been fully realized.

When Queen Mary ascended the throne, in 1553, the Roman Catholic Church was re-established. Nearly three hundred leading Protestants were burned at the stake, and thousands of others had to flee for their lives. From the stake Bishop Hooper commended his wife and child to the care of Bullinger, and Lady Jane Grey took off her gloves on the scaffold, and requested them to be sent to the Swiss preacher as a token of her affection. At this time Zurich was crowded with English refugees, and the Swiss were put to great straits in entertaining them. After the accession of Queen Elizabeth, in 1558, the refugees returned to England, and subsequently Bishops Parkhurst, Jewell, and Horn sent gifts of silver plate in recognition of the kindness shown them by the Swiss. A silver goblet is still in existence, bearing a Latin inscription to the following effect: "The Church of Zurich received the exiles of England during the reign of Mary. Elizabeth acknowledges this with thanks, and reverently presents this goblet to Bullinger."

PETER MARTYR.

According to all accounts the Church of England was, at the beginning of the Reformation, in a deplorable condition. Bucer says there were hardly ten priests in the country who attempted to preach. Cranmer, therefore, invited a number of Reformed theologians to come to England to assist him in his work. The most prominent of these was Peter Martyr (Vermigli), an Italian by birth, who had been a professor at Zurich and Strasburg. He became Professor of Theology at Oxford, where he labored for some years in the face of the bitter opposition. He was very active in the work of revising the Book of Common Prayer. On the accession of Queen Mary he returned to Strasburg, and thence to Zurich, where he died in 1562.

JOHN DE LASKY.

This distinguished leader of the Reformed Church was a Polish nobleman, and a nephew of the Archbishop of Gnesen. His scholarship was remarkable, and Erasmus calls him "a soul without a stain." Though he had early become converted to Protestantism, he lingered long before he finally separated from the Established Church; but when, in 1536, the king of Poland insisted that he should become a Roman Catholic bishop, he made a public profession of the Reformed faith, and left his native country. He was the leading spirit in the Reformed Churches of Northern Europe. To him, more than to any single individual, the Reformed Churches of Poland and Bohemia owe their existence, and his influence was hardly less extensive in the Netherlands and the Rhine provinces of Germany. In 1550 he went to England at the invitation of the king, to become the superintendent of a number of churches which had been founded in London by foreign refugees. He was inclined to extreme simplicity of worship, and therefore did not agree very well with Cranmer, but his influence in England was very extensive. While in London he published a catechism which, says Bartels, was one of the "ancestors" of the Heidelberg Catechism. The liturgies of the Palatinate and the Netherlands were also in great part derived from him. On the accession of Queen Mary, De Lasky left England with a colony of several hundred persons, who, after many trials, found a refuge in Germany. He died in 1560.

MARTIN BUCER.

In 1549 this celebrated reformer was called to England to become Professor of Theology at Cambridge. Cranmer regarded him as peculiarly qualified to assist him in his work, and in this he was not mistaken. The two men had much in common; both were eminently qualified to serve as mediators between conflicting parties, though Bucer was more firm and courageous than the English prelate. Bucer had recently been engaged in an undertaking which had specially prepared him for the work which he was expected to perform in England. Herman V., Archbishop of Cologne, had, in 1541, undertaken to introduce the Reformation into his diocese without making greater changes in the government and ritual of the church than were absolutely necessary. With this intention he secured the assistance of Melanchthon, and especially of Bucer, who was thus led to the study of questions of ritual and government, which were of great importance in his subsequent work. The movement at Cologne was not successful, and the good archbishop was forced to resign his office. On account of his connection with this enterprise, Bucer became especially obnoxious to the emperor, and was, therefore, the more ready to accept Cranmer's invitation. In England he continued his literary labors, and in connection with Peter Martyr was especially employed in the work of revising the English Liturgy. The forms hitherto in use had been closely modeled after the Roman Mass, and it is said to have been at Bucer's suggestion that auricular confession, prayers for the dead, exorcism, anointing with oil, and the authorized use of bright-colored robes, were removed from the Book of Common Prayer.

With all the honors that were shown him, Bucer was not happy in England. He spoke but little English, and his wife was entirely ignorant of that language. His intercourse was therefore limited to the learned, who spoke Latin, and to the German and French refugees.

The climate and mode of living did not agree with him, and his health rapidly declined. He died the 28th of February, 1551, aged 61 years.

We have had room to refer to a few only of the members of the Reformed Church of Germany and Switzerland who were prominent in the organization of the Church of England. It would have been possible to mention others, such as Ochino, Tremellius, and Fagius. For the Church of England we have the most profound respect, but in these latter days we think we observe a tendency in some of its members to ignore their obligations to the churches of the continent. Such persons we would beg to refer to the official letter, quoted by Pestalozzi, and still preserved in Zurich, in which the Swiss churches were, in 1547, informed that the Church of England had adopted the Reformed doctrine of the Lord's Supper. It should also be remembered that, as late as 1618, an English delegation was sent, by the authority of King James I., to the Reformed Synod of Dordrecht in Holland,[1] and that the Protestant Episcopal Church of England was there recognized as one of the Reformed churches.

---

[1] The English delegation to the Synod of Dordrecht consisted of George Carleton, Bishop of Llandaff; Joseph Hall, Dean of Worcester; Samuel Ward, Archdeacon of Taunton; and John Davenant, Professor of Theology at Cambridge.

CHAPTER IX.

Scotland—Before the Reformation—The Great Reformer—Mary, Queen of Scots—The Conclusion of the Work.

In the public square in front of the Parliament House in Edinburgh, there is a stone in the pavement bearing the initials "J. K." There was once a church-yard in that place, and the inscribed stone is supposed to mark the grave of John Knox, who beyond all other men deserves to be called the founder of the Presbyterian Church of Scotland. Yet Knox was a disciple of John Calvin, and had so completely copied his master that he has been called "another Calvin;" while the church which he founded became more thoroughly "Calvinistic" than the Reformed Churches of Geneva, France, or Holland. "The Church of Scotland," says Stähelin, the most recent biographer of the great reformer, "must be recognized as the 'Calvinistic' church, in the fullest sense of the term. Calvin's doctrines and church government were there accepted in the minutest particulars. We find there even his spirit—his sternness, his logical tendencies, his ideas of theocracy and its corollary, the consecrated congregation. It might almost be said, that his personal character was reproduced in Scotland, so that almost every pious Scotch Christian is another Calvin, only different from the original in so far as he is influenced by times and circumstances. All this is, however, owing rather to John Knox than to the direct influence of Calvin." The Reformed Church of the continent, it will be remembered, was derived from three sources—Zurich, Geneva, and the Palatinate. The Presbyterian Church of Scotland, on the other hand, derived its doctrine and government from Geneva alone, and thus preserved many Calvinistic peculiarities, which, on the continent, disappeared with the union of the three original elements. The Church of Scotland was always recognized as one of the Reformed Churches, and yet it was felt to be, in a special sense, the church of Calvin.

BEFORE THE REFORMATION.

The Scotch people are at present so sensible and thrifty, that it is hard to believe that before the Reformation they were regarded as one of the most turbulent races in Europe. The country was rent by intestine feuds, which frequently resulted in civil war. The people were miserable in the extreme, for the country, though so frequently glorified by poets and writers of romance, is really barren. In the midst of general destitution the Church, however, appeared to be prosperous. It had enjoyed the lavish patronage of kings, who looked to it for moral support in their constant conflicts with turbulent nobles. As a close corporation, constantly seeking to increase its possessions, and protected in their enjoyment by the superstition of the people, it seemed as though the whole kingdom must soon become ecclesiastical property. Unfortunately, the Church did not employ its grand opportunities for the advantage of the people. Its enormous wealth was spent in the erection of magnificent monasteries, while the schools were sadly neglected. Even at the University of St. Andrew's, it is said neither Greek nor Hebrew was taught, and a few young men who were ambitious of securing a thorough education were obliged to seek it in foreign countries. The parish priests generally knew nothing but a little Latin, and were therefore theologically unprepared for the coming conflict. They were, however, eager to suppress all opposition to their authority, and during the Middle Ages showed themselves zealous persecutors of the Culdees, who appear to have been adherents of an earlier and simpler form of Christianity. On the first appearance of the Reformed doctrines, the magnates of the church were unanimously in favor of their violent suppression; but as usual persecution failed to accomplish its evil purpose. One of the earliest of the Scotch martyrs was Patrick Hamilton, a near relative of the royal family, who had studied in Germany, and had accepted the doctrines of Luther. He was burned at the stake in 1532. This cruel act not only shocked the people, but roused the nobility to a sense of their danger, when one of their own number could be thus barbarously executed for his theological opinions. The Scotch nobles, it must be remembered, stood in a sort of patriarchai relation to the people. They were at the head of clans, all the members of which bore the same family name with their chief, and regarded themselves as of the same blood. There was, therefore, a community of interest between the nobles and the people, which existed nowhere else in Europe. Gradually a chasm appeared, between the Church and royal family on the one hand, and the nobles, with the great body of the people, on the other. For some years the church continued to rule with a heavy hand, but it cannot have been difficult to to foresee the result of the coming conflict.

THE GREAT REFORMER.

John Knox was born in 1505, but his birthplace is uncertain. He went to school at Haddington and St. Andrew's, but, as he himself says, the schools were so bad that he had to get his real education elsewhere. It is evident, however, that he was regarded as a promising scholar, for he was hurried into the priesthood before he had attained the legal age. Like many others of the Reformers, he was led to the Gospel by studying the writings of St. Augustine. In 1530 the scales fell from his eyes, but it was not till 1542 that he made a public profession of his faith. His violent denunciations of the papacy now made him peculiarly obnoxious to the Catholics, and when a French fleet came to assist the regent, he was taken prisoner and carried away to France. Here he was for nineteen months a galley-slave, loaded with chains and exposed to every manner of indignity. On his release he went to England, where he was for some time a chaplain of King Edward VI., but declined to be made a bishop. When Mary became queen he fled to Geneva, where, in 1554, he for the first time met John Calvin. Knox was delighted with the city and with the great preacher who was its leading spirit. "In other localities," he wrote, "I confess that Christ is truly preached, but nowhere else have I found religion and manners so truly reformed." Though nearly fifty years of age, Knox became a student in Calvin's school, and with great humility studied the ancient languages in the company of boys who were not yet out of their teens. In the meantime he preached to a little congregation of English refugees, who with difficulty provided him with the means of subsistence. Several times he paid short visits to Scotland, but each time returned to Geneva, saying that the time had not yet come. In 1559, however, he exclaimed, "Now Scotland is ripe!" Returning to his native land he became the leader of the Protestants, and in one year the cause was practically gained. In 1560 Parliament declared the Roman system abrogated, and in the same year formally adopted the Scotch Confession.

MARY, QUEEN OF SCOTS.

The tragic fate of Mary Stuart has rendered her a favorite character with poets and novelists, and the question of her guilt or innocence of the crimes charged against her is still debated, but seems no nearer solution than it was three hundred years ago. It will, however, be confessed by her stoutest advocates that her conduct was, to say the least, exceedingly imprudent. When she came to Scotland, in 1561, as the widow of a French king, for the purpose of assuming the government of her kingdom, her grace and beauty charmed all classes. She promised toleration, but it soon appeared that she would employ every means in her power to reestablish the ancient ecclesiastical system. Knox was the special object of her aversion, and on several occasions she tried to have him condemned, under various pretenses; but he defended himself in her presence with such energy and eloquence that she was melted to tears. He was so popular that all her efforts were of no avail, and it became evident that he possessed more real power than royalty itself. For some time Mary's reign was fairly prosperous; but she drew upon herself the bitter enmity of Queen Elizabeth by claiming to be the rightful heir to the crown of England. Then, against the advice of her best friends, she married her weak and wicked cousin, Lord Henry Darnley. Because she would not confer royal power upon her husband, he treated her scandalously, and in company with some of his boon companions murdered her Italian secretary, David Rizzio, in the queen's presence. A year afterwards the house in which Darnley was lying sick was blown up with gunpowder. The guilt of the queen in thus securing the murder of her husband is not clear, but it is certain that she immediately showed great favor to Lord Bothwell, who was universally regarded as the murderer, and three months later married him. It is said she did this under compulsion, but we have not room for all the unsavory details. The people were disgusted, as well they might be, and the natural result was civil war. The queen's party was defeated, and she very foolishly fled to England, to place herself under the protection of her bitterest enemy, Elizabeth. There she was imprisoned, or at least kept under surveillance, for nearly eighteen years. In 1587 she was executed, but it is still an open question whether the death warrant was actually signed by the queen of England. It has been plausibly urged that the English ministers of state were afraid of the vengeance of Mary, in case she should become queen of England by the death of Elizabeth; and that they therefore forged the signature of the latter to the death warrant—an act which Elizabeth did not venture to repudiate in consequence of the state of public feeling in England. However guilty Mary may have been, it is certain that no English court had the right to try and condemn the queen of another country.

THE CONCLUSION OF THE WORK.

After the flight of Queen Mary there was in Scotland a period of confusion and violence. Under the regent Morton an effort was made to establish a diocesan episcopate, but the effort proved a failure, and only intensified the Scottish hatred for every thing that savored of prelacy. Until his death, which occurred in 1572, Knox remained the most influential man in the Church of Scotland, and before he passed away he had succeeded in permanently moulding it to his ideal. The churches were destitute of ornament, and kneeling in worship was forbidden. Prayers were not allowed at the burial of the dead, but the Scriptures were explained daily in the churches. Holidays were abrogated, but the Christian Sabbath was observed with a degree of strictness that had been before unknown. There was a Directory of Public Worship, but it was concerned rather with the matter than the form of the service. The people were thoroughly indoctrinated, and took a profound interest in everything that concerned the church. Stern and strict the Scottish church may have appeared to foreigners, but there can be no question as to the glorious examples of earnest piety which it produced.

The frequent attempts of English monarchs, since the union, to introduce the Episcopal form of government, have but served to intensify the peculiarities of the Church of Scotland. On the continent, for instance, the government of the church was always regarded as a matter of minor importance; but in Scotland it became practically a matter of faith. In the reign of Charles I., those dissatisfied with prelacy in Scotland and England united in subscribing to the "Solemn League and Covenant:" and in 1647 the General Assembly of Scotland adopted the Westminster Confession, which is still its authorized standard of faith.

The Church of Scotland is at present divided into three great divisions: the Established Church, the Free Church, and the United Presbyterians. Whatever may have been the original differences of these bodies they appear to a stranger to be very much alike, and hopes are entertained that they may be finally reunited. There are also, as in America, several minor bodies, which regard themselves as called to offer a special "testimony."

From Scotland the Presbyterian Church has extended to Ireland, America, and Australia. In fact, in almost every region in which the English language is spoken, the Presbyterian Church is a prosperous body, and everywhere it is actively engaged in extending the kingdom of our blessed Lord.

CHAPTER X.

Women of the Reformed Church: Anna Reinhard; Idelette De Bures; Jeanne D'Albret; Charlotte De Bourbon; Catharine Belgica of Hanau; Gertrude von Bentheim; Louisa Henrietta of Brandenburg.

The Reformation has frequently been represented as the exclusive work of men in exalted station. Roman Catholic theologians have been fond of depicting it as a system rudely imposed by the nobility, envious of the wealth of the church, and ignorantly accepted by the people, almost without a single sympathetic emotion. The shallowness of such a view is shown by the enthusiasm and devotion of multitudes of women who, without taking a prominent part in public affairs, proved themselves ready to suffer and die for the cause of the Gospel. In the early history of the Reformed Church we read of the devotion of the women of Geneva, and of the heroism of the women of Holland; and find that in the most trying times the greatest heroes of the faith were encouraged by the self-sacrificing devotion of the women of their households; but it is only in exceptional cases that we can become minutely familiar with the lives of those who by their silent ministrations did so much for the church. Fortunate circumstances have preserved the domestic life of Luther, but we know next to nothing concerning that of the other Reformers. Even such obscurity may, however, have its lessons, and we propose, therefore, to say a few words concerning the wives of several of the men who were most prominent in the early history of the Reformed Church, and then to give a few examples of ladies of exalted station who chose the shame of Christ in preference to the glory of the world.

ANNA REINHARD.

The life of the consort of Zwingli included an unusual portion of affliction. Anna Reinhard had been a beautiful girl of humble station, who had at an early age married a young nobleman, John Meyer von Knonau. The proud family of the bridegroom was bitterly opposed to the union, and he was forced to seek military service in foreign lands. He died in 1515, leaving his widow, with three children, in straitened circumstances. One of the children was a beautiful boy named Gerold, who succeeded in attracting the attention and affection of his grandfather, who afterward made some provision for the support of the widow. When Zwingli met her she was no longer in the bloom of youth, but was dignified in manner and universally esteemed. It is said it was admiration for the boy Gerold that first directed the attention of the great Reformer to the mother. We have no particulars concerning the courtship, but it is certain that the marriage was for some time kept secret. It was dangerous for a priest to marry, as no one could tell what would be the result of the great conflict, so that Anna showed no little courage in linking her fortunes to those of the bold champion of the Reformation. Everything indicates that she became a model wife. She appreciated the grandeur of the work, and therefore took charge of the household and saved her husband as much as possible from those daily cares which might have interfered with his literary labor. During the great controversy of Baden, when, it is said, Zwingli did not go to bed for six weeks, we may be sure Anna was not idle. She was ready at any hour to prepare refreshment for her husband, or for the couriers who generally arrived at midnight. The family life was earnest and solemn; sometimes Zwingli would play on the flute, to the great delight of his wife and children, and it is said, that he often consulted with his wife concerning the proper training of the little ones. With all this, we can hardly suppose that Anna enjoyed much of what is generally known as domestic happiness. It was a period in which there was little time for the cultivation of the amenities of social life, and men and women were alike called to endure hardness for the cause of Christ. As the years rolled on the struggle increased in intensity, and at last came the dreadful catastrophe at Cappel, where, in a single battle, Anna lost her husband, her son Gerold, a son-in-law, a brother, and many other relatives. Could any sorrow be greater than this? That her cotemporaries appreciated her affliction is evident from a mournful ballad, " Frau Zwingli's Lament," which is still extant. Anna lingered seven years after the death of her husband, watching over her children with maternal care, and comforted by seeing them growing up into worthy men and women. Humble and uncomplaining, she was, as really as her husband, a martyr in the cause of truth.

IDELETTE DE BURES.

The domestic life of John Calvin is very obscure. He was twenty-nine years old, and almost at the zenith of his fame, before he thought of marriage. Idelette de Bures, whom he chose to be his wife, was of lofty lineage and high culture, but of a modest and retiring disposition. She was the widow of an Anabaptist, whom Calvin had converted. The union was not the result of violent passion, for as Calvin himself says, he was not "one of that kind." Audin, a Roman Catholic writer, says "he wanted a secretary, a nurse, a cook, a manager;" but there is plenty of evidence to show that Calvin fully appreciated the sanctity of marriage, and chose his wife for loftier qualities than these. His enemies have called him heartless, because when she died he went on with his employments as before; but we may well believe his statement, that unless he had done so he would have been utterly crushed by sorrow. Seven years after her death he still speaks of his great affliction, and he never could be induced to enter into a second matrimonial alliance. He speaks of his wife as an example of all that is beautiful in women. Like an ancient portrait, almost effaced by time, we can hardly discern her features, but enough remains to assure us of the incomparable beauty of the original.

JEANNE D'ALBRET.

We have already referred to Margaret of Navarre, and to the influence which she exerted in behalf of the French Reformation. Her daughter Jeanne D'Albret manifested such courage in the cause of the Huguenots that she has come to be regarded as a national heroine. In her youth she had been very badly treated for her inclination towards Protestantism, and once she was violently beaten by the king, her father. She became the wife of Antoine of Bourbon, and the mother of Henry IV. of France.

Navarre, her ancestral kingdom, was situated directly south of France, on the Spanish border. Part of it had already been seized by Spain, and when it was found that the heiress was a Protestant the pope undertook to dispose of the rest in a similar manner. Her husband, who had hitherto been ostentatious in his Protestantism, now became frightened and sought to make terms with the Catholics, but Jeanne was roused to action. With the courage characteristic of her race, she rode about her kingdom, levying troops, fortifying cities, and inspiring her people to make a bold defence. She issued an edict formally introducing the Reformed religion, and in the midst of war founded schools for the instruction of Reformed ministers. Her influence over the Huguenot soldiery was unbounded, and the enthusiasm which was excited in her behalf was in itself an assurance of victory. No doubt it was, in a great degree owing to the mutual jealousies of France and Spain that she was enabled to sustain herself amid the surrounding storm and strife; but she has left behind her a brilliant fame, and even the Catholics of Southern France know her, after three centuries, as "the good Queen of Navarre." She died in Paris, and though surrounded by bigoted Romanists, she offered her testimony in that solemn hour in the beautiful words: "I believe that Christ is my only Saviour and Mediator, and I expect salvation through no other."

CHARLOTTE DE BOURBON.

It has been remarked by a recent writer, that "The life of Charlotte de Bourbon is one of those romances of real life which give to history all the subtile charm of fiction." She was a daughter of the Duke of Montpensier, who was one of the stoutest champions of the church of Rome. Discovering that she was inclined to become a Protestant her father forced her to enter the convent of Jouarre, of which she soon became abbess. It was not a hard life, and to some persons it might have been fascinating. Her high rank was fully recognized, even within the walls of her convent, and the luxuries and refinements of fashionable life were not absolutely excluded. Charlotte, however, hated the whole system, and, in 1572, escaped in disguise, and found a refuge with the elector of the Palatinate. Here she met the Prince of Orange, who afterward became her husband. During the fiercest portion of the struggle with Spain she stood by the side of her heroic companion, and we read that his household afforded him his chief consolation in that period of unutterable misery. The Prince was several times wounded by assassins before their wicked plans were finally successful. On one of these occasions he was shot through the head, and it was believed that he could not recover. For eighteen days his wife watched over him, and it was chiefly by her tender nursing that his precious life was spared. At the end of that period the nation held a festival of rejoicing for the restoration of their Prince. Charlotte attended the service in the church, but returned home utterly exhausted. In three days she yielded up her life, which it may be said she had sacrificed for her heroic husband. Motley says: " The Prince was saved, but unhappily the murderer had yet found an illustrious victim—the devoted wife who had so faithfully shared his joys and sorrows."

CATHARINA BELGICA OF HANAU.

This excellent lady was a daughter of the Prince of Orange and Charlotte de Bourbon. She was born in 1578, and was married in her eighteenth year to Count Philip Ludwig II., of Hanau. Her husband lived but sixteen years after his marriage, but after his death the affairs of state were wisely administered by his widow until 1627, when she renounced the government in favor of her eldest son. She founded a celebrated literary institution at Hanau, which numbered among its professors such men as Tossanus and the younger Pareus. Her court was always a place of refuge for the oppressed. During the Thirty Years' War her principality was overrun by armies, and she was forced to retire to Holland, where she died in 1649.

GERTRUDE VON BENTHEIM.

Bentheim is a small principality in Westphalia. Though it has long lost its independence, its counts at one time occupied a prominent position among the princely houses of Germany. Count Ernst Wilhelm had remained unmarried until his thirty-eighth year, and the family of his younger brother felt sure of the succession; but in 1663 he married Gertrude von Zelst, who was of noble descent, but was not regarded as of equal rank with her husband. The disappointed younger line tried by every means in their power to have the marriage declared illegal, so that the poor countess was in great trouble. Her husband was a weak man, who had no power to defend himself, and in her extremity she asked the aid of the powerful Roman Catholic bishop of Münster. The bishop was glad of the opportunity, and secured a decree from the emperor by which the countess was exalted to her husband's rank. Then he claimed as his reward that the family should join the Roman Catholic Church. The countess, who was a sincerely pious woman, declined to take this step, but the bishop watched his opportunity, and seized the count while on a journey, and after a week's imprisonment induced him to renounce Protestantism. Then a company of soldiers was sent to take possession of the castle of Bentheim, and as the countess refused to admit them, the bishop followed with 4,000 men. Resistance was in vain, and the countess was taken as a prisoner to Münster. Anticipating the coming evil she had sent her children to Holland, confiding them to the care of the States-General. After many trials she also succeeded in escaping to Holland, where she lived in retirement with her children. Her husband, who had by this time become a thorough Catholic, secured a divorce, and was married to a countess of Limburg. When Gertrude heard of this second marriage, she could no longer sustain the weight of her sorrow, and after three days died of a broken heart.

The people of Bentheim sympathized with their injured countess. They held meetings and determined to remain faithful to the Reformed faith, and it was at this time that the classis of Bentheim adopted a seal, bearing as a device, a representation of our Saviour in the ship, in in the storm on the lake of Galilee, with the inscription in Latin, "Lord save us; we perish," (Matt. viii. 25).

LOUISA HENRIETTA OF BRANDENBURG.

This celebrated poetess was born, Nov. 17th, 1627, at the Hague, in Holland. She was the eldest daughter of Frederick Henry, Prince of Orange, and a granddaughter of the famous Coligni, Grand Admiral of France, who lost his life for his faith at the massacre of St. Bartholomew. Her pious parents gave her an excellent education, but she did not regard it as below the dignity of her station to become familiar with every kind of household labor. At the age of nineteen she was married to Frederick William of Brandenburg, who is called "the Great Elector," and who is properly regarded as the real founder of the kingdom of Prussia. Though he did not assume the royal title, he was as really a king as any one of his successors. Louisa soon proved herself the worthy consort of a great ruler. Her marriage occurred just before the close of the Thirty Years' War, when Germany had been trampled by contending armies until it was almost ruined. The princess labored with all her might to improve the condition of her subjects. She introduced the cultivation of potatoes, and induced some of the best farmers in Holland to remove to Germany and establish model farms. Her popularity was so great that, it is said, almost every female child born during the first years of her reign was called " Louisa."

Though she and her husband were both earnestly attached to the Reformed faith, they labored earnestly for the reconciliation of the two evangelical churches. They refused to promulgate the decrees of the Synod of Dordrecht, which they regarded as an apple of discord.

The domestic life of the royal pair was blessed by mutual affection; but apart from this, it has been said their lives were "a chain of sorrows." Nearly all their relatives died early, and some of them under the most distressing circumstances. There was a succession of dreadful wars, and sometimes it seemed as though their enemies would succeed in destroying them. Their greatest grief was the death of their only son, who died in infancy. For eleven years they had no other child, and it seemed as though the House of Hohenzollern must become extinct. The people appreciated the complications to which such an event must give rise. There would be terrible wars for the succession, and the land must again be given over to ruin and desolation. Hence they, most unjustly, began to regard the princess with aversion, and many wished her out of the way for the good of the country.

All this preyed on the mind of the Electress Louisa. She prayed over it, and at last regarded it as her duty to make a formal application for a divorce. One day she appeared publicly before the Elector and said: "I beg leave to apply for a divorce. Take another wife, who will bless the country with an heir to the throne. You owe this to the wishes of your people." The Elector, however, refused to accept the sacrifice, and replied: "As far as I am concerned, I am determined to keep the vow which I made at the altar; and if it pleases God to punish me and the country, we will have to endure it. Louisa! have you forgotten the words of Scripture: 'What God hath joined together let no man put asunder.'" Then he gave her his hand and said, smiling; "Well! who knows what may yet happen?"

Greatly comforted by the unswerving affection of her husband, Louisa retired to her palace at Oranienburg, where she spent her time in prayer and deeds of beneficence. Her health gradually improved, and in the following year she had a son. Three years later a second heir was granted her, and the latter prince was afterwards Frederick I., of Prussia, the direct ancestor of the present emperor. The prayers of Louisa were answered, and as a memorial of her thankfulness she established an Orphan Asylum, which is still flourishing.

The Electress died June 18th, 1667, soon after the birth of her sixth child, Prince Louis, of Cleves. Some of her death-bed sayings have been recorded. Once she exclaimed: "I am drawing near the harbor! I see the pinnacles of the celestial city! If I should get well, it would throw me back into the stormy ocean." Just before her death she said: "I have passed with Elijah through the storm, the earthquake and the fire. Now I am waiting for the still, small voice." Her last words were: "I hear the still, small voice."

It is as the authoress of a number of hymns that Louisa of Brandenburg is best remembered. The best known of these are, "Jesus meine Zuversicht," and "Ich will von meiner Missethat," which are sung wherever the German language is spoken. The former, it is said, is always sung at the burial of a member of the royal family of Prussia. Some years ago the king presented to the church in which his ancestors used to worship a large bell, which he named "Zuversicht," bearing as an inscription the first two lines of her celebrated hymn, which may be rendered:

"Jesus, my eternal Trust,
And my Saviour, lives forever."

This hymn has been so frequently translated that, in some form, it is probably familiar to most English readers. We give several stanzas, from a version by an unknown author, which, though not very literal, contains much of the spirit of the original:

"Jesus, my Redeemer lives;
  Christ, my trust, is dead no more!
In the strength this knowledge gives
  Shall not all my fears be o'er,
Though the night of death be fraught
Still with many an anxious thought?

"Jesus, my Redeemer lives,
  And His life I once shall see,—
Bright the hope this promise gives;
  Where He is, I, too, shall be.
Shall I fear, then? Can the head
Rise and leave the members dead?

"Ye who suffer, sigh and moan,
  Fresh and glorious there shall reign;
Earthly here the seed is sown,
  Heavenly it shall rise again.
Natural here the death we die;
Spiritual our life on high.

"Only see ye that your heart
  Rise betimes from worldly lust.
Would ye, there, with Him have part?
  Here obey your Lord and trust.
Fix your hearts beyond the skies,
Whither ye yourselves would rise."

CHAPTER XI.

*The Great Theologians—Gomarists and Arminians—The Scho-
lastics—Coccejans or Federalists.*

TRAVELERS in Europe never grow weary of dilating on the architectural grandeur of the great cathedrals. These stupendous structures are so harmonious in all their parts, so wonderful in their artistic execution, that they are at once recognized as works of art of the highest order. Not less wonderful to those who take trouble to examine them are the works of the great theologians who have left us, in great folios, their conceptions of the system of Christian doctrine. Strange and curious their writings may appear to the present generation; full of odd conceits that are not in accordance with modern taste; but there is in them a certain strength and power, a mastering of analytic details, which reminds us irresistibly of the colossal genius of the ancient architects.

The distinguished theologians of the Reformed Church have been so numerous that the mere enumeration of their names and masterpieces would not only be uninteresting to the general reader, but would prove a task too extensive for our present purpose. It is, therefore, possible only to give a brief sketch of several of the early schools by which Reformed theology was elaborated, thus showing that the Church has never been narrow and sectarian, but has on the contrary justified its claim to be regarded as the most liberal of the Protestant Churches.

The work of the Reformers was more polemic than systematic. In most instances their primary object was to defend the Church against the attacks of its enemies, and it was left to a later generation to gather and arrange the trophies of victory.

John Calvin was no doubt the greatest theologian of the era of the Reformation, and his "Institutes" should never be mentioned without respect. His system was further developed after his death by Theodore Beza, Daniel Chamier, Benedict Pictet, and others. It was, however, never completely accepted by the Swiss and Germans. "Two-thirds of the Reformed Church," says Ebrard, "kept itself perfectly free from Calvin's doctrine of absolute predestination." Henry Bullinger, "the wisest man the Reformed Church ever produced," based his system on the Incarnation, as was subsequently done in the Heidelberg Catechism. He was followed by the five great Swiss theologians—Musculus, Aretius, Polanus, Wollebius, and Alting. The theologians of the Palatinate were intimately connected with those of German Switzerland, but most of their literary work was devoted to the defence of the Catechism. The most important systems of Reformed theology produced in Germany during this period were those of Keckermann, Hyperius, and Alsted.

In this way two types of doctrine were gradually developed, the one strictly Calvinistic, the other approaching more nearly to the teachings of Bullinger and Melanchthon. As the age was profoundly interested in theological questions it could not be otherwise than that these systems should be brought into frequent conflict, but it was in Holland especially that the struggle reached its culmination. It would be a weary task to attempt to distinguish between the various shades of doctrine, which in those days furnished questions of the profoundest interest, but which now appear to the general reader as dry as dust. Even the great questions concerning predestination, though they are still occasionally discussed, have lost much of their interest. We have come to feel, with Bullinger, that "Christ is the object and contents of divine predestination," and that it is better to seek for living union with Him than to spend our lives in attempting to fathom the oracles of God. It may, however, not be in vain to say a few words concerning several of the more important schools of doctrine, whose leaders were monarchs in the realm of thought, and whose influence even now cannot be said to have entirely passed away.

GOMARISTS AND ARMINIANS.

We have already referred to the great conflict in Holland, which finally culminated in the great synod of Dordrecht. The titles generally applied to the conflicting parties were derived from Francis Gomarus (1563-1641) and Jacob Arminius (1560-1609) who were rival professors in the University of Leyden. Gomarus claimed to be the special champion of orthodoxy, and insisted that the confessions of the Church could never be changed, and that any deviation from their strict letter must be punished as heresy. Against this interpretation Arminius and his party remonstrated, and they were therefore known as Remonstrants. The main theological questions at issue between the parties were, of course, connected with the doctrine of predestination, but these were by no means the only elements that entered into the conflict. Religious mysteries, which should always be approached with reverence, became the ordinary subjects of political controversy. The struggle soon came to involve questions which concerned the civil government, and the whole community was greatly excited. With the aid of Prince Maurice the Gomarists were finally successful, but their triumph was sullied by many acts of cruelty. It must however be remembered that the conflict was no less political than ecclesiastical, and that it resulted in breaking the power of the hereditary aristocracy of Holland.

A recent writer says: "There was right and wrong on both sides. The doctrines of each party correct and complete those of the other, and each may become dangerous by being exclusively entertained." Ebrard intimates that Arminianism was not so objectionable on account of its doctrine of the decrees, as in consequence of a spirit of rationalism that pervaded the whole system. While, therefore, the Reformed Church of Germany refused to be bound by the decrees of the Synod of Dordrecht, it was equally decided in declining to accept the system of Arminius.

THE SCHOLASTICS.

The great conflict in Holland was followed by a period of stern orthodoxy in which, it was said, "men dreaded the imputation of heresy more than sin." It was not a period of original research, but the teachings of the fathers were gathered and arranged with incredible labor and patience. It would however be a great error to suppose that all this was mere formalism, or that there was a lack of earnest piety. The system was scholastic—it was better suited to the school than to the pulpit, and strongly resembled the mediæval philosophy from which it derived its name, but it produced a series of Christian teachers who are worthy of the highest reverence.

Gisbert Voetius (1589–1676) was undoubtedly the greatest of the scholastic theologians. Nature seemed to have designed him to be a ruler of men, and during his long career he certainly exercised a far greater personal influence than many a crowned monarch. In his youth he had been a delegate to the Synod of Dordrecht, and during his whole life he labored so faithfully to execute its decrees that he was called "the hammer of the Remonstrants." Yet this great man felt the necessity of cultivating a more profound spirit of devotion in the Dutch churches, and it was mainly through his influence that the celebrated French revival preacher Jean de Labadie was brought to Holland, though if he had known how violently the dry bones would be shaken, it is probable the Frenchman would never have been invited. The times were however ripe for a reaction, and it came in the promulgation of another system of doctrine.

THE COCCEJANS OR FEDERALISTS.

Dr. Johannes Coccejus (1605–1669) was a native of Bremen. His family name was Koch, but according to the fashion of the times, he gave it a Latin form. From his earliest youth he was inclined to religious study, and this tendency was strengthened by the training which he received at home. In order to avoid the prevalent rowdyism of the German universities, he studied in Holland, and before he was of age was recognized as an orientalist of the highest order. Called to a professorship in Holland, he soon protested against the prevalent exclusive devotion to the confessions of faith. With the utmost enthusiasm he led his pupils back to the Bible as the only source of our knowledge of the truth. He taught them to devote less attention to the decrees, and more to the covenant which God has established with His people.

In this way Coccejus became the father of what is known in the Reformed Church as "Biblical Theology." Among his disciples were such men as Burmann, Witsius, Lampe, Vitringa, and others, from whom directly or indirectly, many of the early ministers of the Reformed Church in the United States derived their theological instruction.

The contests of the Coccejans and Scholastics were sometimes violent, but they were never as bitter as those of the Gomarists and Arminians. In Holland the Coccejans were soon tolerated, and in Germany their teachings were almost universally accepted.

The Reformed Church has had many schools of doctrine, and we might speak at length of Cartesians, Amyraldists, Wolfians and others. These were not sects but theological parties which served their purpose and then passed away. Their contentions were sometimes fierce, but we believe the only instances of real persecution occurred during the Arminian controversy, and for these the Church is less to be blamed than the State.

We have mentioned but a few of the most eminent early Reformed theologians. Heppe enumerates not less than fifty-three professors who, before the present century, wrote and published systems of theology; and besides these there were many who prepared commentaries on the Heidelberg Catechism. The works of these great men are now but rarely read, but while we enjoy the blessings which we owe to their labors, let us not forget the patient toilers who have hardened the path for our feet.

CHAPTER XII.

The Great Revival—Jean De Labadie—Jodocus Van Loden-stein—The Pietists—Philip Jacob Spener—The Great Hymnologists—Joachim Neander—Gerhard Tersteegen.

THE seventeenth century was a period of gigantic conflicts. At present it is difficult to form an adequate idea of the horrors of the Thirty Years' War, and of the subsequent French invasions. Germany was trodden by contending armies until it was little better than a wilderness; a generation grew up which had no idea of the blessings of peace. There was misery everywhere, and if it had not been for the fact that the Christian faith affords comfort in affliction, it is probable that even the feeble spark that remained would have ceased to glimmer.

Even in Holland, the condition of the Church was very discouraging. The whole ecclesiastical system appeared to be petrified. Folks went to church as their fathers had done, sang their old, unmusical version of the Psalms, and listened to rigidly analytical discourses on the points of Calvinism, but the enthusiasm which had sustained the Church in its hours of trial appeared to have departed. The Church, it was evident, could only be saved by a genuine revival of Christian life; and though when it came it sometimes ran to unwarrantable extremes, it must, as a whole, be regarded as a precious season of refreshing—a blessed rain, that caused the desert wastes to bud and blossom.

Two men were, under the Providence of God, mainly instruments in the inauguration of this great revival. Differing widely in personal characteristics, as well as in their views of the truth, they were both undoubtedly sincere; and though one of them ended his career in wild fanaticism, their united influence was so great and in the main so beneficent, that they deserve a prominent place in the history of the Church.

Jean de Labadie (1610–1674) was a native of Guyenne, in southern France. He is described as having been of small stature, but of a fiery spirit, and possessed of extraordinary eloquence. Having been well educated he was ordained to the priesthood at an early age. An enthusiast by nature, he soon found himself hampered by the services of the Church of Rome. As a pulpit orator he attracted great attention, but when he undertook to organize a brotherhood in the Catholic Church, consisting of those who were truly converted, the Jesuits determined to crush him. In 1650 he entered the Reformed Church, and was for some time pastor of Calvin's Church in Geneva. Here his preaching caused intense excitement. Tens of thousands of people flocked to hear him, and multitudes professed conversion. When he was at the height of his popularity he received a call to come to Holland, for the purpose of awakening the people to a renewed interest in religion. Like most revivalists, he was fond of changing his residence, and became pastor of the French Church at Middleburg. The good men who called him, however, soon discovered their error. His preaching proved a firebrand, which caused a destructive conflagration. He had no difficulty in rousing the people to the highest enthusiasm, but it soon became evident that neither he nor his followers would submit to the rules of the Church. Doctrine, he held, was nothing, and personal experience everything. With regard to the nature of personal consecration his fanaticism knew no bounds. Every true Christian, he said, was bound to preach the gospel, and he insisted that his uneducated followers should renounce all secular business, and go forth to declare the glad tidings.

Labadie was the type and forerunner of a vast multitude of mystics and sectarians, and would hardly be worth mentioning in this connection if he had not started a movement that was greater than himself. Personally, he finally withdrew from the church and sank into obscurity, after founding a fanatical sect which maintained a sickly existence for nearly a century. Among the multitude who were awakened by his preaching there were, however, many who did not imitate him in his excesses, and whose influence on the Reformed Church was most beneficent. The noblest men of the next generation—the men who were shining lights in the midst of the prevailing darkness—were contemptuously called Labadists ; but they only acknowledged the term in so far as to confess that they were converted during the revival which was begun by the preaching of Jean de Labadie. That the current was generally kept within its ancient bounds was, however, owing in great measure to the influence of another preacher of righteousness, whose name is now almost forgotten.

Jodocus Van Lodenstein (1620-1677) was a native of Delft, in Holland. Though educated in theology by Voetius and Coccejus, he had no ambition to be regarded as a great theologian, but rather longed to be instrumental in leading men to Christ. Personally he was more like a mediæval saint than like a Protestant minister, but with all his eccentricities, he was a model pastor. The people called him "Father Lodenstein;" and his earnest piety exerted a more profound influence than the eloquence of many of his contemporaries. Through his exertions strict discipline was maintained in the Dutch churches, and thousands of earnest people were thus kept from becoming sectarians. Lodenstein was the first of the Reformed mystics—of whom Tersteegen was another brilliant example—who, while remaining faithful to the church of their fathers, exercised an influence which extended far beyond its limits. Their peculiarities of practice have been forgotten, but their sincere piety, as expressed in hymns and books of devotion, has remained to bless the Church in all succeeding ages.

THE PIETISTS.

As we have seen, the people who had been awakened by the great revival were at first contemptuously termed

Labadists, but about 1690 it became usual to call them Pietists, from their supposed claims to extraordinary piety. This term was first used among the Lutherans, and it was common to call the same class among the Reformed "die Feinen." The former title, however, prevailed in both churches, and from that day to this it has been commonly but very vaguely employed. Rationalists have unkindly applied it, as a term of reproach, to all earnest Christians. It is a nickname, of course, and as such objectionable; but it may be conveniently used as a general term for all who, during the great revival of the seventeenth and eighteenth centuries, devoted themselves especially to the cultivation of the inner life. Some of these people were wild fanatics, others were quiet, unpretentious Christians, and there never was, and never could be, a sect including these discordant varieties. The term Pietist—like Quietist among the Roman Catholics—is therefore to be applied to a kind of people rather than to any single organized body.

A German writer (Koch) represents the Pietists of the eighteenth century as having consisted of three classes: 1. The Pietists Proper, who remained in connection with the established churches; 2. The Moravians, who were historically derived from the Bohemian Brethren, but who for a time cultivated a Pietistic spirit which was peculiar to themselves; and 3. The Mystics, consisting of many sects, who often ran into the wildest excesses. It is with the first of these classes that we are at present especially concerned.

Philip Jacob Spener (1635-1705) is often called "the father of Pietism," though he was in fact only its most distinguished exponent. He was a Lutheran, but his influence in the Reformed Church was fully as great as in his own. It is principally to him that both churches owe the re-establishment of catechisation and confirmation, which had been universally neglected. Though bitterly persecuted in his day, posterity has accorded him one of the noblest places in the history of the Church. Of course he had many coadjutors, among whom, in the Reformed Church, Theodore Untereyk was perhaps the most prominent.

These men were, in a certain sense, working in the dark, and consequently sometimes employed methods which experience has proved to have been mistaken. They occasionally founded within the church societies or brotherhoods, supposed to consist of those who were truly pious, but such organizations could not fail to result in dissensions. Some of these good people wandered to the very verge of sectarianism, if they did not pass beyond it. With all its imperfections this period was, however, a blessed time in the history of the church. This is especially evident from the multitude of hymns which were then composed. "Spring had come, and all the birds in the forest began to sing."

THE GREAT HYMNOLOGISTS.

Hitherto the Reformed Church had been satisfied to sing the psalms of David, according to the version of

THE GREAT HYMNOLOGISTS. 141

Ambrosius Lobwasser. Indeed, there were many who believed it wrong to sing uninspired productions; but now the time had come when the stream of devotion could no longer be kept within its ancient channels. Foremost among the poets of the Reformed Church was unquestionably *Joachim Neander* (1650–1680), who was very harshly treated for his religious views, and consequently dwelt for several months in a cave, in which he composed his finest hymns. Hardly less eminent as a poet was "the noble mystic," *Gerhard Tersteegen* (1697–1769), who stood on the borders of sectarianism, but who was still in his own way a faithful member of the Reformed Church. He voluntarily lived in extreme poverty, and frequently spent weeks without seeing a single human being, except the little girl who brought him his food. In humility and retirement he composed hymns and devotional books which exerted an extensive influence on the Church. His best hymns are still sung, and even his devotional writings are not entirely forgotten.

Among the later sacred poets of the Reformed Church were such eminent men as Stilling,[1] the Zollikofers,[2]

---

[1] *Johann Heinrich Jung, called Stilling*, (1740–1817) is celebrated in science and general literature, no less than in the annals of the Church. He was a poor tailor's son, but rose to be, not only a professor in the Universities of Heidelberg and Marburg, but a celebrated oculist, and a distinguished writer in defence of Christianity.

[2] *Caspar Zollikofer* (born 1707), pastor at St. Gall, Switzerland, and *George Joachim Zollikofer* (1730–1788), pastor of the Reformed Church in Leipsic, Germany, have bequeathed us many treasures of sacred song.

Lampe,[1] Lavater,[2] and more recently Menken[3] and the Krummachers[4]. Nor should we forget Louisa Henrietta, the illustrious Princess of Brandenburg, and, within the present century, the celebrated Swiss poetesses, Anna Schlatter and Meta Heusser. These are names which have the fragrance of sweet incense—they should be kept in everlasting remembrance. The student of the history of the Reformed Church must, of course, become familiar with its confessions of faith, but he will find its peculiar life most completely reflected in its hymns and books of devotion.

---

[1] *Friedrich Adolph Lampe* (1683-1729), was pastor of St. Ansgar's Church, Bremen. His eloquence was extraordinary, and his influence unbounded.

[2] *John Caspar Lavater* (1741-1801), who was called by Goethe "the best, greatest, wisest, and sincerest of all mortal and immortal men," was for many years pastor of a church in Zurich. He is best known for the most insignificant of his achievements—the supposed discovery of a science of physiognomy.

[3] *Gottfried Menken* (1768-1831), was a celebrated pulpit orator of Bremen.

[4] *Friedrich Adolph Krummacher* (1768-1845) and his two distinguished sons, Friedrich Wilhelm and Emil, have been equally celebrated as preachers and as sacred poets

CHAPTER XIII.

After the Thirty Years' War—The Treaty—The People—The Invasion of the Palatinate and its Consequences—Present State of the Reformed Church.

FOR more than a generation Germany had been the battlefield of Europe. To the Protestants it was a struggle for life or death. Their unfortunate dissensions had prevented them from standing together as they ought to have done in such a crisis, and for a while it seemed as though the imperial generals, Tilly and Wallenstein, would succeed in thoroughly humbling the Protestant league. Indeed, at one time the Protestant cause appeared to be utterly lost, but the brilliant campaign of Gustavus Adolphus, of Sweden, gave matters a more favorable turn.

At last both parties were utterly exhausted, and a peace was patched up in Westphalia, in 1648, which is generally regarded as concluding the Thirty Years' War, but in reality it brought neither peace nor security. Other conflicts followed in rapid succession, and the condition of the people remained utterly miserable.

THE TREATY.

The treaty of Westphalia is often referred to as the occasion when Germany first received religious liberty, but it must not be forgotten that this so-called liberty was granted in accordance with the policy of the French statesman, Richelieu, who sought in every way to divide Germany in order that France might rule the world. In France he had insisted that all must be Roman Catholics, not because he cared for religion, but because he thought unity would promote the strength of the nation. In Germany, on the other hand, he sustained the Protestants, though he fomented dissensions among them. The three principal religious confessions—Catholics, Lutherans, and Reformed—were, according to the treaty, to be recognized by the government; but a clause was inserted by which the Catholic religion was to be maintained wherever there were any people who desired it. In consequence of this proviso, the Jesuits set to work to discover isolated Catholic families in Protestant countries, and a few years afterwards it was found that they had thus introduced the Catholic Church into 1922 Protestant towns and villages. The Protestant princes protested against the trick; but the emperor was on the Catholic side, and he declared that by the terms of the treaty, ecclesiastical matters must no longer be discussed. These encroachments were generally made at the expense of the Reformed Church, which was smaller and less compact than the Lutheran, and consequently less able to resist aggression.

In pursuance of his policy of division, Richelieu secured the recognition of the *quasi* independence of almost every German robber-baron, knowing that these little potentates would in future resist any attempts at consolidation, and thus render Germany powerless for aggression or defence. "The fate of Richelieu," says Hegel, "has consequently resembled that of many other statesmen, inasmuch as he has been cursed by his countrymen, while his enemies have looked upon the work by which he ruined them as the most sacred goal of their desires—the consummation of their rights and liberties."

THE PEOPLE.

The condition of the German people at this period was deplorable in the extreme. It seemed as though wars would never cease. Bands of robbers occupied ruined castles, and the governments were not strong enough to dislodge them. The peasants lived in miserable huts, fearing to make the slightest improvement, lest they should tempt the companies of marauders who roamed over the land in search of booty. A generation had grown up which was rude and ignorant. Fortunately, parents generally regarded it as a religious duty to teach their children to read the Bible and Catechism, and, perhaps, to write a little; but beyond this point their knowledge rarely extended. Their piety assumed a gloomy cast, and thousands were ready to believe the false prophets who were constantly appearing, and who claimed to see signs in the heavens, or elsewhere, indicating the speedy approach of the end of all things. "The government," says Löher, "cared nothing for the people, and almost everywhere the religious party which happened to be in the majority oppressed dissenters. This state of things was worst in the Palatinate, where the electors had changed their religion four times in as many reigns. The whole country was expected to follow the example of its rulers, and whoever was not willing to accommodate himself to this state of affairs could do no better than take up his pilgrim's staff and leave his native land."

The German princes and nobles were in general a multitude of petty tyrants, without enough dignity or culture to render them respectable. Prince Eugene said concerning them: "God forgive them, for they know not what they do; much less do they know what they want; and, least of all, what they are." They voted the taxes, and the burghers and peasants paid them. Since the introduction of the system of employing mercenaries, they had even been released from military service, and now lived from the income of their estates, or rather from the enforced labor of the peasantry, without contributing in any way to the support of the State. "Though the nobles possessed apparent prosperity," says the historian Œser, "they became more and more contemptible. Those of them who remained on their estates maltreated their subjects; those who flocked to the courts held all the important offices, helped to spend the revenues of the State in luxury, and were principally in fault that the German princes degenerated into oriental despots. According to the Imperial Proclamation of 1670, peasants were required to furnish without complaint everything that might be necessary for the sustenance of the army or of their legitimate rulers, and it was ordered that no complaints presented by peasants should be considered in the imperial courts. No property was safe; the peasants and burghers alike laboring only to sustain life; the nobles corrupt, quarreling among themselves, and caring only for the advancement of their houses or the discovery of new sources of revenue."

The condition of the inhabitants of the cities was hardly preferable to that of the peasantry. Many of the cities, it is true, were thoroughly fortified, and had thus escaped the horror of being taken and sacked. It had been their good fortune that the armies were generally ill provided with heavy artillery; but during the long wars the usual avenues of communication had been cut off, and commerce had found other channels. During the Middle Ages the great German cities of the Hanseatic league had monopolized the trade of Europe; but now England, Holland, Denmark, and Sweden had become commercial countries, and the wealth of the great German merchants rapidly melted away. Thousands of tradesmen were thrown out of employment and wandered about in turbulent crowds. The proud patrician families, which had been apt to sneer at the comparative poverty of the nobility, and had known how to maintain their rights in the face of imperial power, were now humbled to the dust, and the law was dictated to them by some miserable little potentate.

The misery of Germany increased the importance of France. Louis XIV. was ambitious of re-establishing the empire of Charlemagne, and after the death of Ferdinand III. in 1657, spent vast sums of money for the purpose of bribing the German princes to elect him emperor; but the majority of the Diet still retained enough national feeling to elect a German. Their choice fell upon Leopold, who was a weak prince, entirely under the influence of the Jesuits and of his prime minister, Lobkowitz, who was known to be a pensioner of France.

Disappointed in his ambition, the French king now determined to retaliate by seizing the Palatinate, which he claimed in the name of his sister-in-law, the Duchess of Orleans, who had been a Palatinate princess.

THE INVASION OF THE PALATINATE.

The valley of the Rhine had been several times overrun by French armies, but the great invasion occurred in 1689. It is said that the French king entertained the foolish notion that he could make a future invasion of France impossible by devastating both banks of the river, and thus protecting his country by making a broad band of desert. At any rate, he knew that he could not permanently hold the Palatinate, and therefore gave orders to his generals to destroy all cities which they were unable to garrison. In one year Worms, Mainz, Speyer, Mannheim, Heidelberg, and many other cities, towns and villages, were either burned or utterly devastated. At Speyer and Worms the churches alone were left standing in the midst of smoking ruins. In the former city the vaults were broken open, the bones of the ancient emperors thrown out, and the French soldiers amused themselves by playing ten-pins with the skulls of Salian monarchs. At Mannheim the very stones of which the city was built were thrown into the Neckar. The castle of Heidelberg, the chief residence of the electors of the Palatinate, was ruined, and its remains still stand as a memorial of that dreadful time.

The misery of the people was indescribable. The French general, Melac, had all the vines on the hill-sides near Heidelberg cut down by his soldiery, thus depriving the peasants of their only means of subsistence. No wonder that, in the Palatinate, the name "Melac" is given to dogs, but only to curs of inferior degree. On one occasion, in the dead of winter, the people of a large district were turned out of their homes, which were immediately committed to the flames. More than one hundred thousand people were rendered homeless. Half naked they wandered into the fields and forests, and many died of starvation. Immense multitudes wandered down the Rhine, and the towns and the cities by the way, in many instances, fed them at the public expense and sent them further. Utterly destitute, they arrived in Holland, and encamped by tens of thousands in the environs of Amsterdam and Rotterdam. The Dutch government and people did all in their power to relieve the distressed, but with all they could do there was great suffering among the unhappy fugitives. Every year there were new French invasions, and the multitude of sufferers increased. What was to be done with them? Many, of course, were gradually scattered over the German empire; others were sent to the Dutch colonies in East India and Guiana; and a few accompanied the companies of sectarians who settled in Pennsylvania at the invitation of William Penn. It was, however, not until the year 1704 that the emigration to America may be said to have fairly begun. "In that year," said Christopher Saur, "after the Duke of Marlborough had defeated the French at Schellenberg (Blenheim), Queen Anne of England invited the suffering Palatines to find a home in America, and transported many thousands of them thither at her own expense." The Queen, however, soon found that she had undertaken a greater task than she could accomplish. Multitudes of Germans flocked to England to avail themselves of the Queen's bounty. The dreadful winter of 1709 had greatly increased the distress which prevailed in the Palatinate, and in the succeeding summer no less than 30,000 people left their native land. They encamped by thousands in the neighborhood of London. As they were ready to work for almost nothing, the lower classes were greatly prejudiced against them, and maltreated them whenever they could find an opportunity.

What shall be done with the Palatines? became the great question of the day. It was said that all the ships in the British navy would not suffice to carry them to America. First of all, the Roman Catholics were separated from the number and compelled to return to Germany. Nearly four thousand of these were sent back at once, each of whom received about four dollars as a gift from the Queen, as a sort of indemnity for his disappointment. The prejudice of the London populace against the Roman Catholics was so intense that unless they had been sent back, the Palatines would have been attacked and probably massacred. The queen and the wealthier classes were exceedingly liberal, and distributed from three to four hundred thousand dollars in charity. Those whose clothes were worn out were dressed at the expense of the queen, and she is said to have distributed 32,000 pairs of shoes. This relief could, however, only be temporary, and the problem of the final disposition of the Palatines was still unsolved. The Duke of Sussex and other noblemen settled some hundreds as laborers on their estates. Between three and four thousand were placed on certain unoccupied lands in the county of Limerick, in Ireland. Among their descendants, it will be remembered, John Wesley made some of his earliest converts, and Embury and Barbara Heck were of Palatinate descent. The great majority were, however, gradually transported to America, and German settlements were founded in most of the British colonies. Those undertaken in the South were not generally successful. At Biloxi the Palatines died by hundreds of yellow fever, and in North Carolina they were massacred by the Tuscarora Indians. It was in

Pennsylvania alone that they found a permanent home; but here they prospered, and finally passed beyond its borders and occupied large portions of adjacent colonies. Hearing of their prosperity, large numbers of Germans and Swiss, who were known to the English by the general name of "Palatines," followed them to the New World, and assisted in laying the foundations of the commonwealth. Some of these brought with them considerable sums of money, while others were extremely poor, but all were frugal and industrious. In humility and patience they labored to subdue the wilderness, and soon became more comfortable than they could ever have become in the Palatinate.

We have spoken at length of the invasion of the Palatinate and its consequences, because most of the sufferers were members of the Reformed Church. The later German emigration was largely Lutheran, but as late as the middle of the last century, it was believed that the Reformed were by far the most numerous of the religious denominations then existing among the Germans of Pennsylvania. In that day of trial multitudes were alienated from the church of their fathers, and in Germany the Reformed Church has never regained the position which it held before this dreadful period.

PRESENT STATE OF THE CHURCH.

In 1817 the Lutheran and Reformed churches of Prussia were, by action of the government, united into a single body, to be known as the "Evangelical Church." According to the terms of the union, there was to be no confessional change—individuals were expected to remain Reformed or Lutheran as they had been before—but in its official relations, the Church of Prussia was to be regarded as a single organization. Congregations which declined to enter the union were, of course, deprived of government patronage. This "Church Union" has gradually extended over Protestant Germany, and now includes the churches which were originally Reformed, with the exception of a comparatively small number of congregations, collectively numbering not more than forty thousand members. The Reformed churches in the Union—by which we mean the churches which still regard themselves as distinctively Reformed, though connected with the Established Church—have, according to an estimate in the "Encyclopœdia Britannica," a membership of 465,120; but from a computation published some years ago in the "Reformirte Kirchenzeitung," of Erlangen, it appears that the actual number may perhaps amount to about one million. The Reformed element in the Evangelical Church of Germany is, however, much more important than these figures would seem to indicate. In many localities the effect of the "Union" has been to obliterate confessional distinctions, and multitudes of Reformed people have become so exclusively identified with the Established Church that they can no longer be separately enumerated. It is, however, acknowledged that a remarkably large proportion of recent German theologians have belonged to the Reformed element; and it has even been recently decided by the imperial courts that the kings of Prussia are still to be regarded as members of the Reformed Church, inasmuch as the union of the churches involved no confessional change.[1]

A "Reformed Alliance," including the various Reformed churches of Germany, has recently been established, and held its first meeting at Marburg, in August, 1884. It will, no doubt, accomplish a great work in advancing the interests of the Church.

The Reformed Church is established by law in Switzerland, Holland and Scotland. It also has many congregations in France, Austria-Hungary, Poland, and the German provinces of Russia. The Dutch colonies have vigorous Reformed churches, and the "Boers," of South Africa, who a few years ago contended so bravely for liberty against the encroachments of the British, are sincerely attached to the same historic confession. Even a superficial account of the national and colonial Reformed churches would require at least a volume. Like "the burning bush," which has been in many lands its chosen emblem, the Reformed Church has passed through the fire but is not consumed, and its teachings are still dear to multitudes of faithful hearts.

---

[1] Cuno's "Gedächtnissbuch Deutscher Fürsten reformirten Bekenntnisses," Barmen, 1884.

BOOK II.
THE REFORMED CHURCH IN THE UNITED STATES.

MICHAEL SCHLATTER.

CHAPTER I.

The Reformed Church in America—A German Reformed Pioneer—William Penn's Mother—Earliest German Reformed Ministers in America.

THE Hollanders deserve the credit of having been the first to establish the Reformed Church in this country. Leaving out of consideration their missions in the Dutch West India Islands, there is every reason to believe that religious services were held on the site of the present city of New York soon after the first settlement of New Amsterdam, in 1614. It has, therefore, been plausibly asserted that "the Heidelberg Catechism was taught in America before the Pilgrims landed on Plymouth Rock." In 1628 the Rev. Jonas Michaelius arrived at New Amsterdam from the West Indies, and organized a congregation of more than fifty communicants. In 1633 he was succeeded by the Rev. Everardus Bogardus, whose fierce conflicts with several Dutch governors became historical.

From the earliest settlement there were some Germans among the inhabitants of New York. These generally soon acquired the language of the people among whom they dwelt, and connected themselves with the Dutch churches. In the course of time, when the number of

German emigrants became greater, many German churches were founded. The history of these churches is very obscure. Some of them were for a time connected with the German Reformed churches of Pennsylvania, others held a sort of filial relation to the Dutch Coetus, but the majority were practically independent. Pastor Gebhard, of Claverack, and others, preached alternately in German and Dutch. Finally the greater part of this German material passed very naturally into the Reformed Dutch Church, and it has been estimated that, at the beginning of the present century, one-third of the members of the latter denomination were of German extraction. The history of the German element in the Reformed Dutch Church is certainly worthy of more attention than it has hitherto received.

A GERMAN REFORMED PIONEER.

The first permanent settlement on the west bank of the Delaware was founded by a Swedish colony, in 1638, forty-four years before the arrival of William Penn. In that year two ships, the "Bird Griffin," and the "Key of Calmar," entered the Delaware and took formal possession of the unoccupied territory on its western bank, in the name of the crown of Sweden. The expedition was commanded by a German named Peter Minuit, who had previously been a governor of New Netherland. Little is known concerning his early history. He was born in Germany, but as his name does not appear to be German it has been suggested that he may have been of

Huguenot descent. It is on record that he had been a deacon in the Reformed Church of the city of Wesel. The office of deacon was, in those days, highly regarded —as it deserved to be—and the fact that he had held it is placed beyond doubt by cotemporary evidence.[1]

Minuit deserves a higher position in history than has been generally accorded him. It was he who inaugurated the policy of fair dealing with the Indians, which was afterwards continued and developed by William Penn; and though the greater part of his settlement was situated within the limits of the present State of Delaware, it was he who purchased from the natives all the land between Cape Henlopen and the falls of Trenton. This treaty was never broken. William Penn, on his arrival, no doubt bought land from the Indians; but he had no occasion to obtain possession in this way of the land on which he founded Philadelphia. It had been included in the original Swedish purchase, and though he had received Proprietary rights from the English government, he purchased the land from the Swedes, who were its prior occupants.

The subsequent history of Minuit is not generally known, and very recently a writer in one of our most prominent magazines ventured to assert that he died at Wilmington. The facts have, however, been recov-

---

[1] See "Kapp's History of Immigration," and Broadhead's "History of New York." In the original Dutch documents, transcribed by the late Mr. Joseph Mickly, it is also stated that Minuit was a deacon of the Reformed Church of Wesel.

ered from the Dutch records, and are thus given in an article on "The Founding of New Sweden," in the "Pennsylvania Magazine of History:" "On the return voyage Minuit visited the West Indian island of St. Christopher, and obtained a cargo of tobacco. He was already prepared to sail away, when he and his captain were invited to pay a visit to a Dutch ship which lay near by, named 'Het vliegende Hert.' (The Flying Deer). While the guests were on board the foreign vessel, there arose a violent hurricane, 'such as occur in the West Indies every six or seven years.' All the ships in the roadstead, to the number of twenty, were driven out to sea; some lost their masts or were otherwise badly damaged, and some absolutely foundered. Among the latter, in all probability, was the ship in which Minuit was, for nothing more was seen of him or of that vessel."

Such was the sad fate of the man who, in the absence of information to the contrary, may be regarded as the earliest pioneer of the German Reformed Church in the United States. The Swedish colony which he led was, of course, Lutheran, but there were many Germans and Hollanders in the country before it came under the dominion of the crown of England. "These," says the historian, Proud, "intermarried with the Swedes, and in course of time became one religious organization; but even at the time of Penn's arrival there was still a Reformed Dutch place of worship at New Castle."

The mother of William Penn was, in her youth, a member of the Reformed Church. She was the daughter of a merchant of Rotterdam, named Jasper, and is said to have been a woman of great strength of mind. Though after her marriage she conformed to the Church of England, her piety was of a type that was most usual in her native country. Her son was induced, by the cold formality of the Church of that period, to ally himself with a sect which occupied the opposite extreme; but he always thankfully acknowledged his obligations to the early teachings of his mother. In his early manhood he visited France, and placed himself under the instruction of the celebrated Reformed theologian, Moses Amyrault. It is well known that the views of Penn were broader and less fanatical than those of the founders of the sect with which he became connected. May we not suppose that this fact was owing, in part, at least, to instruction derived from the sources we have indicated?

EARLIEST REFORMED MINISTERS IN AMERICA.

It was long supposed that either the Rev. George Michael Weiss, or the Rev. John Philip Boehm, was the earliest German Reformed minister in this country, and recent researches assigned priority to the latter. These men were probably the earliest Reformed ministers in Pennsylvania, and by their self-denying labors laid the foundations on which the Reformed Church in the United States is built. There were, however, two ministers whose surnames were very similar, who labored at an earlier date, one to the north, and the other to the south of Pennsylvania.

John Frederick Hager, a Reformed minister, accompanied a body of 2,138 Palatines who, in May, 1709, arrived in London on their way to America. They were sent to New York by Queen Anne, and Hager ministered to the Reformed at East and West Camp, as Joshua Kocherthal did to the Lutherans.[1] He also visited and ministered to the Reformed who removed to the Schoharie and Mohawk settlements, and it is almost certain that he founded the German Reformed church of Schoharie. In Corwin's "Manual," "Hendrick Hagar" is said to have been the pastor at Schoharie and East and West Camp as early as 1711, but this name is evidently erroneously written. Dr. Harbaugh quotes the fact from the diary of the celebrated Indian interpreter, Conrad Weiser, that the latter was married, November 22, 1720, in Schoharie, N. Y., by a Reformed minister named John Frederick Heger, but has no further information concerning him. We regret that so little is known of the career of this early minister; but if any one in the region in which he labored

---

[1] From a "List of Clergy Ordained for the American Colonies," published in the London "Notes and Queries," March, 1884, it appears that John Frederick Hager, "among the Palatines, New York," was ordained December 20, 1709. The rite was performed under the auspices of the Society for the Propagation of the Gospel, but no further particulars are given.

should interest himself in the matter, it ought certainly to be possible to discover more.

Henry Hoeger, a Reformed minister, appears to have accompanied De Graffenried's Swiss colony, which, in 1710, founded New Berne, North Carolina. When the settlement had been scattered by the Tuscarora Indians, he accompanied about fifty of the survivors to Virginia, where they were employed by Governor Spottiswoode. A cotemporary document preserved in "Perry's Historical Collections" relates "That there went out with the first twelve families one minister named Henry Hoeger, a very sober, honest man, of about 75 years of age. But he being likely to be past service in a short time, they have empowered Mr. Jacob Christofle Zollikoffer, of St. Gall in Switzerland, to go into Europe, there to obtain if possible some contributions from pious and charitable Christians toward the building of their church and the bringing over with him of a young German minister to assist the aforesaid Mr. Hoeger in the ministry of religion, and to succeed him when he shall die, and to get him ordained in England by the Right Reverend Bishop of London, and to bring over with him the Liturgy of the Church of England, translated into High Dutch, which they are desirous to use in the public worship. They also seek the support of a minister from the Venerable Society for the Propagation of the Gospel."

These people, it is said, were subsequently organized into an Episcopal parish, with the reserved right to employ their own ministers, and on their own terms.

CHAPTER II.

Pennsylvania Pioneers—John Philip Boehm—George Michael Weis—John Henry Goetschius—John Bartholomew Rieger—Peter Henry Dorstius.

IT would not be easy to write a history of the Germans of Pennsylvania. The English colonies were composed in a great measure of companies whose sentiments were homogeneous, and who occupied extensive territories which they governed to suit themselves. The Germans, on the other hand, had little in common except their language. They came over, not as colonies, but as individuals, seeking a refuge from oppression and misery, and desiring only to be permitted to earn an honest livelihood. When Governor Gordon expressed the fear that "the Germans might give Pennsylvania law and language," and when Archbishop Hering suggested that "they might, by making common cause with the French on the Ohio, drive the English out of the colony," they did not know the people of whom they spoke. They could not even understand the fact that the Germans were divided among themselves in such a manner as to render concerted action impossible.

In order to form a proper conception of the state of affairs at this early period, it is necessary to remember, first of all, the broad distinction which then existed between churches and sects. The sects were first in the field. Prominent among these were the Mennonites, but there were also Dunkers, Schwenkfelders, and sects which have now become extinct. Francis D. Pastorius, who has been immortalized by the poet Whittier, as "The Pennsylvania Pilgrim," and who is generally regarded as the pioneer of the German emigration to America, was in Germany a mystic, and in America a Quaker.

The "church-people"—Lutherans and Reformed—appeared on the scene, at a somewhat later period. They came from widely-separated regions, bringing with them sectional prejudices and peculiarities, and years passed before each of these denominations became a homogeneous people.

We fear it is now impossible to determine with accuracy the time of the establishment of the earliest German Reformed church in Pennsylvania. It appears from the records of the Reformed Dutch church at Churchville, Bucks county—generally called in old records "Southampton" or "Neshaminy"—that the Rev. Paulus Van Vleck, who was then pastor of that congregation, organized a church at Whitemarsh on the 4th of June, 1710. This was, however, a Dutch church, and its historical connection with the German Reformed church of Whitemarsh has not been established. The fact seems to be that the people, in various localities, met and organized congregations, without waiting for the appearance of regular ministers. The most intelligent man in the community was chosen to conduct the services, which generally consisted in reading prayers from a European liturgy, and a sermon [*] from some approved collection. It has been usual to regard the Skippack church[1] (now extinct), in Montgomery county, as the oldest Reformed church in Pennsylvania—though a strong plea has been advanced in favor of the church in Philadelphia—and to fix the date of its organization as 1726 or 1727,[2] but it now appears that the true date must be sought at a somewhat earlier period. From an interesting memorial addressed, in 1728, to the Classis of Amsterdam by the Reformed churches at Falkner Swamp, Skippack and Whitemarsh, it appears that the Rev. John Philip Boehm began preaching at these places at least as early as 1720. Within ten years of this date, nearly a dozen churches were founded, and it seems impossible to ascribe priority to any one of them.

It may be well to give a brief sketch of the career of the ministers who were first in the field, and who may therefore be regarded as the pioneers of the Reformed Church in Pennsylvania.

John Philip Boehm had been a schoolmaster in the

---

[1] Rev Paulus Van Vleck visited Skippack, May 29, 1710, and baptized ten children; but it does not appear that he organized a congregation. See *Records of Neshaminy Church*.

[2] The Reformed church on Race street, below Fourth, Philadelphia, was organized in 1727. The elders then elected were Peter Lecolie, Johann Wilhelm Roerig, Heinrich Weller, and Georg Peter Hillengass.

city of Worms, and having been persecuted by the Roman Catholics, had come to America, not later than 1720. In the memorial to which we have referred, it is stated that shortly after his arrival he had been appointed "Reader," and had served in this capacity for five years. Then he was requested to assume the office of pastor, and accepted the call, as there was no one at hand who was so well qualified for the office. At this time, it is said, his congregations were not aware of the irregularity of their course. For three years Boehm thus continued to serve the churches at Falkner- Swamp, Skippack and Whitemarsh, without regular ordination. In the meantime, however, the Rev. Geo. Michael Weis had arrived in Pennsylvania, and, as the latter was recognized as a regularly ordained minister, there was a division among the people. Some adhered to their former pastor, while others insisted that he had no right to preach. Boehm himself was convinced of the irregularity of his course, and in 1728, his three congregations requested the Dutch Reformed churches of New York to ordain him. The matter was referred to the Classis of Amsterdam, and after considerable delay the request was granted, and Boehm was ordained, in New York, on the 23d of November, 1729, by Rev. Henricus Boel and Gualterius Du Bois. From this time forth Boehm continued in the most intimate relations with the Classis of Amsterdam, and Weiss stood by his side as a faithful coadjutor.

Father Boehm resided in Whitpain township, Montgomery county, and is said to have preached for some time in his own house. From this assembly sprang the congregation which is now known as "Boehm's Church." He also preached in Philadelphia, and made extensive missionary journeys. While preaching in Philadelphia, he became involved in a controversy with Count Zinzendorf, and published several pamphlets.

Though not highly educated, Mr. Boehm was not ignorant, as was sometimes intimated by his opponents. He was withal a man of extraordinary energy, and his extensive influence was fully recognized by the civil authorities. In consequence of the rapid increase in the value of certain lands which he had purchased he became very wealthy, but this fact did not in the least interfere with his work in extending the church. When Schlatter arrived, he found in him a faithful assistant, and he always refers to him with the most profound respect. Mr. Boehm died suddenly, on May 1st, 1749, after having on the previous day administered the Holy Supper to the Egypt congregation.

George Michael Weis or *Weiss* was born about A. D. 1700, at Stebbeck, in the valley of the Neckar, in Germany, and died about 1763, at New Goshenhoppen, Montgomery county, Pa. He was educated at Heidelberg, and came to America as an ordained minister, in 1727, in company with about four hundred colonists, most of whom appear to have been members of the Reformed Church. He organized the Reformed Church of Philadelphia, and also preached at Skippack.

In 1729 Mr. Weis went to Europe, in company with Elder Jacob Reiff, for the purpose of collecting money and good books for the Reformed Churches of Philadelphia and Skippack. As it was somewhat doubtful whether Mr. Weis would return to America, the churches granted a power of attorney to Mr. Reiff, to receive all moneys and otherwise to conduct the mission according to his best judgment. On his return to America the latter delayed to make a settlement, and this led to a protracted suit in chancery. The matter was not finally arranged until after the arrival of Mr. Schlatter, who received from Mr. Reiff a balance of about six hundred and fifty dollars, after which he published a card expressing his entire confidence in Mr. Reiff's integrity.

It is difficult, at this late date, to form a correct judgment on all the particulars of the "Reiff case." After having examined a large number of legal documents we may, however, venture to assert that, though Mr. Reiff may have been careless in keeping his accounts, there is no evidence of dishonesty. A part of the money collected was, perhaps imprudently, invested by him in merchandise which, he believed, could be sold to advantage in Philadelphia, for the benefit of the churches. In consequence of a series of mishaps, which we have no room to relate, these goods were for several years detained in a British custom-house, and could be released only by the payment of a large sum for duties and storage. This detention naturally prevented an early settlement. We do not know the exact amount collected;

but Mr. Reiff's opponents did not charge him with having received more, at the utmost, than from fifteen hundred to two thousand dollars in our present money. As the churches had promised to pay all the expenses of the mission, and as Mr. Reiff also claimed credit for £150, previously advanced by him towards the erection of the church at Skippack, it is evident that the sum remaining after these deductions were made, cannot have been very large. The people had, however, heard exaggerated rumors concerning the amount collected, and it was difficult to persuade them that the churches had received their dues.

Mr. Weis returned to America in 1731, leaving Mr. Reiff in Germany, where he remained one year longer. On his return, Mr. Weis settled among the Germans of New York, laboring chiefly in Schoharie and Dutchess counties. In 1746 he was compelled to flee, in consequence of Indian depredations, and found a refuge in Pennsylvania. Here he took charge of the congregations of Old and New Goshenhoppen and Great Swamp, where he labored faithfully until his death.

John Henry Goetschius (or Goetschy) was a native of Zurich, in Switzerland. Concerning his personal history, we know very little. He was, however, careful to provide the churches which he served with congregational records, in which his name has been preserved.

In 1730, he was pastor at New Goshenhoppen, and entered on the title-page of the church record the names of the congregations which he simultaneously served, viz., Skippack, Old Goshenhoppen, New Goshenhoppen, Swamp, Saucon, Egypt, Macedonia, Mosillem, Oley, Bern and Tulpehocken. What an enormous diocese! In the region which he occupied, there are at present, probably, more than fifty Reformed ministers.

In 1737, Goetschius was ordained, for convenience sake, by the Presbyterian Synod of Philadelphia. He had previously, it seems, been what was known as a *candidatus*, though with the right to administer the sacraments. In 1739, his name disappears from the records, and it was supposed by Dr. Harbaugh that he must have died about this time.

The late Prof. I. D. Rupp, however, once informed us that he had documents by means of which his history could be traced much further. Goetschius, he said, returned to Europe, and a few years later came a second time to America, bringing his family with him. He had a son, John Henry, who came to this country, and was for many years pastor at Hackensack, N. J. Another son, John Mauritius, was at first a physician, but subsequently became pastor of the German Reformed church of Schoharie, N. Y. The elder Goetschius, after his return to America, settled on Long Island, and remained there for several years. The

---

[1] According to Corwin's "Manual," John Henry Goetschius, Jr., was born in 1718, at Liguria, Switzerland. If this date is correct, he was but thirteen years old when his father began to labor in Pennsylvania. Liguria, we presume, is a misprint for Tiguria, the Latin name of Zurich.

time of his death is unknown. Several of his descendants have been ministers of the Reformed (Dutch) Church.

John Bartholomew Rieger was born in the Palatinate, in 1707, and died at Lancaster, Pa., in 1769. He was an educated physician, who had studied at Heidelberg. The time and place of his ordination are now unknown, but he was one of the earliest pastors of the church at Lancaster, and was present at the organization of the first German Reformed Synod held in this country. Very little is known concerning his personal career, but he was the founder of many churches in Lancaster and Lebanon counties.[1]

---

[1] The following communication appears in Christopher Saur's paper for September 16, 1750:

WARNING FROM LANCASTER.

Ministers of unstained character, coming to Pennsylvania with proper testimonials and good intentions, are welcome: The Lord has provided work and bread for them in this country.

On the contrary, the following is generally the fate of vagabond priests in Pennsylvania: They are to wise men of the world a laughing-stock; to wise Christians an abomination; and to those who receive them a burden and a curse—the special delight of Satan.

We warn all well-disposed church-people to beware, because among the multitude of recent immigrants there are some degraded men, deposed babblers, who come hither because they imagine the people are stupid, ministers few in number, and the Church without a "fence," i. e. without a bishop; and that therefore there is no one who can call them to account, or say: *Papa, quid facis?* that is, "Reverend sir, what are you doing?"

Whoever has by his evil conduct become useless to the Church in Europe, and has therefore been deprived of his office and subsistence, can do no good by assuming a pastorate in America.

Peter Henry Dorstius was from about 1731 to 1748, pastor of the only Dutch Reformed charge in Pennsylvania. It was situated on the Neshaminy, in Bucks county, and was generally called Southampton. He married Jane Hogeland, a daughter of Derrick Hogeland, and had three children. In consequence of his proximity to the German churches, he was directed to exercise supervision over them, and to report to the Church of Holland. On September 23, 1740, he visited the Lower Saucon church; and there baptized

It is evident that where such men raise their hearths and altars, there come dissatisfaction, mockery, envy, hatred and contention among people who had previously lived together in peace and harmony.

The Reformed congregation in Lancaster has experienced all this, and by too readily admitting to the sacred office such deposed and excommunicated men, has alienated the flower of its membership (that is, it has disgraced itself), thus losing the support of men who might in their measure have proved as salt to the entire community.

May the Lord Jesus Christ grant to our poor people and their dear children preachers and teachers according to his own heart!

Possibly more hereafter. Let not this be unkindly interpreted.

J. B. RIEGER, *Ref. Minister and President of Coetus.*

In a communication to the same paper, October 16, 1750, Mr. Rieger reminds those who oppose the exercise of discipline in the Reformed churches, that the duty of the Church is defined in the Heidelberg Catechism, which declares in unmistakable language that the ungodly are not to be admitted to the table of the Lord. This is the earliest formal recognition of the authority of the Heidelberg Catechism by a German Reformed minister of this country, which we remember to have seen.

Under date of January 2, 1750, Mr. Rieger contributes some verses to the same periodical, which may perhaps be regarded as the earliest poem published by a German Reformed minister in this country.

several children belonging to members of the Egypt congregation. In the record of the latter church, he is called "Herr Inspektor¹ Peter Heinrich Torschius." Misled by this erroneous orthography, Dr. Harbaugh renders the name "Torsihius," and this name wrongly appears in several lists of deceased ministers.

In 1743, Dorstius was made the bearer of a highly important letter from the Synods of Holland, to the Presbyterian Synod of Philadelphia, inquiring whether it would be practicable to consolidate the Presbyterians, Dutch Reformed and German Reformed, in America, into a single body. In their reply, the Presbyterians tacitly declined to enter into such a union, but "declared their willingness to unite with the Reformed in all efforts to promote the common interests of religion."

Dorstius was not present at the organization of the Synod, but sent a letter of sympathy. The fact is, he was breaking down, physically and morally.² He withdrew from his pastoral charge in 1748, and probably died soon afterwards. In 1755, the Coetus made an appropriation for the reli f of his widow.

---

¹ This title seems to indicate that Dorstius was recognized as "Missionary Superintendent," in consequence of his commission from the Church of Holland. This office was subsequently held by Weis and Schlatter.

² See "Pennsylvania Gazette" for June 9th and June 16, 1748, preserved in the Philadelphia Library.

CHAPTER III.

John Peter Miller—Tulpehocken—The Dunkers—Conrad Beissel and "The Ephrata Brethren"—Beissel's Visit to Tulpehocken—Miller as a Monk.

NEAR the little village of Ephrata, in Lancaster county, Pennsylvania, there may still be seen a cluster of ancient edifices, which are all that remain of the once celebrated cloister of the "Order of the Solitary." In the adjacent church-yard rest the remains of a man who was once a Reformed minister, but who turned aside to become a member and leader of that mystical and fanatical brotherhood.

John Peter Miller was born in the district of Lautern, in the Palatinate, in the year 1710. He was educated at Heidelberg, where Weis and Rieger were his fellow-students. In 1730 he came to America under the auspices of the church authorities of Heidelberg. He was probably what would now be called a Licentiate, but was too young to receive ordination. As there was no ecclesiastical body in the Reformed Church of this country which could confer this rite, he was ordained soon after his arrival by the Presbyterian Synod of Philadelphia. The Rev. Jedediah Andrews, a member of the latter body, has left on record his impression of Miller's extraordinary scholarship.

(175)

"He speaks Latin," he says, "as well as we do our vernacular tongue."

TULPEHOCKEN.

In 1731 Miller became pastor of the Reformed church at Tulpehocken. This was then a somewhat isolated region, which had been settled in a very curious manner. The pioneers had not come from the east, but from the North. They were some of the people who, about 1709, had settled in the colony of New York, at the invitation of Queen Anne.

Ignorant of the language and ways of the country, they had, in New York, become the prey of dishonest men in high station, and a great part of the lands which they had rendered fertile by their toil was taken from them on the pretext of some informality in the title. Having retaliated by beating the officers of the crown, who were sent to dispossess them, they had rendered themselves liable to indictment. At this time they received an invitation from Governor Keith to settle in Pennsylvania, and a company of them entered the wilderness in search of their future home. Reaching the Susquehanna, they built rafts, and on them descended that magnificent river until they reached the mouth of the Swatara. Ascending the latter stream, they came to the beautiful region which was known by the Indian name of Tulpehocken.

For four years, Miller preached to the Reformed people of this place. We have no particulars concerning his ministry, but no doubt he met with many discouragements. In the meantime a mystical brotherhood had established itself at Ephrata, and offered peace to all who withdrew from the world, to serve the Lord in silence and hope. Concerning the sincerity of these people, there could be no doubt. They had voluntarily renounced all worldly ambition, and had submitted themselves to a monastic rule which, for strictness, could hardly be equalled in the Church of Rome. It is more than probable that Miller was familiar, before he came to America, with the religious movements which had finally resulted in this phenomenon, and had been to some extent influenced by them. We can therefore understand how it was, that when he was brought into communication with the "Ephrata Brethren," he was drawn to them by an irresistible influence, so that, renouncing his career of active usefulness, he determined to spend his life in the retirement of the cloister.

The Ephrata society is known to have been an offshoot of the sect which is called by its members "Brethren," or "German Baptists," but is more generally known as "Dunkers." This body in some respects so closely resembles the Mennonites, that certain writers have taken it for granted that they must be derived from them; but this is a mistake, as will become evident when we briefly consider their history.

THE DUNKERS.

At the beginning of the last century the laws against

the Separatists were still rigidly enforced in the greater part of Germany. Their meetings were consequently held in obscure places. In forests or ruined castles they met in secret to hear the doctrines which were forbidden by the State. Such circumstances had a natural tendency to encourage mystery and fanaticism. Teachers appeared who claimed to be divinely inspired, and who perhaps unconsciously clothed their platitudes in mysterious language. The great master of the mystics of the seventeenth century had been Jacob Boehme, who is sometimes called "the inspired shoemaker of Gorlitz." His writings—and especially his "Morgenröthe"—were well suited to the taste of their age, and were studied by learned and unlearned. To many of the Separatists they came with all the force of a divine revelation, and they unhesitatingly accepted them as a key and commentary to the sacred Scriptures. Though the disciples could not fathom the meaning of the master, they had at least the consciousness of standing on the verge of a great mystery, and imagined that through the darkness they could catch glimpses of the "morning-redness" that heralded the everlasting day.

In various places throughout Germany, and in other countries, circles were formed for the study of the Word of God with the aid afforded by the writings of Boehme. The most important of these was the "Philadelphian Society," which, in time, became the fruitful mother of sects. Among the latter, we may mention the "Inspired" (*die Inspirirten*), Ronsdorfers, Ellerians, and others, which were subsequently transplanted to Pennsylvania, but failed to grow on unaccustomed soil. All these sects regarded their leaders as directly inspired, or illuminated by the Holy Spirit.

The increasing tendency towards sectarianism attracted the attention of the civil authorities, and in several countries decrees of banishment were issued against "the mystics." It happened, however, that there were several small districts where the ruling families sympathized with them, and here they found a refuge. The most important of these places was Witgenstein, which consisted of two districts—Sayn-Witgenstein-Witgenstein and Sayn-Witgenstein-Berleburg—which were governed by branches of the same noble family. They are now united, and form the district of Witgenstein, in the Prussian province of Westphalia. The capital of the former district was Laasphe, and of the latter Berleburg. In the former were the villages of Sassamanshausen, Schwarzenau on the Eder, and Elhoff, which became celebrated in the religious annals of the last century.

Count Henry Albert, of Sayn-Witgenstein-Witgenstein, who ruled from 1698 to 1724, was a member of the Philadelphian society, and became the patron of sectarians of every kind. He had three sisters who went so far as to renounce their rank and to devote themselves to mystical studies. The Berleburg family was no less fanatical. The Countess Hedwig Sophia gathered around her the company of men who published the "Berleburg Bible," in eight folio volumes, which is a real storehouse of the German mysticism of the last century.

Count Carl Gustav, a brother of Count Henry Albert, disapproved of the mysticism of his relatives. In formally denouncing them to the imperial authorities, he said: "They live in contempt of the Holy Sacraments, denounce the regular ministry, overturn all human and divine order, and seem ready to play once more the drama of John of Leyden, Knipperdolling, and Thomas Münzer."

The religious condition of Witgenstein at this period must have been pitiable. As the ruling family had repudiated the Reformed faith, it was not to be expected that the people should remain faithful. Religious fanatics came streaming in from every direction, each one preaching his own peculiar heresy. Many of these declared the glories of celibacy, and there were hermitages all over the land. Most eloquent of all the mystics was E. C. Hochman von Hochenau, whose preaching was everywhere attended by multitudes whom he earnestly exhorted to study the Scriptures. From the fact that he publicly declared that "at the Reformation the great Babel had not been destroyed, but had only broken into three heads"—by which he meant the Catholic, Lutheran, and Reformed Churches —it must have been easy to discern the result of studies pursued under the influence of his teachings.

In 1708, eight persons, of whom the most prominent was a miller named Alexander Mack, formed a society for the study of the Bible. Having come to the conclusion that they ought to be baptized by three-fold immersion, they baptized each other in the Eder at Schwarzenau. The society increased rapidly, and a second congregation was founded at Marienborn. The latter body subsequently removed to Crefeld, and in 1719 emigrated to Pennsylvania. Here they prospered, and as the government of Witgenstein had changed, the mother congregation of Schwarzenau followed them in 1729. The whole sect of "Dunkers," or "Dompelars," was in this way transplanted to America.

The "Brethren" now expected to enjoy peace and quiet, but the settlement was hardly effected before it was disturbed by a violent controversy. The man who caused the disturbance was a remarkable character, and his career is worthy of special attention.

CONRAD BEISSEL

was born in 1690, in the village of Eberbach, in the Palatinate. His father died before his birth, and his mother when he was eight years old. We know but little concerning his early life, except that he learned the trade of a baker, and that his master taught him to play the violin. He became a good musician, and wrote verse with extraordinary facility. From his early youth he believed that he was not born for common things, and seems to have exerted an extraordinary influence on his companions. As the Reformed Church, in which he had been brought up, failed to furnish a field for his peculiar genius, he turned to the mystics, and without becoming identified with any one of the sects, became more mystical than his teachers. Disappointed with the reception which was accorded to his message in the fatherland, he sailed to America in 1720, and spent a year in Germantown, working for Peter Becker, who was the preacher of the Dunker congregation of that place. Then he went to Lancaster county in company with a friend, and built a hut in which they lived for some time in voluntary poverty and privation. At this time he visited the Labadist convent at Bohemia Manor, Maryland, and seems to have studied the rules of its peculiar life. In 1724 a little company of Dunkers, led by Beissel's old employer, Peter Becker, came to Lancaster county on a missionary expedition. At first Beissel was doubtful whether he ought to be baptized by a man whom he regarded as so greatly inferior to himself, but he finally determined to allow Becker "to become his John the Baptist." Almost immediately after the baptism, it was discovered that there were doctrinal differences which ought to have been previously discussed. Beissel with his followers formed themselves into a separate congregation, and were popularly known as the "New Dunkers." He published a book, in which he advocated the observance of the Old Testament Sabbath, instead of Sunday, and the schism soon became complete. In all the congregations, however, Beissel had his adherents, who were generally intelligent members, and these in many instances hastened to place themselves under his special direction. They at first encamped around the dwelling of the master, and subsequently built houses there in order that they might constantly enjoy the blessing of his presence.

In 1732 they adopted a conventual rule, and began the erection of monastic buildings. They assumed the garb of Capuchin monks, but the rule was stricter than those of the Roman Catholic orders. All day long they labored unceasingly, and at night their bed was a rough bench, and their only pillow a wooden billet. The master had not studied monasticism in vain. He had organized a society which had no will but his own, and for a time he ruled it with a rod of iron.

Not all of the sect were members of the order. Those who were not supposed to be sufficiently illuminated to embrace the celibate life, were permitted to dwell with their families in the neighborhood, and it is said that nearly all the land within three or four miles of the convent was owned by Beissel's adherents. The congregation, which at one time numbered more than three hundred, was divided into four districts—Massa, Hebron, Zohar, and Cades—and the members voluntarily submitted to as many rules of the brotherhood as were practicable without becoming inmates of the monastery.

BEISSEL'S VISIT TO TULPEHOCKEN.

Though the master was not himself a highly educated man, he was very desirous of drawing into his net a few thoroughly trained theologians. This would not only be flattering to his personal vanity, but would enable him to extend the influence of his order. At first he tried hard to win Rev. J. B. Rieger, the Reformed pastor in Lancaster, but his hopes were disappointed when he heard that Rieger had taken a wife. "O, Lord," he exclaimed, "Thou sufferest them to spoil in my very hands." Then he directed his attention to the young pastor of Tulpehocken. He determined to pay him a visit, and Miller, it is said, received him "as an angel of the Lord." The visit was returned, and finally Miller was immersed, and became a member of the Brotherhood. Beissel also made other converts in Tulpehocken, among whom were Conrad Weiser and three elders of the Reformed church. Weiser soon disagreed with the "Brethren," and withdrew from them, but Miller, after living a short time as a hermit in Tulpehocken, became the most active member of the fraternity.

MILLER AS A MONK.

From the time when Miller entered the Ephrata brotherhood, he seems to have submitted implicitly to his spiritual director, Conrad Beissel. The latter therefore regarded him as a precious instrument. It was through his influence, that after the defection of the first prior, Israel Eckerlin, Miller was chosen to that responsible office. Though at first, through excessive modesty, he declined the position, he was soon re-elected, and from that time he directed the secular business of the society. Beissel, in the meantime, dwelt apart from the brethren, and was supposed to devote his time to spiritual contemplation.

After the death of Beissel in 1768, Miller, or "Brother Jabez," as he was called in monastic life, became the head of the order. There can be no doubt, that to him was principally due the extraordinary activity displayed by its members. They practiced many trades, and owned several grist-mills, a saw-mill, paper-mill, oil-mill, fulling-mill, and we believe, a type-foundry. Their literary activity was remarkable, and they published many books, which are now regarded as among the rarest issues of the American press. Among these was the celebrated "Martyr-Book," which was translated by Miller from Dutch into German, and which was by far the largest volume printed in this country before the Revolution.

Miller maintained an extensive correspondence with eminent men in Europe and America, and was known and respected by the civil authorities. It is said that during the Revolution he interceded with General Washington for the life of a bitter enemy who had given aid to the British, and secured his pardon.

On a tomb-stone at Ephrata, there is a half-obliterated German inscription, of which the following is a translation:

"Here lies buried Peter Miller, born in Oberamt Lautern, in the Electoral Palatinate; came to America as a Reformed preacher in the year 1730; was baptized by the Community at Ephrata in the year 1735, and named Brother Jabez; he was also afterwards a teacher until his end. He fell asleep on the 25th of September, 1796, at the age of eighty-six years and nine months."

As we recently stood by his solitary grave, we could not help regretting that this eminent man was lost to the Reformed Church. If he had remained faithful, his scholarship and energy might have enabled him to accomplish a glorious work. It might have been his privilege to organize the Reformed Church of this country, and to direct, in great measure, the course of its subsequent history. No doubt it was easier to seek a refuge in the cloister, than to grapple with the difficulties that confronted him; but flight is always the refuge of the coward. With all his learning he must have been a weak man. Otherwise he would neither have become the willing slave of a religious charlatan, nor have exchanged the pure doctrines of the Reformation for the vague mysticism of a fanatical dreamer.

Before the death of Miller, the "Order of the Solitary" had commenced to decline, and a few years later it practically ceased to exist. In 1814 the property was legally transferred to the society of "The German Seventh-day Baptists," which now numbers considerably less than fifty members. Even these are divided into two parties, who are engaged in litigation for the control of the property. The end cannot be far distant.

The reasons for the downfall of the Ephrata brotherhood are not hard to determine. Its European resources had dried up, and celibacy prevented a younger generation from taking the place of those who passed away. The society was entirely separated from the general life of the Church. A branch that is severed from the stem may put forth an abundance of foliage, but it has no root, and must finally wither away.

CHAPTER IV.

" The Congregation of God in the Spirit"—Antes—Bechtel—Brandmiller—Rauch—Lischy.

IN speaking of the condition of the Presbyterian Church in America during the last century, Dr. Sprague reminds us, in his "Annals," that we cannot properly understand it without remembering that there were almost from the beginning two parties, which differed widely as to their views of church polity. These were respectively known as the "Old Side" and the "New Side." The former, laid great stress on purity of doctrine; it insisted on the strict observance of law and order, and regarded a thorough education as essential to ministerial efficiency. The latter, though it included many learned men, was inclined to relax the ancient rules by admitting to the ministry pious men who had not enjoyed the advantages of a systematic education. Deeply impressed with the deplorable religious condition of the people, the latter party would gladly have sent forth a multitude of evangelists, in the hope of thus winning them for the cause of Christ. Naturally they were somewhat impatient of the restraints imposed upon them by the existing order; and though, in most instances, they held to the ancient confessions of the Church, it was evident that they regarded the doctrinal side as of much less importance than the practical.

Of course there were dangers on both sides. On the one hand was formalism, on the other fanaticism. It was difficult to steer between these dangers, and the best men sometimes fell into one or the other extreme.

The condition of the Reformed Church a few years later was analogous to that of the Presbyterian. In some respects, indeed, these differences were more strongly marked in the former Church than in the latter. The early Presbyterians were mostly Scotch or Irish, so that their social life and early training had been very similar. The Reformed people, on the contrary, came from many countries, and had naturally brought with them a large number of local peculiarities. These were not less evident among the ministry than among the people. In the Fatherland there had been schools of theology by scores, and their peculiar features had impressed themselves upon their disciples. Thus, it is evident that ministers who came from districts in which Pietism had been prevalent, were inclined to what may be denominated the "New Side," while others who in their own way were no less earnest and devoted, regarded the preservation of the purity of Christian doctrine as the highest function of the ministry.

When Boehm and Weis placed themselves under the protection of the Church of Holland, and formally recognized its symbols of faith, their course did not command the universal approval of the Reformed people of Pennsylvania. It was believed by many that the Dutch synods would insist on a rigid adherence to the Belgic confession and the Articles of Dordrecht. This dissatisfied element, which might have been called the "New Side," was principally influenced by those who were active in the organization of the "Congregation of God in the Spirit."

The religious condition of the German people of Pennsylvania was deplorable. The wildest forms of fanaticism were rampant, while the great body of the people, disgusted by these extravagancies, and destitute of proper means of religious instruction, was fast falling into a condition of hopeless irreligion and unbelief.

It is not surprising that under these circumstances some of the best of the Germans should have looked around for some means of promoting unity among Christians, and thus presenting a strong front to the attacks of the enemy. As early as 1738 John Adam Gruber, of Oley, had issued an address calling for some sort of union. Gruber was, however, a member of the sect of "the Inspired," and the people were not disposed to accept him as a leader. The idea was then taken up by Henry Antes, and under his leadership it for a while promised to become a powerful movement in the direction of Christian unity.

Antes was certainly a remarkable man. Descended

from an eminent family in Europe, he had come to America with his parents in early manhood. "In appearance and dress," says one of his descendants, "he was an enormous German farmer, and in language and manners a courtier of the *ancien regime.*" He was a miller and a millwright, but soon became an active man of business. "His services," says Mr. H. S. Dotterer, in a valuable series of articles on his career, "were called into requisition in the selection of lands, the negotiation of purchases, the drawing of wills, and the settlement of estates. His prudence and integrity in the performance of duties requiring acquaintance with business formalities and knowledge of financial matters were recognized throughout the then limited bounds of the inhabited parts of the province."

Antes entered into religious affairs with characteristic energy and enthusiasm. In 1736 we find him ministering to the Reformed people of Oley. It is not certain that he preached at this time, but he went from house to house and led the people in singing and prayer. In the same year he made the acquaintance of the celebrated Moravian missionary, Spangenberg, who was staying at the house of Christopher Wiegner, in Skippack. At that old Schwenkfelder homestead he frequently met a company of godly men, representing many forms of faith, who were all earnest in the promotion of the kingdom of God. For a while he continued to hold his membership in the Reformed church at Falkner Swamp, but the time came when

Boehm and Antes could no longer agree. Boehm, however, said of him, in the midst of the subsequent controversy: "So far as Henry Antes and myself are concerned, he knows full well how our hearts were formerly bound together in a cordial love for the divine truth of our Reformed teachings. This love, for my part, I have not forgotten, and although I have been deeply wounded by him, I shall never forget to beseech the Almighty in my prayers, to bring him, together with all the erring ones, by the power of the Holy Ghost, back to the right."

When the Reverend George Whitefield, the greatest revival preacher of modern times, visited Pennsylvania, in 1740, he was entertained at the house of Antes, and preached there to a great multitude of people. The Moravian bishop, Petrus Boehler, preached in German on the same occasion. Thus Methodists and Moravians fraternized at the home of "the pious Reformed man of Frederick township."

When Count Zinzendorf arrived in Pennsylvania, in 1741, Antes was among the first to welcome him. To him, he presented his plan of promoting unity among the churches. It is said that the Count did not at first fully approve of it, possibly anticipating that it might result in the establishment of a body that would be unfavorable to the Unity of the Brethren. He therefore gave his consent to the enterprise rather reluctantly, but soon became its leading spirit. In December, 1741, Antes issued a call for a meeting of "those who could give a reason for the faith that was in them," to be held in Germantown, on New Year's Day. This meeting was followed, during the succeeding years, by six others. The plan of union elaborated at these meetings was called "The Congregation of God in the Spirit." It was founded in strict accordance with Zinzendorf's theory of Tropes, according to which every one might retain his denominational peculiarities, while at the same time he stood in connection with a higher unity. There was, for instance, no intention of destroying the Lutherans, Reformed, or Mennonites, as religious denominations, but they were to be united by means of the confederation of those who had reached the highest grade of spiritual perception. Though the fact was rather implied than expressed, the Moravians were to be the controlling power in the whole movement. Zinzendorf had no idea of establishing a sect, but to him it appeared beautiful that there should be within the Church a community of elect souls who would more and more withdraw themselves from worldly affairs to live a life like that of the angels in heaven.

At first it seemed as though this well-meant movement would prove successful. Many excellent men welcomed it, and Zinzendorf and his coadjutors proceeded to ordain ministers for the Lutheran and Reformed Churches. They presumed to do this for the Reformed Church by virtue of authority given them by the Reformed antistes (or bishop) Jablonsky, of

Berlin, who was also a bishop of the ancient Moravian community. In this way they ordained, as Reformed ministers, Henry Antes, John Bechtel, John Brandmiller, Christian Henry Rauch, Jacob Lischy, and possibly others. As the confessional basis of its Reformed churches, the "Congregation" laid down the Decrees of the Synod of Berne. Bechtel prepared and published a catechism which claimed to be founded on these decrees, and which was intended to supplant the Heidelberg Catechism. Then there came a time of fierce conflict. Zinzendorf and Boehm engaged in a controversy which was too bitter to be creditable to either party. The Reformed congregations were excited, and refused to be served by ministers who stood in the "Unity." Gradually most of these ministers, with some of their members, withdrew from the Reformed Church and fully identified themselves with the Moravians. Antes was for some time a resident of Bethlehem, but finally became dissatisfied and returned to his farm in Frederick township, Montgomery county, where he died in 1755. It is not known whether he ever renewed his relations with the Church of his fathers. Some of his children were Reformed, and others Moravian. Bechtel, Brandmiller, Rauch and other ministers became fully identified with the Moravian Church. Lischy remained a while in the Reformed Church, and preached in York county. Always impatient of the restraints of law and order, he was accused of moral delinquency and became independent of all ecclesiastical connections. Finally, when the Reformed and Lutheran Churches were severally consolidated by the labors of Muhlenberg and Schlatter, the last vestiges of the "Congregation" were entirely swept away.

It is not hard to determine the reasons for the failure of this well-meant scheme. Apart from other grounds, it is evident that, whatever may have been its original motives, it was in its subsequent development entirely foreign to the spirit of the Reformed and Lutheran Churches. And yet who will say that it did not accomplish an important purpose? In that dark and dreary time even this shaking of the dry bones was in itself a promise of the coming resurrection.

CHAPTER V.

Michael Schlatter—Birth and Education—Sent to America by the Synods of Holland—Pastor in Philadelphia—Missionary Journeys—The Organization of the Coetus—The Rival Congregation in Philadelphia—Schlatter's Mission to Europe—The Charity Schools.—Later Years—The Character of his Work.

THE arrival of Michael Schlatter in America, on the 1st of August, 1746, was an important event in the history of the Church. Hitherto the scattered Reformed congregations had been in a lamentable state of confusion. A few congregations in eastern Pennsylvania recognized the authority of the Church of Holland, but there was practically no bond of union between them. The mission of Weis and Reiff had called attention to their miserable condition, but had not been instrumental in relieving it. The Synods of Holland, therefore, regarded themselves as fortunate in being able to secure the services of a worthy Swiss minister to take charge of their missionary work in America, and thus to bring order out of the existing chaos.

Michael Schlatter was born in St. Gall, Switzerland, October 8, 1685. He was respectably connected, being related through his mother with the celebrated Zollikofer family. In his youth he enjoyed excellent educational advantages, but seems to have been by nature better suited to be a pioneer than a scholastic recluse. After completing his course in the university, he was for some time a teacher in Holland, where he was

SCHLATTER'S COAT OF ARMS AND SIGNATURE.

ordained to the ministry, and then successively served as assistant minister at several places in his native land.

HIS MISSION TO AMERICA.

During his résidence in Holland, Schlatter had become familiar with the language of the country, and had no doubt made many friends.[1] When the Synods

---

[1] At this time he began to write his name "Slatter," after the Dutch fashion, and this orthography he retained until his relations with the Dutch synods were terminated. A signature in possession of the author, dated 1767, is written "Schlatter."

of Holland, in 1746, sought a successor to Dorstius and Weis, as Superintendent of Missions in Pennsylvania, it was but natural that they should remember the young Swiss minister who appeared so well suited to this peculiar work. He responded to their invitation with alacrity, and on the 1st of June, 1746, sailed from Amsterdam for his field of labor. After a voyage of exactly two months, during which he narrowly escaped shipwreck on Cape Sable, he arrived at Boston on the 1st of August, where he was kindly entertained by the Honorable I. Wendel, an eminent Holland merchant.

Full of enthusiasm, Schlatter rested only four days at Boston, and then started on his journey by land to Philadelphia. In New York he was very kindly received, but after spending a few weeks with his Dutch brethren he hastened on to his destination. On the 6th of September he arrived in Philadelphia, where the Reformed people received him with great rejoicing. It was not his intention at first to become a settled pastor; but the need of ministers was so great that, within a few months of his arrival, he was induced to accept a call from the Reformed Churches of Philadelphia and Germantown. He refused, however, to accept any salary for the first year, "in order," he says, "that by deeds I might convince them that I did not serve them merely for the sake of my bread."

MISSIONARY JOURNEYS.

During this period Schlatter made extensive missionary journeys, visiting the widely scattered churches in Pennsylvania, New Jersey, Maryland and Virginia. The work was difficult and sometimes dangerous, and could only have been accomplished by a person of indomitable energy and perseverance. He informs us that he traveled more than eight thousand miles, not reckoning his voyage across the ocean. By rude bridle-paths he took his way through the forests from one settlement to another, enduring privations of which we cannot form an adequate conception. Wherever he went he called the people together, and, after preaching the Gospel, induced them to pledge themselves to pay a specified amount for the support of a settled minister. No doubt many of these people had hitherto failed to appreciate the necessity of providing for the salary of a pastor. Unwearied by the difficulties that confronted him, Schlatter organized the congregations into pastoral charges. Some of these were of enormous extent, and in more than one instance their territory now furnishes room for an entire classis; but the field had been traversed, and it was now possible to build up the Church in an orderly manner.

THE ORGANIZATION OF THE COETUS.

In accordance with the instructions which he had received from Holland, Schlatter immediately prepared the way for the establishment of a Coetus,[1] or Synod. The

---

[1] The term Coetus, as applied to an ecclesiastical body, is derived from John de Lasky, who, in 1544, established the Coetus of Emden. It properly differs from a Synod in being a purely advisory body, though the two terms are often interchangeably employed.—*Goebel*, I., 333.

preliminary meeting was held in Philadelphia on the 12th of October, 1746. Besides Schlatter, Weiss, Boehm, and Rieger were present. The first regular meeting was, however, convened in Philadelphia, on September 29th, 1747. Thirty-one members, including elders, were in attendance. The opening sermon was preached by the Rev. J. B. Rieger.

From this time onward, except for several years during the Revolutionary War, the meetings of the Coetus were regularly held. The proceedings were reported to the Synods of Holland, and no action could be final without their approval.

THE RIVAL CONGREGATION IN PHILADELPHIA.

While Schlatter was absent on his missionary journeys, there was trouble brewing in his church in Philadelphia. In September, 1749, the Rev. John Conrad Steiner, of Winterthur, Switzerland, arrived in Philadelphia. He was a pulpit orator of considerable celebrity, having published a volume of sermons in Europe. The Germans of Philadelphia were captivated by his eloquence, and a party was soon formed which desired to make him pastor instead of Schlatter. The result was a conflict between the Schlatter and Steiner parties, which was brought before the civil authorities, and was finally decided in favor of Schlatter. The Steiner party built a new church on Race street, below Third, but Steiner remained there only a few years, and then removed to Germantown, Pa., and subsequently to Frederick, Maryland. The new congregation in Philadelphia maintained a sickly existence until 1759, when the members returned to the mother church. Steiner accepted a call to the pastorate of the united congregation, but died three years later. Though in many respects a worthy man, his conduct towards Schlatter is not to be defended. His extant correspondence with Otterbein shows him to have been self-willed and impatient of authority.

SCHLATTER'S MISSION TO EUROPE.

At the request of the Coetus, Schlatter in 1751 went to Europe for the purpose of presenting the cause of the destitute German Churches in America. His mission was very successful, especially in Holland. A sum of money, amounting to £12,000, was collected and invested for the benefit of the American churches. Though the greater part of this amount was contributed in Holland, other countries also sent gifts, and even the poor Palatinate gave about three hundred dollars. Schlatter's mission was a complete success, and in 1752 he returned to America, bringing with him six young ministers.[1] He also brought seven hundred Bibles for distribution to churches and families.

THE CHARITY SCHOOLS.

The success which had attended the labors of Schlatter in Holland and Germany, suggested an extensive

---

[1] The names of the ministers who accompanied Schlatter to America were Otterbein, Stoy, Waldschmid, Frankenfeld, Wissler, and Rubel.

educational movement in behalf of the Germans of Pennsylvania. Rev. David Thomson translated Schlatter's "Appeal" into English, and a number of philanthropists organized in England a "Society for the Promotion of the Knowledge of God among the Germans." In order to attract attention to the scheme, the condition of these Germans was grossly exaggerated. They were not only represented as ignorant beyond comparison, but as fast becoming "like unto wood-born savages." It was even suggested that unless their children received an English education, they might finally become rebellious and drive the English from the continent of America. In consequence of these imputations, the Lutherans, in 1754, and the Reformed, in 1756, adopted resolutions expressing their indignation at such insinuations.

Even at this early period this charitable movement had become, to some extent, political. A very large sum of money was collected—said to have amounted to £20,000—which was placed in the hands of trustees for the establishment of "Charity Schools" among the Germans. These trustees consisted mainly of the colonial aristocracy, who made no secret of their intention to employ the schools as a means of breaking the alliance which had hitherto subsisted between the Germans and the Quakers. No doubt, when they rode about in their coaches, to establish schools, they did not do much to conciliate the recipients of their bounty. Charity schools were established in Lancaster,

Reading, York, Easton, New Hanover, and Skippack. Schlatter was persuaded to become superintendent of schools, but he was powerless in the face of the opposition that had been aroused against them. Christopher Saur, the celebrated printer, denounced them in his paper, insisting that they were intended to prepare the way for the establishment of the Church of England. The Germans consequently became greatly excited, and held meetings in which they resolved not to patronize the charity schools. It must be confessed that they had some reason to be dissatisfied. Though they had founded a parochial school in close connection with almost every one of their churches, they were stigmatized as hopelessly ignorant. No wonder that Christopher Saur was not willing to rest quietly under this imputation, when at his great publishing house in Germantown, he was printing more books than any other publisher in the American colonies. The conduct of the Germans, in refusing to avail themselves of the benefits of the charity fund, was perhaps unwise; but it is not surprising that they were incensed at being represented, in the old and new world, as proper subjects to be bribed and cajoled by a foreign charity. "It was," says Dr. Harbaugh, "in a measure, at least, a just indignation; and we feel disposed first to blame them somewhat for a lack of humility, and then to praise them more for their manliness and sense of honor."

In the midst of this excitement, Schlatter was personally the chief sufferer. His official position as superintendent of the charity schools rendered him the main object of popular hatred. For some time the Lutheran and Reformed ministers sustained him, but the people were so greatly excited that his influence was entirely destroyed.

The charity schools proved an utter failure. What finally became of the funds it is impossible to say. As the interest alone could be applied to the schools, it would seem as though the principal must have remained intact. "Those who had control of the funds," says Dr. Harbaugh significantly, "no doubt found some more promising object to which to apply the capital." The Holland fund, on the contrary, was securely invested in Europe, and from its income the Reformed Churches for many years received valuable aid.

Utterly disheartened, Schlatter became a chaplain in the British army, and was present in 1757 at the siege of Louisburg. After his return to Pennsylvania, in 1759, he lived in retirement at a place which he called "Sweetland," at Chestnut Hill, near Philadelphia. He preached in neighboring churches, but took no active part in the affairs of the Church. During the Revolution, he earnestly sided with the Americans. As he was still nominally a Royal chaplain, he became especially obnoxious to the British, and was for some time imprisoned, much of his property being wantonly destroyed. He died in October, 1790.

The portrait of Schlatter, which was saved from the British by his daughter Rachel, represents a man with strongly-marked Swiss features, seated before an open Bible. He is said to have been of small stature, but exceedingly active and versatile. Though his public life was confined to a few years, the results of his work were extraordinary. If his plans had not been spoiled by men who cared nothing for his labors, but employed him for political purposes, and thus compassed his ruin, he would no doubt have accomplished a gigantic work for the literary advancement of his people. Rejected by his own generation, Schlatter died in poverty and obscurity, but at last his Church has learned to do justice to his memory, and his name will never be forgotten.

CHAPTER VI.

The Decline—The Lost Churches—Streaks of Daylight.

THE period immediately succeeding the failure of the Charity Schools was a time of gloom and depression. It would be more pleasant to hasten on to the contemplation of brighter days, but this period really furnishes a key to much of our subsequent history. There were many causes that contributed to this unhappy condition. Schlatter had withdrawn from active co-operation with the Coetus, and the body which had previously suffered from his unpopularity was now deprived of his talents and energy. The enthusiasm which is an essential condition of great enterprises had almost disappeared. In 1757 there were but six ministers who attended the meeting of Coetus. On that occasion, it is true, Rev. J. C. Steiner, pastor at Frederick, Maryland, reported that he had travelled 2,690 miles in visiting vacant churches, but such isolated efforts could not meet the wants of the Church.

It must also be confessed that there were serious dissensions which stood in the way of concerted action. Steiner and Stoy were probably the most prominent ministers in the Church. Both were well educated, but they were high-spirited, eccentric, unwilling to submit to authority, and sometimes came into violent collision.

Every year from fifteen hundred to three thousand guilders were sent from Holland in aid of the German Reformed Churches. It was a noble act of charity, and no doubt accomplished much good; but the money was distributed by a committee of Coetus, and there were frequent complaints with regard to the apportionment. Finally, these troubles were overcome by dividing the money equally among the recipients. Not many documents of this period have been preserved, but these show that in the opinion of some of the best men, the condition of the Church appeared to be almost hopeless. The pious Otterbein, who had come to America in 1752 in company with Schlatter, was greatly discouraged. In a letter, written in 1759, in which he expostulates with Steiner for his disorderly conduct in Philadelphia, he says: " It is true the condition of the Coetus is discouraging. But ought you, in deference to the Synods (of Holland) to have acted in this manner? And if the Coetus had resisted their decision, which I do not anticipate, you might then have acted according to your conscience and have been excusable. Why do we constantly annoy each other? Why do we misunderstand each other? What will be the final result of all this? When I consider our whole cause, I feel too certain that God has given up the pastors and people."

THE LOST CHURCHES.

If Schlatter's missionary labors had been continued and extended, the Reformed Church might have been established in almost every one of the colonies. There were far more German settlements than is now generally supposed, and the Huguenots of the South would have been glad to be connected with the Reformed churches, especially as many of them had not come directly from France, but had found a refuge in Germany before they emigrated to America. It may be well briefly to survey a part, at least, of 'the territory in which the Reformed Church might have successfully labored.

Far to the North, in Nova Scotia, there was a considerable German settlement. These Germans had been brought there in 1753, and were at first greatly discouraged by the coldness of the climate and the sterility of the soil. After dreadful sufferings they grew prosperous, and built the town of Lunenberg. In 1770 they appealed to the Coetus to send them a minister, and two years later they sent a delegate to Germany to collect money for their church. Despairing of obtaining a pastor in any other way, they finally selected a pious fisherman, named Bruin Romcas Comingoe, who was ordained by ministers of the Church of Scotland. He labored faithfully until 1819, when he was succeeded by the Rev. Mr. Moschell, who came directly from Germany. After his resignation in 1837, the congregation connected itself with the Presbyterian Church.

At Waldoborough, in Maine, there was a settlement as early as 1739, consisting principally of Lutherans and Reformed. They built a union church, and as the Reformed were in the minority, were served for many years by Lutheran ministers, who administered the communion to the Reformed members according to the form which they preferred. German services were maintained until 1850, but the young folks grew up English, and the whole congregation finally passed over to the Congregationalists.

The towns of Frankfort and Kennebec, in Maine, and of Leyden, in Massachusetts, were founded by Germans. Even in New England, we believe that by earnest missionary labor the Reformed Church might have been firmly established.

In the colony of New York there were many German Reformed churches. The church on Nassau street, in the city of New York, numbered among its pastors such men as John Michael Kern, Dr. J. Daniel Gros, and Dr. Philip Milledoler, who were famous in their day. Gebhard preached at Claverack, and Foehring at Montgomery.. At Schoharie, where Hager and Weis had labored, there was a succession of German ministers, who were virtually independent. At various places in the Mohawk Valley there were German congregations, for which John J. Wack preached irregularly for many years, but they finally passed over at last to the Reformed Dutch Church. The congregations in the State of New York, which are now connected with the Reformed Church in the United States were, we believe, all founded at a later date.

The German Reformed element in New Jersey was by no means insignificant. In Amwell, Hunterdon county, there was a large congregation which is said to have been founded in 1740. Here Dr. Caspar M. Stapel preached, and in 1762 published an edition of Lampe's "*Wahrheitsmilch*," which was probably the first bound volume issued by a Reformed minister in this country. Northward from Amwell, through the German Valley, extended a long line of Reformed churches, in some of which Schlatter preached. In 1763 the consistory at Amwell suggested to the synods of Holland to send over a few more ministers, and to organize a Coetus of New Jersey, including, we suppose, both the German and Dutch churches. If this had been done, we do not doubt that the Reformed would have become the leading denomination in all that region. The lack of ministers and the fact that the English language soon supplanted the German in New Jersey, were the principal reasons why the Reformed churches were neglected and lost. A few were gathered by the Reformed Dutch Church, and some became Presbyterian, but most of them were disbanded and scattered.

It is far from New Jersey to Virginia, and we might find many places to linger on the way. There is, however, no part of the country in which the Reformed Church has suffered more, than in the "Old Dominion." The present Classis of Virginia includes some prosperous charges and many excellent and intelligent people, but it must be confessed that the Church has lost greatly by neglecting its early opportunities. As early as 1711 Governor Spottiswoode founded a German settlement in Rockingham county, and in 1736 Samuel Jenner, of Berne, Switzerland, under the auspices of the "Helvetic Society," built the village called "Eden," on the Roanoke. These are but examples of early settlements before the great stream of German immigration began to pour into the valley of the Shenandoah. As we have seen, there were Reformed ministers among these people, but it is now impossible to discover the extent of their labors. The churches which they founded were almost immediately taken up by the Episcopal Church. The latter was in those days the Established Church in the colony, and as the episcopate had not yet been established in America, the Germans found it easy to "conform," and thus their churches became entitled to receive a government stipend.

Farther south, there were Reformed people among the earliest settlers. In North Carolina, two Swiss gentlemen, De Graffenried and Michel, founded New Berne in 1710, and in 1732, John Peter Purry, of Neufchatel, laid out Purrysburg. A large German Church was established in Charleston, S. C., under the pastorate of the Rev. Dr. J. J. Zubly, who subsequently removed to Savannah, Georgia, and founded the congregation which is now known as the Independent Presbyterian Church. There it was his custom, for many years, to preach regularly in

German, English, and French. In an extant letter, written in 1755, he mentions the fact that he has received a letter from Schlatter, requesting him to attend a meeting of the Coetus "so as to be placed in proper ecclesiastical relations," and he seems to express an intention of accepting the invitation, but there is no evidence that his purpose was ever accomplished.

The Reformed Church has still a classis in North Carolina; but it no longer holds its earliest settlements, and in South Carolina and Georgia it has not a single congregation. The last of the South Carolina congregations was lost to the Reformed Church about fifty years ago.

It is not necessary to take a more extended survey. The causes of the decline which almost immediately succeeded the establishment of the Church in this country, have already been partially indicated. The most important reason, was, however, the lack of ministers. If the large sums which were in Europe contributed in aid of the American churches, had been devoted to the endowment of a good literary and theological school, we believe it would have been better, in the end, for pastors and people.

STREAKS OF DAYLIGHT.

We believe the minutes of the Coetus between 1764 and 1770 are no longer extant. Those of the latter year, which are in the library of the Historical Society, at Lancaster, Pa., plainly indicate that a great change had come over the Church. Of the early ministers Leydich, Waldschmidt and Du Bois alone remained. Otterbein was at the time absent on a visit to Europe. A new generation had appeared upon the scene, and there was a promise of better things to come.

Nicholas Pomp, who was at this time the President of the Coetus, was a man of unusual talents. While pastor at Falkener Swamp, he wrote a book in which he defended the doctrines of the Reformed Church against the insidious teachings of a popular book, the "Everlasting Gospel" of Paul Siegvolck. His son, Thomas Pomp, was for many years pastor at Easton, Penna.

Equally eminent were C. D. Weyberg and William Hendel. Their earnestness and piety were never called into question, and the value of their labors cannot be too highly estimated. In 1788 the college of New Jersey conferred upon both these excellent men the honorary degree of Doctor of Divinity.

The other ministers present at the Coetus were Gros, Faber, Witmer, Dallecker, Gobrecht, Foering, and Henop. Bucher was absent on account of illness. These were earnest and faithful men, who may be said to have inaugurated a brighter era in the history of the Church. Dr. Weyberg had undertaken the task of preparing young men for the ministry, and at this meeting it was reported that Mr. Casper Wack had already pursued his studies for three years under his direction.

CHAPTER VII.

The Church in Maryland—The Rev. William Otterbein and the "United Ministers."[1]

ABOUT the year 1770, the Reformed Church in Pennsylvania began to show signs of improvement, but the condition of the congregations in Maryland was less encouraging. Most of the latter churches were independent, and their relation to the rest of the Coetus had not been properly defined. As late as 1773 the "Fathers" in Holland declared that Maryland did not fall under their jurisdiction; but they made no objection to the reception by the Coetus of the congregations situated in that province. It was felt that something ought to be done for Maryland, where the people were everywhere clamoring for religious instruction. The lack of ministers was great, and the Coetus, therefore, so far relaxed its rules as to ordain several pious laymen for this special work. The means at hand were, however, entirely inadequate, and we have every reason to believe that the Coetus heartily welcomed the organization, in 1774, by the Rev. William Otterbein and other Reformed min-

---

[1] An article by the author, entitled "Otterbein and the Reformed Church," was published in the *Reformed Quarterly Review* for January, 1884. To this article we refer our readers for copies of original documents, and for further information concerning the subject here discussed.

isters, of societies, whose main object was to promote discipline, and to aid pastors in the work of cultivating vital piety among their people.

William Otterbein[1] was born June 3, 1726, at Dillenburg, in Nassau, Germany. His father and grandfather were Reformed ministers, and five of his brothers also assumed the sacred office. He was one of the band of six young ministers who, in 1752, accompanied Schlatter to America. Immediately on his arrival he was called to the pastorate of the church of Lancaster, which was then, next to Philadelphia, the most important Reformed congregation in Pennsylvania. At this place he built a church, and, under the direction of Coetus, performed much missionary labor. After leaving Lancaster, in 1758, he was for two years pastor at Tulpehocken, and then assumed charge of the Reformed church at Frederick, Maryland.[2] Here, as at Lancaster, a church and parsonage were erected, which in their day were regarded as buildings of a very superior order.

From 1765 to 1774, Otterbein was pastor of the Reformed church at York, Pennsylvania. In 1770 and

---

[1] In baptism he was named "Philip William," but for some unknown reason he dropped the first of these names in later life.

[2] On the 19th of April, 1762, while he was pastor at Frederick, Mr. Otterbein was married to Miss Susan Le Roy, of Lancaster, Pa. She was a daughter of Abraham Le Roy, a native of Switzerland. Her sister Elizabeth was subsequently married to the Rev. Dr. W. Hendel, Senior. Mrs. Otterbein died April 27, 1768, and was buried in Lancaster. Her husband remained a widower for the rest of his life.

1771 he was absent on a visit to his relatives in Germany, but his people would not give him up, and the Church was supplied, at their request, by members of Coetus.

We are inclined to doubt the stories which are related concerning the " big meetings " which Otterbein is said to have conducted at this early date. He was no doubt more inclined to " Pietism " than some of his brethren, though not to such a degree as to come into conflict with them; and it is, of course, possible that he may occasionally have participated in " union meetings ;" but it accords better with ascertained facts to believe that those meetings which have become historical occurred somewhat later than has been generally supposed. Tradition is almost certain to antedate events.

In 1774, Mr. Otterbein accepted a call from the Second Reformed Church of the city of Baltimore. This congregation had seceded from the First Church after a protracted conflict, and had been served for some time by the Rev. Benedict Schwob. The latter was not an educated man, but having begun to preach in the hope of supplying the pressing need of the churches of Maryland, he developed remarkable talents as a pulpit orator, and after several applications to the Coetus, was finally ordained. A party in the church of Baltimore was greatly pleased with his earnest and enthusiastic preaching, and desired to displace their pastor, the Rev. John Christopher Faber, in order to secure his services. It turned out that Mr. Faber had more friends than had been supposed, and their efforts proved unsuccessful. Then the dissatisfied party withdrew and organized the second congregation.

For a long time neither party had regarded the separation as final, and by mutual consent the whole matter was referred to Coetus for adjudication, though the church of Baltimore had hitherto been independent. Every possible means was employed to restore peace, and several times it appeared as though the desired object had been attained; but after each attempted reconciliation, the struggle began anew. Mr. Faber finally accepted a call from Taneytown, but the First Church irregularly called Rev. W. Wallauer as his successor, and thus forfeited the good opinion of the Coetus, whose sympathies were for a time entirely with the Second congregation. After the withdrawal of Mr. Schwob, in 1773, the latter Church called Mr. Otterbein, but the Coetus still hoped to reunite the congregations, and at first declined to confirm the call "because the one party was too greatly prejudiced against him." The elders of both congregations then extended a call to the Rev. William Hendel, D. D., but the First Church refused to confirm the action of its delegates, and the Second, evidently felt itself authorized to renew its call to Mr. Otterbein, who finally accepted it. In 1775 this call was confirmed by Coetus, which formally expressed its satisfaction at learning that "his labors are blest, and the opposing party cease from strife." Both congregations were subsequently recognized as standing in regular connection with the Coetus.

In 1771 Francis Asbury, the pioneer of American Methodism, arrived in this country. As is well known, he did not propose to establish a separate religious denomination, but, in furtherance of the great movement inaugurated by Wesley and his coadjutors, he founded societies whose sole condition of membership was "a desire to flee the wrath to come and be saved from sin." The sacraments were not administered in these Methodist societies, but the class system was introduced, and some of the leaders then appointed subsequently became earnest Methodist ministers.

Soon after his arrival Mr. Asbury became acquainted with Mr. Schwob, and was by him introduced in 1774 to Mr. Otterbein. We can well conceive how great must have been the impression made on Otterbein and Schwob by the intimate acquaintance of such a man as Asbury. Their views of religious truth were very similar, and it was but natural that they should agree concerning the methods of its promulgation. Wesley's plan of founding societies and holding class-meetings cannot have been new to Mr. Otterbein. It was based on the old idea of the "*ecclesiola in ecclesia*," which had been familiar to the Reformed people of Germany since the days of Jean de Labadie. In some instances such societies had accomplished much good, and as in Europe the State was careful to preserve the external organization of the Church, it was but rarely that they resulted in schism.

What was more natural than that Otterbein and

Schwob should conceive the idea of introducing the system advocated by Mr. Asbury into the German Reformed churches? It seemed to furnish an answer to what was then a burning question, especially in Maryland. If it was not possible to obtain regular pastors, why should not the people help themselves by organizing class-meetings in their respective churches, under the direction of worthy leaders, who would, at least in some measure, promote devotion in the Church and exercise proper discipline?

That this class system was actually introduced is evident from the minutes of five conventions, found by the author in November, 1882, among the records of St. Benjamin's church, near Westminster, Md. These conventions were held from May, 1774, to June, 1776, by six Reformed ministers, who called themselves "United Ministers." The ministers were Wm. Otterbein, of Baltimore; Benedict Schwob, of Pipe Creek; Jacob Weimer, of Hagerstown; F. L. Henop, of Frederick; Daniel Wagner, of York, Pa., and Wm. Hendel, of Tulpehocken, Pa.[1] It appears that the work was at this time confined to the Reformed Church, and that it was conducted peaceably, with the co-operation of most of the churches in Maryland and of several in Pennsylvania. The members of the larger congrega-

[1] On the 4th of June, 1776, the "United Ministers" licensed Henry Weider, one of their earliest class-leaders, to preach the Gospel. The certificate of licensure is still extant. Weider was subsequently pastor of Reformed churches in Adams county, Pa.

tions were generally divided into two classes, but in smaller churches a single class was deemed sufficient. Some of the classes convened in the church, but others held their meetings at the houses of their leaders.

There are, so far as we know, no extant documents bearing on the progress of this remarkable religious movement between the years 1776 and 1789. It is, however, more than probable that soon after the former date peculiarities of doctrine and worship began to appear which greatly affected the character of the " unity." The conferences instituted by the " United Ministers " became " great meetings " of the type which are familiar from the early history of Methodism. Among those who became most profoundly interested were men who were not connected with the Reformed Church, and who had no intention of becoming identified with it. It was evident that a new type of Church life was in process of development, and most of the ministers and members of the Reformed Church therefore gradually withdrew from the organization. This process was no doubt facilitated by the fact that during the latter part of the Revolutionary war the meetings we e interrupted by the disturbed state of the country.

Otterbein probably regarded the matter in a somewhat different light. Like Zinzendorf, when he founded the " Congregation of God in the Spirit," he seems to have imagined that the Christians of various denominations might participate in a " higher unity " without renouncing their original ecclesiastical relations. He therefore continued to take a profound interest in the movement which he had helped to inaugurate, but at the same time was careful to remain in regular standing in the Coetus of the Reformed Church.

For thirty-nine years Mr. Otterbein was pastor of the Second Reformed Church of Baltimore. During a part of this period he occupied a position which is at present hard to comprehend. He was not independent of ecclesiastical relations, as has sometimes been suggested, but was a member of Coetus in good and regular standing. At the same time he labored as an evangelist, especially in Maryland, and was regarded as one of the leaders in the religious movement which he had helped to inaugurate. One at least of the original class-leaders, Geo. Adam Gueting, was brought by him to the Coetus and there ordained to the ministry. Otterbein evidently had no idea of establishing a separate religious denomination; it was to him a "society" rather than a Church, and therefore from 1789 to 1804, he did not hesitate to act as one of its superintendents.[1]

For a long time the "Brethren," with whom Mr. Otterbein labored, were popularly known as "New Reformed," though Martin Boehm, and others of their most prominent leaders, had no connection with the Reformed Church. In 1804 there occurred an event which, it has been said, "drove the wedge of separation." The Rev. G. A. Gueting, whom Otterbein had introduced into

---

[1] Otterbein was also favorable to the Methodists, and in 1784 assisted Dr. Coke in the ordination of Mr. Asbury.

the Reformed ministry, became an enthusiast of the most pronounced type, whose preaching was attended by extraordinary excitement. Under his auspices were chiefly held the "great meetings" on the Antietam, which are not yet forgotten. In this respect he went much further than Mr. Otterbein, whose disposition was more quiet and reflective. Gueting became more and more irregular, and as he did not heed the admonitions of Synod, was finally excluded by a vote of twenty to seventeen. This action of the Synod has been sharply criticised, but it is hard to see how, with proper self-respect, that body could have acted differently. There was no reflection cast on the personal character of Mr. Gueting, but the type of religion which he represented was certainly foreign to that of the Reformed Church, and it is possible that he did not expect or desire a different action on the part of the Synod. He continued to labor in the manner which pleased him best, and his memory is greatly cherished in the Church of the "United Brethren in Christ."

Otterbein attended but a single conference of the "Brethren" after the exclusion of Gueting from the Reformed Synod. This was in 1805, after which date, it has been said, "he withdrew from the active work." It is true that he was advanced in years; but, as he continued in charge of his congregation until his death, which occurred in 1813, eight years later, this suggestion as to the cause of his absence is not entirely satisfactory. Is it not at least possible that after the Synod had spoken in the case of Gueting, he felt that he could no longer attend these conferences without placing himself in a position of antagonism to the body to which he owed his first allegiance? There can, however, be no doubt that he was warmly attached to the "Brethren," and that the latter to the end regarded him with unlimited veneration. He must have foreseen that a new denomination was unavoidable, and one of his last official acts was to assist in giving it a settled ministry by the rite of ordination. Thus he sent it forth with his benediction, but personally preferred to remain in the Church of his fathers. It will be remembered that J. D. Aurand, Henry Hiestand, Thomas Winters, and perhaps others who had participated in the early conferences, also decided to remain in the Reformed Church, of which they became worthy and efficient ministers. Winters says in his autobiography: "During this time" (between 1809 and 1815) "I was strongly urged to go into the organization of a new church, which was then in process of formation, and which did actually come into being; but like the great Otterbein, whom I greatly loved and esteemed for his piety and talents, I preferred rather to live and die in the Reformed Church."

There can be no doubt that Mr. Otterbein continued a member of the Reformed Synod until the end of his life. He attended its meeting held in Baltimore in 1806, one year after he was present for the last time at a conference of the "Brethren," and his name was always retained on the roll of its members. In August, 1812, he said to the Rev. Isaac Gerhart: "I too am a member of the Synod of the German Reformed Church, but cannot attend on account of old age." He was at that time eighty-six years old. His congregation was, however, so thoroughly permeated by the spirit of the movement in which its pastor had at one time been actively engaged, that after his death it became possible to alienate it from the Reformed Church, to which it properly belonged. With reference to the personal excellence of Mr. Otterbein there can be no difference of opinion. Even those who differed from him with respect to the methods which he pursued, were impressed by his unaffected piety and attracted by his benevolent disposition. The religious movement in which he took so prominent a part was well meant, but it grew beyond its original plan, and carried him further than he had intended. It is, however, pleasant to know that he was treated by the Synod with the utmost kindness and consideration, and that to the end of his life he remained in full communion with the Reformed Church.

CHAPTER VIII.

*The Reformed Church in the Revolution—Baron Steuben—
Patriotic Ministers—The Loyalists.*

THE War of the Revolution is the most fascinating period of our national history. It has been greatly embellished by poetry and tradition, and its stirring scenes afford frequent employment to the imaginative writers of the present generation. Possibly, in the dim light of the past, some of the personages of that momentous epoch have been magnified beyond their due proportions; but patriotism demands that we should give reverence to the memory of the men who achieved our national independence.

The prominence of the German element in the revolutionary struggle will hardly be called into question. There were German regiments in the Continental army,[1] and even among the generals of "the line" there were some who derived their lineage from the Fatherland. Several of these, like De Kalb and De Woedtke, were old soldiers whose church relations it might be difficult to determine. Muhlenberg was, of course, a Lutheran.

---

[1] We have been told by aged people, that when the German soldiers marched into battle they sang a song with the refrain:
"England's Georgel, Kaiser, Koenig,
Ist für GOTT und uns zu wenig."

Of the others, there were several who appear to have been of Reformed descent,[1] but there was at least one celebrated German general who was a faithful member of the Church:

BARON STEUBEN.

Frederick William, Baron von Steuben, was born in Magdeburg, Germany, on the 15th of November, 1730. His father, who was a distinguished officer, took him early to war, so that at the age of fourteen he was a cadet in the Prussian army.

The earlier years of Steuben's manhood were spent in the service of Frederick the Great, who first raised Prussia to the rank of one of the great powers of Europe. Having fought gallantly in the Seven Years' War, he accepted the position of Grand Marshal at the Court of one of the minor German potentates. Here he remained for ten years, varying the monotony of his duties by making extended journeys in company with his prince. At the end of that time he found, however, that the little court was getting too hot to hold him. The prince and his subjects were Roman Catholics, while Steuben was always an outspoken Protestant, and it was therefore natural that his intimate relations with the prince were productive of much jealousy. Steuben discovered the

---

[1] Gen. Nicholas Herkimer, "the hero of Oriskany," was the son of a Palatine, and resided at Burnetsfield, where Rev. G. M. Weis was once pastor. His will is signed "Nicholas Herckheimer," and this was, no doubt, the proper orthography.

storm while it was brewing, and prudently retired before it had reached its height. After spending some time at several of the German courts, he determined, in 1777, to pay a visit to friends in England. On the way he made, in Paris, the acquaintance of Franklin and Deane, the American commissioners, who invited him to accept a commission in America. They felt that the young republic needed such a drill-master as the baron, to bring order out of the chaos of the Continental army.

It was long before Baron Steuben could make up his mind to accept the invitation; but he had seen so much of the hollowness of courts, that he felt irresistibly drawn towards the struggling colonists. At last he set sail in a vessel that was full of articles which were contraband of war. They had a long and dangerous passage. The ship was three times on fire, and the hatches full of gunpowder. Once the crew mutinied, and the passengers were compelled to quell the disturbance.

On the 1st of November, 1777, they arrived at Portsmouth, New Hampshire, whence the baron and his suite were compelled to proceed on horseback to York, Pa., where Congress was then in session.

For a while the baron appeared greatly depressed, not understanding a single word that was spoken by the people; but when they arrived in Pennsylvania he seemed like another man. The tones of his mother tongue fell like music on his ear. At York he was received with open arms. His recommendations were laid before Congress, and he was directed in the most complimentary manner to proceed to Valley Forge, to report to General Washington.

It was the most gloomy period in the Revolution. The soldiers were ill-clad and discontented, and there were probably but few who anticipated the success of the American cause. Washington appointed Steuben to the office of Inspector-General, and he at once set about the work of re-organizing the army. He drilled the men almost incessantly, which, he said, was good for them, as it kept them from freezing. In a few weeks the army was drilled; and "after this," says Lossing, "the Continental regulars were never beaten in a fair fight."

General Steuben did his full duty to the end of the war, commanding a division in several battles, and finally directing the trenches at the siege of Yorktown. It was long before he received any compensation for his services, in consequence of the impoverished condition of the national treasury. The States of New York, Pennsylvania and New Jersey, however, presented him with tracts of wild land, and, in 1790, the general government added an annuity of twenty-five hundred dollars.

Baron Steuben survived the war of the Revolution eleven years, during which time he resided in the city of New York, generally spending the summer months on his land in Oneida county. He was a ruling elder of the German Reformed Church in Nassau street, of which Rev. Dr. Gros was pastor. The whole community treated him with the utmost respect, and it is related that during a riot the angry crowd made way for him to pass, and gave " *Three cheers for Baron Steuben!* "

After the baron's death, his aide, General North, very properly erected a tablet in the church of which he had been a member, bearing the inscription: "Sacred to the memory of FREDERICK WILLIAM AUGUSTUS, BARON DE STEUBEN, a German; Knight of the Order of Fidelity; Aid-de-Camp of Frederick the Great, King of Prussia; Major-General and Inspector-General of the Revolutionary War; esteemed, respected and supported by Washington. He gave military skill and discipline to the citizen soldiers, who, fulfilling the decree of Heaven, achieved the Independence of the United States. The highly polished manners of the Baron were graced by the most noble feelings of the heart. His hand, open as day for melting charity, closed only in the strong grasp of death. This memorial is inscribed by an American, who had the honor to be his aide-de-camp, the happiness to be his friend. Ob. 1795."

Though Baron Steuben had his faults, like other men, all our authorities agree in declaring him to have been as brave and honorable a German as ever crossed the ocean. The Reformed Church should not cease to do honor to the memory of her distinguished son.

PATRIOTIC MINISTERS.

The ministers of the German Reformed Church connected with the Coetus, appear to have been generally earnest advocates of independence. In their official communications with Holland it was not to be expected that they should express themselves freely on the questions at issue, but it is to be observed that they speak of the British as "the enemy." Days of fasting and prayer were appointed, and their proceedings have throughout a melancholy tone. Tradition has it that some of the ministers in preaching on these fast-days, chose texts which sufficiently expressed their political sentiments. Rev. John H. Weikel, pastor of Boehm's church, Montgomery county, Pennsylvania, got into trouble at the beginning of the war by preaching on the text: "Better is a poor and wise child than an old and foolish king who will no more be admonished." Ecclesiastes, iv. 13.

Rev. C. D. Weyberg, D. D., of the Race street Reformed church, Philadelphia, was imprisoned for his patriotism, and his church occupied by British soldiers. He had not only preached patriotic sermons to the American soldiers, but had subsequently addressed the Hessians on the justice of the American cause; and it is asserted that unless he had been silenced, the whole body of mercenaries would have left the British service. On the first Sunday after his liberation he suggestively addressed his congregation on the words, "O God! the heathen have come into Thine inheritance: Thy holy temple have they defiled." *Psalm* lxxix. 1. The text had a certain appropriateness, for it is recorded that the church had been so greatly injured by the British occupation, that the cost of repairing it was fifteen thousand two hundred dollars.

PATRIOTIC MINISTERS. 231

Several other German Reformed ministers are also entitled to revolutionary honors. Schlatter, it will be remembered, was imprisoned for his sympathy with the American cause. Hendel was accompanied by armed men when he went to preach in Lykens Valley—the guards standing at the door to protect him from the

WEYBERG AMONG THE SOLDIERS.

Indians, who had become hostile through British influence. Rev. John Conrad Bucher, who had been a military officer during the French and Indian war, and had resigned his position to become a minister of the gospel, certainly visited the army and preached to the soldiers, if he was not a regular chaplain. Rev. J. C. A. Helffenstein was pastor at Lancaster at the time when the captive Hessians were kept there, and it frequently became his duty to preach to them. "On one occasion," says Dr. Harbaugh, "he preached on the text, Isaiah, lii. 3; 'For thus saith the Lord, Ye have sold yourselves for nought and ye shall be redeemed without money.' 'This sermon caused a good deal of excitement and offence among the captives. On another occasion he preached a discourse in the church, in the evening, on the words: 'If the Son make you free, ye shall be free indeed,' when the excitement was so great that it was deemed necessary to accompany him home with a guard. Once he preached to the American soldiers on their departure for the scene of conflict from the words: 'If God be for us, who can be against us?'"

We have no room to speak at length of all the members of the Reformed Church who distinguished themselves during the Revolutionary struggle, but we cannot refrain from referring to an incident which illustrates the patriotism of the Reformed people of Philadelphia. When General Richard Montgomery was killed in the famous attack on the city of Quebec, Dr. William Smith delivered his eulogy in the Race street Reformed Church, on February 19, 1776. "At that time," says Dr. Van Horne, the present pastor, "the opinions of citizens were very much divided on the subject of the war, and no greater proof of their loyalty to the American cause could be given by pastor and people than the opening of their new and highly-prized house of worship for this purpose."

In 1789 the Coetus, assembled in Philadelphia, addressed a communication to General Washington, congratulating him on his election to the Presidency, and at the same time expressing sentiments of the most exalted patriotism. In his reply, the General declared himself extremely gratified by this expression of good will, and presented to the Coetus his most cordial wishes for the prosperity of the Reformed churches.

We may mention, in this connection, that in 1793, during the prevalence of the yellow fever in Philadelphia, Gen. Washington made his home for several months in the family of Rev. Dr. F. L. Herman, then pastor of the Reformed Church in Germantown. At that time the General frequently attended worship in the Reformed church when the services were held in English, and there is a tradition that he once received the communion with the congregation. When the great chieftain died, a memorial address before the Society of the Cincinnati, consisting of the officers of the Revolution, was delivered in the Reformed church on Race street, Philadelphia, by Major William Jackson, who had held the position of Secretary in the Convention which formed the Constitution of the United States.

THE LOYALISTS.

A century has passed, and we may now venture to express a few words of pity for those Americans who opposed the cause of Independence and persisted in their allegiance to the King of Great Britain. For the men who took up arms against their native country we can have but little sympathy; but among those of more pacific disposition there were some of the foremost men in the colonies, who, for their devotion to a mistaken principle, were compelled to sacrifice their possessions and to seek a refuge in a foreign land.

It may appear strange to the present generation, that among those who were contemptuously called Tories, there should have been men of German birth, who cannot be supposed to have been moved by natural affection for the British monarchy. It should, however, be remembered that these men had but recently taken an oath of allegiance to the crown of England, by which they regarded themselves as permanently bound. They failed to see that this oath was of the nature of a contract which had already been broken by the tyranny of Great Britain.

In each of the German denominations there were a few ministers and members who were regarded as Loyalists. Of these we will mention two Reformed ministers whose brilliant usefulness was utterly destroyed in the manner which we have just indicated.

John Michael Kern was a native of Manheim, in Germany. After receiving a thorough education he was sent to this country in 1763, by the Consistory of Heidelberg, to take charge of the German Reformed Church on Nassau street, New York. We do not know whether he became a member of the Coetus, as the minutes of that period are lost; but the fact that his favorite pupil and successor, Dr. Gros, was a member of that body, renders it more than probable. At the beginning of the Revolution Mr. Kern became an enthusiastic loyalist, believing that in America neither church nor state was prepared for independence. Unable to sustain himself in New York, where his congregation held opposite political principles, he removed to Montgomery, and soon afterwards to Halifax, where he remained till long after the close of the war. In 1788 he came to Pennsylvania and located in Rockhill township, Bucks county, where he died March 22d of the same year. He had sacrificed his all, and, poor and heartsick, he came to lay his bones among his own people.

John Joachim Zubly, D. D. (name also written Zubley, Zübli, and Züblein), was briefly mentioned in a previous chapter. He was born at St. Gall, Switzerland, August 24, 1724. His father emigrated to Carolina with his family in 1726. The son was taken back to Europe, educated at Halle, ordained at Chur in 1744, and then returned to America.

His first charge was in Pennsylvania, but the locality is now unknown. In 1754 we find him at Charleston, S. C., and about 1758 at Savannah. The degree of Doctor of Divinity was conferred upon him in 1770 by the College of New Jersey. At this time his correspondents were among the foremost men of the country—his influence in Georgia was very great, and at the beginning of the Revolution he found himself compelled by circumstances to take an active part in public affairs.

On the 4th of July, 1775, Dr. Zubly preached an eloquent sermon, afterwards published in Philadelphia, before the Provincial Congress then assembled in Savannah. The title-page bears the suggestive Scriptural motto: "Ephraim shall not envy Judah, and Judah shall not vex Ephraim." *Isaiah* xi. 13.

On the 10th of July, 1775, Dr. Zubly and four others were selected to represent the Colony of Georgia in the adjourned session of Congress, which convened in Philadelphia in September of the same year. He declined to accept the appointment unless his congregation should give its consent. A committee was then sent to consult with the people, and they finally agreed "to spare their minister for a time for the good of the common cause."

For three or four months Dr. Zubly was a member of the Continental Congress. At this time he wrote his Appeal to the Earl of Dartmouth in behalf of the Liberties of America. In his answer to Paine's "Common Sense," occurs the following passage, which sufficiently indicates the nature of his political sentiments: "The author looks upon an entire separation from Great Britain not as a *last remedy*, but as a new and dangerous disease; and earnestly prayeth that America, in that connection, may soon and forever enjoy that constitution and freedom which her representatives so justly claim."

Early in 1776, while Congress was engaged in discussing the question of independence, Samuel Chase, of Maryland, publicly accused Dr. Zubly of holding treasonable correspondence with Sir James Wright, Colonial Governor of Georgia. How much truth was contained in this accusation it might now be impossible to determine; but it is hard to understand how such correspondence—which may have been entirely personal—could be construed as treasonable, previous to the Declaration of Independence. Soon afterwards Dr. Zubly suddenly left Congress and returned to Georgia, for the purpose of using his influence in opposition to a separation from the mother country. He must, however, have soon discovered that he had mistaken the signs of the times. His great popularity vanished almost immediately, even in the place of his residence. In 1777 he was banished from Savannah with the loss of half of his estate. He found a refuge in South Carolina, where he remained until the royal government was reestablished in Georgia in 1779. Then he resumed his ministerial charge in Savannah, and there abode until his death, which occurred July 23, 1781. Two of the streets of Savannah, Joachim and Zubly, are named after him, and one of the hamlets of the town, St. Gall, yet records the name of his native place in Switzerland.

If Dr. Zubly had remained in Congress a few months longer, he would have become a Signer of the Declaration of Independence. In that case his memory would, no doubt, have been highly cherished, especially by the German people of the United States. Though his career is now almost forgotten, let us not refuse to grant him a place among the worthies whose names adorn the history of the Reformed Church.

CHAPTER IX.

After the Revolution—Rev. John William Weber—Educational Movements—Franklin College—The Last Years of the Coetus.

THE years intervening between the close of the Revolution and the adoption of the Federal Constitution furnish few materials for the history of Church or State. The country had not yet recovered from the effects of the war, and the States were practically independent, hardly recognizing the authority of Congress. It is, therefore, not surprising that in this gloomy period the Reformed Church should have manifested but few signs of vigorous activity. The most important event was, perhaps, the settlement in 1783, of Rev. John William Weber, as pastor of several congregations which had been recently organized in Westmoreland county, Pennsylvania. He was the founder of the Reformed Church in Greensburg, and was the first minister of any denomination who preached regularly in Pittsburg. Mr. Weber may, therefore, be regarded as the pioneer of the Reformed Church west of the Alleghanies, and it was a graceful act when the Westmoreland classis, in 1874, erected a handsome monument to his memory.

The difficulty of securing educated ministers for service in America had rather increased than diminished. In 1786 Frederick L Herman and George Troldenier, the last of the missionaries sent by the Synods of Holland, arrived in this country; and indeed, for many previous years the number of ministers arriving from Germany had been so small that it was impossible to depend upon this source of supply. To send young men to the Fatherland to be educated was dangerous and expensive, and in this country there was no institution where the course of instruction was believed to be suited to the requirements of German students[1]. In the hope of meeting these wants, Dr. J. C. Kunze, of the Lutheran Church, of Philadelphia, had established a classical school, which was finally superseded by the German department of the University of Pennsylvania, conducted by Dr. Helmuth. This bilingual arrangement did not work very well, and it was not expected to be permanent. In New York Dr. Gros held, besides his pastorate, a professorship in Columbia College, and instructed a few German students, among whom were Milledoler and the younger Hendel. These arrangements could, however, only meet the wants of isolated students, and more extensive educational facilities were imperatively demanded. Neither the Reformed nor the Lutheran Church felt itself strong enough to establish a literary institution, and both Churches, therefore, welcomed an enterprise of a more general nature which proposed to provide facilities for higher education for the entire German community.

---

[1] In 1782 the Coetus requested the Synods of Holland to establish a High School in Pennsylvania for the education of ministers of the Gospel. The reply to this request is not known.

FRANKLIN COLLEGE.

The beginning of the year 1787 was believed to be especially auspicious for the foundation of a German college. The country had now in some degree recovered from the Revolution, and was about to adopt a Federal Constitution. Many ancient prejudices had passed away, and there was a kindly feeling towards the Germans for their patriotism during the war of independence. The leading ministers of the Lutheran and Reformed Churches were on terms of affectionate intimacy; and it was believed that by their co-operation with the members of the German Society of Philadelphia, who were deeply interested in the movement, an important work could be performed for the literary advancement of the German people. It was, of course, never intended to establish a purely German institution; but it was believed that by the cultivation of both languages it might be possible to bring the German and English citizens more closely together, and thus to advance the social and literary interests of the entire community.

Benjamin Franklin, the most eminent citizen of Pennsylvania, was instrumental in the establishment of many philanthropic institutions. Among these we may mention the Philadelphia Library, the Pennsylvania Hospital, the American Philosophical Society, and the University of Pennsylvania. It would be ungracious, we think, to refuse to recognize him as the founder of Franklin College. Though advanced in years, he took a deep interest in the new institution, and was the largest individual contributor to its endowment.

It was expected by the friends of the proposed institution that the Legislative Assembly would make a considerable appropriation towards its endowment. In this expectation they were disappointed. By the incorporating act, ten thousand acres of land lying within the boundaries of the present counties of Lycoming, Venango, and Bradford, in the State of Pennsylvania, were granted to the college, the expenses of surveying to be paid out of the treasury of the State. In February, 1788, an act was passed for "vesting the public storehouse and two lots of ground in the borough and county of Lancaster in the trustees of Franklin College for the use of said institution." The donated lands were at that time unsalable, and the old storehouse required extensive alterations before it could be used as a college-building. We have no means of knowing how large a sum was raised by private subscription, but it is evident that it was utterly inadequate to its intended purpose. Many years passed before the land which had been granted by the Legislature became sufficiently valuable to be sold to advantage, and thus to furnish the nucleus of a respectable endowment.

Though the Legislature had granted the public storehouse at Lancaster for a college-building, it was found necessary to make an addition to the original structure. The laying of the corner-stone was performed by Benjamin Franklin, and was one of his latest official acts. On this occasion he was accompanied by a French author, Hector St. Jean Crèvecœur, who, in his book ("Voyage dans la Haute Pennsylvanie,") has preserved a record of the event. He says, "In the year 1787 I accompanied the venerable Franklin, at that time Governor of Pennsylvania, on a journey to Lancaster, where he had been invited to lay the corner-stone of a college which he had founded there for the Germans." The author then proceeds to give an account of a conversation with Franklin concerning the origin of the American Indians. It is a pity that he did not rather speak at length of the exercises attendant upon the laying of the corner-stone.

When the college-building was ready to be occupied, the institution was formally opened in the most impressive manner. Several copies of the programme are still extant, one of which is in the possession of the author. It is printed both in German and English, on the same sheet. There was a grand procession in which many dignitaries participated. The Reformed Coetus, which was then holding its annual meeting in Lancaster was present in a body. The German part of the programme includes several beautiful original hymns which were probably composed by Rev. Dr. Helmuth. There is also an English ode of unknown authorship, which was sung on the occasion, and which we quote as illustrative both of the literary tastes of the period and of the exalted expectations of the friends of the new college :

1. Strophe.

Hail, ye Banks of Conestogoe!
 Fertile, favor'd Region, hail!
Chosen seat of FRANKLIN COLLEGE,
 What but Good can here prevail?
Science never comes alone,
 Peace and Plenty,
Heaven itself support her Cause!

1. Antistrophe.

Creator, hail! thy Light and Glory
 Rejoice the Good, the Bad dismay,
Dispel the mists of Vice and Folly,
 And consecrate this happy day.
Now doubly bless the favor'd Region,
Where Science joins with mild Religion,
To raise their grateful Hymns to GOD.

2. Strophe.

By Jehovah's care protected
 The Fabric gains a height sublime;
Truth expands its bright effulgence,
 Error seeks another clime.
All its base and dark attendants,
 Superstition,
Pride and Discord fly from Truth.

2. Antistrophe.

All in the glorious work assisting,
 We build on Christ the corner-stone;
The walls may bear diverse directions,
 The building still shall be but one.
Devotion pure and peaceful science,
United, bid their foes Defiance,
While Time remains the work shall stand.

Sermons were preached by the Rev. Dr. H. E. Muhlenberg and the Rev. Joseph Hutchins, rector of the Episcopal church—the former in German and the latter in English. Both sermons were published in pamphlet form, the latter not until 1806, nineteen years after its delivery. In his discourse Mr. Hutchins took occasion to recommend that the new institution should be prevailingly English. "As the limited capacity of man," he said, "can seldom attain excellence in more than one· language, the study of English will consequently demand the principal attention of your children." However innocent such utterances may now appear to have been, they were hardly prudent under the circumstances. It would have been better to employ language like that of Benjamin Rush in his " Essay on the Germans," written two years later: "Do not contend with their prejudices in favor of their language. It will be the channel through which the knowledge and discoveries of the wisest nations in Europe may be conveyed into our country."

The first board of trustees of Franklin College consisted of the following gentlemen: Hons. Thomas Mifflin and Thomas McKean, Revs. John H. C. Helmuth, Caspar Weyberg, Henry Muhlenberg, William Hendel, Nicholas Kurtz, George Troldenier, John Herbst, Joseph Hutchins, Frederic Weyland, Albertus Helffenstein, W. Ingold, Jacob Van Buskirk, Abraham Blumer, Frederic Dallicker, C. E. Shultz, F. V. Meltzheimer, Messrs. John Hubley, Joseph Hiester, Casper Schaffner, Peter

Hoofnagle, Christopher Crawford, Paul Zantzinger, Adam Hubley, Adam Reigart, Jasper Yeates, Stephen Chambers, Robert Morris, George Clymer, Philip Wager, William Bingham, William Hamilton, Benjamin Rush, M. D., William Rawle, Lewis Farmer, Christopher Kucher, Philip Groenwaldt, Michael Hahn, George Stake, Sr., and John Musser.

This was a very intelligent and distinguished body. The clergymen named were generally the foremost men in the Lutheran and Reformed Churches. Included in the list were a number of eminent Revolutionary officers and four of the Signers of the Declaration of Independence.

The charter, as granted by the Legislature, appears at first sight to have been sufficiently liberal and comprehensive. The faculty and board of trustees were authorized to grant such degrees in science and the liberal arts "as are usually granted in other colleges in America and Europe." The college was authorized to hold property and receive bequests, "provided always the same do not exceed in the whole the yearly value of ten thousand pounds, valuing one Portugal half Johannes, weighing nine penny-weight, at three pounds."

Though apparently so liberal, the charter was in some respects cumbrous and defective. Fifteen of the Trustees were required to be members of the Lutheran Church, fifteen of the Reformed, "the remainder to be chosen from any other society of Christians." The

President of the college was to be forever chosen alternately from the Lutheran or Reformed Church, unless the trustees should "unanimously agree to elect and appoint two or more persons in succession of the same religious denomination, or some suitable person of any other society of Christians." In guarding the various interests represented, various minute regulations concerning meetings and elections were introduced into the charter, which subsequently interfered materially with the successful working of the institution. The Faculty as originally constituted was able and enthusiastic. The Rev. Dr. H. E. Muhlenberg, the celebrated botanist, was the first President, and the Rev. Dr. W. Hendel served as Vice-President. The Rev. Frederick V. Melsheimer, "the father of American Entomology," had special charge of the German department. Prof. Stewart gave instruction in the English branches, and Prof. J. C. W. Reichenbach taught Mathematics. A little later, Prof. James Ross took charge of the department of Ancient Languages, and it was while he was connected with the college that his celebrated Latin Grammar was written.

There is no evidence that Franklin College ever formally graduated students or conferred degrees in the liberal arts. This was probably due to the exalted ideas of the faculty concerning the proper requirements of academic distinction. It was, however, customary for many years to hold an annual festival, which in many respects resembled a modern commencement. From the reports of these festivals published in the papers of the day, it appears that among the earliest students were young men who subsequently became influential ministers in the Lutheran and Reformed Churches. Among those who became Reformed ministers we may mention J. C. Becker, J. T. Faber, Jr., and Philip Gloninger.

The school was well patronized from the beginning. In 1788 there were 125 students, of whom upwards of twenty studied the ancient languages. In order to extend the advantages of the institution as widely as possible, the rates of tuition were very low, so that the receipts for tuition for the first session were only £40, and for the second £70. There were three salaried teachers who received about £410. It is not surprising, therefore, that the treasurer, John Hubley, Esq., at the end of the first year, reported a deficit of £244. In a letter to Dr. Benjamin Rush, of Philadelphia, the treasurer says, "I wrote to you some time ago how poorly our college stands, and how far we are in arrears. These arrears are increasing daily, and unless you gentlemen in Philadelphia will put your shoulders to the wheel we must inevitably perish, and that soon." .

It is evident, therefore, that the chief trouble was financial. Professor Melsheimer writes, "If the Germans will take an interest and increase the endowment, the institution will soon be among the most prosperous in the State." The German papers of the day contain many appeals for aid, as well as bitter complaints against the people for their lack of interest in this important enterprise. The fact is, the time for success on so extensive a scale had not yet arrived. A large portion of the German population of Lancaster county was not favorable to higher education, and even the Lutherans and Reformed were not generally enthusiastic. They were warmly attached to their native language, and feared that the new institution would make the English language more prominent than the German. If either of the Synods had possessed supreme control, it is probable that arrangements would have been made to meet the deficiencies of income by special contributions from the churches, but neither body was properly conscious of its responsibility, and each depended upon the other. Franklin College was therefore neglected, and the trustees could discover no other way of preventing utter ruin than by contracting its operations. It has been assumed by some writers that the college was closed, but this is a mistake. The Rev. Dr. F. A. Muhlenberg,[1] who was himself a professor at a comparatively recent period, says concerning it, "The school, it must be admitted, was constantly kept open, so that parents resident in that vicinity seldom stood in need of a place where their children could receive, at least, a respectable classical education." Sometimes, however, there was but a single professor, who received a small stipend from the Board, but depended in great measure on the fees received for tuition. The institution became a local academy, and

---

[1] "Educational Efforts of the Pennsylvania Synod," Evangelical Review, April, 1859.

was of little advantage to the Church in general. Its property was, however, increasing in value, and it finally became possible to establish a college upon the old foundation.

THE LAST YEARS OF THE COETUS.

Though America had for some years been separated from Great Britain, the connection of the German Reformed Churches of Pennsylvania with the Synods of Holland still remained unbroken. The latter continued to take a profound interest in the welfare of the American churches, occasionally writing letters full of affectionate counsel. In conducting this correspondence, the difference of language was sometimes annoying. It was expected that the reports of the meetings of Coetus should be written in the language of Holland, but after the pioneers had passed away it was often difficult to find a secretary who was sufficiently familiar with that language to write it with fluency. Latin was occasionally substituted, but this did not entirely remove the difficulty, for, as one of the German ministers complains, "it is difficult to choose between writing in a language which one has never properly learned or in another which one has in great measure forgotten." During the later years of the correspondence the secretaries of Coetus sometimes ventured to write German; but this was not supposed to be agreeable to the "Fathers" in Holland, very few of whom could understand that language.

The German churches of America owe a debt to the Synods of Holland which they can never repay. For more than half a century the latter continued their benefactions without any possible anticipation of a return. It must have been a weary task to review the minutes of the German Coetus, and to give advice in cases whose difficulties they could not always perfectly appreciate. Sometimes they were disappointed in the men whom they had commissioned to labor in America, but they were never discouraged. In the whole history of the Church there is no better example of genuine philanthropy. That the kindness of the Dutch Synods was gratefully acknowledged is very certain. When the Dutch Churches of New York and New Jersey were about to sever their connection with Holland, in 1771, they invited the German congregations to unite with them in the formation of a Synod; but the latter declined in consequence of their affection for the " Fathers" who had shown them so much kindness.

With all the aid furnished from Holland, and possibly to some extent in consequence of it, the Coetus remained a very inefficient body. Its resolutions were not final until they had been received and approved in Holland, and sometimes several years passed before a decision could in this way be reached. Even with the neighboring Coetus of New York there was no official communication except through the Synods of Holland. In America the demand for ministers far exceeded the supply; but it was under many restrictions, and by special permission only, that the Coetus was authorized to add it to its numbers. At last it assumed the responsibility of performing the rite of ordination. The young men who were thus introduced into the ministry were probably not very favorably regarded in Holland, and became clamorous for a separate ecclesiastical organization. In 1791 they secured the adoption of the following action :

"*Resolved*, That the Coetus has the right at all times to examine and ordain those who offer themselves as candidates for the ministry, without asking or waiting for permission to do so from the Fathers in Holland."

At the same meeting it was resolved to continue to send a report of the proceedings, accompanied with suitable explanations, "as may be necessary." This was equivalent to a declaration of independence, as the proceedings were to be sent merely as a matter of courtesy, and not for revision. In 1792 the Coetus went a step further by directing Domines Pomp and Hendel to prepare a Synodical Constitution. This was practically the end of the Coetus; for in the next year the Synod held its first meeting, and by the adoption of the "Synodalordnung," became an independent body.

CHAPTER X.

The Synod of the German Reformed Church—"Die Synodalordnung"—The First Hymn-book—The Conflict of Languages—Correspondence with other Denominations—Condition of the Church—Unionistic Tendencies—Signs of Progress—The Classes.

On the 27th of April, 1793, the Synod convened for the first time, in Lancaster, Pennsylvania. The whole number of German Reformed ministers was at that time twenty-two, of whom thirteen were present at this meeting. The separation from Holland was now completed by the adoption of a resolution to substitute a friendly letter for the usual annual report of proceedings; and the body which had been hitherto called "The Coetus of Pennsylvania," was henceforth to be known as "The Synod of the German Reformed Church in the United States of America." The most important action was, however, the adoption of the "Synodal Ordnung," or Rules of Synod. Many of these rules are found in the present Constitution of the Reformed Church, but others have long since become obsolete. Ministers who had been sent to America by the Synods of Holland, or who might hereafter be sent, were entitled to membership; while those who came from other parts of Europe were to present certificates of ordination and testimonials of good conduct. Candidates for licensure and ordination were required to be well grounded in the ancient languages, except in special cases when the applicant was more than twenty-five years of age, and was otherwise well prepared for the sacred office. The powers of the President of Synod were carefully guarded, but he seems to have been a more influential personage than he is at present. He had not only the sole privilege of calling special meetings, but it was his duty to visit ministers who appeared to be going astray, for the purpose of reprimanding them, either privately or in the presence of two or three ministers. If a minister lived a vicious life, it became the duty of the President to suspend him from his office until the next meeting of Synod. The Secretary who performed his duties satisfactorily was to be elected President of Synod in the following year. Pastors were required to present reports of their ministry, as is now done at the meetings of Classes, and the elders were questioned concerning the state of the churches, not only formally, but minutely. At every session of Synod a private meeting was held, in which the orthodoxy of the sermons which had been preached during the convention was discussed, and private difficulties between the members were considered and settled.

In 1800 an additional series of rules was adopted by which the Synod was made to consist of ordained ministers, Licentiates, and Catechists. Catechists, like licentiates of the present day, were not allowed to administer the sacraments. They were frequently directed by Synod to supply vacant congregations, but were required to keep a diary in which their labors in the ministry were carefully recorded. This document was annually examined by Synod, and if found satisfactory the catechist either received permission to continue his labors for another year or was advanced to a higher grade in the ministry. Licentiates were authorized to administer the sacraments, and could serve congregations; but their license was annually renewed, and at the meetings of Synod they were required to occupy back seats. They were also required to present a manuscript sermon annually to Synod, for inspection and review. Ministers sometimes remained licentiates for several years before receiving ordination. Thus they were for a long time on trial, and were not admitted to the possession of all the privileges of the sacred office until they had made full proof of their ministry. There were instances when young men entered upon the ministry with great enthusiasm, but afterwards became convinced that they lacked the requisite degree of courage and perseverance for the proper prosecution of the work. Such men could withdraw while they were licentiates without incurring censure, but after they were ordained it was universally acknowledged that they were bound to devote themselves exclusively to the ministry to the end of their lives. These rules appear to have been wisely adapted to the necessities of the Church.

CATECHISMS AND HYMN-BOOKS.

During the colonial period little attention had been given to cultus. As early as 1762, as we incidentally learn from a cotemporary document,[1] the Palatinate Liturgy was employed in all the churches, and though individual ministers occasionally employed other formularies with which they had become familiar in the Fatherland, the general practice remained the same until long after the beginning of the present century. As a symbol of faith the Heidelberg Catechism maintained its position unquestioned from the beginning; but in the instruction of youth it was sometimes supplemented by the catechisms of Basel and Nassau-Siegen. At a somewhat later period catechisms, based on that of Heidelberg, were prepared and published for local use by F. L. Herman, Samuel Helffenstein, J. C. Becker, Samuel Hess, and others.

The earliest American edition of the Heidelberg Catechism in the German language, of which we have any knowledge, was printed by Christopher Saur in 1752. A fine edition of the large "Palatinate" was issued in Philadelphia, in 1762, by Peter Miller & Co. The first edition of the catechism in the English language, for the use of the German Reformed Churches, was printed in 1810 by Starck and Lange, of Hanover, Penna.

The hymn-book most frequently employed during the colonial period was known as that of "Marburg," from the place of its original publication. It was, we think,

---
[1] Mayer MSS. 1, 15.

the best hymn-book then in use, containing more of the hymns of the Primitive Church than was usual in those days. This book was several times reprinted by Christopher Saur. It is one of the finest specimens of the typography of that celebrated printer, containing, besides the Psalms and Hymns, the Heidelberg Catechism, Morning and Evening Prayers, Gospel and Epistle lessons, and the History of the Destruction of Jerusalem.

It appears evident that this book was printed by Saur as a private speculation, though for some years it was extensively used in the churches. During the Revolution Saur's publication house was confiscated, on account of the Toryism of its owner, and his books necessarily became scarce. The preparation of a hymn-book was therefore absolutely necessary, and in 1793 the Synod appointed a committee to attend to this important work. The committee consisted of Dr. Hendel, Helffrich, Blumer, Wagner, Pauli and Mann. The resolution adopted by Synod reads:

"*Resolved*, That a hymn-book be prepared, of which the Psalms shall be taken from Lobwasser and Spreng's improved version, and the Palatinate hymn-book shall form the basis of the hymns, with this difference only, that some unintelligible hymns be exchanged for better ones."

It is evident that the work of revision and alteration became much more extensive than was originally intended. The preface says: "We have chosen the most edifying and best known hymns in the Marburg and Palatinate hymn-books, composed by Joachim Neander, Friedrich Adolph Lampe, Caspar Zollikofer, and other godly men among the Protestants. To these we have added a number of edifying spiritual songs, taken from the hymn-books recently published in various parts of Germany. The metres are arranged throughout according to the Palatinate hymn-book."

This collection, entitled "*Neues und Verbessertes Gesangbuch*," was printed by Steiner and Kammerer, Philadelphia, 1797. It was an unfortunate period for the preparation of a hymn-book, and it was probably well that it was based on older collections. As it is, it contains a few hymns which were evidently composed under the Rationalistic spirit which was then prevalent in Germany. Others contain expressions which would be offensive to a more modern taste; but with all its imperfections, the book was creditable to its compilers. It was re-printed in numberless editions; each with a frontispiece representing the Psalmist playing on his harp. Michael Billmeyer, of Germantown, was for many years the publisher. Its use in some of the churches must have continued longer than is generally supposed, inasmuch as a handsome edition was printed as recently as 1850, by Enos Benner, of Sumneytown, Pennsylvania.

THE CONFLICT OF LANGUAGES.

In 1804 the church in Philadelphia requested Synod "to come to their assistance in their present sad condition, inasmuch as a total separation is to be feared from the fact that there is a strong party among them who desire an English sermon every two weeks." This may be regarded as the beginning of a conflict which continued for many years.

There had, indeed, been English preaching here and there in the German Reformed churches some years earlier. Not to speak of Zubly, in Georgia, and Gebhard, in New York, it is known that when the Rev. Caspar Wack became pastor of the churches of New Jersey, in 1782, he found it necessary to preach English. A few years later the Rev. Dr. Herman held regular English services in Germantown, Pennsylvania. It is hardly possible that all this could have occurred without some difference of opinion; but it was in Philadelphia that the dissensions first became violent, and thus forced themselves upon the attention of Synod. A few years later similar troubles broke out in other cities; and it would be difficult to overestimate the losses which the Church was in this way made to suffer. If there had been ministers at hand who could have preached in both languages, much of this trouble might have been avoided; but there were probably not half a dozen members of the Synod who could employ the English language with any degree of fluency. It is easy enough now to see that affairs were badly managed, and that trivial personal advantages were often made to stand in the way of the best interests of the Church; but we fail to appreciate the difficulties of the situation. The Synod may have been weak, as has been asserted, but it should be remembered that it had neither men nor money. It is, therefore, not surprising. that though it constantly counseled peace, the dissensions continued, and that the problem was left to work itself out as best it might. Possibly, this was all that could justly be expected, and it must be acknowledged that the course of history in the Reformed Church has, in this respect, not been very different from that in other churches where a change of language became unavoidable. It is, however, impossible to regard the mistakes and losses of this dreary period without sentiments of deep regret.

CORRESPONDENCE WITH OTHER CHURCHES.

In 1803 a letter was received by the Synod of the United States from the Rev. Dr. J. H. Livingston, requesting that young ministers be sent to the destitute German Reformed Churches in the State of New York, and at the same time suggesting that a fraternal correspondence be opened between the German Reformed and Reformed Dutch Synods. The kindest feelings had always subsisted between the two bodies, but a correspondence by the exchange of delegates was then inaugurated which was for many years peculiarly intimate and affectionate. It may appear strange that these two branches of the Reformed Church were not organically united, but there were serious difficulties in the way. Though both Churches were equally attached to the Heidelberg Catechism, the German body did not deem it desirable to increase the number of its confessions by subscribing to the Belgic Confession and the Articles of the Synod of Dordrecht, which it regarded as the exclusive possession of the Church of Holland. Besides this doctrinal difference, there was also a practical difficulty in the way of union. The two Churches occupied different territory, and did not at first employ the same language. There was but little personal communication between their members, and it was even difficult to induce ministers to serve as corresponding delegates, on account of the extensive journey which such an appointment involved.

A similar correspondence with the German Lutheran Ministerium of Pennsylvania grew out of an invitation from the latter body to the Reformed Synod, in 1817, to unite in the annual celebration of the Festival of the Reformation on the 31st of October. Though the Reformed Synod took no decisive action on the subject thus presented, it at the same meeting directed a committee of conference to attend the meeting of the Lutheran Synod, for the purpose, especially, of considering the propriety of unitedly founding a literary institution. The correspondence thus inaugurated was subsequently extended to several Lutheran Synods, and was thus maintained until a comparatively recent period.

In 1823 a correspondence was opened with the General Assembly of the Presbyterian Church. It was on this occasion agreed that ministers or members who might be under discipline in one of the corresponding bodies should not be admitted to membership in the other. The two Churches were, however, to remain "separate and independent." On this basis corresponding delegates were annually appointed or elected by each body; and during the period of "the great schism" a delegate was sent by the Reformed Synod impartially to the General Assembly of each of the "schools."

The Synod of Ohio, before the establishment of the General Synod corresponded regularly with the Synod of the United States, and occasionally with other ecclesiastical bodies. At present the General Synod generally attends to this kind of correspondence, though each of the District Synods possesses its original privileges in this respect, if it chooses to exercise them.

At the meeting of the General Synod held in 1884, delegates were elected to the following corresponding bodies: The General Synod of the Reformed Church in America; the General Assembly of the Presbyterian Church; the General Synod of the Evangelical Lutheran Church; the Quadrennial Provincial Synod of the Moravian Church; and the Evangelical Synod of North America.[1] Though the "correspondence with Sister Churches" has possibly failed to accomplish all that was expected of it by its original promoters, it is a pleasant feature in our synodical assemblies, while at the same time it testifies to our belief in the essential unity of Christian believers.

---

[1] The latter body is popularly known as "The German Church-Union of the West."

It cannot be doubted that during the first two decades of the present century, the German Reformed Church in this country was in a discouraging condition. The first generation of ministers had mostly passed away, to be succeeded by others whose educational advantages had been very limited. Their theological training had been in most cases entrusted to a preceptor who had perhaps been educated in Germany, but who in many years of pioneer service had possibly forgotten much of what he had learned in his youth, and was at any rate unable to keep up with the more recent developments of theologic science. The latter fact may not have been an unmixed evil, as in this way the Church was preserved from the ravages of the Rationalism which was then devastating the Fatherland. Some preceptors were conscientious, and gave their pupils a course not only in theology, but also in philosophy and the ancient languages; but there were others who did no more than to allow them the use of their rather limited libraries, and who appear to have been mainly solicitous of obtaining the fees paid by their students, or of using them as assistants in the pastoral labor of an extensive charge.

We have no desire to reproach the Fathers for their shortcomings. No doubt the difficulties appeared insuperable, and the best was done that was possible under the circumstances; but it is easy to see that the wants of the Church could not be met in any such fashion. A few men of great natural ability overcame by persistent study many of the difficulties with which they were forced to grapple, and to their energy and devotion we owe the preservation of the Church at this momentous crisis. The condition of affairs was, however, sufficiently discouraging to dishearten the most courageous. The German immigration had almost ceased, and the denominational consciousness of the Churches in America had not yet awakened; and though the number of ministers and members was gradually increasing with the development of the country, it really seemed as though the German Reformed Church had no separate mission.

UNIONISTIC TENDENCIES.

The mutual relations of the Reformed and Lutheran Churches were at this time peculiarly intimate. They occupied the same territory, and in many places worshiped in the same building. The knowledge of the people concerning denominational distinctions was generally limited to certain minor matters of ceremonial observance.[1]

---

[1] If a Pennsylvania farmer had at this time been asked to point out the difference between the Reformed and Lutheran Churches, he would probably have said: "In the Lord's Prayer the Reformed say '*Unser Vater*,' and the Lutherans say '*Vater unser;*' and further on in the same prayer the Lutherans say '*Erlöse uns von dem Uebel,*' and the Reformed '*Erlöse uns von dem Bösen.*'" He might also have referred to the fact that the Lutherans generally use unleavened bread in the Lord's Supper; and if particularly well instructed, he might have mentioned the variation in the division of the Ten Commandments which is found in the Catechisms of the two Churches.

Union churches, which were once exceptional, had become exceedingly numerous, and in certain sections of the Church they are still almost universal. From one point of view it is, of course, pleasant to see two congregations worshiping in the same church; but it has been proved by experience that this · arrangement is not conducive to their highest interests, and the synods of both Churches have consequently expressed their disapproval of the continued erection of union churches. It is, at best, as when two families occupy the same dwelling; the opportunities of pleasant social communication are more than counterbalanced by the dangers of interference and collision to which each family is necessarily exposed.

In the period to which we have specially referred, it must be confessed that many ministers of the Reformed and Lutheran Churches favored the organic union of these two bodies, not because they had reached a proper doctrinal basis for such union, but because they knew little and cared less about the questions at issue between them.[1]

The union of the Lutheran and Reformed churches of Prussia, in 1817, was not without its effect in America, and during the succeeding years frequent

---

[1] These unionistic tendencies are illustrated by the resolution adopted by the Reformed Synod in 1812, to support the "Evangelical Magazine," founded by the Rev. Dr. Helmuth, and the formal approval by the same body, in 1817, of the "Gemeinschaftliche Gesangbuch"—a compilation prepared by irresponsible parties for use in union churches.

conferences were held in the hope of reaching a similar result. In 1824, when the consideration of the subject had begun to languish, a communication was received from the Lutheran Ministerium, urging the Reformed Synod to devote renewed attention to the union of the Churches, and to labor earnestly for its speedy consummation. Indeed, it is probable that an effort would have been made to follow the European example, if it had not been for the fear expressed in an almost cotemporary document, that "some pastors and churches of each denomination would stand aloof, and that the result would thus be to introduce a new denomination without decreasing the number already in existence." The Reformed Church has always favored union when effected upon a proper basis; but it is questionable whether, if introduced at the time and under the circumstances to which we have referred, it would have produced the beneficent results which its promoters fondly expected.

SIGNS OF PROGRESS.

It must not be supposed that during this period of depression there were no signs of progress. The most hopeful feature was a general longing for better things, which, although expressed in abortive resolutions, was a prophecy of future advancement. There was especially an earnest desire for the establishment of a Theological school and the publication of a religious periodical. The time for these things had not yet fully come, but the seed was sown from which they subsequently grew.

THE CLASSES.

Notwithstanding the difficulties which it was compelled to encounter, the Church had increased in numbers until about seventy ministers were connected with Synod. The difficulty of bringing them together at Synodical meetings was fully appreciated, and it was suggested that ministers residing outside of Pennsylvania might organize Classes, electing a single delegate annually to represent them at Synod. Nothing came of this until 1818, when a committee was appointed to divide the Synod into districts or Classes. In 1819 the division was effected, and each Classis was permitted to choose a name for itself. These Classes, eight in number, held their first meeting on the fourth Sunday after Easter, 1820. The names respectively assumed by them were: Philadelphia, Northampton,[1] Lebanon, Susquehanna, West Pennsylvania, Zion, Maryland, and Ohio.[2] From these pioneer Classes[3] all the Classes at present in con-

---

[1] In 1824 the Classes of Philadelphia and Northampton were united by Synod and constituted a single classis.

[2] The Synod of Ohio, which was derived, as will be seen hereafter, from the Classis of Ohio, did not establish Classes within its bounds until 1842. The Classes organized at this time were Miami, Lancaster, Columbiana, Sandusky, Westmoreland, and Erie.

[3] Several of these Classes are now extinct. The following list of additional Classes constituted by the Synod of the United States prior to the organization of the General Synod, with the year of their earliest meeting, may be useful as a matter of reference:

Virginia, 1824 (dissolved 1830); East Pennsylvania, 1826; North Carolina, 1830; Philadelphia (new), 1836; Virginia (new), 1839; Mer-

nection with the General Synod may be regarded as directly or indirectly derived.[1]

With the organization of the Classes, in 1820, the second period of the history of the Reformed Church in this country comes to a close. Hitherto its organization can hardly be said to have been completed. If the Reformed Church owes its Synods to Zwingli, the Classes are derived from Calvin and the Church of France. In Holland and the Rhine Provinces of Germany they were introduced at least as early as 1571, and whether known as Classes or Presbyteries, they have everywhere been recognized as of fundamental importance to our system of government. Their introduction into the German Reformed Church of this country, therefore, appropriately marks the time of its awakening to the nature of its mission, and of an earnest determination to labor for its accomplishment.

---

cersburg, 1840; New York, 1840 (?); Goshenhoppen, 1841; Lancaster, 1852; East Susquehanna, 1856; West Susquehanna, 1856; Clarion (organized by Synod of Ohio, 1850, transferred to Synod of U. S., 1857); St. Paul, 1861.

[1] In 1884 the number of Classes in connection with the General Synod was fifty-two, but several additional Classes have since been organized.

CHAPTER XI.

The Theological Seminary—Popular Opposition—" The Free Synod"—Repeated Failures—The Seminary Founded at Carlisle—Removed to York, Pa.—The Seminary and College at Mercersburg.

AT the Synod at Hagerstown, Md., in 1820, a plan was adopted for the establishment of a Theological Seminary. This was a consummation towards which the best men in the Church had looked forward with intense longing, and it is perhaps not surprising that on this occasion their enthusiasm carried them beyond the limits of ordinary prudence. In fact, they almost seem to have imagined that the work could be accomplished by the simple adoption of a resolution. On the ground of vague promises and of still more uncertain expectations, it was taken for granted that the income of the new institution would be from the first greatly in excess of its expenses, and the Rev. Philip Milledoler, D. D., of New York, was immediately elected Professor of Theology, at an annual salary of two thousand dollars. Frederick, Maryland, was selected as the location of the new institution. Subscriptions for its endowment were solicited, but unfortunately most of these were made conditional on Dr. Milledoler's acceptance. It was supposed that in this way large contributions would be secured from the

Doctor's personal friends in New York; but this proved a mistake, and the labor of several years was lost.

Dr. Milledoler, though at this time connected with the Reformed Dutch Church, had been in his early ministry a member of the German Reformed Synod. He was in the zenith of his fame, and being equally familiar with the German and English languages, it was believed that he would not only gain the confidence of the Germans, but by his personal influence give the new Theological Seminary a prominent position among the institutions of the land. No doubt this estimate of Dr. Milledoler's abilities was correct; but we cannot approve his course on this occasion. For two years he retained the call, leaving the Synod under the impression that he would certainly accept it; but finally he declined and became Professor of Theology and President of Rutgers College, in New Brunswick. This was a grievous disappointment, and for a while it seemed as though the project of establishing a German Reformed Theological Seminary had proved an utter failure.

POPULAR OPPOSITION.

In many parts of the Church the people failed to appreciate the necessity of establishing a theological institution, and indeed regarded it with great suspicion. The most ignorant could not fail to see that great movements were in progress in all the churches. Theological and Literary institutions were springing up in various directions; ministers advocated the work of missions, and organized societies for its advancement. Colporteurs traversed the country distributing Bibles and tracts; and Sunday-schools were beginning to be generally established. All these things came so rapidly that they attracted the attention of the entire community. It was a "shaking of the dry bones," that was offensive to those who were "at ease in Zion." Demagogues created the impression, in uneducated communities, that the ministers had formed a vast conspiracy to deprive the people of their liberty. The collections taken up for benevolent purposes, it was said, were soon to be succeeded by taxes, to be rigorously exacted for the support of the Church. Traditions concerning the tyranny of the State Churches of Germany, at the beginning of the last century, were sedulously revived, and a state of feeling was thus created of whose intensity we can hardly form a proper conception. Everything of which the Synods approved was regarded as suspicious; and theological seminaries became especially objectionable because the most eminent ministers were enthusiastic in their behalf. Books in opposition to Synods were written by Carl Gock and others, and these elicited replies which only added to the prevailing excitement. Anti-synod conventions were held at intervals for several years—the most important of them in 1829—and some churches resolved that they would "employ" no minister who remained a member of Synod. The latter churches, in many instances, became the prey of deposed ministers or unordained vagrants, and were thus made to suffer for their folly. Many years passed before the Church in eastern Pennsylvania was thoroughly pacified; and indeed it is questionable whether the evil results of this period of excitement have even now entirely disappeared.

"THE FREE SYNOD."

Closely connected with the troubles we have endeavored to describe, but by no means to be identified with them, was the schism which was generally known as "The Free Synod." Its founder and chief promoter was the Rev. F. L. Herman, D. D., the last of the missionaries sent to this country by the Synods of Holland. He was a thoroughly educated man, who had for many years been prominent in the councils of the Church. Among the ministers who had been employed in instructing candidates for the ministry, he was one of the most active, and his ability as an instructor was generally recognized. In his parsonage at Falkener Swamp he had organized a theological school, which was familiarly known as "The Swamp College." Students were required to remain under his care at least three years, and during this time he not only instructed them in theology and kindred sciences, but in the rudiments of the ancient languages. The course would now be regarded as incomplete, but it was probably the best that could under the circumstances be reasonably expected. When the Church determined to establish a Theological Seminary, many of Dr. Herman's friends regarded him as the person best suited to be the first Professor of Theology, and regretted that in its choice the Synod should have gone beyond the limits of the Church; but his name was never publicly proposed, and we would be far from intimating that he entertained any personal aspirations in this direction.

When the Synod adopted the "Plan for the Establishment of a Theological Seminary," in 1820, the following resolution was adopted:

"*Resolved*, That no minister shall hereafter have the privilege of receiving a young man in order to instruct him in theology, but may only direct him in his preliminary studies."

We have no hesitation in characterizing this resolution as at least premature, for it should be remembered that the seminary was only "on paper," and had as yet no actual existence. As Dr. Herman was at this time the only minister who had any considerable number of students under his care, the resolution was supposed to be aimed at him and his incipient institution.

Dr. Herman now began to oppose the proposed Theological Seminary, basing his opposition principally on its proposed location at Frederick, Maryland, which, in his opinion, was too far distant from the centre of the Church. The controversy which ensued became personal, and caused unpleasant feelings. Next year (1821) the Synod suspended Dr. Herman's gifted but wayward son, Frederick, from the ministerial office, and though there could be no question as to the justice of the sentence, it is said to have been communicated to the father in terms which proved offensive. Dr. Herman and his friends immediately withdrew from the meeting of Synod and returned home without permission, for which acts they were severely censured by resolution. Though the Synod afterwards formally requested them to declare their intentions there was no doubt that a schism had already occurred, and when Messrs. F. L. Herman, C. G. Herman, H. Dieffenbach, and J. C. Guldin were finally excluded from membership, these ministers had been for some time associated as members of the " Free Synod."

We have not space to give a full account of the history of this schismatic body. Its first title was "The Synod of the Free German Reformed congregations of Pennsylvania;" but this was subsequently changed to "The German Reformed Synod of Pennsylvania and Adjacent States." From various causes the organization grew very rapidly. All of Dr. Herman's students were now licensed and ordained by this Synod, though some of them soon connected themselves with the parent body. We have in our possession a list of the names of fifty-seven ministers who were at various times members of the "Free Synod," and more than one hundred congregations are recorded as having been in connection with it. Among the latter were churches in New York, Philadelphia, Allentown, Carlisle, and other important places. The schism was therefore by no means contemptible.

The prosperity of the "Free Synod" was, however, more apparent than real. Its younger members felt that they had been placed in a position of antagonism to the progressive Christian spirit of the age. Their Synod had been founded on personal grievances and consequently lacked the elements of permanence. Missionaries were sent to the Far West, as well as to the northern counties of Pennsylvania; and it was proposed to establish a church-school on the manual-labor plan in Cumberland county, where a friend had offered to donate two hundred and fifty acres of land for this purpose. All these enterprises, however, only served to show that there was no real community of interest. With the increase of numbers, the looseness of the organization became more apparent, and many of its best members longed for union with a stronger body.

Many years ago—when most of the leading members of the "Free Synod" were still living—an article giving a full account of the healing of the schism was published in "The Messenger." As its statements were at the time fully verified by the author, there need be no doubt concerning their correctness. We therefore do not hesitate to quote the concluding paragraphs of this article:

"In the year 1836 the Free Synod met in Salem church, Philadelphia. Rev. T. H. Leinbach was elected President of the meeting. Dr. Herman was in the city, but was able to attend only a part of the sessions on account of illness. It was during his absence, on the afternoon of Tuesday, September 6, 1836, that the subject of church-union was brought to the attention of Synod. One of the brethren—whose name, for obvious reasons, we decline to mention—stated that he had conferred with the younger Milledoler, and as a result of their deliberations he begged leave to offer a resolution to the following effect:

"'*Resolved*, That this Synod take measures to unite with the General Synod of the Reformed Dutch Church.'

"At the conclusion of the remarks made in support of this resolution, there was silence for several minutes. Each felt that this was a moment of paramount importance, in which a hasty decision might jeopardize the interests of a large portion of the Church. At last, Rev. J. S. Dubbs, of Allentown, arose and stated that he too was in favor of union, but of union with the Synod of the German Reformed Church. 'We are German Reformed,' he said, 'and not Dutch Reformed; and a union with the latter body would be productive of endless confusion and of bitter heart-burnings. I propose, therefore, that this Synod—laying aside all personal feelings, and looking only to the best interests of the Church—take such measures as will best promote our re-union with the General Synod of the German Reformed Church.'

"After these remarks there was again an interval of silence. Then Rev. J. S. Ebaugh, of Carlisle, requested the mover of the latter resolution to commit it to writing. This was done, as will be seen by referring to page 13 of the published minutes, from which we translate as follows:

"'Rev. J. S. Dubbs presented the following preamble and resolution:

"'WHEREAS, The division which has occurred in the Reformed Church has been productive of many differences, which were unpleasant to both of the existing Synods, and which must have been painful to every right-thinking mind; and,

"'*Whereas*, We believe that a general desire exists that these differences should now be adjusted; therefore,

"'*Resolved*, That the Reverend Synod send three delegates to the General Synod of the German Reformed Church, to confer concerning terms of re-union, and to report the result of their deliberations to the Synod, which is to meet in Pottstown, Pa., in 1837, for final consideration.'

"The above resolution was supported by the mover with extended remarks. He was then followed, in a similar strain, by Rev. Dr. Bibighaus, Rev. J. C. Guldin, Rev. J. S. Ebaugh, and others. After considerable discussion, the resolution was adopted. Three delegates were then appointed to present this action to the General Synod, which was about to convene at Baltimore, Md. The delegates appointed were Revs. J. S. Dubbs, C. G. Herman, and J. C. Guldin.

"When the time arrived for the meeting of the Synod at Baltimore, Rev. C. G. Herman was detained at home; but the other delegates proceeded to fulfill the duty which had been imposed on them. At Baltimore they were received, as it were, with open arms. Their overtures were referred to a committee consisting of Rev. J. C. Becker, D. D., Rev. I. Gerhart, Rev. B. C. Wolff, D. D., and Elders George Hess, Jr., and James Grimes. This committee reported favorably to the reception of the Free Synod *in a body*, and their report was unanimously adopted. Synod also adopted a minute expressive of its gratitude to Almighty God, and of its 'sincere joy at the prospect of a union so essential to the best interests of the Church.' The delegates then returned home—much encouraged by their reception and by the action of Synod—to report to the body that had commissioned them.

"The last Free Synod was held in Pottstown, Pa., in 1837. At this meeting the delegates presented their report, but soon found that unexpected opposition awaited them. Dr. Herman was understood to be opposed to re-union, and though aged, his influence was still extensive. It soon, however, became evident that the days of the Free Synod were numbered. Most of its members were now determined to return to the General Synod, under all circumstances, and the continued existence of the Free Synod became, therefore, almost an impossibility. After considerable discussion, the report of the delegates received the necessary ratification, and the 'Free Synod of Pennsylvania and Adjacent States,' thus became an integral part of the 'Synod of the German Reformed Church in the United States.'"[1]

---

[1] An Independent Synod, composed in part of former members of the "Free Synod," maintained a sickly existence for some years in central Pennsylvania. It is said to have included some Lutheran elements, and was popularly known as the "Stiely Synod," from the prominence of the brothers Isaac and Philip Stiely in its organization.

A SECOND FAILURE.

Though Dr. Milledoler's declination had shattered the best hopes of the friends of the proposed Theological Seminary, they were not disposed to give up the work in despair. If the project could not be carried out on its projected scale, it might possibly be done in a more modest manner. It was, therefore, immediately resolved, in 1822, to found the new institution in Harrisburg, Pennsylvania, against which location it was presumed there could be no objection. The Professor of Theology, it was proposed, should be elected pastor by the congregation in Harrisburg, and the Synod, on its part, pledged itself to contribute to his support the annual sum of five hundred dollars in addition to his pastoral salary.

A serious obstacle to the success of this promising scheme was found in the fact that there was no vacancy in the pastorate of the church at Harrisburg. The Rev. John Weinbrenner had for several years been pastor of that congregation, and of several others in its immediate vicinity. He was a man of considerable talent, possessing unusual oratorical ability, who had taken great interest in the proposed establishment of a Theological Seminary, and had pledged himself to contribute in its support, for ten years, the annual sum of two hundred dollars. Recently he had, however, become an enthusiastic advocate of what were known as "New Measures," carrying the revival system to an extreme that was unusual in the Reformed churches. Some of the members of his church had, therefore, become dissatisfied, and the Synod was convinced that it would be well for him to seek another field of labor. The Consistory of the church at Harrisburg must have had the same opinion, for they expressed their willingness to accept the Professor of Theology as their pastor, provided that the position was first vacated by the resignation of Mr. Weinbrenner. The latter, however, asked time for consideration, and no further action was then taken.

Next year (1823), the subject was taken up again. The Synod renewed its resolution to establish a Theological Seminary at Harrisburg, and at once proceeded to elect a professor. On the first ballot the votes were equally divided between three candidates—Rev. Drs. S. Helffenstein, J. C. Becker, and L. Mayer. Then Dr. Mayer withdrew his name, and Dr. Helffenstein was chosen.

The troubles in the church in Harrisburg still continued, and these, no doubt, were not without influence on the mind of Dr. Helffenstein, who finally declined the call extended by Synod. Mr. Weinbrenner became more and more alienated from the doctrine and practice of the Reformed Church, and at last founded a separate denomination, whose members call themselves "The Church of God," but are popularly known as "Weinbrennerians." He was treated very leniently, in the hope that he would be brought to recognize his errors; but when it was finally announced to the Synod, convened in Mifflinburg, in 1828, that Mr. Weinbrenner had refused to heed its citations, and was even then preaching against the doctrine of Infant Baptism, his name was reluctantly erased from the roll of members.

In consequence of the declination of Dr. Helffenstein, and of the contemporaneous troubles in the church at Harrisburg, the second attempt to establish a Theological Seminary proved a failure. It was a season of gloom and depression, and some of the best men in the Church seriously contemplated the necessity of seeking a home in some other ecclesiastical connection. Fortunately for the Church, their discouragement was not of long duration. It proved to be the darkness that precedes the dawn.

THE SEMINARY FOUNDED AT CARLISLE.

At the Synod convened in Bedford Pa., in 1824, a communication was received from the Trustees of Dickinson College—then under the control of the Presbyterian Church—inviting the Reformed Church to establish its Theological Seminary at Carlisle, in close connection with the literary institution which they represented. The college was to furnish suitable rooms for the use of the Seminary, and to permit theological students to attend the lectures of certain of its professors free of charge. In return for these favors, the Professor of Theology was to occupy the chair of History and German Literature in the college. The scheme certainly looked promising, and we are not surprised to find that the Synod immediately accepted it. The call to Dr. Helffenstein was renewed, with the proviso that, in case of his non-acceptance,

LEWIS MAYER.

a similar call should be extended to the Rev. Lewis Mayer, pastor of the Reformed church of York, Pa. Helffenstein declining, Mayer was called. The latter having accepted the call, the Theological Seminary was opened on the eleventh day of March, 1825, at Carlisle, Pa. The first class of students numbered five, of whom the late Rev. John G. Fritchey was the last survivor. The annual salary of the Professor of Theology was fixed at $700, which was to be paid out of the Treasury of Synod.

The position of Professor was, under these circumstances, by no means attractive, and the Church was fortunate in being able to secure the services of Dr. Mayer. He was in many respects an extraordinary man. In his youth he had enjoyed few opportunities of literary culture, but perseverance had enabled him to surmount unusual obstacles. He was not only an excellent classical scholar, but was familiar with several modern languages, besides German and English, and took great interest in the study of certain branches of Natural Science. In Theology he was fully abreast with his American cotemporaries; and though subsequently accused of varying on minor points from the accepted standards, it is affirmed by competent judges that this divergence was more apparent than real. In the main his system agreed with the current Reformed theology of his day; and his memory is justly revered in the institution of which, with great self-sacrifice, he helped to lay the foundations.

At first the Seminary enjoyed the support of but a portion of the Church, and even among its friends there were many who were doubtful with regard to its ultimate success. It was therefore necessary to resort to extraordinary means to secure funds for its endowment. During the summer of 1825 Rev. James R. Reily, one of the most zealous friends of the Seminary, visited Germany to solicit contributions towards an enterprise that was so intimately related to the welfare of emigrants from the Fatherland. He was very kindly received, especially in Holland, Prussia, and Switzerland, and collected $6,700, in money and books. One of the most liberal contributors was His Majesty, Frederick William III., King of Prussia, and many volumes presented by him are still in the library of the Seminary. About the same time Rev. J. C. Beecher, of Shepherdstown, Va., succeeded in this country in collecting a handsome sum for the endowment of the Semimary, and thus, it is said, saved it from financial ruin.

The arrangement with Dickinson College, at Carlisle, did not prove satisfactory. The college was financially involved, and found itself unable to provide proper accommodations for the Seminary. On the other hand, the college students did not desire to study German, and Dr. Mayer, therefore, found himself unable to make a proper return for even the scanty favors which had been shown him. For these, and other reasons, it was concluded, in 1829, that Carlisle was not a satisfactory location for the Theological Seminary. The effects of the institution were still few in number, and their removal was easily accomplished.

THE SEMINARY AT YORK, PA.

The Seminary was re-organized at York, Pa., on the 11th of November, 1829, and was conducted in this place until the autumn of 1837. It was a time of many trials, caused principally by financial embarrassment. During all this time the institution was in charge of Dr. Mayer, assisted, in 1831, by the Rev. Daniel Young, and subsequently by Dr. Frederick A. Rauch. The number of students who completed their theological course during this period was thirty-five.

As most of the students had not received an academic training, the professors found it necessary from the beginning to impart instruction in the different branches of a preparatory course. The way was thus gradually prepared for the establishment, in 1831, of a classical department, which was known as the High School of the Reformed Church.

As the High School became prosperous, there was a general desire to raise it to the rank of a college. At this time the trustees of Franklin College, in which the Reformed Church still retained a third interest, made liberal offers for the removal of the High School to Lancaster; but as the institution would, at that place, have been under the control of several denominations, and as the connection of a theological seminary with Franklin College was not desired, the invitation was respectfully declined. Proposals were received from the citizens of Mercersburg, and at the Synod of Chambersburg, in 1835, these proposals were accepted. The literary institution was at once removed to Mercersburg, but the seminary remained two years longer in York, under the care of Rev. Dr. Mayer.

MARSHALL COLLEGE.

This institution was organized in Mercersburg in

accordance with a charter granted by the Legislature of Pennsylvania, which at the same time voted an appropriation of twelve thousand dollars to its endowment. It was named in honor of Chief Justice John Marshall, who was then in the zenith of his fame, but died in the same year.

FREDERICK A. RAUCH.

The Rev. F. A. Rauch, Ph. D., who had previously been principal of the High School, became the first president of Marshall College.[1] He was born in Hesse Darmstadt in 1806, and had been thoroughly educated at the

---

[1] Dr. Rauch's portrait is believed never to have been taken from life, but after his death an imperfect sketch of his features was made by one of his friends. From this sketch all existing portraits are derived, and it is well understood that they fail to do justice to the original.

University of Marburg. For a short time he was professor extraordinary at Giessen, but came to America in 1831, on account of political complications in his native land. After serving for some time as Professor of German in Lafayette College, he was called by the Reformed Church to take charge of its classical institution. He continued in this position until his death, which occurred March 2, 1841. In 1840 he published his work on "Psychology," which may be said to have introduced this science to the attention of American students. A more extensive work on "Ethics" was left unfinished. A volume of his sermons, entitled "The Inner Life of the Christian," was subsequently edited and published by Rev. Dr. E. V. Gerhart. Dr. Rauch's remains were removed from Mercersburg to Lancaster in 1859, and were solemnly re-interred in Lancaster Cemetery. A handsome monument to his memory has been erected in front of the college-building.

In 1837 the unnatural separation of the College and Seminary was brought to a conclusion by the removal of the latter institution to Mercersburg. Dr. Mayer, who was unwilling to go with the Seminary, resigned and remained in York. From this time, for many years, the history of the two institutions runs parallel, and may be simultaneously considered.

THE SEMINARY AND COLLEGE IN MERCERSBURG.

For one year the whole course of theological instruction was in charge of Dr. Rauch, and in 1837-38 there was but one student in the Seminary. Then Dr. Mayer, at the urgent request of Synod, consented to resume his place; but he remained in Mercersburg only one year and, in 1839, finally withdrew. In the same year a call to a professorship was extended to Dr. J. C. Becker, of Northampton county, Pa., but he declined to leave his

THEOLOGICAL SEMINARY.

pastoral work. Dr. Rauch's failing health warned the church that the powers of a single individual, however capable, were unequal to the task of performing the twofold duty of Professor of Theology and President of Marshall College. Accordingly, at a special meeting of the Synod, held in Chambersburg early in 1840, the vacant chair of Professor of Systematic Theology was

JOHN WILLIAMSON NEVIN.

filled by the election of the Rev. John Williamson Nevin,[1] D. D., then Professor in the Theological Seminary at Alleghany, Pa. After due consideration he accepted the appointment, and entered upon its dutes in the month of May of the year of his election. " This change of position" says one of his recent biographers, " was not considered to be of itself any change of denominational faith, only a transition from one section of the general Reformed confession to another, and took place accordingly with the full approbation and favor of the friends of Dr. Nevin in the Presbyterian Church, and under the advice of Dr. Archibald Alexander, his former theological instructor at Princeton."[2]

During his residence in Alleghany, Dr. Nevin had begun to study the German language, and to take a profound interest in German Theology. He was therefore better prepared than most English divines to understand the proper character of the Reformed Church, and to enter intelligently upon the special work to which he had been called. " The death of Dr. Rauch, in 1841, made it necessary for Dr. Nevin to assume the tempo-

---

[1] *John Williamson Nevin, D D., LL. D.*, was born in Franklin co., Pa., Feb. 20, 1803. Graduated in Union College, 1821. Studied Theology at Princeton, and was for two years assistant teacher there, during which time he wrote "Biblical Antiquities." Professor in the Theological Seminary at Alleghany, Pa., 1829-1839. Professor of Theology in Mercersburg, 1840-1851, and President of Marshall College, 1841-1853. President of Franklin and Marshall College, 1865-1876. He died at Caernarvon Place, near Lancaster, Pa., June 6, 1886.

[2] Ellis and Evans's " History of Lancaster County." p. 424.

rary presidency of the college, which was afterwards made permanent, and which position he filled for ten years without receiving any salary."[1] "In 1843," says the writer from whom we have just quoted, "he became involved in what has been known as the 'Anxious Bench controversy,' through the publication of his tract called 'The Anxious Bench,' directed against the use of certain means and methods employed extensively at the time among different denominations in the service of religious revivals, which has been regarded as the beginning of the movement since spoken of as the Mercersburg Theology."

For three years after the death of Dr. Rauch, Dr. Nevin, assisted only by a teacher, of Hebrew, had sole charge of the Theological Seminary. There was, however, an earnest desire in the church to aid him by securing a German professor to carry on the work which had been begun by the lamented Rauch.

In 1843 the Synod unanimously elected to this position the Rev Dr. F. W. Krummacher, of Elberfeld, Prussia. As Dr. Krummacher was the most celebrated pulpit orator of Germany, they would not have ventured to extend the call without previous assurances that it would be favorably considered. Rev. Drs. T. L. Hof-

---

[1] In 1841 the German Reformed Church celebrated the Centennial anniversary of its organization in this country. The date was arbitrarily chosen, and the celebration was by no means universal; but the offerings of the churches, which were mainly appropriated to Marshall College and the Theological Seminary, were of great advantage to these incipient institutions.

feditz and B. S. Schneck were appointed commissioners to present the call in person. They sailed for Europe in the following May, and were very cordially received in the Fatherland. Dr. Krummacher, however, finally felt constrained to decline, especially as the Prussian government expressed a decided disinclination to his removal. Unwilling to return to America without having accomplished their mission, the commissioners consulted with some of the leading divines of Germany, and were by them directed to the Rev. Philip Schaff, Ph. D.,[1] who was at that time a professor extraordinary in the University of Berlin. On their return to America the delegates proposed his name to the Synod, and he was unanimously elected. He was installed Professor of Church History and Biblical Literature, in the city of Reading, on the 25th of October, 1844.

Dr. Schaff's inaugural address, "The Principle of Protestantism," was published in German and English, and at once attracted extraordinary attention. Its ability was universally recognized, but it contained views concerning its subject which, however well known in Europe, appeared new to American readers, and provoked no small amount of adverse criticism. They even led to an investigation on the part of the Synod, in 1845, which resulted in an almost unanimous expression of confidence in the orthodoxy of the professor.

---

[1] Philip Schaff, D. D., LL. D., was born at Chur, Switzerland, Jan. 1, 1819. He is at present a Professor in the Union Theological Seminary in New York, and has an international reputation as a distinguished theologian and author.

The succeeding years were marked by intense theological and literary activity. The two professors, Drs. Nevin and Schaff, labored together in perfect harmony, and their united influence was felt far beyond the limits of the Reformed Church. In 1846 Dr. Nevin published "The Mystical Presence, a vindication of the Reformed or Calvinistic Doctrine of the Holy Eucharist;" a book which has been regarded as marking an epoch in the history of American Theology. This was followed in 1847 by "The History and Genius of the Heidelberg Catechism," and in 1848 by a tract entitled "Antichrist, or the Spirit of Sect and Schism." In the latter year Dr. Schaff began the publication of the "*Kirchenfreund*, a monthly magazine devoted to the interests of the German Churches of America; and in 1849 Dr. Nevin was instrumental in founding the "Mercersburg Review," of which he remained the editor and chief contributor until 1853. During the same period, Dr. Schaff wrote his History of the Apostolic Church," which appeared in German in 1851, and was subsequently translated into English, under the direction of the author, by the Rev. Edward D. Yeomans. The same writer, during his connection with the Theological Seminary at Mercersburg published a "German Hymn-Book" (1859); "America, its Political, Social, and Religious Character" (1854); "Germany, its Universities and Divines" (1857); "History of the Christian Church of the First Three Centuries" (1858); besides various minor tracts and essays.

The remarkable literary activity of the professors at Mercersburg naturally attracted great attention. German Theology and Philosophy were in those days comparatively unknown in this country, and it is not surprising that their introduction should have induced controversy and opposition. The subjects discussed were profoundly interesting, and were treated with unusual freedom of thought and expression.

It is not our purpose to consider in detail the long controversies which were thus inaugurated, In a general way it may be remarked that the questions which were under discussion belonged rather to the Church in general than to any single denomination, and that there is hardly an ancient and historical church in the world which has not been shaken by the conflicts which they induced.

In the Reformed Church these controversies were conducted with extraordinary energy and ability. Gradually the utterances of the Professors at Mercersburg and their coadjutors came to be known as "Mercersburg Theology"—a term which was at first introduced by its opponents, but was subsequently tacitly accepted by its friends. It did not properly designate an organized theological system, but a movement in the life of the Church; and consequently left room for injudicious and extreme utterances on the part of professed friends, which did it more harm than the attacks of its most violent opponents.

It is probably still too soon to express a judgment

with reference to what has been called "Mercersburg Theology" and the controversies connected with it For those who desire to study the questions involved, there is a whole literature, consisting of the controversial publications of the period. No doubt there were errors on both sides, and on both sides there were individuals who renounced the Church of their fathers because they felt themselves unable to mould its faith and direct its counsels. The faith of the Reformed Church was, however, studied not only by ministers, but by the people; and its historical relations to other Christian denominations came to be intelligently comprehended. The Heidelberg Catechism, which had in great measure been crowded out of practical use by catechisms prepared by individual ministers, was now reëstablished in the affections of the people, not in name only, but in spirit and truth. It was a great blessing that in these controversies there was no tendency on either side towards the rationalism which had been so prevalent in Europe, but that through many difficulties and trials the Church was evidently struggling onwards towards a clearer apprehension of the central verities of the Christian faith. For these and other reasons, we have no hesitation in affirming that the period of "the Mercersburg movement" was not a time of retrogression but of genuine advancement.

In 1853, Marshall College was removed to Lancaster,[1]

---

[1] Marshall College, while at Mercersburg, held high rank as a literary institution. The number of students was large, and nearly two hundred

but the Theological Seminary remained in Mercersburg until 1871. Dr. Nevin had retired in 1851, but Dr. Schaff continued in connection with the latter institution until 1865. Rev. Bernard C. Wolff, D. D., held the chair of Systematic Theology from 1852 to 1864. He was succeeded by Rev. Henry Harbaugh, D. D., who occupied the position until his death, which occurred in 1867. Rev. E. E. Higbee, D. D., was Professor of Church History and Exegesis from 1865 to 1871. In 1868, Rev. E. V. Gerhart, D. D., was chosen to fill the place vacated by the death of Dr. Harbaugh. He was the only member of the faculty who accompanied the Seminary to Lancaster.

In 1857 the Synod established a Theological Tutorship, partly by a fund invested in Germany, the gift of Baron von Bethman-Hollweg, which had been made available for this purpose, and partly by gifts from individuals and Classes. The successive incumbents while the institution was in Mercersburg were William M. Reily, A. M., and Jacob B. Kerschner, A. M.

The largest contributions to the endowment of the institution received during this period were a bequest of ten thousand dollars from the estate of Mr. Daniel Kieffer, of Berks County, and a gift of five thousand dollars from Miss Ann E. Keller.

---

were graduated in the regular classical course. The difficulties which necessitated the acceptance of propositions of union from Franklin College, were purely financial. It is believed that a book will soon be prepared in which the history of our literary institutions will be more minutely related than is possible in the present volume.

In 1871, Rev. Thomas G. Apple, D. D., was elected Professor of Church History and Exegesis, and Rev. F. A. Gast, D. D., was appointed tutor. Two years later (1873) the tutorship was changed to a full Professorship, and Dr. Gast was elected professor. The faculty is now constituted as follows: Rev. E. V. Gerhart, D. D., Professor of Systematic and Practical Theology; Rev T. G. Apple, D. D., Professor of Church History and Exegesis; and Rev. F. A. Gast, D. D., Professor of Hebrew and Old Testament Theology.

When this Theological Seminary was organized there were about eighty ministers in connection with the (German) Reformed Church in the United States; now there are nearly eight hundred. Other theological institutions have since been established, and these have done their full share in the work of supplying the Church with an educated ministry; but an important part of this progress and success is naturally due to the institution which was first in the field, and which now numbers about four hundred ministers upon its roll of graduates. In 1884 the Synods of the United States, Pittsburg, and the Potomac, each resolved to provide for the endowment of an additional professorship. When this work is completed there will be six professors in connection with the institution, and its efficiency and influence will be greatly increased. The demand for thoroughly educated ministers has never been more urgent than it is at present, and we therefore trust that our Theological Seminaries will continue to enjoy the favor of the Church.

CHAPTER XII.

The Synod of Ohio—Western Theological Seminary—Literary Institutions in the East and West.

WE have now reached a period when the materials of history become abundant. It may be said, in a general way, that it was a time of gradual growth and advancement, though a large portion of the Church as yet failed to appreciate the importance of unity and co-operation. We can only refer to a few of the subjects which occupied the attention of the Church, and in considering them we crave the liberty of frequently departing from a strictly chronological order.

THE SYNOD OF OHIO.

We have already referred to several of the pioneers of the Reformed Church in the Great West. The first Reformed minister settled within the limits of the present State of Ohio is believed to have been the Rev. Jacob Christman, who began to labor in Warren county in 1803. In the following year (1804) that truly apostolic man, the Rev. John Jacob Larose, entered upon the field, and for many years his extensive missionary journeys were a source of comfort to hundreds of isolated members of the Church. In 1812 the Synod resolved "to send certain ministers into the western country, to visit the members of our Church residing there," and "that a collection be taken up in each congregation for their support." The ministers appointed to this service were William Hendel, Jr., and J. W. Dechant. Hendel was subsequently excused, but Dechant began his labors in Ohio in 1816. Gradually the number of ministers increased, and in 1819, when the Synod of the United States was divided into Classes, it was possible to form a Classis of Ohio. The Classis was formally organized at Lancaster, Ohio, on the 1st of May, 1820, and at that time included five ministers, fifty congregations, and about eighteen hundred communicants. Four years later this Classis, at its meeting in New Philadelphia, O., on the 14th of June, 1824, resolved itself into a synod, under the title of "The German Evangelical Reformed Synod of Ohio." On this occasion but eight ministers were present, and as the number was so small, we may as well enumerate them. Their names were J. P. Mahnenschmidt, Thomas Winters, George Weiss, Benjamin Faust, Henry Sonnedecker, Daniel Rahauser, David Shearer, and William Reiter. John Jacob Larose and Simon Riegel are noted as absent, and John Peter Dechant as having died within the year. David Winters, J. Descombes, and John Pence, were admitted to membership at the same meeting. These ministers may be regarded as the pioneers of the Synod of Ohio.

The occasion which induced the division from the parent Synod was almost identical with that which had originally caused the separation of the latter from the Church of Holland. In both cases the superior body regarded the ordination of ministers as its special prerogative, and declined to grant this privilege to a subordinate organization. In 1823 the Classis of Northampton applied to the Synod of the United States for permission to examine a candidate (Mr. Philip Zeiser), and "if found qualified to ordain him to the gospel ministry." The Synod, however, declined to grant the request, and officially declared that "no candidate shall in future be examined and ordained except by Synod." As might have been expected, the members of the Classis of Ohio, who were farthest distant from the centre of the Church, felt aggrieved by this decision. It was impracticable, they declared in their published protest, to require candidates for the ministry to undertake a long and expensive journey for the purpose of receiving ordination from the hands of the Synod. "The money expended in traveling over the mountains," they said, "might be applied to much better advantage in building up the Church at home."

As there seemed to be little hope that the Synod would rescind its action, the only course which suggested itself to the Classis of Ohio was to declare its independence, and to assume the privilege to which it believed itself justly entitled. There was but little personal feeling involved in this action; it was the cutting of a knot which the Classis found itself unable to untie.

The course taken was irregular, but it may be regarded as to some extent warranted by urgent necessity.

For some years after the separation there was, it is true, a certain coldness between the two Synods, and they had but little direct communication; but each regarded the other as belonging to the same Church, and ministers were dismissed from one to the other without hesitation. The Synod of the United States, having in the meantime granted to its Classes the privilege of performing the rite of ordination, several times invited the Synod of Ohio to resume its former classical relations; but the latter felt that it had a special mission, and was naturally unwilling to occupy a subordinate position. In 1837 the Classis of West Pennsylvania, which had hitherto belonged to the Synod of the United States, became connected with the Synod of Ohio, and the latter thus became a much stronger and more efficient body. Its territory had, however, become greatly enlarged, and the difficulty of convening its members was accordingly increased. The charges were widely scattered, and the ministers who resided on the frontiers often endured great dangers and privations on their way to the place of meeting. With a view of decreasing these difficulties, and of promoting the efficiency of its practical operations, the Ohio Synod, during its annual sessions at Lancaster, Ohio, in June 1839, divided its territory into three District Synods which were to meet annually, and constituted itself a General Synod, to meet every third year.

This arrangement, it seems, did not prove satisfactory, and three years later it was abandoned. In that year (1842) the Triennial General Synod of Ohio convened at Canton, and proved a very important assembly. It entered largely into the work of reconstruction and re-adjustment, and exerted an important influence on the general life of the Church. A plan of co-operation with the Synod of the United States by the interchange of delegates was adopted, and, in place of its own, it adopted the Constitution of the latter body. This system of correspondence was continued until the organization of the present General Synod rendered it no longer necessary.

In doctrine and discipline there was, at this time, no important difference between the East and West. At the time of its organization the Synod of Ohio had declared its unalterable attachment to the Heidelberg Catechism and the ancient usages of the Church, and had, in 1832, published a Constitution which fully harmonized with this profession. The doctrinal and practical questions which claimed the attention of the synods were generally the same, though slightly varied by local circumstances. Thus, for instance, in the West the conflict concerning the propriety of employing extraordinary measures for the promotion of revivals of religion was more intense than in the eastern portion of the Church, and even resulted in the formation, in 1846, of the "German Independent Synod of Ohio," which after a separate existence of six years re-united in a body with the Ohio Synod. As a general thing there was, in all sections of the Church, great reverence for the ancient landmarks, though there were many who recognized the danger of falling into a state of heartless formalism, and some who in their opposition to this evil suffered their zeal to outrun the bounds of their discretion. "It is evident," says Dr. I. H. Reiter, with reference to the early days of the Ohio Synod, "that the idea of the supernatural and the divine elements of Christianity was not ignored or discarded. This appears from certain facts and official acts. The fathers, as foreshadowed in the parochial reports, as well as in the synodical records, were not only 'churchly,' but faithful to the customs of the Church, to the practice of catechisation, and to the proper use of the means of grace. The ordinances of divine appointment were valued and observed. In 1830, with the view of giving due prominence and significance to the Divine Ordinances, the Synod made it the duty of every minister to make proper account of the worship of the sanctuary and to administer the Lord's Supper at least twice in each year in all the congregations. And from the reports of baptisms, it is evident that this ordinance was generally observed."

"It also appears from the official record, that due regard was had for the leading Church Festivals, such as Christmas, Good Friday, Easter, and Pentecost; and, in 1837, it was resolved 'that Good Friday be observed throughout the Church as a day of prayer.' This evinces a spirit of true devotion and consecration, as well as churchliness."[1]

THE WESTERN THEOLOGICAL SEMINARY.

As early as 1834 the Synod of Ohio had officially declared that it entertained "the exalted intention of establishing an institution for the education of worthy young men for the gospel ministry, that the vacant places of the West may be filled with the Word and Gospel of Life." Years passed before this laudable purpose could be consummated. In 1838 there was an attempt to establish a Theological Seminary at Canton, Ohio. The Rev. J. G. Buettner, Ph. D., a well educated German, had become pastor of several congregations in the vicinity of the latter place, and it occurred to the Synod to employ his services in the instruction of candidates for the ministry. He was accordingly elected Professor of Theology, and an annual stipend of $250 was promised him for his educational work. Though a man of some scholastic ability, Dr. Buettner appears to have been unable to adapt himself to American life, and in 1839 he resigned his congregations and soon afterwards returned to Europe. With his departure the incipient institution ceased to exist. Nine years later, in 1848, another attempt was made to establish a Theological Seminary, and this time the chosen location was Columbus, Ohio. The Rev. A. P. Freeze was elected Professor, but for various reasons his work proved

---

[1] "*Ref. Quarterly Review*," 1879, p. 156.

unsuccessful, and he resigned. After several other abortive attempts, the Synod, in 1850, resolved to found Heidelberg College at Tiffin, Ohio, and in connection with it to establish a Theological Seminary. The first Professor of Theology was the Rev. Dr. E. V. Gerhart, then of Cincinnati, Ohio, who formally opened the latter institution in May, 1851, with two students. Since that time the Seminary has been steadily at work, and the increased prosperity of the Reformed Church in the West is in great measure due to its labors. For ten years after the organization there was but one professor to attend to the full course of study: Dr. E. V. Gerhart from 1851 to 1855, and Dr. Moses Kieffer, from 1855 to 1861. In the latter year Dr. Herman Rust was called to a second professorship. Dr. Kieffer resigned in 1868, and in the succeeding year Dr. J. H. Good was chosen his successor. Since that time the Faculty has consisted of Dr. J. H. Good and Dr. Herman Rust. The course of instruction is thorough and complete, and the institution is in every respect worthy of the confidence and affection of the Church.

LITERARY INSTITUTIONS.

The work of the ministry demands thorough preparation, and the Reformed Church is therefore profoundly interested in the prosperity of her Literary Institutions. The Theological and Classical department of study can never be sundered without serious loss; the one will always remain the proper complement and completion of the other. It is not without reason, therefore, that ministers connected with the Faculties of our Literary Institutions are recognized as performing the full duties of their ministry, and that contributions to the support of these institutions are acknowledged to be gifts of Christian charity in the fullest sense of the term. It may perhaps be well to conclude the present chapter by enumerating the Literary Institutions in the East and West which are at present engaged in the service of the Church.

Franklin and Marshall College, at Lancaster, Pa., was founded in 1853 by the consolidation of two older institutions, of which it is, therefore, the proper historical continuation. Marshall College was for the purpose of this union removed from Mercersburg and united with old Franklin College, whose early history has already been somewhat minutely related. In this way it became possible to use the endowment of Franklin College for the purposes for which it had been originally intended.

The amount paid according to agreement to the trustees of Pennsylvania College, at Gettysburg, for the Lutheran interest in Franklin College, amounted to $17,169.61. This sum was collected in the Reformed Churches, and the endowment of Franklin College thus remained intact. At the same time the one-third interest supposed to belong to the "outside community" was formally transferred to the Reformed Church. Since that time the largest individual additions to the endowment have been derived from the legacy of Mr. Lewis Audenried, of Philadelphia, and the donation of the Wilhelm family, of Somerset county. The College has also recently received a very acceptable gift of $10,000 from Mrs. James M. Hood, of Frederick, Maryland, for the erection of an Astronomical Observatory, which is to be known as "Daniel Scholl Observatory," in memory of the deceased father of the donor. The Reformed Church has in many ways testified to its interest in the prosperity of the college, and during the Tercentenary year (1863) no less than thirty thousand dollars were collected for its endowment.

This institution is a college of the old classical type, and has no irregular or mixed Classes. The number of students is, therefore, probably, somewhat smaller than it would otherwise be; but perhaps for this very reason it has been more easy to maintain a high educational standard. Its published course of studies, it is believed, will compare favorably with those of similar institutions in other parts of the country. The Rev. Dr. Thomas G. Apple is President.[1]

Heidelberg College, at Tiffin, Ohio, was founded in 1850, in close connection with the Western Theological Seminary. It is said that a large majority of the ministers of the Ohio Synod were educated in this institution. It provides several complete courses of instruction, and

---

[1] The successive Presidents have been Dr. E. V. Gerhart, from 1854 to 1866; Dr. J. W. Nevin, from 1866 to 1876; and since the latter date Dr. Thomas G. Apple.

also furnishes superior advantages for the education of young women. Though, like our other institutions, this college struggled for years with financial difficulties, it has now in great measure surmounted them, and the outlook is hopeful and encouraging. A new college building costing about $50,000 has recently been erected. The first President was Dr. E. V. Gerhart, who was succeeded by Drs. M. Kieffer and G. W. Aughinbaugh. This office is now held by the Rev. George W. Williard, D. D. The financial interests of the institution have been greatly promoted by its agent, Elder Henry Leonard, familiarly known as "The Fisherman," who has for many years labored faithfully for the advancement of the cause of higher education in the Reformed Church.

Catawba College was founded at Newton, North Carolina, in 1851, by ministers and members of the Reformed Church. Having lost a large part of its resources during the war, this institution now claims only the humbler title of "Catawba High and Normal School," and in its chosen sphere is doing excellent work. We are, however, more familiar with its earlier name, and prefer to give it here. "An effort has been made to endow the institution so as to make it a full college." The President is the Rev. J. C. Clapp, D. D

Ursinus College, at Freeland (or Collegeville), Montgomery county, Pa., was founded in 1869, under the Presidency of the Rev. J. H. A. Bomberger, D. D. During its brief history this institution has been instrumental in affording the advantages of liberal culture to a large number of young men, and recently arrangements have been made by which young women are admitted to similar educational privileges. It has been recognized and commended by the General Synod and the Synod of the United States. Connected with the college is a Theological Department, which is undei the immediate charge of three professors. Although under no formal synodical control, this institution fully acknowledges its amenability to the jurisdiction of the Reformed Church.

Our space is necessarily so limited that we can hardly do more than mention a number of additional educational institutions which are engaged in the service of the Church:

Mercersburg College had its origin in a desire to utilize the buildings left vacant by the removal of Marshall College from Mercersburg to Lancaster, and also to meet the educational wants of the section of the Church in which these buildings are located. It has performed a good work, and at present is carried forward as an Academy or Collegiate Institute, but has an important mission to perform in this character. The Rev. Dr. G. W. Aughinbaugh is President.

Palatinate College, at Meyerstown, Pa., of which the Rev. W. C. Schaeffer, A. M., is President, also had its origin in a desire to provide for the education of the young, under the care and guardianship of the Church. Like the institution at Mercersburg, it aims to provide an education for those who do not intend to pursue a full college course, and also to prepare students for one of the classes in college. These institutions are under the care of the Church, and are worthy of support.

"*Calvin College*," at Cleveland, O., and the Collegiate Department of the "*Mission House*" at Sheboygan, Wis., are mentioned elsewhere in this volume in connection with the German work in the West. The amount of good which they have accomplished is incalculable. At Dakota, Ill., the "*College of Northern Illinois*" has been founded, and in Kansas "*Wichita University*" will soon be ready to receive students. The two latter institutions will, no doubt, perform a work of great importance. Thoroughly educated ministers are especially necessary on the frontiers, where the foundations of the Church ought to be broadly and firmly laid. As we can hardly expect the young men of the remote West to come to our Eastern institutions, it becomes our duty to provide for their education in the region in which they are expected to labor. This is the special work which these new institutions have undertaken, and we have no doubt it will be thoroughly performed.

Other schools which enjoy the support and patronage of the Reformed Church are Clarion Collegiate Institute, Rimersburg, Pa.; Juniata Collegiate Institute, Martinsburg, Pa.; and International Academy, Portland,

Oregon. Parents who send their children to such schools may feel assured that they will receive a faithful Christian training.

Female education, we regret to say, has not, in the Reformed Church, received the attention which it demands. An intelligent mother is the best pledge for the intelligence of her family; and if our Church is to exert the social influence which is her due, we must provide for the education of the young women who will be the mothers of future generations. Three institutions are specially devoted to this important work: Allentown Female College and Greensburg Female Collegiate Institute, both in Pennsylvania, and Claremont Female College, at Hickory, North Carolina. We need more such schools, and those which we have should be better patronized. It is utter folly to send children to be educated at distant and irresponsible institutions, because the eye of the parent happens to have been caught by a specious advertisement; when an education more thorough and better suited to their subsequent surroundings could be obtained for them under the fostering care of their own Church. We have personally known parents who have thus placed their children under the care of strangers, only to discover, when it was too late, that their dear ones had not only been alienated from their affections, but had imbibed the infidel principles which are now so prevalent in many parts of our country, and which to the faith of a Christian are worse than death.

We do not believe that the number of our literary institutions should be decreased, in order to add strength to the few that remain. We live in a great country, and there is plenty of room for all worthy educational enterprises. At the same time it will be cheerfully conceded that new educational institutions should be founded only after mature consideration and where the necessities of the Church imperatively demand them.

Though it is pleasant to contemplate the advancement of our educational interests during the past half-century, it should not be forgotten that the Reformed Church was late in the field, and has been compelled to struggle with peculiar difficulties. The colleges of certain other denominations have, especially of late years, received large endowments, and have consequently been able to provide the means for advanced study in special departments, which are very expensive, and are consequently beyond our reach. In the regular course of scholastic training, which is essential to a thorough preparation for the ministry, or the ordinary pursuits of life, we do not believe that any one of the literary institutions of our country is in advance of those which are under the special care of the Reformed Church; but the advantages presented by wealthier institutions to students in special courses are not without attractions, and our institutions must struggle hard to hold their own. An endowment which would have been regarded as very respectable fifty years ago is now considered small. As we are naturally desirous of affording to the young men and women of the Reformed Church the best advantages which the country can afford, it is necessary that the endowments of our literary institutions should be increased until they compare favorably with those of the schools of other influential denominations. Our deficiency in this respect has thus far been in a great degree compensated by the ability and self-sacrificing devotion of the men who have been engaged in the work of education; but renewed efforts are necessary to enable us to maintain the position which is our due. There is, in fact, no interest in the Reformed Church which more loudly appeals to the benevolence of its members than the cause of education. We should not only seek to elevate our literary institutions beyond the reach of pressing want. It is in our power to make them the glory of our Church and of the nation. Let us not rest satisfied until this work is thoroughly accomplished.

CHAPTER XIII.

The Widows' Fund—Home Missions—The German Church in the West—Foreign Missions—Beneficiary Education.

The revival of ancient charities occupied the attention of the Church simultaneously with the establishment of its theological and literary institutions. Some of these had been for years in a languishing condition, but earnest men now began to direct new streams of life into the ancient channels.

THE WIDOWS' FUND.

The Fund for the Relief of the Widows of Ministers is the oldest of the charitable institutions of the Reformed Church in the United States. It was founded as early as 1755 by the Coetus of Pennsylvania, which obtained permission from the Synods of Holland to apply to this laudable purpose certain unexpended remainders of the annual stipends. There are no consecutive records of the manner in which the income of the Fund was applied in those early days, but no doubt it brought relief to the stricken household of more than one minister who had fallen at his post. The fund thus created gradually increased in value, and soon after the separation from Holland, was made the special charge of the "Society of Guardians for the Relief of Ministers and their Widows," which was incorporated in 1810 by the Supreme Court of Pennsylvania. The charter appears to have been cumbrous and defective, and the work of the society was circumscribed. In 1832, when the Synod appointed Dr. B. C. Wolff and others a committee to inquire into the condition of the society, it was found that there were but three surviving members, and that but two widows were receiving its benefits. The surviving members were the Rev. Caspar Wack, William Hendel, D. D., and Samuel Helffenstein, D. D. These aged ministers held a conference with the synodical committee at Falkner Swamp, in 1833, and cheerfully agreed to transfer the funds under their control to Synod, under the sole condition that the widows who were then receiving annuities should not be deprived of them. The Synod expressed a desire that the society should be perpetuated, and by its direction certain changes were made in the charter, which rendered its benefits applicable to destitute ministers and the widows of ministers throughout the entire Church, instead of confining them to the State of Pennsylvania, as had been hitherto the case. Since that time the society has continued to exist, though it has never been supported as it deserves. In 1849 the initiation fee was changed from £2, Penna. currency, to $5, and the annual dues fixed at $3. The payment of $60, in addition to the initiation fee, constitutes a minister a life member. In special cases the widows of ministers who were not members of the society may be made partakers of its benefits. Though the annuities are necessarily small, they have in many instances prevented great suffering, and it is to be hoped that by the liberality of the church the benevolent operations of the society may soon be greatly extended.

HOME MISSIONS.

The Reformed Church has always been, in a peculiar sense, the Church of Missions. It is for this reason that the soil of almost every country of Europe was once crimsoned by the blood of her martyrs, and that when her children crossed the ocean they were so speedily followed by faithful ministers of the Gospel. As the establishment of the German Reformed Church of this country had been in great measure due to the prevalence of the spirit of missions in the Fatherland, it might, perhaps, have been expected that the American Church should, in turn, engage in this great work with peculiar enthusiasm. In fact, however, the Church awoke but slowly to a sense of its duty. In a weak, spasmodic way, the Synod attempted to respond to the earnest appeals of the infant churches on the frontiers, and several ministers were at an early date commissioned to visit the vacant congregations of the South and West, receiving for their services a small stipend from the treasury of the Synod. Until 1826 the Synod annually appointed a committee on Missions. In the latter year this committee, through its secretary the Rev. James R. Reily, presented a lengthy report, including a diary written by the Rev.

John Rudy, who had been sent by the committee to visit the vacant churches of South Carolina. From this report it appeared that there were not less than eighty-four vacant churches within the bounds of the Synod. These are enumerated in the following condensed extract from the report:

"*Pennsylvania*: 5 vacant congregations in Butler, Warren, and Venango counties. Also others, concerning which the committee can give no certain information.

"*Ohio:* 4 vacant congregations in Butler county, on the Miami river; 7 formerly served by Rev. Mr. Dechant.

"*Virginia:* 7 vacant congregations in Pendleton county; 5 in Botetourt county; 2 in Loudon county; and others widely scattered.

"*North Carolina:* 4 vacant congregations in Ashe county; 4 in Rowan county; 6 in Lincoln county.

"*South Carolina:* 8 vacant congregations in Newberry, Lexington, and Richland districts.

"*Tennessee:* 12 vacant congregations on the French Broad river.

"*Kentucky:* 5 vacant congregations in the southern part of the State.

"*Indiana:* 5 vacant congregations in Washington and Harrison counties.

"*Illinois:* 5 vacant congregations in Union county.

"*Missouri:* 5 vacant congregations in Capberedo[1] county; formerly served by Mr. Weyberg."

The committee concluded its report by suggesting the appropriation of the sum of $200 from the synodical treasury for the work of missions during the current year. The interest awakened by the discussion of the subject led, however, to more decisive action, and by the direction of Synod, the Board of

---

[1] Probably Cape Girardeau county.

Domestic Missions was organized in Frederick City, Maryland, on the 28th of September, 1826.[1] Popular prejudice was, however, so strongly arrayed against all enterprises of general benevolence, that the Synod was careful to explain that participation in this movement was to be wholly voluntary. It was to be known as a "Missionary Society," and to be supported by the contributions of local auxiliary societies, established at such places as might be deemed advisable. This society was to have general direction of the work of missions, and to enjoy the privilege of recommending to Synod young men whom it might deem qualified for missionary work, for examination, licensure, and ordination. The plan thus recommended was not practically carried out, and the association instituted under the auspices of Synod was known as the "Board of Missions."

For some years the "Board" received but little sympathy and support from the churches, and frequently it neglected to prepare an annual report. Its proceedings were, however, published in the "Magazine," a publication which was founded for the special purpose of awakening an interest in the cause of Missions. In 1835 the "Board" reported that, during the past year, it had received benevolent contributions to the amount of $97.20¼, and had expended $54.31, leaving a balance of $42.89¼. It would, however, be a mistake to suppose that this small sum represented

---

[1] See Minutes of Synod, 1827, p. 41.

the whole amount of the annual contributions of the Church for the cause of Missions. Pastors or members of indigent Western churches could without difficulty collect far more on a single visit to their friends in the East, than was contributed by the whole Church to the enterprises of the Board of Missions. In this way many thousands of dollars were gathered for church extension of which no public record has been preserved. Of course, this state of affairs was favorable to the schemes of plausible impostors, who sometimes succeeded in collecting large sums of money before their wickedness could be exposed. Gradually it dawned upon the consciousness of the churches that it would be better to direct the stream of their contributions into a regular channel, and the receipts of the Board of Missions were consequently increased. In 1841 the contributions amounted to $153.94; a year later to $650; in 1845 the amount of offerings was $1,577.62. In the latter year the Board of the Synod of Ohio was organized, but for some years its existence was hardly more than nominal. Ten years later (1855) the offerings of the whole Church, East and West, amounted to $3,771.11. From this time, however, the increase of offerings was rapid, and the work of the Boards became more extensive. The churches began to take a more profound interest in the subject, and instances of self-sacrificing devotion became numerous. Some of the ablest men in the Church devoted themselves to the work, and many a widow's mite was voluntarily given to increase its treasury.

In 1873 the Eastern Synod and the Synods of Pittsburgh and the Potomac formed what has since been known as the "Tri-synodic Union." These three Synods elect a "Superintendent of Missions," who as the executive officer of the Board has the general supervision of all its missions. In unifying the work, and in giving it a new impulse, the labors of the successive Superintendents have proved successful. The "Joint Board" elects from its number four persons, who, with the Superintendent of Missions, form the Executive Council. Among the results of the labors of the "Tri-synodic Union," may be mentioned the organization of the Classes of California and Oregon, and the recent establishment of a promising mission among the Swiss colonists at Valparaiso, in South America.

The four Synods which are not embraced in this "Union" are equally interested in the work of Missions, and through their several Boards are laboring earnestly for its advancement. A summary of the labors of all the Boards is presented triennially to the General Synod.

The "*Ursinus Union*" is an association for religious and benevolent purposes, including in its membership many of the patrons and friends of Ursinus College. Besides the support which it has afforded to the latter institution, it has contributed largely to Home Missions and other objects of general benevolence.

Throughout the entire Reformed Church in the United States the cause of Home Missions is annually receiving greater attention. From the Report of the Board of Home Missions to the General Synod in Baltimore, in May 1884, we learn that "there are now one hundred and forty-two missions under the care of the different district boards, and that the amount raised and expended for their support during the past three years is $77,989.70. This is forty-eight missions and $22,951.61 more than were reported to the General Synod which met at Tiffin, Ohio, in May 1881." Though the amount of contributions is greatly exceeded by that of several other denominations, which have a larger membership, "it will be seen," in the language of the Report, "that considerable advance has been made in the great work of Missions, for which there is reason of thankfulness to the God and Father of our Lord Jesus Christ."

The Harbor Mission, at New York, which was inaugurated by the General Synod in 1866, is one of the most interesting of the special enterprises of the work of Home Missions. It has accomplished much good in protecting worthy immigrants from the impositions to which they are exposed, and in aiding them to find homes in Christian communities. It certainly deserves more attention than it has hitherto received.

There is one department of the great work of Missions which in its importance has transcended all others, and has proved peculiarly fruitful. Its success has indeed been so wonderful, when we consider the grandeur of the results in comparison with the meagreness of the means employed for their attainment, that we do not hesitate to say that it deserves to occupy one of the brightest pages in the history of the Reformed Church For the facts contained in the following sketch we are indebted to a Western pastor who was himself one of the most eminent laborers in this interesting field:

THE GERMAN CHURCH IN THE WEST.

The origin and rise of the German Western Church must under Divine Providence, be chiefly attributed to the Eastern Church in Pennsylvania, as the solid basis; to the Western Church, as the missionary and progressive agent; and to the German element, as the instrument of patient and and self-denying work. The three men who were chiefly instrumental in this work all came from Pennsylvania. Dr. M. Stern, who was most active in missionary labor, had spent several years in studying and teaching in Mercersburg, and had served congregations in the Classis of East Pennsylvania before he removed to Ohio. Dr. H. A. Muehlmeier, the founder of the "Missionshaus" in Wisconsin, studied Theology in Mercersburg. Dr. H. J. Ruetenik, the originator of the German Publishing House, at Cleveland, Ohio, entered the ranks of the ministry as a member of East Pennsylvania Classis. In 1853 these three men first met at a meeting of Tiffin Classis, Ohio; and from this meeting are to be dated the beginnings of the great work which, in the course of thirty years, has resulted in the formation of three German Synods, with forty thousand members and all the institutions necessary to effective Church-work.

MAX STERN.

Soon after this meeting Dr. Stern removed to Crawford county, the very heart of the German population of Ohio. Here he found the religious elements with which the German Church of the West has had to deal almost everywhere. There were " New-Measure Men," zealous but strongly tincured with Methodism; Separatists, who had brought their Pietism and Mysticism from the secluded valleys of Germany; and liberal Unionists, who thus far had been contented members of the Lutheran Church, but were being driven out of it by its rising Lutheran consciousness. Dr. Stern preached Christ crucified, the central life of faith; he inculcated the authority and ordinances of the visible Church; he catechised the young and educated them to become active Church-members. This course met the spiritual wants of large numbers of people, and he succeeded in building up four flourishing charges in this county alone. He was also constantly at work encouraging missionary labor through all the Western region.

Dr. Muehlmeier went to Sheboygan, Wisconsin. Having here, as a missionary, established a sound and prosperous church, he accepted a call from a rural congregation in the vicinity, consisting of pious people from Lippe, in Germany. These people had emigrated thither in a body, bound together by their love for the Heidelberg Catechism, and by their strong and sweet Christian experiences during a time of genuine revival at their old home. Finding less necessity for home work in his charge than most other ministers, he turned his attention to the great missionary work around him. Wisconsin was then rapidly filling up with German immigrants. They came in great numbers, and found work, bread, and all the good things of this life, but neither churches nor ministers. To supply this want, Dr. Muehlmeier looked in vain to the churches in Ohio and in Pennsylvania, for neither of them had German ministers to spare. Ministers had, therefore, to be prepared for the work. Thus the "Missionshaus" originated, where young men were instructed by Dr. Muehlmeier and one or two neighboring ministers, who received no salaries for their services. They fed their pupils at their own tables, and clothed them at their own expense, aided by the small contributions which they were able to obtain for this purpose from Christian friends. Gradually the number of friends increased; a house was built; teachers could be salaried, so as to devote their full time to this work; and, what was worth more than all, a Christian home was established, whose pure air and edifying intercourse built up its inmates in all things spiritual. There are at present (1884) more than sixty students in this institution, which is under the superintendence of the Rev. Dr. Muehlmeier. In all Wisconsin there were in 1854 but three German Reformed ministers. Now this state alone contains two Classes, with forty ministers, and two more Classes have been organized in adjacent States.

Dr. Ruetenik, after some missionary work in Toledo, Ohio, was called to a professorship in Tiffin. But the great wants of the German population did not allow him to remain satisfied with scientific work. To help his brethren in their missionary efforts he commenced, at his own expense, the publication of the German "Evangelist," at first a small monthly paper, which, however, gradually grew to a weekly of 6,000 subscribers, to which was added, afterwards, the publication of a Sunday-school paper now numbering 20,000 subscribers, a monthly for adults, books, etc. In short, out of these small beginnings a Printing House has grown whose annual sales now amount to $30,000, and which is almost free of debt. In order to give his whole time to the German work, Dr. Ruetenik, in 1860, removed to Cleveland, where he soon afterwards organized the First German Reformed congregation of that city. Now the Reformed Church has seven congregations there, numbering together two thousand members.

While these men continued in their work, others, possibly less known by men, but not less in heaven, labored in other places, and after many vicissitudes succeeded in planting churches.[1] Missouri, Nebraska, Minnesota, and Iowa, are at present the names of the frontier Classes.

At first the German work was pursued in connection with Synods which were prevailingly English. It was, however, thought better to have distinctly German Synods, which might devote all their attention to this work. As early as 1856 a number of German ministers formed a "Conference," which met annually

---

[1] By mentioning a trio of representative men, the writer, of course, does not mean to discriminate between them and their earnest and eminent fellow-laborers. Dr. J. H. Klein, for instance, has from the beginning been zealously and wisely active in the general administration of the affairs of the Church, and is still prominent in its councils. If space permitted, it would be a fascinating task to trace the record of the self denying toil of the eminent men upon whom the mantle of the fathers has fallen.

for mutual counsel and encouragement. As the work of Missions continued to prosper, the want of a Synodical organization was felt more and more. The Synod of Ohio was frequently importuned to grant its sanction to the movement, and in 1866 a resolution was passed by which the organization of a German Synod was fully authorized. A number of Classes, prevailingly German, in northwestern Ohio, Indiana, Illinois, and Wisconsin, were formed into the Synod of the Northwest, but this Synod did not include the German elements of eastern and southern Ohio. These retained their connection with the Ohio Synod, because the places where the Northwestern Synod met appeared to be too far distant. Only recently, in 1882, when permission was granted by the General Synod, the two German Classes, Cincinnati and St. John's, united with two Classes of the Synod of the Northwest, Heidelberg (Central Ohio), and Erie, in the formation of the Central Synod. The latter is a German body of fifteen thousand members. The Northwestern Synod numbers fourteen thousand, and the German Synod of the East, ten thousand.

Besides the institutions above mentioned, these German Churches sustain Calvin College, in Cleveland, and an Orphan Asylum in Fort Wayne. There are also two Societies for mutual aid in cases of death, with about 1,500 members. A missionary among the Indians in Wisconsin is chiefly sustained by their contributions. The Home Missionary Board of the North Western and

Central Synods receives about $3,000 annually, in contributions; and the Board of Church Extension about $500. The gifts to the "Missionshaus" and Calvin Institute amount annually to about $5,000. Including contributions to the Orphan Asylum and Indian Missions, the German Reformed Churches of the Northwest average $12,000 in annual contributions for Christian Benevolence.

FOREIGN MISSIONS.

In the work of Foreign Missions, the Reformed Church in the United States has accomplished less than might have been justly expected. A partial explanation of this humiliating fact may be found in the extraordinary extent of its Home Missionary field. The immigration from foreign lands was so enormous that the resources of the Church were utterly insufficient to provide for its most pressing spiritual necessities. With this work constantly at hand, it is perhaps not surprising that the Church should not have felt itself so strongly drawn to labor among the heathen as it might have been under different domestic conditions. It is however pleasant to know that of late years the interest taken in Foreign Missions has become far more general, and that the Church is making earnest efforts to retrieve the past.

The Board of Foreign Missions was organized at the Synod held in Lancaster, Pa., in 1838. During the first year the amount of contributions was $811.13¼. In

1842 the Rev. Benjamin Schneider, a missionary of the American Board of Foreign Missions who had been since 1834 located at Broosa, Asia Minor, connected himself with the Reformed Church, of which he had been a member in his early youth. This was done with the approval of the American Board, for the special purpose of promoting the interests of the cause of Missions in the Reformed Church. In this respect the anticipations of the friends of the cause were not disappointed. For many years Dr. Schneider was mainly supported by the contributions of the Reformed Church, while the Missions which he served remained under the care of the American Board.[1] In 1849 he removed from Broosa to Aintab, Syria, where his labors were greatly blessed. Two large congregations were established, and in 1862 sixteen native ministers had been raised up in Aintab alone.

The German Reformed Church, in 1865, withdrew its contributions from the American Board. For several years. the subject of Foreign Missions, on this account, received less attention; but many of the churches contributed to the support of the missionaries of the German Evangelical Missionary Society at Bisrampore, India. The most prominent of these missionaries is the Rev. Oscar Lohr, until recently a member of the Classis of New York.

---

[1] It is pleasant to note that, in 1845, the Schwenkfelders, a small religious denomination in Montgomery county, Pa., contributed $273 to the Reformed Board of Foreign Missions for the support of the Mission at Broosa.

BENEFICIARY EDUCATION. 329

In 1878 the Board selected Japan as a proper place for missionary labor, and the following year the work was formally begun. The following are the names of missionaries sent out with the date of their arrival at Yokohama:

Rev. Ambrose D. Gring and wife, June 6, 1879.
Rev. Jairus P. Moore and wife, October —, 1883.
Rev. William E. Hoy, December 1, 1885.
Miss Lizzie R. Poorbaugh, July 22, 1886.
Miss Mary B. Ault, July 22, 1886.
Rev. David B. Schneder, December 23, 1887.

On the 31st of January, 1888, the Board elected Miss Emma F. Poorbaugh to sail for Sendai, Japan, during the summer of 1888. In Tokio we have two congregations, and five mission stations in the immediate vicinity. In Sendai one church, a Theological School and a Ladies' Seminary. In Yamagata there is a flourishing boy's school, under the charge of Rev. J. P. Moore and wife. There are five or six ordained native ministers, eight or ten evangelists or catechists, and between ten and eleven hundred communicants.

The Mission among the Winnebago Indians, to which we have already alluded, has also been aided by the Board of Foreign Missions.

BENEFICIARY EDUCATION.

The necessity of assisting indigent young men in the work of preparing for the Gospel ministry has been recognized in all ages of the Church. It is, in fact, absolutely essential to the prosperity of the Church, and Beneficiary Education is therefore universally regarded as a proper object of Christian beneficence. Disguise it as we may, the ministry is ordinarily a life of hardship and privation, and has but few attractions for those who regard wealth and luxury as essential to their happiness. In this country, at least, the sons of wealthy parents but rarely devote themselves to this service; and though there are many young men who struggle upwards through unnumbered difficulties, without receiving financial aid from the Church, until they finally reach the sacred office, there are others who without such assistance must fail to attain the object of their hopes. With all that we can do, the number of candidates for the ministry is utterly inadequate to the necessities of the Church; and self-preservation—if no higher motive—should induce us to contribute to the small stipend which is annually granted to our beneficiaries.

The financial aid given for this purpose partakes of the nature of a loan, which the recipients are expected to repay as soon as they are able. Though the Church has sometimes been disappointed in those whom she has aided, no student of our history can deny that many of our ablest men were once beneficiaries, and that they have by their labors abundantly repaid the cost of their education.

Even in the last century the Synod on several occasions aided young men in the prosecution of their studies by appropriations from its treasury, and this excellent practice was never entirely discontinued. After the establishment of the Theological Seminary, this special interest was placed in charge of the Board of Visitors, which first presented a detailed report of its operations as a Board of Beneficiary Education in the year 1841. For many years the late Rev. Dr. S. R. Fisher served as Treasurer of the Board of the Synod of the United States, and since his death the same position has been worthily occupied by his son. The several Synods and Classes vary to some extent in their manner of conducting this work, so that it is somewhat difficult to collect its exact statistics; but we believe it to be more actively prosecuted than ever before, and the excellence of its results is evident throughout the Church.

CHAPTER XIV.

Publications—Parochial and Sunday-schools—Orphan Homes.

THE minutes of the Coetus held in Philadelphia on the 27th of September, 1748, were published in accordance with a resolution adopted by that body.[1] We regret that not a single copy of this pamphlet is extant, as it was, in all probability, the earliest official publication of the Reformed Church in the United States. It is not probable that the minutes were published in subsequent years, and more than half a century appears to have passed before the labors of the press were again called into requisition. Hymn-books and Catechisms were issued by individuals, either on their personal responsibility or by special agreement with the authorities of the Church. Several original volumes were also published by Reformed ministers, but these do not properly fall within the scope of our present inquiry. The late Rev. Dr. S. R. Fisher says, in his "History of Publications,"[2] "I have not been able to discover any evidence that the German Reformed Church, as such, was engaged in any direct publication efforts prior to the year 1805. It was in that year that she first published her 'Synodal Ord-

---

[1] Mayer MSS., p. 11.
[2] Reformed Quarterly Review, January, 1885.

nung,' which had been adopted in 1793, together with some addenda which had been made in 1800. The Minutes of Synod began to be published in German in 1817, and after 1825 in German and English."

SAMUEL REED FISHER.

The first periodical publication was the "Magazine of the Reformed Church," which appeared at Carlisle, Pa. in 1828, under the auspices of the Board of Missions For three years it was published monthly in pamphlet form. Then it was changed into a small quarto, and called "The Messenger of the Reformed Church," but still published monthly. From July 1834 to July 1835 it appeared semi-monthly. At the latter date it was changed to a weekly, and its publication transferred to Chambersburg, Pa. Until this time the editor was the Rev. Dr. Lewis Mayer, except for a short time when his place was supplied by the Rev. Daniel Young.

Since the removal to Chambersburg "The Messenger" has been the principal English periodical of the eastern portion of the Reformed Church. Its first editor was the Rev. Dr. B. S. Schneck, who held this position until 1840 when he was succeeded by the Rev. Dr. S. R. Fisher. In connection with many other duties, Dr. Fisher, who was an indefatigable worker, edited "The Messenger" from 1840 to 1875, assisted by the Rev. Dr. B. S. Schneck from 1848 to 1852; the Rev. Samuel Miller, from 1852 to 1857; the Rev. Dr. B. Bausman, from 1858 to 1861; and the Rev. Dr. G. B. Russell, 1869 to 1871. From 1875 to 1888 the Rev. Dr. P. S. Davis was editor-in-chief, assisted by three synodical editors.

A German magazine, entitled "Evangelische Zeitung" was started, in 1832, by the Rev. Dr. S. Helffenstein of Philadelphia. It was subsequently edited by the Rev. John H. Dreyer; but having become disorderly in its course towards Synod, it was formally disowned by that body in 1833.

The Rev. Dr. D. Zacharias published a small German paper called "Der Herold," in Harrisburg, in 1834; but it was soon discontinued for want of patronage. In 1836 the Rev. Dr. B. S. Schneck commenced the publication of " Der Christliche Herold," and in 1837, the Rev. Dr. John C. Guldin began to issue " Die Evangelische Zeitschrift." The latter two papers were, in 1837, transferred to the Board of Missions and instead of them, " Die Christliche Zeitschrift " began to appear. The title of this paper was subsequently changed to " Reformirte Kirchenzeitung," and having been united with the " Evangelist," it is now published at Cleveland, Ohio, under the editorship of the Rev. Louis Praikschatis. Its successive editors, while it was connected with the Eastern Board of Publication, were Rev. Dr. B. S. Schneck, Rev. S. Miller, Dr. N. Gehr, and J. G. Wittman.

" Der Reformirte Hausfreund " has, by the authority of Synod, been published, since 1866, in Reading, Pa. Its editor is the Rev. B. Bausman, D. D.

" The Reformed Quarterly " is a continuation of the " Mercersburg Review," founded in 1849. It is devoted to the higher departments of theological inquiry, but labors also in the interest of science and literature. The editors are the Rev. Drs. T. G. Apple and J. M. Titzel.

" The Guardian " was founded in 1850, at Lewisburg, Pa., by Dr. H. Harbaugh, as a magazine for young men and women. Its successive editors have been Henry Harbaugh, B. Bausman, J. H. Dubbs and H. M. Kieffer.

" The Christian World," issued at Dayton, Ohio, by the Reformed Publishing Company, is the principal English periodical of the Reformed Church in the West. It is a continuation of " The Western Missionary," which was founded in 1848 by the Rev. Dr. J.

H. Good. Rev. E. Herbruck and Rev. M. Loucks are the present editors. In January, 1885, the Reformed Publishing Company began the publication of "The Interior," a literary magazine of a high order.

We have not space even to enumerate the titles of all the periodical publications of the Reformed Church. According to a list published in the "Almanac for the Reformed Church" (1884), they are twenty-one in number; fifteen are English and six German. Nearly one-half of these are devoted to the cause of Sunday-schools.

The "Printing Establishment" at Chambersburg, Pa., is now known by tradition only to many of the younger members of the Church. It was, however, for many years an important institution, and its destruction during the civil war was a loss which has perhaps never been fully appreciated. Founded in 1840 by the Board of Missions, it had struggled along for several years under great difficulties, and soon became financially involved. In 1844 the Board of Publication was organized for the purpose of taking special charge of this interest, but the condition of the "Establishment" did not improve. At last, in 1848, the Synod became hopeless, and resolved to wind up the whole affair, and it seemed as though the labor of years would be utterly lost. In the very darkest hour three ministers came forward and proposed to form a company to carry on the Printing Establishment as an individual enterprise, receiving it as it was, with all its liabilities, and obligating themselves not only to carry on the publications of the Church, but to pay an annual bonus for the privilege. The ministers thus associated were the Rev. Drs. Moses Kieffer, B. S. Schneck, and S. R. Fisher, subsequently known as the firm of M. Kieffer & Co. The Synod was only too glad to accept these propositions, and for fifteen years—until January 1, 1864—"the firm" had charge of the publications of the Church. The work had been undertaken under great difficulties, but was nobly accomplished. Not only were the financial difficulties removed, but the establishment became a valuable possession. In 1854, on the renewal of its contract, the firm voluntarily transferred to the Synod one-half of this property, and ten years later disposed of its entire interest in the concern to the same body at a price much lower than its real value. The course of the firm of M. Kieffer & Co. was recognized as most liberal, and the Synod spontaneously added to the purchase money the sum of one thousand dollars, which may be regarded as a testimonial of gratitude for many years of faithful service.

The printing establishment was now entirely in the hands of the Church, and its future appeared exceedingly promising. The Board of Publication procured new presses, and all the material necessary for a first-class publishing house. The Church had long desired the publication of denominational literature, and now, it was believed, the time had come when its wishes could be gratified. The men who had formerly so wisely conducted the publications of the Church were to be continued in their respective stations, and under their guidance success appeared almost a certainty.

Suddenly a calamity occurred which in a few hours swept away the accumulations of years. It was during the civil war, and Chambersburg, which was near the border, had been several times visited by the forces of the enemy, but the inhabitants had suffered no injury, and felt no premonition of the coming evil. On the morning of the 30th of July, 1864, a detachment of the Southern army entered Chambersburg and laid the greater portion of the town in ashes. "In the general destruction," says Dr. Fisher, "our beautiful printing establishment, with all its valuable contents, was involved. Nothing was saved from the general wreck, except the stereotype plates and the principal account-books, which were in a large fire-proof vault, built in the previous spring for the use of the establishment. Thus was the labor of years wantonly destroyed. The loss, at a moderate estimate made at the time, footed up at nearly $43,000."

The destruction of the printing establishment left the Church without the necessary facilities for issuing its periodicals, and Dr. Fisher, at the direction of the Board, proceeded to Philadelphia to make the best arrangements which were possible under the circumstances. It was an undertaking of great difficulty, but Dr. Fisher was so energetic and successful that, after an interval of only four weeks, the periodicals were once more in the hands of their subscribers.

From this time forth the history of the Board of Publication is so well known that it is not necessary to consider it minutely. We need only say that the Rev. Dr. S. R. Fisher was the efficient business superintendent until his death, since which time the position has been held by his son, the Rev. Charles G. Fisher. The latter has recently by purchase and lease secured the privilege of publishing the books and periodicals of the church for a term of years. The contributions received from the Church, together with what was realized from the sale of the lot in Chambersburg and the State appropriation for the relief of the sufferers, were not even sufficicient to compensate the Board for its loss, much less to enable it to undertake important enterprises. Besides successfully conducting the periodicals of the Church, it has, however, issued a number of instructive and devotional volumes, some of which have enjoyed an extensive circulation.

We have already, in other connections, referred to the work of the Reformed Publishing Company in Dayton, and the German Publishing House in Cleveland, Ohio. Though we cannot consider their operations in detail, we are happy to be assured that they are actively and successfully engaged in the performance of their important functions. We fear, however, that the Church has not yet learned fully to appreciate the importance of properly encouraging its publication interests. In these days it ought not to be necessary to insist upon the power of the Press; and it is very certain that the Church cannot fully accomplish her mission without employing that power to the utmost in the service of her blessed Lord.

PAROCHIAL AND SUNDAY-SCHOOLS.

The German churches, in Europe and America have always devoted much attention to the instruction of the young. They are emphatically "the Catechetical churches," and have been more frequently reproached for the unusual stress laid by them on this subject than for any supposed neglect of duty. In our earlier history, religious instruction was always regarded as an essential part of education. When our fathers established a church, they almost invariably founded a parochial school at its side. They generally built a house which contained a large school-room, and at the same time served as a comfortable residence for the teacher. In many instances the latter had the use of a farm which belonged to the congregation, besides receiving a small annual stipend for playing the organ in the church, and whatever sums were paid him by parents for the tuition of their children. The children of the poor, as a rule, received instruction free of charge.

The secular learning imparted was perhaps inadequate, if judged by the standards of the present day; but there was no lack of religious training. The author well remembers one of these schools which it was his privilege to attend in early youth. Every morning the scholars gathered from miles around in the long, old-fashioned school-room, and joined in the united repetition of the Apostles' Creed and the Lord's Prayer. The Scripture lesson for the day was read, and then the master led in prayer. Twice a week the Ten Commandments were repeated, and certain hours were regularly devoted to instruction in the Catechism, preparatory to the pastor's Catechetical lectures, which were regarded as a direct preparation for Confirmation and the Holy Communion. In the evening the school was closed with singing and prayer. How earnestly all united in singing the ancient German choral: "Ach bleib bei uns, Herr Jesu Christ!"

> "Lord Jesus Christ, abide, we pray!
> The evening comes, we've spent the day.
> Thy blessed word and sacrament
> May we preserve unto life's end!"

From such a school the transition to the Church was easy. Every Sunday the pastor gathered the young folks around him in the church, and instructed them for an hour before the regular services; the afternoon was reserved for the Sunday-school, which was still in a somewhat incipient condition. Though there have been many changes, we are glad to know that in some of our oldest churches the ancient custom of Sunday catechisation is still maintained, without, of course, suffering it to interfere with Sunday-school or the regular courses of catechetical lectures.

When we remember how carefully our fathers provided for the religious instruction of their children in the way which we have indicated, we cannot be surprised that Sunday-schools were rather slow in making their way into the Reformed Churches. The earliest German Reformed Sunday-school of which we have any knowledge, was organized with forty scholars, in the church on Race st., near Fourth, Philadelphia, on the 14th of April, 1806. The Sunday-school of the First Reformed Church of Baltimore, was not founded until 1822; and about the same time schools were established in a number of churches of Pennsylvania and Maryland.

Though there was at first some popular opposition to Sunday-schools, especially in rural districts, their excellence was long since universally recognized. Many of our most eminent ministers have taken great interest in the Sunday-school, and as a result of their literary labors we have had a long series of catechisms, hymn-books, and periodical publications. Books for the library, illustrative of the social and religious life of the Reformed Church, are, however, still a *desideratum*. Of late years Conventions, devoted to the advancement of the cause of Sunday-schools, have been held in various parts of the Church, and have certainly done much good in directing attention to this important interest.

The minutes of the General Synod for 1884 report 1,378 Sunday-schools with 114,720 scholars. Some of these schools are, however, in all probability, held in union churches, and therefore do not belong exclusively to the Reformed Church. This is a fact which should be kept in mind in computing the average amount of their benevolent contributions and the possible extension of our periodical literature. Many Reformed Sunday-schools have recently manifested great interest in the work of Foreign Missions, and the increased contributions to this cause are in great measure due to their active benevolence.

ORPHAN HOMES.

In 1863 the Rev. Emanuel Boehringer,[1] pastor of a small mission church at Bridesburg, Philadelphia, was moved by Christian sympathy to admit several homeless orphans to his family circle. This was purely an act of faith, for he himself was very poor in this world's goods; but his faith proved all sufficient. Christian friends came to his aid, and he was thus enabled to found the Orphans' Home, which was for some time known by the name of "The Shepherd of Lambs," but is now called "Bethany." One year later the founder and his faithful wife entered into their heavenly rest, but their work was not suffered to fail. As the location at Bridesburg was found unsuitable, the Home was, in 1867, removed to Womelsdorf, Berks county, Pa., where it has greatly prospered. Even the destruc-

---

[1] Mr. Boehringer and the author of this volume were simultaneously ordained at Harrisburg, Pa., on the 23d of October, 1859, during the sessions of Synod. They met for the first time at the altar, and after the services they separated, never to meet again in this world.

tion of the buildings by fire, on the night of November 11, 1882, turned out to be a blessing in disguise; for the affliction opened new streams of benevolence, and a new and beautiful structure has arisen from the ashes. The Home has a good farm, and there is no debt; but the running expenses are, of course, large, and to provide for these the free-will offerings of Christians are the only resource. At present the orphans in the institution number about sixty, and this number the Board desires, as soon as possible, to increase to at least one hundred. The number of applications is large, and the accommodations in the new building are ample; it remains for the friends of the orphans to extend the blessings of the Home by their beneficence.

St. Paul's Orphans' Home at Butler, Pa., was founded in 1868, and derives its support principally from the Synods of Pittsburgh and Ohio. It is reported as being in an excellent condition. "Its location is healthy, its surroundings are beautiful, and its management is of the very best order." As in other similar institutions, children are most frequently received at an early age, and are then carefully trained until they reach the age of from thirteen to fifteen years, when they are indentured into good Christian families, where they will be still further prepared to become useful members of society. At present the number of orphans is about thirty-six, and this number will be increased as rapidly as the means at hand will allow.

The Reformed Orphans' Home, near Fort Wayne,

Indiana, is under the special patronage of the Central Synod and the Synod of the North West. Having but recently been founded, the number of orphans is not large; but the churches have been liberal, and the prospects of the institution are excellent.

"Zoar," at Detroit, Mich., admits adults as well as orphans. Besides a considerable number of children, twenty-one aged persons were recently members of this Christian family.

The cause of the orphans appeals directly to our warmest sympathies, and is consequently regarded with special favor. It has not only proved a blessing to hundreds of poor children, who have been saved from suffering and sin and taught the truth of Christ; but it has otherwise conferred blessings upon the Church. In days of dissension, when brethren found it difficult to labor together, the cause of the Orphans remained a precious bond of unity. It not only softened the asperities of theological controversy, but directly fostered the Christian charity which is the fairest blossom of our faith. We are, therefore, not surprised to behold the prosperity and rapid extension of this excellent work. The field is practically limitless, and the number of applicants would no doubt be increased ten-fold if the means were at hand for their support. We hope the stream of charity which flows in this direction may increase until thousands are partakers of the blessings which it brings.

CHAPTER XV.

Doctrine—Discipline—Cultus.

THE doctrine of the Reformed Church is best studied in its history. Though it has had many theological schools, which have varied greatly in their modes of expression and in the doctrines which they specially intoned, we believe the Church as a whole has been faithful to the great truths which were promulgated in her name in the sixteenth century and for which so many of her children suffered and died.

It has sometimes been objected to the Reformed Church that she has but few distinctive peculiarities; yet is not this, after all, her chief glory? She does not, in any sectarian fashion, exalt a single doctrine at the expense of all the rest, but seeks to hold the whole truth in due and harmonious proportion. Nor should it be forgotten, that most of the denominations which so closely resemble the Reformed Church are of much more recent origin, and have copied the model which she provided them in doctrine, discipline, and cultus. "Imitation is the sincerest homage."

As regards doctrinal standards, the Reformed Church in the United States holds "that the Holy Scriptures of the Old and New Testament, which are called canonical scriptures, are genuine, authentic, inspired, and therefore divine scriptures; that they contain all things which relate to the faith, the practice, and the hope of the righteous, and are the only rule of faith and practice in the Church of God; that consequently no traditions, as they are called, and no mere conclusions of reason, which are contrary to the clear testimony of these scriptures, can be received as rules of faith or of life." It receives, however, the Heidelberg Catechism, believing "the doctrine of the Catechism to be the doctrine revealed to us in the Bible." The Catechism, according to its own statement, rests upon the Apostles' Creed. With the various confessions adopted by other branches of the Reformed Church, we have no controversy; but find no necessity for a more definite declaration of doctrine than that which is contained in the Heidelberg Catechism. It contains "all things which it is necessary for a Christian to believe;" it allows all proper liberty in the development of the truth; and withal is full of Christian charity.

At the very beginning, the Catechism points with special emphasis to Christ as the source of redemption and salvation. It teaches substantially the old Augustinian doctrine of natural depravity and salvation by free grace alone, which, as we have seen, was the doctrine not only of Calvin but of all the chief Reformers. It does not, however, teach a decree of reprobation, and as a whole directs our attention rather to the work of our Lord Jesus Christ than to the decree in accordance with which it was accomplished. The German branch of the Reformed Church accordingly allows freedom for more moderate views on the subject of predestination than are usual in the more strictly Calvinistic Reformed churches. We are, however, by no means Pelagian or Arminian.

With regard to the sacrament of the Lord's Supper, the Reformed Church teaches, in accordance with the Catechism, the *spiritual* real presence of the body and blood of Christ in the Holy Eucharist, for believers only. It does not hold, as has sometimes been asserted by its opponents, that the sacrament is a mere memorial of the sufferings and death of Christ. Not "in, with, and under" the visible elements, but by the working of the Holy Ghost, "who dwells both in Christ and in us," we become by faith "partakers of the true body and blood of Christ." As has already been shown, the Reformed Church in the United States, in common with all the other branches of the same historical confession, differs on this point from the doctrine of Luther.

The Reformed Church regards the children of Christian parents as belonging to the covenant and people of God, and therefore considers them proper subjects for Christian baptism. In this respect she differs from the various Baptist communities. The Church insists that her ministers shall carefully instruct the young in the teachings of the Catechism, as the best means of preparing them for confirmation and admission to the Lord's Table. Confirmation, as practiced in the Reformed Church, is regarded as a solemn and appropriate rite. It is not, however, considered a sacrament, and when members are received by certificate from denominations in which this rite is not practiced, it is not usual to require them to receive confirmation. While the Church lays stress on the importance of experimental religion and Christian experience, it regards faithful instruction in the truths of God's word as the best means to be used in leading to this end. The authorized teaching of the Church is conveyed by the Heidelberg Catechism, to which those who desire to become acquainted with our doctrines are always referred.

ORGANIZATION AND DISCIPLINE.

The Protestant Churches of the continent of Europe have always laid special stress on the preservation of purity of doctrine, while they regard external organization and the ritual of worship as matters of minor importance. Calvin and Bullinger advised their friends in foreign countries to maintain the truths of the Gospel even with their blood, but in matters of external organization to accommodate themselves to the policy of the government. This advice was given on the ground that, while the Scriptures emphatically teach the necessity of order and discipline, they nowhere enjoin a particular form of church-government. That every Christian minister is a bishop in the sense of the New Testament was universally acknowledged, and the fact that so little is said on the subject by way of command led the churches to the conclusion that, while the general principles of church-government are unchangeable, particular features may be regulated by Christian expediency. At first the Reformed people found great difficulty in attaining to complete organization. In many countries they were compelled to worship secretly; but as often as possible they held Synods consisting of ministers and delegates from the isolated "churches under the cross." "As the effect of persecution," says Dr. Demarest, "they were determined, when the time came for organization, to have much of the popular element in the Church constitution, and much of simplicity in public worship." The system of government which had grown up in Switzerland, and was finally elaborated by Calvin, was gradually accepted by most of the Reformed Churches. It avoided the extreme of tyranny on the one hand and of independency on the other, and was especially well suited to the government of a Church which had little to hope from the favor of the state. In some countries, where the relations of the Church with the civil power were more intimate than elsewhere, the government of the Church became practically a function of the civil power, and its more popular features were never fully realized; but though this condition of affairs was regarded as unfortunate, it was on purity of doctrine that the unity of the Church was believed chiefly to depend.

In accordance with their chosen system of government, the Reformed churches still hold that all ministers are equal in office, and elect and institute ruling elders and deacons, who represent the people, and are at the same time partakers in a degree of the functions of the ministry.

The Reformed Church, therefore, differs from the Episcopalians, who are governed by diocesan bishops, and from the Congregationalists, who teach the independence of each congregation. The questions of presbytery, episcopacy, and independency, are, however, according to Dr. Schaff, "questions of polity, not of dogma," and the German churches have never made them the subject of extended discussion.

In England and Scotland the case has been different. The Church of England at first acknowledged the validity of the ordination of the ministers of other Protestant churches, and held "that episcopacy is not the only, but the best form of government, and necessary not for the being, but only for the well-being of the Church."[1] But there came a time of great conflict, in which questions concerning church-government were exalted beyond their original significance. The kings of the Stuart family unwisely attempted to force episcopacy upon the reluctant people of Scotland, and in the struggle which ensued, the question of church-government came to be regarded as a matter of paramount importance. The doctrinal aspects of the questions at issue were earnestly discussed, and the difference

---

[1] Schaff's "Harmony of the Reformed Confessions," p. 27.

was made much greater than Knox and Cranmer ever anticipated.

The German Reformed congregations, on their organization in America, naturally followed in the main the pattern which was provided for them by the Churches of Holland and the Rhine provinces of Germany. This pattern became traditional, and the differences between the Constitutions of the several congregations were but trifling. More than a century, however, passed away before the Church, as a whole, adopted a Constitution. In an able report presented by the Rev. Dr. T. L. Hoffeditz to the Synod of the United States, in 1839, it is stated that there was even at that time no document in existence which could properly be called the Constitution of the Reformed Church. The "Synodalordnung," to which we have already referred, was properly a series of rules of order for the government of Synod. A provisional "Discipline" had been adopted by the Synod in 1828, but it was never formally sanctioned by the Church. The "Constitution" was not adopted until 1845. It was principally the work of the Rev. Dr. Samuel R. Fisher, who, during his life-time, was regarded as the chief authority for its exposition. It is felt to be imperfect in various minor particulars; and the Church has for a series of years been engaged in the work of its revision. Though the desired consummation has not yet been attained, it is believed that it cannot now be far distant.

Though it would be manifestly beyond our province

ORGANIZATION AND DISCIPLINE. 353

to furnish an abstract of the Constitution, it may not be out of place to say a few words concerning the organization of the Reformed Church in the United States. In its general features it closely resembles that of the other Reformed Churches. The affairs of each congregation are committed to a consistory, consisting of the minister, elders, and deacons. The elders and deacons are elected for a term of years. The minister and elders constitute the "spiritual council," which attends to the reception and dismissal of members, exercises discipline, and has a general supervision over the spiritual interests of the congregation. In a few congregations there is a Board of Trustees which holds the property in the name of the congregation; but this arrangement has frequently caused trouble, and such matters are much better left in the hands of the Consistory. The ministers and one elder from each pastoral charge within a certain district constitute the Classis, which in its nature and functions closely resembles the Presbytery in the Presbyterian Churches. A certain number of delegates, clerical and lay, from each Classis within a specified district, constitute the Particular Synod, which meets annually. The number of delegates from each Classis is proportioned to the number of ministers which it includes. A Synod may meet in general convention, including all the ministers within its bounds, whenever it regards this as desirable, and has resolved to do so at a previous meeting.

There are at present eight Particular, or District. Synods, of which five are prevailingly English and three

German. The oldest of these is still known as "The Synod of the United States," though it has long since ceased to occupy a field as extensive as its title indicates. Out of its territory have been constituted the Pittsburg and Potomac Synods, and the German Synod of the East. In a similar way the Synod of Ohio, which once exercised supreme jurisdiction over the Reformed Churches of the West, has become the mother of the Synod of the North West and the Central Synod. Since 1863 the Particular Synods are under the supervision of the General Synod, which meets triennially, and is a court of the last resort in judicial cases. We need hardly add that our discipline is purely spiritual, and extends not only to the ministers, but to all the baptized members. The humblest member of the Church who feels aggrieved by the decision of an ecclesiastical body may carry his case by appeal or complaint to a higher court. The Reformed Church has always, in her standards, declared the necessity of excluding from her communion "those who by confession and life declare themselves infidels and ungodly," but at the same time guards with loving care the rights and privileges of the weakest of her children.

CULTUS.

Hymn-Books. The gradual awakening of the Church to a sense of its mission in this country brought with it an earnest desire for improvement in cultus, or worship. The "Neues und Verbessertes Gesangbuch" was now old, and the worthlessness of the "Gemeinschaftliches Gesangbuch" had become apparent. In some parts of the Church, congregational singing had almost become a "lost art." In many churches, after the reading of the entire hymn by the minister, each line was announced and sung separately, and frequently, it must be confessed, the minister and organist were almost the only persons in the congregation who audibly joined in singing. Occasionally the volume of sound was increased by the jingling of little bells, attached to alms-bags (*Klingelsäcke*) which were fastened to long poles and handed around by the deacons to receive the collection. An improvement in church-music was certainly eminently desirable; and the Synod of the United States accordingly, in 1841, appointed a committee to prepare an improved edition of the German hymn-book. The committee, however, proceeded to form a new collection, and the result of their labors was the publication, in 1842, of the "Sammlung Evangelischer Lieder," which was popularly known as the "Chambersburg Hymn-book." It was, unfortunately, hastily prepared, without proper familiarity with the principles of hymnology; and though extensively used for some years, it never gained a permanent place in the affections of the Church. The hymn-book which is at present in general use in our German churches was prepared in accordance with a resolution adopted in 1857 by the Synod of the United States. In consequence of certain difficulties concerning the place and terms of its publication, the book was issued as a private enterprise, in 1859, by the chairman of the committee, the Rev. Dr. Schaff, who had made the collection. Two years later, in 1861, it was formally adopted by the two Synods of the Reformed Church. It is generally recognized as a collection of the highest order.

In the English churches the hymn-book of the Reformed Protestant Dutch Church was at first generally used; but in 1830 the Synod adopted a collection known by the general title of "Psalms and Hymns," which had been made by a committee of the Maryland Classis. The appendix was added three years later. It was a very respectable collection, considering the time of its publication, and compared very favorably with those which were then in use in other denominations.

Within the past decade this book has been in great measure superseded by two collections, " Hymns for the Reformed Church" and "Reformed Church Hymnal," These were prepared after careful study of hymnologic sources, and, we believe, are fully accomplishing their purpose in promoting the devotion of the Church. Collections of music to accompany our hymn-books, both German and English, have also been published, and there is every indication that the Church is now taking a profound interest in the culture and development of sacred song.

Liturgies. Though the Reformed Church, during her entire history, has showed a marked preference for forms of worship which are simple and unpretentious, she has also insisted that everything should be done "decently and in order." In her religious services she has followed the general order of the Church-year, faithfully observing the great festivals of the Church, especially Christmas, Good Friday, Easter, Ascension Day and Pentecost. Her oldest liturgies date from the days of the earliest of the Reformers; and though in various European countries the forms of worship differed greatly, the desirability of having such offices for the guidance of the Church was never seriously questioned. In the administration of the sacraments, and other sacred rites, it was deemed especially important that the form of words should be settled by the Church; and the fact was generally recognized that divine ordinances may be easily, though perhaps unconsciously, profaned, when the manner of their administration is left to the individual tastes of the officiating minister.

In this country, as we have seen, the worship of the Reformed churches was at first conducted in general accordance with the Palatinate Liturgy, with which most of the pioneers had been familiar in Europe. This liturgy, however, needed thorough revision to render it suitable for permanent use in this country; and this, unfortunately, it did not receive. It was not re-printed in America, and after a while became quite rare. Then there came a time of great confusion in the ordering of public worship. Some ministers, in the performance of their official acts, employed the liturgies of various European countries, while others used manuscript collections of unknown origin, which had perhaps been given them by their preceptors at the beginning of their ministerial career. The practice of the churches of different sections of the country varied greatly even where the service was entirely "free," and the result was a general looseness in everything concerning ceremonial observance, that was universally deplored.

The first attempt to remedy the existing evil was the publication, in 1841, of a "Liturgy" prepared by the Rev. Dr. Lewis Mayer, as chairman of a committee appointed by the Eastern Synod. It was, in fact, simply a book of forms, for the use of ministers on special occasions. Though not without merit, it must be confessed that the "Mayer Liturgy" failed to meet the wants of the Church. It was, perhaps, too didactic to be acceptable either to ministers or people; but it should be remembered that it was prepared at a time when in this country but little attention had been given to liturgic study.

The general desire of the Church for a new liturgy soon began to find expression in various ways, and in 1848 was formally brought to the attention of the Eastern Synod by a request from the Classis of East Pennsylvania. The importance of the subject was fully appreciated, and in the following year, 1849, it was referred to a committee consisting of the most eminent men in the Church. In the hands of this committee the work of forming a new liturgy progressed but slowly, for difficulties presented themselves at almost every step of the way. There were differences of opinion with regard to the principles on which it was desirable that the liturgy should be constructed; but the committee persevered, under the instructions of Synod, and published, in 1857, the "Provisional Liturgy," which, from a literary point of view, was at once recognized as a work of a high order of excellence. According to its preface, it carried with it no "binding obligation," and was "put forth for the purpose of meeting and satisfying, if possible, what was believed to be a growing want of the Reformed Church." That the "Provisional Liturgy," with all its undeniable excellencies, did not meet the wants of the Church, soon became evident, and the question of its revision was brought to the attention of the Synod. This revision may be regarded as having been, in some measure, the occasion of the liturgic controversies which for many years occupied the attention of the Church. From another point of view they may, however, be regarded as a continuation of the doctrinal controversies to which we have already alluded. Though these conflicts were in many respects unfortunate, it cannot be doubted that the Church was roused by them to a high degree of literary activity. Even now, a member of any denomination who desires to become historically familiar with the subject of Christian cultus, cannot do better than to study the publications of the Reformed Church during this momentous epoch.

At the first meeting of the General Synod, in 1863, the Synod of Ohio received permission to prepare a liturgy, and the Eastern Synod was recommended to go forward in the work of revising the "Provisional Liturgy." In accordance with this resolution, the "Order of Worship" appeared in 1866, and the "Western Liturgy" in the following year. These works also appeared, with necessary modifications, in the German language. At last, in 1878, the General Synod committed all the questions which had been in controversy to a special commission, which was known as the "Peace Commission." In answer to the prayers of thousands, this commission was, with the blessing of Heaven, instrumental in restoring peace to the Church. As one of the results of its labors, it has published the "Directory of Worship," which was by the General Synod, held in Baltimore, Md., in 1884, submitted to the Classes for adoption or rejection. In 1887 it was formally adopted, and will now serve as the *normal* directory of worship, as its name indicates, but there will be no disposition to use it in an exclusive way. The Church will practically continue to occupy the position which it has held from the beginning. It will value and use its liturgy, but will in no way abridge the liberty which is the privilege of pastors and people.

It is a remarkable fact that notwithstanding all the sufferings which the Church endured during its reason of trial, it increased with remarkable rapidity. We have in 1884 three times as many ministers as we had in 1848, and the increase in our membership has at least maintained a corresponding proportion. We therefore recognize the hand of Providence in this period of our history, as we do in every other; and do not doubt that through all its troubles the Church was struggling upward to a higher stadium of religious life.

CHAPTER XVI.

Tercentenary Celebration—General Synod—Conclusion.

THE year 1863 was in many respects the most brilliant in our denominational history. Though it occurred in the midst of a dreadful civil war, when the Church might have been expected to languish rather than to prosper, the fact remains that there was at this time a remarkable development in every department of Christian activity. In the Tercentenary Celebration we have the proper conclusion of the formative period of our American ecclesiastical history; in the establishment of the General Synod we behold the beginning of an epoch of growth and advancement which has not yet reached its highest comsummation.

THE TERCENTENARY CELEBRATION.

The earliest suggestion with respect to the propriety of celebrating the 300th anniversary of the formation and adoption of the Heidelberg Catechism, was offered in 1857, by the Rev. Dr. H. Harbaugh, in the first volume of his "Lives of the Fathers." Two years later the suggestion was renewed by the Rev. Dr. P. Schaff, at a meeting of the Classis of Mercersburg, and being sent up to Synod in the form of a request, was by that body referred to a committee, of which the Rev. Dr.

Harbaugh was chairman. The plan as elaborated by this committee was comprehensive beyond anything the Church had hitherto attempted. The celebration was to be, first of all, "a sublime festal service to God;"

HENRY HARBAUGH.

but it also demanded that the Church should throw its devout, joyous, and zealous energies into all it proposed to do during the festival year. It involved the holding of a Convention on the 19th of January, 1863; the enrollment of all the members of the Church, and the reception of memorial free-will offerings from those who desired to present them; and the preparation and publication of several important volumes having special reference to the celebration.

The Convention by which the Year of Jubilee was inaugurated, met on the evening of the 17th of January, in the historic church on Race street, below Fourth, Philadelphia, of which the Rev. Dr. J. H. A. Bomberger was then pastor, and continued in session six days. The Rev. Dr. J. W. Nevin was elected President, and the Rev. Dr. S. R. Fisher and L. H. Steiner, M. D., served as Secretaries. Original essays on subjects connected with the history and doctrines of the Heidelberg Catechism, contributed by some of the most eminent divines in Europe and America, were read before the convention and afterwards discussed. The European contributors were the Rev. Drs. C. H. Hundeshagen, of Heidelberg; J. J. Herzog and J. H. A. Ebrard, both of Erlangen; C. Ullmann, of Carlsruhe, and G. D. J. Schotel, of Leyden, Holland. Essays were also read by the following ministers of the Church in this country: B. S. Schneck, T. C. Porter, H. Harbaugh, Theodore Appel, Thos. G. Apple, M. Kieffer, E. V. Gerhart, G. B. Russell, D. Gans, B. Bausman, J. H. A. Bomberger, B. C. Wolff, and Thos. De Witt, of the Reformed Dutch Church, New York. The convention was large and enthusiastic, and was in every respect a fitting introduction to the joys and labors of the year.

Inspired with zeal, the pastors and delegates returned home, and proceeded to inaugurate Tercentenary festivals in the several churches. By the co-operation of the Eastern and Western Synods, the celebration became general, and many a church was decked with green and decorated with symbols which indicated the nature of the festival. The people learned more concerning the Church of their fathers than they had ever heard before, and their affections were naturally more warmly enlisted in its behalf. The enrollment of members was pretty general, and liberal gifts to benevolent causes were in many instances spontaneously offered. It had been feared by many that the enrollment would in many sections be unfavorably regarded, but these anticipations of evil were not realized. Men, women, and children, were pleased to know that they were individually recognized by the Church, and reflected with satisfaction on the fact that their names would be recorded with her membership in the Year of Jubilee.

The Tercentenary free-will offerings, as reported in the following year, amounted to $108,125.98 from the Eastern Synod alone. This amount would have been regarded as respectable in any American denomination, but in the Reformed Church it was an immense advance on everything that had preceded it, and it need hardly be said that it gave a renewed impetus to every enterprise of Christian benevolence.

Literary activity characterized the Tercentenary year in a remarkable degree. The Tercentenary edition of the Heidelberg Catechism, generally known as the "Triglot," was prepared by a committee of which the

Rev. E. V. Gerhart, D. D., was chairman. It contains, besides a valuable historical introduction, the standard text of the Catechism in Old German, Latin, Modern German, and English, printed in parallel columns. The book was issued in excellent style, by Scribner, of New York, and is probably the finest edition of the Catechism ever published.[1]

The Tercentenary Monument, a large volume containing the Proceedings of the Tercentenary Convention and the essays read on the occasion, was published by M. Kieffer & Co., in English and German. It is a great storehouse of valuable materials, and is still deserving of careful study.

It was also proposed to publish a "Digest of the Minutes," but this work still remains a *desideratum*. A book of this kind, in which all the decisions of our Synods, from the beginning, might be found arranged for ready reference, would manifestly be of great value. Renewed attention has recently been directed to the subject, and it is hoped the "Digest" will be speedily completed. "The Historical Society of the Reformed Church" was organized in accordance with a resolution of the Tercentenary Convention. It has succeeded in accumulating a library of considerable value, but has not received the sympathy and support which it evidently deserves.

Other subjects to which the attention of the Church

---

[1] As a preparation for this work, an edition of the Catechism in Latin was published in 1852 by Dr. L. H. Steiner, a member of the committee.

was specially directed during the Tercentenary year were the organization of the Board of Church Extension —for the purpose of aiding struggling congregations in the work of erecting church-buildings—the founding of Orphan Homes, the extension of the work of the Boards of Publication, and, last but not least, the organization of the General Synod. The formal conclusion of the festival season was the Convention held in Reading, Pa., from the 21st to the 25th of May, 1864. This body was mainly occupied in summing up the work of the year, but at the same time offered valuable suggestions concerning future growth and advancement. The results of the Tercentenary Celebration may even now be regarded with unmingled satisfaction. It may, indeed, be said that in the most inclement season of our national history our Church put forth the blossoms whose ripening fruit we are now beginning to enjoy.

THE GENERAL SYNOD.

The first meeting of the General Synod in Grace Church, Pittsburg, Pa., on the 18th of November, 1863, certainly constitutes an important era in the history of the Reformed Church. It is chiefly owing to this event that the German branch of the Reformed Church in this country, instead of being broken up into a number of "asteroidal fragments," as they have been called by an eminent divine, has become a single organized body which, if not one of the largest denominations, at any rate holds an honorable position for numbers and influence among the churches of the land.

The manner in which the General Synod came to exist was somewhat remarkable. There had been, since 1844, a Triennial Convention composed at first of delegates from the Reformed Dutch Church and the two German Reformed Synods. The functions of this body were purely advisory. There was, indeed, an understanding concerning coöperation in the work of Domestic Missions, but it does not seem to have led to important practical results. The Reformed Dutch Church having withdrawn from the Convention after its second meeting, it was, at the suggestion of the Synod of Ohio, continued in a somewhat modified form by the two German Reformed bodies. Various plans were suggested for the strengthening of the bond, until at last in a happy hour it was proposed that it should be replaced by a General Synod. The subject was in 1860, referred to the Classes, with many misgivings as to the result; but the awakening enthusiasm of the Church for the approaching Tercentenary carried the measure by a large majority. It was recognized as essential to the development and prosperity of the Church, and subsequent history has abundantly proved the wisdom of the decision.

Change of Title. In the annals of the colonial period the name of the Church rarely appears. Individual congregations were called "Evangelical Reformed" or only "Reformed," and the ecclesiastical body was known simply as "The Coetus of Pennsylvania." On the organization of the Synod a more distinctive title became necessary, and for the purpose of distinguishing it from the Reformed Dutch Church, the term "German Reformed" was introduced. As long as the German language was solely employed in public worship, the name had a certain practical value, though it was recognized as unhistorical; but as the use of English became more general, its influence was felt to be too limiting and repressive. It was argued that the word "German," as used in the official title, had a tendency to retard the growth of the church in English communities, while it could have no special value for the German churches, inasmuch as their language sufficiently indicated their national origin. On the other hand, there were many excellent people who were loath to part with a name which had become endeared to them by many years of use, and which was so suggestive of an honored ancestry. An effort was made to substitute the word "Evangelical" for "German," but it proved a failure. The question of the omission or retention of "the foreign patrial adjective" caused, for some years, considerable discussion in both branches of the Reformed Church, but was finally decided by both in the same way. The German Reformed Church is now the "*Reformed Church in the United States*," and the Reformed Dutch Church is the "*Reformed Church in America*," a difference in title we conceive to be purely accidental. The most recent conference of committees on the subject of the organic union of these two branches of the Reformed Church was held in Philadelphia on the 2d of April 1888, and the prospects of ultimate union now appear exceedingly promising. The chief obstacle in the way of union has hitherto been the difference in doctrinal standards to which we have already referred.

The Peace Commission. The labors of the commission to which, under the blessing of God, was committed the work of restoring peace to the churches, which had been greatly disturbed by the long controversies which we have mentioned, have proved so eminently successful that they should always be remembered with heartfelt gratitude. The report presented by this Commission to the General Synod convened in Tiffin, Ohio, in 1881, and then unanimously adopted, is in our opinion a document of great historical and doctrinal importance. It deserves, we think, to be rescued from the comparative obscurity of the files of the Minutes of Synod, and to be placed within easy reference of ministers and members of the church, by whom it should be frequently and carefully studied. The report is as follows:

" *To the General Synod of the Reformed Church in the United States:*

FATHERS AND BROTHERS IN THE LORD:—The Commission authorized by the action of the General Synod at Lancaster, Pennsylvania, A. D., 1878, and constituted by the concurrent act of the six District Synods, in the spirit and interest of the original action, met and organized in Harrisburg, Pennsylvania, on the 26th day of November, A. D., one thousand eight hundred and seventy-nine, as directed:

The weighty matters entrusted to its solemn and prayerful deliberation by the Church, were considered during the period of eight days; and after having arrived at a unanimous result, under the manifest guidance of the Spirit of Truth, the Commission adjourned.

Your Commissioners, in now most respectfully reporting their action to your reverend body for adoption, venture to express the hope that a like unanimity may characterize its endorsement of the same, as a basis to a solid and endurable peace.

In order to the restoration and maintenance of "the unity of the Spirit in the bond of peace, as one body and one spirit, even as we are called in one hope of our calling, one Lord, one Faith, one Baptism, one God and Father of all, who is above all, and through all, and in all" (Eph., iv. 3–6), "it seemed good unto us, being assembled with one accord" (Acts, xv. 55), in the light vouchsafed to us of God, to subscribe to the following:

I. DOCTRINE.

The Reformed Church in the United States unites in the confession of her adherence to the doctrines of the Holy Scriptures as set forth in the Heidelberg Catechism, taking the same in its historical (or original) sense; and declares that any departure from the same is unauthorized by the Church; and renewedly directs all her ministers, editors and teachers of theology, "faithfully to preach and defend the same."

This action is not to be so construed as to forbid, or interfere with, that degree of freedom in Scriptural and theological investigation which has always been enjoyed in the Reformed Church.

In presenting the above as a basis for peace in the Church, we are not unmindful of the fact that more than this might be expected. We believe that the theological contest that has gone forward in our Church for over a quarter of a century, with earnestness and zeal, has resulted, now that it has substantially come to a close as we hope, in bringing the Church to a deeper apprehension of the truth. It would seem proper, therefore, that an attempt should be made to summarize, in some general way, this result. We, therefore, submit the following, as embodying certain points on which this Commission is able to harmonize, and thus contribute towards a substantial agreement throughout the whole Church in the peace period upon which we are now entering:

I. We recognize in Jesus Christ and His sacrifice for fallen man, the foundation and source of our whole salvation.

II. We hold that the Christian life is begotten in us by the Word of God, which is ever living, and carries in itself the power to quicken faith and love in the heart, through the Holy Ghost.

III. We do not regard the visible Church as commensurate and identical with the invisible Church, according to the Roman theory, nor do we think that in this world the invisible Church can be separated from the visible, according to the theory of Pietism and false Spiritualism; but while we do not identify them, we do not, in our views, separate them.

IV. We hold that in the use of the holy sacraments the grace signified by the outward signs is imparted to those who truly believe, but that those who come to these holy sacraments without faith, receive only the outward elements unto condemnation.

V. We have come to a clearer apprehension of the fact that the Christian life is something broader and deeper than its manifestations in conscious experience.

VI. We hold the doctrine of justification through true faith in Jesus Christ, according to which only the satisfaction, holiness and righteousness of Christ is our righteousness before God, and that we can not receive and apply the same to ourselves in any other way than by faith only.

VII. We hold the doctrine of the ministerial office, according to which the ministers of the Church are not lords of faith, but servants, messengers, heralds, watchmen of Christ, co-workers with God, preachers of the Word, and stewards of the mysteries of God.

VIII. We hold the doctrine of the universal priesthood of believers over against all Romanizing tendencies to priestly power, while we also assert the proper recognition of the ministerial office in the Church of Christ.

IX. We affirm our confidence in the truth of Protestantism over against the errors of Rome on the one hand, and against the errors of rationalism and infidelity on the other.

X. All philosophical and theological speculations (in the Church) should be held in humble submission to the Word of God, which, with its heavenly light, should illumine and guide the operations and researches of reason.

II. CULTUS.

With reference to cultus, we recommend to the General Synod, at its next regular meeting, the inauguration of measures for the formation of a committee properly representing the different Synods and the various theological tendencies existing in the Church, whose duty it shall be to prepare an Order of Worship, containing such offices as may be required for the services of the Church, the said committee to report the result of its labors, as soon as their magnitude and importance will allow, to the General Synod for approval and adoption, as required by the Constitution of the Reformed Church in the United States.

And we recommend further, that pending the adoption of such Order of Worship, the various Liturgies now in use in the Church be allowed in public worship, provided none of them be hereafter introduced into any congregation without the consent of a majority of its communicant members, nor when (in the judgment of the pastor and Consistory), such introduction would be injurious to the best interests of the congregation; and that, until the Church shall adopt a new hymn-book for the use of all its congregations, any of the hymn-books now approved by one or more of the District Synods, may be used by any particular congregation in public worship.

III. GOVERNMENT.

With reference to Government we recommend:

1. That all the judicatories of the Church be requested, in the appointment of their Boards and Committees, to pay regard only to fitness for the position.

2. That the General Synod, as soon as it sees its way clear and the general peace and quietude of the Church sufficiently established, take the proper steps for a thorough revision of its Constitution, Rules, and By-laws, in order:

(*a*) To create a more perfect organic relation between the different judicatories of the Church, completing themselves in their head, the General Synod.

(*b*) To provide for a supervision by the General Synod over all the theological institutions of the Church, by the appointment of a duly authorized Committee or Board of Visitors, empowered at any time, when deemed necessary, to examine into the doctrine, cultus, and management of said institutions, and to report to each session of the General Synod; said Board of Visitors, however, not to interfere with any arrangement or authority of the respective District Synods, or their boards or committees.

(*c*) To provide some mode by which all cases of appeal, involving only facts and individual disputes, shall be excluded from the General Synod, so that such only as relate to controversies on doctrine, cultus, and constitutional construction may be brought for a final hearing before that body.

And we recommend further, that the General Synod be requested to direct the attention of the Church at large to the importance of an undivided effort for her extension, and to engage diligently and zealously in the work of Missions, looking forward to a more concentrated and co-operative action in that direction in the future.

In testimony whereof we, the Commissioners, representing the different Synods of the Reformed Church in the United States, hereunto subscribe our names, at Harrisburg, Pennsylvania, this third day of December, in the year of our Lord one thousand eight hundred and seventy-nine.

Ministers.	Elders.	Synods.
CLEMENT Z. WEISER,	DANIEL W. GROSS,	Synod in the United States.
THOMAS G. APPLE,	WILLIAM H. SEIBERT,	
FRANKLIN W. KREMER,	RUDOLPH F. KELKER,	
JEREMIAH H. GOOD,	ANDREW H. BAUGHMAN,	Synod of Ohio.
LEWIS H. KEFAUVER,	BENJAMIN KUHNS,	
HERMAN J. RUETENIK,	FREDERICK W. SCHEELE,	Synod of the Northwest.
PETER GREDING,	HENRY TONS,	
JOHN M. TITZEL,	CHRISTIAN M. BOUSH,	Synod of Pittsburg.
JOSEPH H. APPLE,	THOMAS J. CRAIG,	
SAMUEL N. CALLENDER,	HENRY WIRT,	Synod of the Potomac.
G. WILLIAM WELKER,	LEWIS H. STEINER.	
JOHN KUELLING,	WILLIAM D. GROSS,	German Syn. of the East."

We are not surprised that on the adoption of this

report—so fraught with blessings to the churches—the General Synod rose to its feet and sang with one voice the grand old doxology: "Praise God from whom all blessings flow!"

Alliance of Reformed Churches. At the meetings of the "Alliance of the Reformed Churches holding the Presbyterian system," convened in Philadelphia in 1880, and in Belfast, Ireland, in 1884, the Reformed Church in the United States was well represented. On these occasions papers were read by several of our ministers. The Alliance includes delegates from most of the Reformed Churches throughout the world, and will no doubt accomplish great good, not only in bringing nearer together the scattered members of the same historical confession, but in promoting the great cause of Christian unity.

Zwingli Festivals. The year 1884 was rendered memorable in many Reformed Churches, by the celebration of the 400th anniversary of the birth of the Reformer, Ulric Zwingli. These delightful festivals are still fresh in the memory of our readers, so that we need not enlarge upon them. It will be remembered how the people on these occasions thronged the churches, and listened with delighted attention to the fascinating story of the Swiss hero. The Providence of God, as illustrated in the continued existence of the Church in whose early history Zwingli occupies so prominent a position, filled many Christian hearts with responsive gratitude. It is indeed, marvelous that the natal-day of a man who was born before the discovery of America, in an obscure village of an obscure land, should still be enthusiastically celebrated. It illustrates the dying words of that great man in a manner which he never anticipated: "They may kill the body, but they cannot kill the soul!"

CONCLUSION.

When a weary pilgrim approaches the end of his journey, he finds it pleasant to rest awhile on some commanding eminence, and to look back over the road on which he has traveled. He does not forget his toils and trials, but it is with special pleasure that he remembers the clear fountains and shady groves which refreshed him by the way. So, when we contemplate the history of the Reformed Church in the United States, we behold some things which we regret, but there are more which call for devout gratitude. It is not without pain that we recall the "lost churches;" that we remember how in great cities and extensive districts of country, where our Church was once hopefully founded, it is now almost unknown. When we contemplate the immense work which, as a Christian denomination, we are especially called to perform, we think it would have been better if so many of our brethren had not departed from us in our days of trial. The larger denominations, with which they generally became identified, could have flourished without them, while in the Church of their fathers they might have accomplished a grand and glorious work. It is, however, pleasant to know that, in some instances at least, the fields which were once ours are well cultivated, though not by the descendants of those who reclaimed them from the wilderness.

> "Yes! Though a stranger must receive them,
> For blessings still to Heaven we call;
> Thy dews, O Lord! Thy rain and sunshine,
> In Thine own season, grant them all!"

We profoundly regret that in the Reformed Church in the United States so many years elapsed before the importance of the work of missions was properly appreciated; and that, even now, we fall short of our duty in this respect. Hundreds of churches have been formed out of our material by other denominations; and this work is still going on, especially among the recent immigrants from the Fatherland. No one is able to do this work as well as we, who are already allied to this people by the ties of kindred and a common faith. It is, therefore, not only the duty but the privilege of every minister and member of the Reformed Church to labor with might and main in the work to which we appear to be especially called. It has been said that the destinies of the world are in the hands of those who labor. If we were as earnest, active, and laborious as we ought to be, it would be easy to extend our borders, and at the same time to bring a new tribute to our blessed Lord.

While we regret the errors of the past, we are profoundly grateful for the blessings we have enjoyed. Our forefathers came to this country poor exiles, many of them dependent for a time upon the bounty of strangers.

Earlier settlers had generally chosen land which was easily cleared, so that the Germans were compelled to attack the forests which occupied the interior of the country. The result proved that the soil which had sustained great trees was best suited for agricultural purposes, but who can form an adequate conception of the toil and privation which the task of clearing it involved? For years the Germans dwelt in comparative solitude, exposed to the attacks of hostile savages. Industry and economy made them rich, and the descendants of the poor " Palatines " have come to enjoy a degree of temporal prosperity of which their fathers never dreamed.

When the German pioneers began to erect their little forest chapels, the churches of New England had already enjoyed a prosperous history of more than a hundred years; and even in Pennsylvania several English denominations, though considerably more recent, were firmly established. The Germans, as we have seen, had few traditions in common. Those of them who belonged to the Reformed Church had been members of the established churches of several European countries, and had not been trained to habits of Christian benevolence. Years passed before they could be moulded to a compact body, and it was much longer till they acquired the denominational spirit which in this country is necessary to prosperity, if not essential to continued existence. It is, however, a remarkable fact that since the establishment of its Theological Seminaries, the Reformed Church has grown with unexampled rapidity. In the past twenty-five years the numbers of its ministry and membership have more than doubled. But this is not all. The prominent position taken by the Reformed Church in Theologic science during this period has been very generally acknowledged, and we are but repeating the words of a distinguished divine[1] of a sister denomination when we say, that "there is no church in the land which has produced a larger number of well-trained theologians."

What now is our prospect for future growth and advancement? We answer that it was never so promising as it is to-day. The Reformed Church is no more to be regarded as foreign or provincial, and her doctrines need only to be known to be commended. Her firmness in the maintenance of Christian truth, conjoined with the abundant charity with which she regards all other branches of the Church of Christ, cannot fail to gain responsive sympathy. With her glorious history, her broad but comprehensive standards of faith, and her simple but devout worship, there is surely no reason why multitudes of wanderers should not accept from the Reformed Church the home which she so freely offers.

The work of Missions, which has already proved so successful, is hardly more than begun. It has, indeed, been asserted that the number of members of the Reformed Church who are scattered like lost sheep throughout the vast expanse of our country is greater than that

---

[1] The late Rev. Dr. C. P. Krauth, in conversation with the author.

of those who have already been gathered into her congregations. English and German churches might readily be established in many places if we could supply them with pastors and had means to sustain them for a few years, until they become strong enough to help themselves and others. Our efforts in behalf of the French, Bohemians, Hungarians and Russians, many of whom are members of our Church, have hitherto been imperfect and unsatisfactory, but among all these nationalities there is room for successful labor. " The harvest truly is great, but the laborers are few: pray ye therefore the Lord of the harvest that He would send forth laborers into His harvest."

It is a precious privilege to be a member of the Church whose fortunes we have attempted to delineate. " Noble descent," it has been said, " should be a pledge of exalted deeds." When the children of the Reformed Church become familiar with her brilliant history, when they sincerely love the truth for which the martyrs died, can they fail to be moved to deeds of high and holy activity?

One of the most ancient emblems of the Reformed Church represents a lily blooming in the midst of thorns. Even in the history of the Church in the United States the truth which it conveys has been fully exemplified. Through trials innumerable she is gradually coming forth into the sunlight and putting forth beautiful flowers. There will be troubles in the future as in the past, but He who has preserved us hitherto will guide us safely to the end.

APPENDIX.

1. NECROLOGY.
2. MEETINGS OF SYNODS.
3. COMPARATIVE STATISTICS.

NECROLOGY.

1709-1885.

ABBREVIATIONS: B. or b., signifies born; d., died; ed., educated; stud., studied; Grad., graduated; col., college; Theol. Sem., Theological Seminary; ab., about; lic., licensed; ord., ordained; past., pastor; miss., missionary or mission; sup., supply or supplied; ch. or chg., church or charge; Cl., classis; Syn., synod; w. c., without charge; Ref. D., Reformed Dutch; Presb., Presbyterian, or presbytery; P. E., Protestant Episcopal; M. Col., Marshall College; F. and M. Col., Franklin and Marshall College; Heid. Col., Heidelberg College; Ger., Germany; Switz.. Switzerland. Other abbreviations will, we think, be readily understood. Variations in the orthography of surnames are given in brackets.

JOHN ACKERET, b. Canton of Thurgau, Switz., Feb. 22, 1824; d. Millersburg, O., Sept. 13, 1869. Lic. 1849; ord. 1850. Past. Mount Eaton chg., C., 1850-'69.

JOHN D. ADAMS, b. Hesse, Ger. Past. Sunbury, Pa., Middle Creek, etc., 1808-ab. 1813. Deposed 1813.

CHARLES H. ALBERT, b. Lehigh co., Pa., 1824; d. Texas, 1869. Grad. M. C., 1848. Theol. Sem., Mercersbnrg, 1851. Lic. 1851; ord. 1852. Pres. Catawba Col., N. C. Entered P. E. Ch. Author of " Youth's Phantasies," Chambersburg, 1847.

JOHN E. ALBERT, b. 17—; d. York Springs, Pa., 1856. Lic. ab. 1818; ord. ab. 1819. Past. St. John's ch., York co., and Zion and Salem, in Adams co., Pa., 1819-'32.

GEORGE M. ALBRIGHT, b. Maytown, Lancaster co., Pa., April 3, 1829; d. New Lisbon, O., Feb. 22, 1879. Theol. Sem., Lancaster. Lic. 1861; ord. 1864. Allen co. mission, O., 1864-'66. Past. Tarlton chg. 1866-'68; New Lisbon, O., 1863-'77; Wilton chg., Iowa, 1877-'78.

JACOB ALLEBORN, lic. 1844, "Free Syn." Miss., Kensington and Rising Sun, 1837; Bath, Pa., 1838. Name erased, 1843.

CHARLES L. A. ALLARDT, received 1833, West Penn. Cl. from Europe. Past. 1834, Columbiana co., Ohio; then at Cleveland and Delaware, O. Name disappears from minutes, 1845.

JOHN GEORGE ALSENTZ, b. Palatinate, Ger.; d, Montgomery co., Pa., 1769. Ed. at Heidelberg. Ord. by Synods of Holland. Came to America 1757. Past. Germantown, Pa., 1758-'62; Wentz's, Boehm's etc., Montgomery co., Pa., 1762-'69. Sup. Amwell, N. J , 1760.

NECROLOGY. 383

J. B. ALTERMATT, stud. Freiburg, Switz. Received minor orders in R. C. Church. Member of Cl. of Erie, 1843, and past. at Sheldon, N. Y.

JOHN ALTHOUSE (*Althaus*), lic. Free Syn., 1825; ord. 1826. Past. Indiana, Armstrong, Jefferson, and Clearfield cos., Pa., 1826-'45; Niagara and Erie cos., N. Y., and Black Creek, Canada, 1845.

WILLIAM AMDYKE (*Amdicken*), lic. and ord., Cl. of E. Pa., 1821. Past. Huntingdon co., Pa., 1826. Without charge, 1834.

HENRY ANTES, b. 1701, probably at Freinsheim, Rhenish Bavaria; died, Frederick twp., Montgomery co., Pa., July 20, 1755. See p. 190.

JOHN ARDUESER, b. Graubünden, Switz., 1844; d. May 17, 1874. Ed. as a schoolmaster. Taught in Italy. Came to America, 1866. Stud. Theol. Inst. of the Evangelical Synod of the N. W., 1868. Lic. 1869, Syn. of Ohio. Ord. by Iowa Cl. Past. Plainfield and Charles City, Iowa, 1869-'71 ; Linton, Ind., 1871-'72. Died while on a visit to Switzerland.

JOHN AULT, b. Annville, Lebanon co., Pa., April 1, 1836; d. Littlestown, Pa., July 26, 1880. F. and M. Col., 1857; Theol. Sem., Mercersburg, 1858. Lic. 1858, Cl. of Lebanon; ord. 1858, Cl. of Zion. Past. Trindle Spring chg., 1858-'59; Loudon and St. Thomas, 1859-'63; Mechanicsburg, Pa., 1863'-73; Christ ch., Littlestown, etc., 1873-'80. Author of several historical pamphlets.

HENRY AURAND, b. Reading, Pa., Oct. 4, 1806; d. Lena, Stephenson co., Ill., Oct. 8, 1876. Stud. Dickinson Col. and Princeton Theol. Sem. Sup. Presb. ch., Taneytown, Md., 1833-'34. Pastor Ref. ch., Carlisle, Pa., 1834-'49. Afterwards at Sulphur Springs, New Berlin, New York City, and Columbia, Herkimer co., N. Y. Removed to Illinois, sup. Astoria, Fulton Co., and other vacant charges.

JOHN DIETRICH AURANDT, b. Maiden Creek, Berks co., Pa., Nov. 8, 1760; d. Huntingdon co. Pa., April 24, 1831. Soldier in the Revolution, 1778-'81. For many years engaged in secular employments. Licensed to exhort by " United Brethren in Christ." Applied to Synod U. S. for licensure, 1801 ; but directed to prosecute his studies. Lic. 1806; and ord. 1809. Past. Buffalo Valley; Huntingdon co., 1804-'30.

DOMINICUS BARTHOLOMAEUS, came to America, 1748. Past. Tulpehocken, 1748-'57. For several years a great sufferer. In 1759 Coetus made an appropriation for his relief.

HENRY S. BASSLER, b. Lower Milford, Lehigh co., Pa., Aug. 11, 1804; d. Millersburg, Pa., Feb. 17, 1883. Preceptor, Rev. J. W. Dechant. Theol. Sem., Carlisle, Pa., 1827-'29. Lic. by Synod U. S., 1829. Past. Beaver Dam, Snyder co., 1829-'33; Hilltown, Bucks co., etc., 18 3-'43 ; Lykens Valley, 1843-'51 ; Millerstown, Lehigh co., etc., 1851-'54; Lykens Valley (second time), 1854-'56; Pleasant Grove, Ind , 1856-'58; Forreston, Ill., 1858-'59 ; Berrysburg, Pa., 1859-'65; Zionsville, Lehigh co., Pa., 1865-'71 ; Hegins, 1871-'77.

JOHN BAUMUNK, b. Reichenbach, Hesse-Darmstadt, Ger., Feb. 15, 1824; died Indianapolis, Ind., Sept. 16, 1857. Came to Penna. with his parents, 1837. Preceptor, Rev. J. G. Zahner, D. D. Lic. and ord., Miami Cl., 1852. Pastor Poland, O., 1852; Millville, O., 1852 ; Seymour, Jackson co., Iowa, 1856.

JOHN AD. BAYER, b. in Rhine Bavaria. Recd. by West Pa. Cl., 1831. Past Youngstown, 1831-'33; Meadville, 1833- ab. '36; Dansville, N. Y., ab. 1836-'44; Fort Wayne, Ind., 1845.

JACOB BEAR (*Baer*), b. —, Pa., Mar. 4, 1810; d. West Point, Iowa, Feb. 1, 1855. Theol. Sem., 1835. Lic. and ord. 1836. Past. Spring Mills, Centre co., Pa., 1830.

Oxford, Adams co., 1837; Shanesville, O., 1840; West Point, Lee co. Ia., ab. 1846-'55.

FREDERICK BECHER, b. Ger., —. Past. Shrewsbury, York co., Pa., 1836; Wilkesbarre, 1838; later at Bloomfield, Perry co. Name disappears from minutes, 1840.

JOHN BECHTEL, b. Bergstrasse, Pal., Ger., Oct. 3, 1690; d. Bethlehem, Pa., Apr. 16, 1777. Came to Pa., 1726. Began to preach irregularly at Germantown, Pa., in 1728; regularly called, 1733. In 1742 ord. a Reformed minister in the "Congregation of God in the Spirit." See page 194.

JOHN BECK, D. D., b. York, Pa., Apr. 10, 1830; d. Easton, Pa., Apr. 19, 1877. M. C., 1848; Theol. Sem., Mercersburg, 1850. Lic. by Synod, 1850; ord. same year, by Maryland Cl. Past. Funkstown, Md., 1850-'54; Easton, Pa., 1854-'77. President of Synod U. S. at the time of his death.

CHRISTIAN LUDWIG BECKER, D. D., b. Anhalt Cöthen, Ger., Nov. 17, 1756; d. Baltimore, Md., July 12, 1818. Stud. at Cöthen and Halle. *Candidatus Theologiæ*, Bremen, 1779-'93. Published sermons and theological works. Came to America, 1793. Ord. 1794. Past. Easton, etc., 1794-'95; Lancaster, Pa., 1795-1806; Baltimore, Md., 1806-'18. Author of "Sammlung Geistreicher Predigten," Baltimore, 1810.

JACOB CHRISTIAN BECKER, D. D., son of the preceding; b. Bremen, Ger., Jan. 14, 1790; d. Bethlehem, Pa., Aug. 18, 1858. Came to America with his parents, 1793. Stud. Franklin Col., Lancaster, and with his father. Lic. and ord., Syn. U. S., 1808. Past. Manchester, Md., 1808-'11; Allen, Moore, etc., Northampton co., Pa., 1811-'58. See page 287.

JACOB BEECHER, b. near Petersburg, Adams co., Pa., May 2, 1799; d. Shepherdstown, Va., July 15, 1831. Grad. Jefferson Col., Canonsburg, Pa., 1824. Theol. Sem., Princeton, N. J. Lic. and ord., Synod U. S., 1826. Pastor Shepherdstown, Martinsburg, and Smithfield, Va., 1826-'31. See page 283.

AUGUSTUS L. W. BEGEMAN, b. Bremerhöhe, Hanover, Ger., July 14, 1810; d. Columbus, O., Sept. 4, 1848. Stud. Gymnasium of Emden. Read Theol. privately in Germany and Holland. Came to America, 1833. French teacher at Washington Col., Pa., 1833-'34. Lic. and ord., Classis of West Pa., 1834. Past. Washington co., Pa., 1834-'36; Orangeville, O., 1836-'40; Wooster, O., 1840-'43; Columbus, O., 1843-'45; Mansfield, O., 1845-'47.

FREDERICK P. BEIDLER. Stud M. C. Miss., Patton, Mo., 1850. Entered Ref. D. Ch., 1854. Past. South Bend, Ind., 1854-'55.

WILLIAM CROSBY BENNET, b. Long Island, N. Y., Apr. 14, 1804; d. Boiling Springs, Cumberland co., Pa., April 12, 1870. Theol. Sem., York. Lic. and ord., Syn. U. S., 1832. Miss. to North and South Carolina, 1832-'34. Past. Davidson co., N. C., 1834-'37; Shippensburg, Pa., 1837-'39; Newville, Lisbon, etc., 1839-'44; East Berlin and Oxford, 1844-'46. Sup. churches in Cumberland co., Pa., 1846-'49; Liverpool, Perry co., 1849; Cumberland co., 1849-'50. Agt. for church periodicals 1854-'70.

CHRISTIAN BERENTZ, b. Baltimore, Md., ab. 1794; d. Grandview, Washington co., O., March 23, 1879. Lic. and ord., Synod U. S., 1829. Past. Johnstown, etc., Pa., 1829-'42. Removed 1842 to Hillsboro, Highland co., O., and then to Grandview. Without regular pastoral charge, but made extensive missionary journeys.

JOSEPH F. BERG, D. D., b. June 3, 1812, Antigua, West Indies, where his

NECROLOGY.

parents were Moravian missionaries; d. New Brunswick, N. J., July 20, 1871. Stud. in England aud at "Moravian Seminary." Called to the pastorate of Salem's Reformed church, Harrisburg, 1835. Lic. and ord., Synod U. S., 1836. Past. Harrisburg, Pa., 1836. Prof. of Ancient Languages, M. Col., 1836-'37. Past. First Ref. ch., Phila., 1837-'52. Entered Ref. D. Church. Past. at Seventh and Brown sts., Phila., and Prof. in the Theol. Sem., New Brunswick, N. J. Editor of "Protestant Quarterly," and author of "Chiistian Landmarks," etc.

ABRAHAM BERKY (*Berge*), b. Pa., 1806; d. New York City, Aug. 1, 1867. Lic., Free Synod of Pa., 1828; ord. by the same body, 1830. Past. Flatland, etc., Bucks co., Pa., 1830-'34. Agt. for Sunday-school Union, 1834. Past. Berks co., Pa.; Northampton co.; Wilkesbarre, Pa.; Hilltown, Pa.; Dansville, N. Y.; Rochester, N. Y.; Detroit, Michigan. Dismissed to Ref. D. Ch., 1852. Pastor 2d Ger. Ref. D. ch., New York city, 1872-'65. .

HERMAN BEUSSEL, b. Germany, 1820; d. Williamsburg, N. Y., Aug. 13, 1849. Stud. Mission Institute, Langenberg, near Elberfeld, Prussia. Lic. and ord., Cl. of N. Y., 1848. Past. Williamsburg, N. Y., 1848-'49.

HENRY BIBIGHAUS, D. D., b. Bedminster, Bucks co. Pa., Aug. 2, 1777; d. Phila., Aug. 20, 1851. Organist and teacher, Lehigh co., and afterwards in Race St. congregation, Phila. Preceptor, Dr. Samuel Helfenstein. Lic. and ord., "Free Synod," 1824. Past. Salem's ch., Phila., 1824-'51.

FREDERICK W. BINDEMAN, b. Germany. Preceptor, Rev. J. W. Dechant. Lic., Synod U. S., 1824. Ord. ab. 1825. Past. Hanover, Christ ch., and Lischy's, York co., Pa., 1826. Susp. 1827. Deposed 1828.

JOHN BIPPUS, b. Boll, Würtemberg, Ger., June 2, 1815; d. Leesville, O., May 21, 1872. Came to America, 1837. Lic. and ord., Tiffin Cl., 1864. Past. Galion, O., 1864-'68.

BITTHAHN. See *Pithan*.

JAMES BLACK, Presbyterian minister, received 1834 by Cl. of Maryland. In 1839 returned to the Presb. Ch. Died 1860, at Shepherdstown, Va.

ABRAHAM BLUMER, b. Graps, Switzerland, Dec. 25, 1736; d. Lehigh co., Pa., April 23, 1822. Stud. at Basel. Ord. 1756. Chaplain to a Swiss regiment in the Sardinian service, 1757-'66. Asst. pastor and teacher, 1766-'70. Sent to America in 1770 by the Synods of Holland. Past. Allentown, Pa., Egypt, etc., 1771-1801. Declined a call to the pastorate of the French Ref. ch. of N. Y.

CHARLES LOUIS BOEHME (*Boehm*), b. Ger.; d. ab. 1786. Came to America 1770, with Rev. A. Blumer. Preached French in Phila. Past. Lancaster, Pa., 1771-'75; Hanover, 1775-'81; Baltimore, Md., 1781-'82. Secretary of Coetus, 1772.

JOHN PHILIP BOEHM, b. Palatinate, Ger., —; d. Montgomery co., Pa., May 1, 1749. Earliest Reformed preacher in Pa. See page 166.

EMANUEL C. BOEHRINGER, b. Buergach, Würtemberg, Ger., May 29, 1823; d. Bridesburg, Phila., Oct. 25, 1864. Came to America ab. 1858. Stud. Theol. privately. Lic. Cl. of Phil., 1859. Ord. Synod U. S., 1859. Ger. missionary Norfolk and Richmond, Va., 1861-'63. Removed to Phila 1863. Founded the Orphans' Home at Bridesburg—since removed to Womelsdorf, Berks Co.—and remained in charge until his death. Established and edited the "Laemmer-Hirte."

FREDERICK W. BOETTICHER, b. Prussia. Ord. in Europe. Received, Synod of Ohio, 1835. Past. Captain's Creek, Belmont co.. O., 1835-'39. Name disappears from the minutes, 1840.

NECROLOGY.

GEORGE ROGER, b. Rowan co., N. C., Dec. 15, 1782; d. Cabarrus co., N. C., June 19, 1865. Preceptors, Samuel Weyberg and Andrew Loretz. Ord. 1803. Past. Rowan and Cabarrus co.'s, N. C., 1803-'30. Preached also in South Carolina, and supplied a part of his charge after his resignation. Lived many years in retirement.

HERMAN BOKUM, b. Königsberg, Prussia, Jan. 2, 1807; d. Germantown, Pa., Aug. 5, 1878. Ed. in Europe. Came to America, 1825. Prof. of German and French in University of Pa. Lic. Syn. U. S., 1842. Ord. Cl. of Lebanon, 1843. Past. Columbia and Marietta, Pa., 1843-'44. Removed to Cincinnati, and in 1855 to Kn ·xville, Tenn. Chaplain in the army, and Commissioner of Immigration for Tennessee. Past. German ch., Atlanta, Ga., 1869-'73. Returned to Phila., and engaged in missionary labor. Published "German Grammar," and a German translation of McIlvaine's "Evidences of Christianity."

WILLIAM WILSON BONNEL, b. 1819; d 1850. Recd. from Presb. Ch., Cl. of Mercersburg, 1842. Past Chambersburg, 1842-'44. Dism. to Presbyterian Church.

WILLIAM BOOS. Arrived from Europe, 1771. Pastor Reading, Pa., 1771-'82; also in 1789. Preached at various times in a number of churches in Berks co., Pa. During a part of his ministry he was independent of Coetus.

DAVID BOSSLER, b. Snyder co., Pa., April 15, 1800; d. York, Pa., May 14, 1875. Preceptor, Rev. James R. Reily. Lic., Synod U. S., and ord., 1821. Past. Emmittsburg, Gettysburg, etc., 1821-'33; Dauphin co., Pa., 1835-'52; German ch., York, Pa., 1852-'68. Agt. for the Theol. Sem., F. and M. Col., and the Ref. Ch. Publication Board.

BENJAMIN BOYER, b. Montgomery co., Pa., Feb. 4, 1792; d. Nov. 15, 1864. Served in the war of 1812. Preceptor, Dr. S. Helffenstein. Lic. and ord., Synod U. S., 1821. Past. Pinegrove, etc., 1821- ab. '29; Northumberland co., Pa., ab. 1829-'33; Selinsgrove, ab. 1833-'43; Armstrong co., Pa., 1843; Meadville, Pa., etc., 1844-'50; Mercer co., Pa., 1850-'53 or '54.

DANIEL G. BRAGONIER, b. near Hagerstown, Md., Oct. 10, 1808; d. Shepherdstown, W. Va., Oct. 23, 1868. Theol. Sem., York, 1834. Lic., Synod U. S., and ord. 1834; Past. Clearspring chg, Md., 1834 ab. '39; Winchester, Va., ah. 1839-'42; Shepherdstown, Martinsburg, etc., Va., ab. 1843-'56.

G. H. BRANDAU, b. Homburg, Ger. Came to America, 1833. Past. Ger. (Ind.) ch., Louisville, Ky., 1834-'41. Lic. "Free Synod," 1835. Entered the Lutheran Church.

JOHN BRANDMILLER, b. Basel, Switz., Nov. 24, 1704; d. Bethlehem, Pa., Aug. 16, 1777. Served in the French army. Joined the Moravians, 1738. Came to America, 1741. Ord. a minister of the Reformed branch of the "Congregation of God in the Spirit," 1745. Preached at Allemaengel, Berks co., and Donegal, Lancaster co., Pa. Printer in Bethlehem. Accidentally drowned.

NATHANIEL E. BRESSLER, b. Lower Mahantango twp., Schuylkill co., Pa , Sept. 7, 1821; d. Dauphin co., Mar. 8, 1877. Lic. and ord., Susquehanna Cl., 1846. Past. Armstrong Valley chg., Dauphin co , Pa., 1846-'77, with an interval of three years, during which he served the 2d ch., Harrisburg.

JOHN BROWN, D. D. (*Braun*), b. near Bremen, Ger., July 21, 1771; d. Bridgewater, Va., Jan. 26, 1850. Came to America, 1797. Preceptor, Philip Stock. Lic Synod U. S., 1800. Ord. 1803. Labored about 48 years in the Valley of Virginia. For 35 years the only Reformed minister in that region, except the pastor of Shepnerdstown charge. Author of "Circular-Schreiben," Harrisonburg, 1818.

PETER BRUECKER, b. Düsseldorf, Ger., 1826; d. Sandusky, City, O., Jan.

NECROLOGY. 387

16, 1854. Came to America ab. 1849. Theol. Sem., Mercersburg, 1850-'51: Lic. and ord., Tiffin Cl., 1852. Past. Sandusky City, F., 1852-'54.

MARTIN BRUNNER, b. Phila., 1795; d. Lancaster, Pa., 1852. Preceptor, Dr. S. Helfenstein. Lic. Syn. U. S., 1816; ord., 1819. Past. Sunbury, Pa., etc., 1816-ab. 1827; Hagerstown, Md., etc., 1827-'32; Lancaster, Pa., 1832- ab. '40. One of the compilers of first Eng. Ref. Hymn-book.

JOHN CONRAD BUCHER, h. Schaffhausen, Switz., June 10, 1730; d. Lebanon, Pa., Aug. 15, 1780. Stud. at St. Gall, Basel, Göttingen, and Marburg. Came to America ab. 1756, and entered the British military service. Ab. 1763 resigned his commission and became a minister. Ord. by Coetus. Royal Chaplain. Past. Carlisle, etc., ab. 1763-'68; Lebanon, Pa., etc., 1768-'80. Founded many churches. See pages 213 and 231.

J. G. BUETTNER, Ph. D., b. Ger. Ord. West Penn. Cl. 1835. Past. Osnaburg and Massilon, O., 1838-'39. Elected Prof. of Theol., 1838, in the Seminary founded in Canton. Returned to Europe. Conducted a controversy with Frederick Muench, of Missouri, and wrote a book on America.

JACOB BURKHOLDER, b. Bedford co., Pa., Aug. 29, 1823; d. Indiana, Aug. 17, 1875. Preceptor, Rev. H. Heckerman. Lic. Illinois Cl., 1862. Ord. St. Joseph Cl., 1869. Past. Union chg., De Kalb co., Ind., 1869. West Jefferson chg., Williams Co., O., 1870; Miami and Kosciusko cos., Ind., 1871-'75.

THORNTON BUTLER, b. Catawba co., N. C., Oct. 4, 1820; d. Anna, Ill., Nov. 2, 1870. Grad. M. Col., 1846; Theol. Sem., Mercersburg, 1848. Lic. and ord., North Carolina Cl., 1848. Past. Lexington, N. C., etc., 1848-'53. Without charge, 1853-'58. Past. East Rowan chg., N. C., 1858-'68; Anna, Ill., 1868-'70.

JOHN CARES, b. Turbut twp., Northumberland co., Pa., Sept. 1811; d. York, Pa., April 5, 1843. Theol. Sem., York, Pa., 1830-'32. Lic. and ord., Synod U. S., 1832. Past. York, Pa., 1832-'43. President of Synod U. S. at the time of his death.

ANDREW CARROLL (*Garrol*), b. Switz., 1782; d. Bloomfield, Ind., 1857. Ord. in Switz. Received, Syn. of Ohio, 1842. Past. Holmes co., O., 1842-'44; Fort Wayne, Ind., 1844; Holmes co., O., 1845; Bloomfield, Ind , 1856.

JOEL CAREY, b. June 1, 1814; d. Napoleon, O., Sept. 21, 1849. Lic. Maumee Cl., 1847; ord. Syn. of Ohio, 1848. Miss. Napoleon, O., 1848-'49.

ADOLPH BERNHARD CASPER, b. Halberstadt, Prussia, Nov. 2, 1810; d. New Berlin, Pa., June 5, 1882. Son of Prussian Court Preacher. Came to America, 1836. Lic., 1837; ord., Syn. U. S., 1833. Past. York co., Pa., 1837-'39; Mifflinburg, New Berlin, etc., 1840-'60.

CHARLES CAST, b. Ettlingen, Baden, Ger., Feb. 22, 1815; d. Egg Harbor, N. J., Jan. 2, 1883. Univ. of Freiburg and Heidelberg. Ord. to R. C. Priesthood, 1845. Came to America. Admitted to Ref. Ch., 1852. Past. of several charges.

JOSEPH CHIPMAN, Lic. Synod U. S., 1828. Teacher of the Academy, Lebanon, Pa.

LUDOVICUS CHITARA. This man, once an Augustinian monk, applied to Coetus for ordination, 1786. Referred to Holland, but the response was not favorable. Called a Reformed minister in extant documents, but it is doubtful if he was ever ordained.

AARON CHRISTMAN, b. Lower Saucon, Northampton co., Pa., June 4, 1826; d. Phila., Mar. 28, 1860. Stud. M. Col. Lic. Susquehanna, Cl., 1850; ord. Mercersburg Cl., 1851. Entered P. E. Church.

JACOB CHRISTMAN, b. 1744; d. Warren co., O., Mar. 11, 1810. Lic. and ord.,

NECROLOGY.

Synod U. S., 1792. Pastor of six congregations in North Carolina. In 1803 he went to Ohio, and is said to have been the first Ref. minister in that State.

J. T. CLARK, lic., "Free Synod," 1830.

JOHN M. CLEMENS, b. New Berlin, Pa., Jan. 27, 1838; d. Conyngham, Pa., Sept. 11, 1880. Stud. F. and M. Col. Theol., Mission House, Sheboygan, Wis. Lic. Sheboygan Cl., 1866. Ord. Zion's Cl., 1866. Past. Littlestown, Pa., 1866-'69; St. Clair, Pa., 1869-'71; Conyngham, Pa., 1871-'80.

WILLIAM F. COLLIFLOWER, b. Cavetown, Md., Feb. 14, 1814; d. Frederick, Md., April 30, 1882. Theol. Sem., York, Pa. Lic. and Ord., Cl. of Md., 1836. Past. Millcreek ch., Va., 1837-'39; Woodstock, Va., 1839-'42; Glade ch., Md., 1842-'50; Manchester, Md., 1850-'59; Jefferson, Md., 1859-'69; Bloomfield, Pa., 1869-'72; Sulphur Springs chg., Pa., 1872-'74; Hagertown, Md., Second ch., 1874-'77; Abbotstown, Pa., 1877-'80; w. c., 1880-'82.

BRUIN ROMCAS COMINGOE, d. ab. 1819. Ord. by ministers of Scotch Presb. Church of Nova Scotia, 1770. Past. Ref. ch., Luneburg, N. S., 1770-1819. See page 208.

WILLIAM CONRAD, b. Hagerstown, Md., Aug. 11, 1808; d. Berlin, Somerset co., Pa., Feb. 16, 1865. Grandson of Rev. Henry Giesy. Stud. High School and Theol. Sem., York, Pa. Lic. and ord., West Penn. Cl., 1835. Past. Salisbury, etc., 1835-'41; Berlin chg., 1841-'59; Beams chg., 1841-'62. Author of a work on "Baptism."

WILLIAM E. CORNWELL, b. Phila., Dec. 8, 1807; d. Princeton, N. J., March 29, 1857. Lic. 1836 and ord. 1838, Phila. Cl. Past. Kensington, ch., 1838-'42; Pleasantville, etc., 1842-'50. Resigned and became a Baptist.

JOHN H. CRAWFORD, b. Carrol co., Md., July 23, 1801;. d. Middleburg, Augusta co., Va., Oct. 9, 1864. Theol. Sem., Carlisle, 1828. Lic. and ord., Synod U. S., 1828. Past. Guilford and Orange cos., N. C., 1828-'40; Lincoln co., 1840-'57; Augusta co., Va., 1857-'64.

DAVID CROOKS, b. Pa., March 12, 1820; d. Lincoln co., N. C., Jan. 24, 1859. Stud. Marshall Col. Theol. Sem,, 1837. Lic. Zion's Cl., 1838; ord. N. C. Cl., 1839. Past. Davidson chg., N. C., 1839-'45; Lincolnton chg,, 1845-'59.

JOHN JACOB WILLIAM DAHLMAN, b. Elberfeld, Prussia, June 29, 1801; d. Phila., Aug. 1, 1874. Came to America, 1848. Stud. privately. Lic., N. Y. Cl., 1851; ord.. 1852. Past. Evangelical ch., Lancaster, Erie co., N. Y., 1852-'53; Arnheim, O., 1853-'58; Ger. Presb. ch., Jamaica, L. I., 1858— —; Ref. (D.) ch., Melrose, N. Y., 1861-'63; Glassborough, N. J., 1863-'69; Bridesburg, Pa., 1869-'71.

ABNER DALE, b. near Boalsburg, Centre co., Pa., Nov. 17, 1829; d. Armstrong co., Pa., Jan. 16, 1875. Grad. M. Col., 1852. Theol. Sem., 1856. Lic. Mercersburg Cl., 1856; ord Clarion Cl., 1857. Past. Fairview ch., Armstrong co., Pa., 1857-'60; Reimersburg, 1860-'61; Mercer co. miss., 1862-'66; w. c., 1866-'70; then recalled to his first charge.

FREDERICK DALLICKER (*de la Cour*), b. in Europe, Feb. 2, 1738; d. Falkner Swamp, Montgomery co., Pa., Jan. 15, 1799. Came to America ab. 1757. Past. Amwell, N. J., 1770; Rockaway, etc., ab. 1770-'82; Goshenhoppen, Pa., 1782-'84; Falkner Swamp, 1784-'99.

CHARLES LEWIS DAUBERT, b. Ger. Stud. Theol. in Europe. Lic. Free Syn. of Pa., 1831; ord. 1832. Past. 1834, at Lawrenceville, Allegheny co., Harmony, Butler co., Pa., etc. Past. Wheeling, Va., 1839. Name mentioned in Minutes Syn. O., 1847.

NECROLOGY. 389

J. W. DAVIS, lic. Free Syn. 1835; ord. 1837. Dismissed to Presb. of Brooklyn, 1839.

WILLIAM F. P. DAVIS, b. Paradise twp., York co., Pa., Oct. 1, 1831; d. Reading, Pa, June 11, 1883. Grad F. and M. Col., 1861; Theol. Sem., Mercersburg. Lic. and ord., Zion's Cl., 1863. Past. Abbottstown chg., Pa., 1863-'71; Sinking Spring, etc., Berks co., 1871-'83.

JACOB WILLIAM DECHANT, b. Kreuznach, Ger., Feb. 18, 1784; d. Lancaster co., Pa., Oct. 5, 1832. Came to America, 1805. Preceptor, Rev. C. L. Becker, D. D. Lic. and ord., 1808. Past. Bucks and Lehigh cos., Pa., 1808-'15; miss. to Ohio, 1815-'19; Montgomery co., Pa., 1819-'32. Died of cholera on his way home from a meeting of Synod.

JOHN PETER DECHANT, brother of the preceding, b. Kreuznach, Ger., 1782; d. Champaign co., Ohio, 1824. Lic. and ord. Syn. U, S., 1822. Past. Champaign co., etc., O., 1822-'24.

J. PETER DECKER, Past. Chestnut Hill, Monroe co., Pa., 1832-'55.

SOLOMON K. DENIUS, b. Baltimore co., Md., Aug. 11, 1798; d. New Castle, Ind., Sept. 29, 1878. Preceptors, Dr. C. L. Becker and J. Geiger. Lic. and ord., Syn. U. S., 1821. Past. Boonsboro, Md., 1821-31; Bedford, Pa., 1831-'36; Berlin, Pa., 1836- —. Removed to the West, laboring successively at Somerset, Bakersville, Germantown, West Alexandria, and Camden, Ohio, and at New Castle, Ind.

DR. DE QUENAUDON, lic. "Free Synod," ab. 1834. Doctor of Medicine, residing in Berks co., Pa. Preached occasionally, but was never pastor of a charge.

JACOB DES COMBES, b. Coblentz, Ger., Feb. 17, 1798; d. Butler co., O., Oct. 6, 1845. Stud. in Germany. Came to America, 1820. Preceptor, Rev. Geo. Weiss. Lic. and ord., Syn. of O., 1824. Past. of congregations in Ohio and Indiana. Author of a small volume on "Baptism."

JACOB DIEFFENBACH, b. Va., Feb. 27, 1784; d. Espytown, Pa., Apr. 13, 1825. Preceptors, Rev. Henry Dieffenbach and C. L. Becker, D. D. Lic. and ord., Syn. U. S., 1807. Past. Berks and Lehigh cos., Pa., 1808; Union co., 1808-'11; Lehigh co., 1811-'15; Bloomsburg, 1815-'22; Espytown, 1822-'25.

HENRY DIEFFENBACH, elder brother of the preceding. Ord. Syn. U. S., 1802. Past. of churches in North Carolina. First Sec. of "Free Synod," 1822, and pastor of Jerusalem ch., Berks co., Pa. Removed to Ohio, 1826. Died ab. 1839.

JACOB FOLLMER DIEFFENBACHER, b. Northumberland co., Pa., Dec. 18, 1802; d. Harmony, Pa., Feb. 4, 1842. Stud. Theol. Sem., Carlisle, Pa. Lic. and ord., Syn. U. S., 1828. Past. Sharpsburg and Boonesboro, Md., 1828-'30; Mercersburg, Pa., 1830-'32; Woodstock, Va., 1832-'39; Harmony, Pa., 1839-'42.

N. DODDS. Preceptor, Rev. S. Helfenstein, D. D. Lic. Syn. U. S., 1829.

PETER HENRY DORSTIUS, past. Ref. (Dutch) church, Southampton, 1731-'48. First Missionary Superintendent. Visited German churches, 1740. Commissioner to Presb. Synod, 1743. Died before 1755. See page 173.

ABRAHAM H. DOTTERER, b. Boyertown, Pa., Nov. 4, 1840; d. New Hanover, Pa., Aug. 24, 1870. Grad. F. and M. C., 1867. Theol. Sem., 1869. Lic., Cl of Phil., 1869. Ord. East Sus. Cl., 1869. Past. Sunbury, Pa., 1869-'70.

HERMAN DOUGLASS, sup. York, Pa., 1845 or 1846. Without charge, 1846.

ROBERT DOUGLASS, b. Ireland, Oct., 1807; d. near Shepherdstown, W. Va., Aug. 20, 1867. Came to America ab. 1828. Entered Ref. church, Baltimore, Md Theol. Sem., York, Pa. Lic. Syn. U. S., 1833. Past. Shepherdstown and Martinsburg, Va., 1833-'46; Jefferson, Md., 1846-'50; Boonsboro, Md., 1850-'56; w. c., 1856-'65; Mt. Moriah, Md., 1865-'67.

G. WILLIAM DREES, stud. Germany. Lic. Cl. of Bentheim, Hanover, 1836. Ord. as miss., Syn. U. S., 1846.

JOHN H. DREYER, b. Ger., 1768; d. 1840. Past. Baltimore, Md., 1806; Forsyth st. ch., N. Y., 1812-'14; w. c., 1814-'24. Editor of " Evangelische Zeitung," 1830-'34. Went to Europe. Afterwards past. of a church in Bremen, Ger.

SAMUEL DUBBENDORF, b. Ger., —; d. Selinsgrove, Pa., 1800. Came to America as chaplain of Hessian troops ab. 1776. Past. Germantown, Pa., 1777-'80; Lykens Valley, 1780-'80; Carlisle, Pa., 1790-'95; Lykens Valley, 1795.

JOSEPH S. DUBBS, D. D. (*Dubs*), b. Upper Milford, Lehigh co., Pa., Oct. 16, 1796; d. Allentown, Pa., Apr. 14, 1877. Preceptor, Rev. F. L. Herman, D. D. Lic., Free Syn. of Pa., 1822; ord. 1823. Past. Windsor, Eppler's, etc., Berks co., Pa., 1822-'31; Zion's ch., Allentown, Pa., 1831-'61; Egypt, Jordan, etc., 1831-'66. See page 276.

JONATHAN DU BOIS, d. 1771. Past. Ref. (Dutch) ch. at Southampton, Pa., 1730-'71. Member of Coetus of Pa.

JOHN S. EBAUGH (*Ibach*), b. York co., Pa., Apr. 19, 1795; d. N. Y. city, Nov. 2, 1874. Preceptor, Dr. S. Helffenstein. Ord., Syn. U. S., 1818. Miss. N. C., 1818-'19; Carlisle, Pa., 1819- ab. 1833. Entered " Free Synod," 1831. Genl. Agt. of American Bible Society, 1835. Published " Heavenly Incense," an English version of Zollikofer's Prayer-book. W. c., 1839-'44. Past. Forsyth st. ch., N. Y., 1844-'51. Founded "Industrial School," N. Y., 1854.

GEORGE CHRISTIAN EICHENBERG, b. Rinteln, Hesse, Dec. 25, 1816; d. Weissport, Pa., June 12, 1880. Came to America, 1844. Lic., Cl. of E. P., 1845; ord., 1848. Past. Weissport ch., 1848-'80. Susp. 1863.

PETER EISENBERG, d. ab. 1805. Ord., Syn. U. S., 1800. Pastor at a place called " Grove."

GEORGE EPPERT, lic., Free Synod, 1829. Labored in Virginia.

DAVID B. ERNST, b. near Hanover, Pa., July 4, 1815; d. Bath, Pa., Mar. 11, 1877. Grad. Mar. Col., 1841. Theol. Sem., Mercersburg, 1844. Lic., Susq. Cl., 1844; ord., Westmoreland Cl., 1844. Past. Somerset chg., 1844-'49; Saegertown, Crawford co., 1849-'75; Moore township, Northampton co., 1875-'77.

JOHN ERNST, b. Feb. 22, 1744; d. Berlin, Pa., Aug. 30, 1804. Grandfather of the preceding. Labored in York co., Pa.

ADAM ETTINGER, d. York co., Pa., ab. 1810. Lic., Synod U. S., 1803; ord., 1805. Past. at Abbotstown and Hanover, Pa. Said to have participated in the " United Brethren" movement.

NATHAN EVANS, b. Apr. 21, 1822; d. Fostoria, O., Feb. 2, 1848. Lic. Sandusky Cl., Syn. O., 1846; ord., 1847. Past. Rome, etc., O., 1847-'48.

JOHN CHRISTOPHER FABER, b. Ger. ab. 1731; d. 1796. Past. First ch., Baltimore, Md., 1757-'71; Taneytown, 1771. See page 216.

JOHN THEOBALD FABER, b. Toggenburg, Palatinate, Feb. 13, 1739; d. Nov. 2, 1788. Sent to America by Synods of Holland, 1766. Past. New Goshenhoppen, etc., 1766-'79; Lancaster, Pa., 1779-'84; Indianfield, 1784-'86; N. Goshenhoppen, etc., 1786-'88. Taken with fatal illness while preaching at New Goshenhoppen.

JOHN THEOBALD FABER, Jr., son of the preceding; b. Goshenhoppen,

NECROLOGY.   391

Sept 24, 1771; d. there, Jan. 31, 1833. Stud. Franklin Col., Lancaster. Preceptor, Dr. W. Hendel. Lic. and ord., Coetus Pa., 1792. Past. N. Goshenhoppen, etc., 1792-1807; Bethany ch., Lancaster co., Pa., 1807-'19; N. Goshenhoppen, etc., 1819-'33. Died suddenly while preaching at New Goshenhoppen.

BENJAMIN FAUST, b. Pa., Nov. 19, 1797; d. Stark co., O., Nov. 19, 1832. Ord. ab. 1819. Past. Canton O., etc., 1819-'32.

JOHN FELIX, lic. Syn. U. S., 1717; ord. 1819. Past. Northumberland and Schuylkill cos., Pa., 1819-'23; Union co., 1823-'25. He then irregularly left his charge, and his subsequent history is unknown. In the minutes of Synod for several years his name is marked "vermisst," or "missing."

THOMAS FERRELL, died Carrollton, O., Nov. 29, 1875. Received from the Church of the "United Brethren" by the Cl. of Sandusky. He served no pastoral charge in the Reformed Church.

SAMUEL J. FETZER, b. Woodstock, Va., Sept. 14, 1820; d. Rowan co., N. C., Aug. 8, 1861. Stud. Mercersburg, 1839. Preceptor, Rev. D. Feete. Lic. and ord., Virginia Cl., 1842. Past. Zion's, Grace, etc., 1842-'46; Pendleton co., Va., 1846-'50; Augusta chg., 1850-58; West Rowan ch., N. C., 1858-'61.

GEORGE A FICKES, b. Bedford co., Pa., Apr. 15, 1820; d. De Kalb co., Ind., Apr. 26, 1865. Stud. Tiffin, O.; lic. and ord., Westmoreland Cl., 1857. Past. Grantsville, Md., 1857-'59. Removed to Fremont, O.; w. c., 1859-'63; Plymouth, Ind., 1863-'64; De. Kalb co., Ind., 1865.

PETER S. FISHER, b. near Reading, Pa., Oct. 11, 1804; d. May 22, 1873. Preceptor, Dr. F. L. Herman. Lic., Free Synod, 1825; ord., 1826. Past. Dauphin co., 1826-'32; Centre co., 1832-'57; Tohickon chg., Bucks co., 1857-'73.

RICHARD A. FISHER, b. Heidelberg twp., Berks co., Pa., Oct. 25, 1805; d. Lykens Valley, Pa., Jan. 27, 1857. Preceptor, Dr. F. L. Herman. Lic. and ord., "Free Synod," 1826. Past. Sunbury chg., 1827-'54; w. c., 1854-56; Lykens Valley, 1856-'57. Cousin of the preceding.

SAMUEL REED FISHER, D. D., b. Norristown, Pa., June 2, 1810; d. Tiffin, O., June 5, 1881. Grad., Jefferson Col., Canonsburg, Pa., 1834. Theol. Sem., York, Pa., 1836. Lic. and ord., Syn. U. S., 1836. Past. Emmittsburg, Pa., 1836-'39. Superintendent of Publication Interests, 1840-'81. Editor of "The Messenger," 1840-75. Synodical Editor, 1875-'81. Stated Clerk, Syn. U. S., 1840-'81. Treas. Board of Ed., 1838-'81. See page 333.

CHRISTIAN F. FOEHRING, b. Hanover, Ger., 1736; d. Millstone, N. J., Mar. 29, 1779. Came to America, 1742. Preceptor, Dr. C. D. Weyberg. Lic., Cl. of N. Y., R. D. Ch., 1770. Past. Germantown, Whitpain, etc., 1770-'72; New_York, Forsyth st., 1772; Montgomery, 1773-'74; Millstone, N. J., 1774-'79.

JOHN AUGUSTUS FOERSCH, b. Ger., —; d. in New York. Lic. and ord., Syn. U. S., 1833. Past. successively in Chambersburg, Washington, D. C., and New York City. Author of "Zwingli's Leben," Chambersburg, 1837. Became a Rationalist. Deposed from the ministry ab. 1839. Reinstated 1842, and subsequently again deposed.

THEOBALD FOUSE, b. Blair co., Pa , Dec. 26, 1802; d. Huntingdon co., Aug. 23, 1873. Lic. and ord., Mercersburg Cl., 1842. Past. Woodcock Valley, etc., 1842-'73.

GEORGE F. FOY, lic. and ord., Susq. Cl., 1851. Past. Bellefonte, Pa. Dep., 1854. Died Johnstown, Pa., ab. 1857.

THEODORE FRANKENFELD, b. Ger. D. Frederick, Md., ab. 1757. Came to America with Schlatter, 1752. Past. Frederick, Md., 1853-'57.

NECROLOGY.

HENRY A. FRIEDEL, b. Hamburg, Ger , Sep. 8, 1823; d. Harrisburg, Pa., Jan. 15, 1883. Came to America, 1848. Stud. at Mercersburg. Lic. and ord., Miami Cl., Syn. of O., 1860. Preached in the West; then Bethlehem ch., Phila. Entered Ref. (D.) Ch. Labored in N. J. and N. Y. Returned to Ref. ch., U. S., Zwingli ch., Harrisburg, Pa., 1883.

JOHN B. FRIEHE, a convert from the Roman Catholic Church. Lic. Free Syn., 1836.

YOST HENRY FRIES, b. Nassau-Dillenberg, Ger., Apr. 24, 1777; d. Mifflinburg, Pa., Oct. 9, 1839. Came to America, 1803. Preceptor, Rev. Daniel Wagner. Lic. Syn. U. S., 1809; ord. 1813. Past. York co., Pa., 1810–'12'; Mifflinburg, Brush Valley, etc., 1812– —. Published several sermons.

JOHN G. FRITCHEY, b. Dauphin co., Pa., Feb. 6, 1802; d. Lancaster, Pa , Mar. 12, 1885. Theol. Sem., Carlisle, 1825–'28. Lic. and ord., Syn. U. S., 1828. Past. Lincolnton, N. C., 1828–'40; East Berlin, Pa., 1840–'45; Mechanicsburg, 1845–'52; Taneytown, Md , 1852–'65. Removed to Lancaster, Pa. Sup. Manheim, Millersville, New Holland, etc., Lancaster co., Pa.; Zwingli ch., Harrisburg, 1880.

WILLIAM FULTON, preceptor, Dr. J. Helffenstein. Lic., Phila. Cl., 1852. Past. Phœnixville, Pa. Entered Presb. Ch , 1854. Chaplain of Scott Legion Regt., 1867. Manayunk Ref. D. ch., 1865–'69.

HENRY FUNK, b. near Hagerstown, Md., May 7, 1816; d. Bloomsburg, Pa., Apr. 16, 1855. Grad. Marshall Col., 1841. Theol, Sem., Mercersburg, 1844. Lic. Maryland cl.; ord. Susquehanna Cl., 1844. Past. Bloomsburg chg,, Pa., 1844–'55.

JOHN GASSER, refused membership by Coetus, 1752. Preached some time in Carolina. Returned to Europe.

CORNELIUS GATES, d. Minisink, N. Y., 1863. Lic., Syn. U. S., 1833; ord., Md. Cl., 1834. Entered Ref. D. Ch., 1840.

JOHN GABRIEL GEBHARD, b. Waldorf, Ger., Feb. 2, 1750; d. Claverack, N. Y., Aug. 16, 1826. Stud. Heidelberg and Utrecht. Came to America, 1772. Past. Whitpain and Worcester, 1772–'74; N. Y. City, 1774–'76; Claverack, N. Y., 1776–1826.

JOHN GERBER, a native of Switzerland. Stud. at Basel. Miss. in Africa. Past. Basil, O., 1835; Newark, O., 1835–'40.

ISAAC GERHART, b. near Sellersville, Pa., Feb. 12, 1788; d. Lancaster, Pa., Feb. 11, 1865. Preceptor, Dr. S Helffenstein. Lic., Syn. U. S., 1813. Past. Union co., Pa., 1813–'18; Lykens Valley, 1816–'43; Ger. ch., Frederick, Md., 1843–'49; Manheim, etc., Pa., 1849–'56. President of Board of Missions. Published "Church Harmonia."

JOHN HENRY GERHART, b. Montgomery co., Pa., Dec. 23, 1782; d. Hatfield, Pa., Nov. 11, 1846. Preceptor, Dr. S. Helffenstein. Lic., Syn. U. S., 1812; ord. 1815. Past. Bedford, Pa., 1812–'30; Hilltown, Pa., 1830.

JACOB GEIGER, b. Allentown, Pa., Oct. 17, 1793; d. Manchester, Md., Oct. 19, 1848. Preceptor, Dr. J. C. Becker. Lic., Syn. U. S., 1817; ord., 1819. Past. Manchester, Md., etc., 1819–'48.

GEORGE GEISTWEIT, b. Pa., 1761; d. York, Pa., Nov. 11, 1831. Preceptor, Dr. F. L. Herman. Lic. and ord., Syn. U. S., 1794. Past. Sunbury, etc., Pa., 1794–1804; York, Pa., 1804–'20; w. c., 1820–'31.

HENRY GIESY, b. Lichtenau, Ger., Apr. 13, 1757; d. Berlin, Pa., Mar. 24, 1845. Lic. and ord., Coetus Pa., 1782. Past. Loudon co., Va., 1782–94; Berlin, Pa., 1794–1833; w. c., 1833–'45.

NECROLOGY.

NICHOLAS E. GILDS, b. Frederick co., Md., Apr. 17, 1819; d. Mechanicsburg, Md., Mar. 5, 1879. Lic., Va. Cl., 1850; ord., Columbiana Cl., O., 1851. Past. Carrollton, O., 1851-'54; Rimersburg, Pa., 1854-'56; St. Clairsville, Pa., 1856-'65; Taneytown, Md., 1865-'67; Mechanicstown, Md., 1867-'76.

WILLIAM GILPIN, b. Schuylkill co., Pa., July 1, 1821; d. Broken Sword, O., Jan. 16, 1882. Lic. and ord., Illinois Cl., 1862. Past. Hickory, Ill., 1863-'68; Macon chg., 1868-'72; Union ch., Fairfield co., O., 1873-'78; Broken Sword ch., 1879-'82.

SHERIDAN GITTEAU, received 1841, Cl. of Md., from Presb. Ch. Dism. to Presb. Ch., 1843.

PHILIP GLONINGER, b. Lebanon, Pa., Feb. 17, 1788; d. Sept. 10, 1816. Stud. Franklin Col. Preceptor, Dr. C. L. Becker. Lic. and ord., Syn. U. S., 1808. Past. Harrisburg, Pa., 1808-'16.

JOHN CHRISTOPHER GOBRECHT, b. Angerstein, Ger., Oct. 11, 1733; d. Hanover, Pa., Nov. 6, 1815. Came to America, 1753. Preceptor, Rev. J. G. Alsentz. Lic. and ord., Coetus, Pa., 1766, Past. Tohickon, etc., Pa., 1766-'79; Hanover chg, Pa., 1779-1806.

JOHN GOBRECHT, b. Lancaster, Pa., Dec. 10, 1773; d. Lehigh co., Pa., Mar. 5, 1831. Son of the preceding. Preceptors, Rev. V. Melsheimer, P. Stock and W. Hendel. Lic. and ord., 1794. Syn. U. S. Past. Asst. at Hanover, etc., 1794-1802; Past. Allentown, etc., Pa., 1802-'31.

JOHN HENRY GOETSCHIUS, (*Goetschy*). A native of Zurich, Switz. Pastor at New Goshenhoppen, Pa., and many other churches, 1731-ab. 1739. Ord. Presb. Syn , Phila., 1737. See p. 170.

WILLIAM A GOOD, b. Philadelphia, July 15, 1810; d. Reading, Pa., Feb. 9, 1873. Theol. Sem , York, Pa. Lic. and ord., Cl. Lebanon, 1833. Rector Prep. Dept. Marshall Col., Pa. Past. Hagerstown, Md., York, Pa., etc. For many years engaged in the work of education.

DIETRICH GRAVE, b. Ger. ab. 1776; d. Shippensburg, Pa., Mar. 22, 1833. Lic. and ord., Syn. U. S., 1820. Past. Uniontown and Taneytown, Md.. 1820-'29; Woodstock, Va., 1829-'32; Shippensburg, Pa., 1832-'33.

DANIEL GRING, b. Berks co., Pa., Feb. 8, 1811; d. York, Pa., May 31, 1882. Theol. Sem , York, Pa. Lic. and ord., 1835. Past. Paradise chg., Pa., 1835-'53; Shrewsbury chg, 1853-'80.

JOHN DANIEL GROS, D. D., (*Gross*) b. Palatinate, Ger., 1737; d. Canajoharie, N. Y., May 25, 1812. Past. Allentown, etc., Pa., 1764-'70 ; Lower Saucon ch., 1770-'72; Kingston, N. Y., 1772-'83 : Forsyth st. ch., N. Y., 1783-'95. Prof. of German in Columbia Col., N. Y., 1784-'95, and of Moral Philosophy, 1787-'95. Author of " Natural Principles of Rectitude," 8vo., 1795.

GEORGE ADAM GUETING, (*Guething* or *Geeting*), b. Nassau, Ger., Feb. 6, 1741, d. Maryland, June 28, 1812. Came to America, 1753). Taught school on the Antietam. Preceptor, Rev Wm. Otterbein. Ord. Coetus, Pa., 1783. Deposed 1804. Prominent among the "United Brethren in Christ."

JOHN C. GULDIN, D. D., b. Berks co., Pa., Aug. 1799; d. New York City, Feb. 18, 1863. Preceptor, F. L. Herman, D. D. Lic. and ord., Syn. U. S., 1820. Member of Free Synod, 1822-'36. Past. Trappe, etc., Pa., 1820-'41; Grindstone Hill ch., 1841. Ger. Ev. Mission, N. Y., 1842. Dism. to Ref. (D.) ch. in America.

SAMUEL GULDIN. A Swiss minister, great-grandfather of the preceding, settled in Pennsylvania early in the last century. Probably independent.

SAMUEL GUTELIUS, b. Manheim, Pa., Oct. 22, 1795, d. Lykenstown, Pa., July

NECROLOGY.

17, 1866. Preceptor, Rev.Yost Henry Fries. Lic. and ord., Syn. U. S., 1822. Past. Paradise ch. Pa., 1822-'28; Hanover ch., 1828-'38, Gettysburg ch., 1838-'43, Conway st. ch., Baltimore, Md., 1843-'46; Abbotstown ch., Pa., 1846-'51; Emanuel's ch., 1851-'53; w. c., 1853-'54; Freeburg, Pa., 1855-'60: w. c., 1861-'62; Tremont (supply) 1863; Lykens Mission, 1864-'66.

HENRY N. B. HABLISTON, b. Baltimore, Md., ab., 1794; d. Baltimore, Md., April 2, 1870. Stud. St. Mary's Col., Md. Preceptor, Dr. C. L. Becker. Lic. and ord., Syn. U. S., 1815. Missionary, Westmoreland co., Pa., 1815-'17. Past. Shrewsbury, Pa., 1819; Shippensburg, 1824. Suspended, 1828. Restored, 1847. Past. Manheim, Pa., 1847-'48. Missionary in Illinois, 1850-'51. Deposed, 1853.

NICHOLAS P. HACKE, D. D., b. Baltimore, Md., Sep. 20, 1800; d. Greensburg, Pa., Aug. 25, 1878. Went to Germany, 1806; returned to America, 1816. Preceptors, Rev. Drs. C. L. and J. C. Becker. Lic. and ord., Syn. U. S., 1819. Past. Greensburg chg., Pa., 1819-'78.

JOHN FREDERICK HAGER, (*Heger*). Probably the earliest German Reformed minister in America. Accompanied Palatines to London, 1709. Came to New York and preached at East and West Camp. Ord. Dec. 20, 1709. Preached at Schoharie, N. Y., 1711. See page 162.

JOHN WILLIAM HAMM, b. York co., Pa., August 5, 1800; d. Manchester, O., April 3. 1872. Preceptors: Rev. Drs C. L. Becker and S. Helffenstein. Lic. and ord., Syn. U. S., 1822. Past. Newville, Pa., 1822-'24; Manchester, O., 1824-'72.

JACOB W. HANGEN, b. Philadelphia, Mar. 5, 1805; d. near Trappe, Pa., Feb. 23, 1843. Preceptor, Rev. J. W. Dechant. Ord. Syn. U. S., 1825. Past. Columbia and Warren, N. Y., 1825-'30; Root, N. Y., 1830-'40; Hilltown, etc., Pa., 1840. Trappe chg., Pa., 1841-43.

HENRY HARBAUGH, D. D., b. near Waynesboro, Franklin co., Pa., Oct. 28, 1817; d. Mercersburg, Pa., Dec. 28, 1867. Stud. Marshall Col., 1840-'41; Theol. Sem. Mercersburg, 1843. Lic. Syn. U. S.; ord., Susquehanna Cl., 1843; Past. Lewisburg, Pa., 1843-'50; Lancaster, Pa., 1850-'60; Lebanon, Pa., 1860-'63. Prof. of Didactic and Practical Theology, Mercersburg, Pa., 1863-'67. Published "The Sainted Dead (1848); "The Heavenly Recognition" (1851); "The Heavenly Home" (1853); "Union with the church" (1853); "The Birds of the Bible" (1854); "Life of the Rev. Michael Schlatter" (1857); "The Fathers of the German Reformed Church in Europe and America," 2 vols. (1857-1858); "The True Glory of Woman" and " The Lord's Portion" (1858); "Poems" (1860); "The Golden Censer" (1860); "Hymns and Chants" (1861); Christological Theology" (1864). Posthumous publications; " Harbaugh's Harfe," a collection of his poems in the German dialect of Pennsylvania, edited by Rev. B. Bausman, D. D , (1870); and "The Fathers of the German Reformed Church," vol. 3, edited by Rev. D. Y. Heisler, D. D., (1872). Author of "Jesus, I live to Thee," and other hymns. Also wrote many articles for periodicals. Founded " The Guardian," a monthly magazine, 1850. Editor of " The Guardian " 1850-'66. Editor of "The Mercersburg Review" 1867. Contributed the Lives of Reformed Ministers to Dr. McClintock's " Theological Cyclopædia."

FREDERICK W. HESSELMAN, Ord. Cl. of New York, 1849. Past. Buffalo, N. Y., 1849-'50.

DAVID HASSINGER, b. Meyerstown, Pa., 1791; d. Ickesburg, Pa., March 3, 1858. Preceptor, Rev. Dr. S. Helffenstein. Lic. Syn. U. S., 1823; ord. 1824. Past. Newville, Pa., 1824—ab. 1829; Orwigsburg, Pa., 1829-; Pottsville, Pa., ab. 1830-'56 Remove ' to Perry co., 1856. W. c., 1856 '58.

PETER HAUCK. Member of St. Joseph's Cl., Syn. of O., 1851-'52.

NECROLOGY. 395

WILLIAM HAUCK, b. North Carolina—; d. Missouri—. Lic. Syn. U. S., 1814; ord. 1818. Past. North Carolina, 1814-'19; Wythe co., Va., 1819-; Davidson co., N. C., 1830; Forks, S. C.; Peck's ch., N. C., 1836. Suspended ab. 1836.

ANTHONY HAUTZ, b. Ger., Aug. 4, 1758; d. Grotton, N. Y., 1830. Came to America, with his parents, 1768. Preceptor, Dr. W. Hendel. Catechist 1786. Ord., Coetus, Pa., 1787. Past. Lancaster co., 1786-'88; Harrisburg, Pa., 1788-'97; Carlisle, Pa., 1798-1804. Seneca co., N. Y., 1804-'15. W. c., 1815-'30.

JOHN HAUTZ, b. Pa., ab. 1799; d. Bernville. Pa., Dec. 28, 1832. Lic. and ord., Syn. U. S., 1828. Past. Northumberland, Schuylkill, and Berks counties, Pa.

HENRY HECKERMAN, b. Chambersburg, Pa., Jan. 7. 1817; d. Bedford, Pa., April 5, 1876. Grad. Marshall Col., 1844. Lic. Cl. East Pa., 1845; ord. Mercersburg cl., 1845. Miss. Bedford co., 1845-'47. Past. Huntingdon ch., 1847-'50; Bedford ch., 1850-'71; without ch., 1871-'76.

DAVID HEFFELFINGER, b. Cumberland co., Pa., 1816; d. Fayetteville. Pa., July 23, 1860. Stud. Marshall Col. and Theol. Sem., Mercersburg. Lic. and ord., Goshenhoppen Cl., 1848. Past. Brownbacks ch., Chester co., Pa., 1848-'55; Newville, Pa., ch., 1855-'60; Grindstone Hill, Pa., 1860.

JOHN EGIDIUS HECKER, b. Dillenberg, Nassau; d. Northampton co., Pa., 1775. Ordained in Europe. Pastor of congregations in Northampton co., Pa. Independent.

ELIAS HEINER, D. D., b. Taneytown, Md., Sept. 16, 1810; d. Baltimore, Md., Oct. 20, 1863. Theol. Sem., York, Pa. Lic. and ord., Syn. U. S., 1833. Past. Emmittsburg, Md., ch., 1833-'35; First ch., Baltimore Md., 1835-'63. Pub. "Sermon on the Life of Rev. John Cares" (1843); "Centenary Sermon" (1850); "Memoir of Rev. L. Mayer, D. D.," as an Introduction to his History of the German Reformed Church (1851): "Reminiscences of a Quarter of a Century" (1861).

JOHN C. ALBERTUS HELFFENSTEIN, b. Mossbach, Palatinate, Feb. 16, 1748; d. Germantown, Pa., May 17, 1790. Son of Peter, Church Inspector at Simsheim. Studied at Heidelberg. Came to America in 1772, with his step-brother Rev. J. H. Helffrich and Rev. J. G. Gebhard. Past. Germantown, Pa., 1772-'73; Lancaster, Pa., 1776-'79; Germantown, (2d time) 1779-'90. Several volumes of his sermons have been published.

SAMUEL HELFFENSTEIN, D. D., eldest son of J. C. Albertus; b. Germantown, Pa., Apr. 17, 1775; d. North Wales, Pa., Oct. 17, 1866. Preceptor, Dr. W. Hendel, Sr. Lic., Syn. U. S., 1796; ord., 1797. Past. Boehm's ch., Montgomery co., Pa., 1796-'99; Race st. ch., 1799-1831. Sup. Lower Saucon, 1833-'37; w. c., 1837-'66. Author of "Didactic Theology," and many pamphlets. See page 279.

CHARLES HELFFENSTEIN, third son of J. C. Albertus; b. Germantown, Pa., Mar. 29, 1781; d. Reading, Pa., Dec. 19, 1842. Preceptor, Dr. C. L. Becker. Lic. and ord., Syn. U. S., 1801. Past. Berks co., Pa., 1801; Goshenhoppen, 1802; Ephrata, ab. 1803-'c8; Hanover and Berlin, York co., ab. 1808-'26; Rockingham co., Va.; Mechanicsburg, Pa., 1830-'34; w. c., 1834-'42.

JONATHAN HELFFENSTEIN, fourth son of J. C. Albertus; b. Germantown, Pa., Jan. 19, 1784; d. Frederick, Md., Sept. 29, 1829. Preceptor, Dr. C. L. Becker. Lic., Syn. U. S., 1805; ord., 1807. Past. Carlisle, Pa., 1805-'11; Frederick, Md., 1811-'29.

ALBERT HELFFENSTEIN, Sr., fifth son of J. C. Albertus; b. Germantown, Mar. 13, 1788; d. Shamokin, Pa., Jan. 30, 1869. Preceptor, Dr. C. L. Becker. Lic. and ord., Syn. U. S., 1808. Past. New Goshenhoppen, Pa., 1808-'11; Carlisle, Pa.,

1811-'19; First ch., Baltimore, Md., 1819-'35. Removed to Ohio, 1835. Entered P. E. Church, 1836. Returned to the Reformed Ch., 1851. Past. Elizabethtown, Pa., 1851-'53; w. c., 1853-'69.

SAMUEL HELFFENSTEIN, Jr., eldest son of Dr. Samuel; b. Philada., Jan. 13, 1800; d. North Wales, Pa., May 21, 1869. Grad. University Pa., 1820. Stud. Theology with his father and at New Brunswick. Lic. and ord., Syn. U. S., 1822. Past. Shepherdstown, Va., etc., 1822-'25; Assistant, Frederick, Md., 1825-'28; w. c., 1828-'34; Boehm's ch., etc., 1834-'44; w. c., 1844-69'.

ALBERT HELFFENSTEIN, Jr., second son of Dr. Samuel; b. Philada., Mar. 14, 1801; d. North Wales, Pa., Sept. 12, 1870. Grad. Univ. Pa., 1820. Preceptor, Dr. Samuel Helffenstein. Lic. and ord., Syn. U. S., 1822. Asst. in Phila., 1822. Past. Harrisburg, Pa., 1824- ab. 1830; Germantown, 1830-'36; Hagerstown, Md., 1840-'43; Third ch., Phila., 1843-'46. Sup. New Holland chg., Pa., 1852-'58; Maytown, Pa., 1859-'60; w. c., 1860-'70.

JACOB HELFFENSTEIN, D. D., third son of Dr. Samuel; b. Phila., 1802; d. Germantown, Pa., Mar. 17, 1884. During his pastorate, and mainly through his influence, the congregation at Germantown, Pa., was alienated from the Reformed Church.

JOHN HENRY HELFFERICH (*Helffrich*), b. Mosxbach, Ger., Oct. 22, 1739; d. Lehigh co., Pa., Dec. 5, 1810. Stud. at Heidelberg. Sent to America by Synods of Holland, 1772. Past. Weissenburg, Lowhill, Heidelberg, Kutztown, and other churches in Lehigh and Berks cos., 1772-1810.

JOHN HELFFERICH (*Helffrich*), son of John Henry; b. Weissenburg, Lehigh co., Pa., Jan. 17, 1795; d. there, April 8, 1852. Preceptor, Dr. S. Helffenstein. Lic., Syn. U. S., 1816; ord., 1819. Past. Weissenburg, Lowhill, etc. (part of his father's charge), 1816-'51.

ERASMUS H. HELFRICH, b. Lehigh co., Pa., d. Philada. Stud. Mercersburg. Lic. and ord., East Pa. Cl., 1848. Past. Northampton co., Pa., 1848-'57. Deposed 1858.

JEREMIAH HELLER, b. —, Oct. 22, 1807; d. New Jefferson, O., Nov. 3, 1876. Theol. Sem. York, Pa. Lic., Maryland Cl., 1837; ord., 1838. Past. Pendleton co., Va., 1838-'47; McConnellsburg, Pa., 1847-'51; St. Clairsville, Pa., 1851-'56; Martinsburg, Pa., 1856-'58; Fremont, O., 1858-'64; Jenner's Cross Roads, Pa., 1864-'67; Sydney and Tarlton, O., 1867-'71; Hillsboro, O., 1873; Germano, O., 1875; New Jefferson, 1876.

WILLIAM HENDEL, Sr., D. D., b. Palatinate, Ger.; d. Philada., Sept. 29, 1798. Ord. in Germany. Sent to America by the Synods of Holland, 1764. Past. Lancaster, Pa., 1765-'69; Tulpehocken, 1769-'82; Lancaster, 1782-'94; Philada., 1794-'98. Died of yellow fever. See page 213.

WILLIAM HENDEL, Jr., D. D., son of the preceding; b. Lancaster, Pa., Oct. 14, 1768; d. Womelsdorf, Pa., July 11, 1846. Grad. Columbia Col., N. Y.; Theol. Sem., New Brunswick, N. J. Also instructed by Drs. Gros and Livingston. Lic., Syn. U. S., 1792; ord., 1793. Past. Tulpehocken, Pa., 1793-1823; Womelsdorf, 1823-'29; w. c., 1829-'46.

JOHN CHARLES HENEMAN, b. Harhausen, Nassau, Ger., June 4, 1815; d. Glade, Jackson co., O., Sept. 14, 1884. Stud. Mission House, Barmen; Theol. Sem., Mercersburg. Lic. and ord. Westmoreland Cl., 1848. Past. Jefferson co., etc., Pa., 1848-'51; Brown co., O., 1851-'52; Columbus, O., 1852-'56; Beaver ch., O., 1857-'84.

FREDERICK L. HENOP, b. Germany, —; d. Frederick, Md., 1784. Past. Easton, Pa., ab. 1764-'70; Frederick, Md., 1770-'84. Accepted a call to Reading, Pa., but died suddenly.

NECROLOGY.

AUSTIN HENRY, b. near West Alexandria, O., Aug. 17, 1845; d. Canal Winchester, O., April 6, 1885. Grad. Heid. Col., 1870. Theol. Sem., Tiffin, 1872. Lic., Syn. of O.; ord., Lancaster Cl., O., 1872. Past. Kinnick-Kinnick chg., O., 1872-'82; Winchester chg., 1882-'85. President of Synod of Ohio at the time of his death.

FREDERICK LEBRECHT HERMAN, D. D. (*Herrmann*), b. Gusten, Anhalt-Cöthen, Ger., Oct. 9, 1761; d. Upper Hanover, Montgomery co., Pa., Jan. 30, 1848. Stud. Univ. of Halle. Assistant pastor at Bremen, 1782-'85. Sent to America by Synods of Holland, 1786. Past. Easton, Pa., 1786-'90; Germantown and Frankford, 1790-1802; Falkner Swamp, Pottstown, etc., 1802- ab. '42. Pub. "Catechismus," etc. See page 272.

CHARLES GEBLER HERMAN, eldest son of Dr. F. L.; b. Germantown, Pa., Oct., 24, 1792; d. Maxatawny, Berks co., Pa., Aug. 4, 1863. Lic. and ord., Syn. U. S., 1810. Past. Kutztown, etc., Berks co., Pa., 1810-'61. Pub. "Der Sänger am Grabe," etc.

FREDERICK A. HERMAN, second son of Dr. F. L.; b. Germantown, 1795; d. Turbotville, Pa., Oct. 30, 1849. Lic., Syn. U. S., 1815; ord., 1818. Past. New Holland, Pa., 1818-'21. Suspended, 1821.

AUGUSTUS L. HERMAN, third son of Dr. F. L.; b. Montgomery co., Pa., June 11, 1804; d. Reading, Pa., Dec. 31, 1872. Lic., "Free Synod," 1822; ord., 1823. Past. Berks co., Pa., 1823-'72. Published Zollikofer's "Prayer-Book."

REUBEN T. HERMAN, fourth son of Dr. F. L.; b. Montgomery co., Pa., —; d. Norristown, Pa., —; Ord. "Free Synod," 1829. Past. Baumstown, etc., 1829-'36. Subsequently without charge.

LEWIS C. HERMAN, fifth son of Dr. F. L.; b. New Hanover, Montgomery co., Pa., Oct. 13, 1813; d. Carlisle, Pa., July 13, 1884. Lic., "Free Syn.," 1831; ord., 1833. Past. Friedensburg, Pa., 1833-'38; Pottstown, 1838.

OSCAR C. S. HERMAN (son of Rev. J. S. Herman, and great-grandson of Dr. F. L.); b. Kutztown, Pa., Dec. 2, 1848; d. Sept. 5, 1873. Grad. F. and M. Col., 1869; Theol. Sem., Lancaster, 1872. Lic., E. Pa. Cl., 1872.

WILLIAM HERR, b. Allen co., Ind., Aug. 1, 1848; d. Prospect, O., Sept. 19, 1878. Grad. Heidelberg Col., 1872. Lic. and ord., 1873. Past. Broken Sword ch., 1873-'77; Second Marion ch., 1877-'78.

DANIEL HERTZ, b. Dauphin co., Pa., Apr. 23, 1796'; d. Ephrata, Pa., Sept. 22, 1863. Preceptor, Dr. S. Helffenstein. Lic., Syn. U. S., 1823; ord., 1824. Past. Ephrata chg., Lancaster co., Pa., 1823-'68. His charge for many years included a great part of the present Bethany and New Holland charges.

HENRY HESS, b. Bucks co., Pa., Jan. 21, 1811; d. near Mansfield, O., Aug. 12, 1875. Stud. Theol. Sem., Canton, O., 1838. Past. New Lisbon, O.; Trumbull co.; Delaware. Entered the Presb. Ch. After eight years returned to the Reformed Ch. Then past. Delaware (2d time), Galion, Larue, Shelby, Mansfield; Pleasant Valley. Bucks co., Pa., 1868-'74.

SAMUEL HESS, b. Northampton co., Pa., Dec. 25, 1804; d. Hellertown, Pa., Nov. 23, 1875. Preceptor, Dr. J. C. Becker. Lic. and ord., Syn. U. S., 1827. Past. Blue ch,, Apple's, etc.. 1827-'68.

HENRY HIESTAND. In 1812 he was an itinerant preacher of the "United Brethren in Christ." Lic. and. ord., Syn. of Ohio, 1828. Miss. to New Orleans, 1830. Spent several years in Europe. Having been dropped from the roll for absence, he appeared before the Syn. of O., in 1836, and was reinstated. Was permitted to return to Europe and remain a member of the Synod. Revivalist.

WILLIAM HIESTER, b. Bern township, Berks co., Pa., Nov. 11, 1870; d. Lebanon, Pa., Feb. 8, 1828. Preceptor, Rev. Daniel Wagner. Lic., Syn. U. S.. 1798; ord., 1799. Past. Lancaster co., Pa., 1798–1808; Lebanon, etc., 1800–'28.

JOHN HILLEGAS, b. Montgomery co., Pa., Nov. 12, 1800; d. Carollton, O., June 28, 1828. Removed to Ohio, with his parents, 1816. Preceptor, Rev. Geo. Weiss. Lic. and ord., 1826. Past. Carrollton, O., 1826–'28.

JESSE HINES, b. York, Pa., Nov. 2, 1806; d. Reedsburg, O., Jan. 29, 1879. Preceptor, Rev. J. Schlosser. Lic., Sandusky, cl., 1845; ord. Columbiana Cl., 1846. Past. Reedsburg, O., 1846–'55; Nankin, 1856. Johnson's Corner, 1862; Hiawatha, Kansas, 1870. Afterward resided at Akron, and Reedsburg, O.

LEBRECHT L. HINSCH, b. Anhalt-Cöthen, Ger., 1769; d. Piqua, O., Aug. 1864; aged 95 years. Stud., Univ. of Halle. Lic. at Bremen, 1789. Sent to America by the Synod of Holland, 1793. Ord., Syn. U. S., 1794. Past. Creagerstown, Md., 1794–1804. Arendt's ch., Adams co., Pa., 1804–'34; Piqua, Miami co., O., 1834–43; w. c., 1843–64.

JOHN JACOB HOCK, First settled Reformed minister at Lancaster, Pa., 1736–'37.

JOHN JACOB HOCHREUTINER, b. St. Gall, Switzerland; d. Phil., Oct. 14, 1748. Sent to America by Synods of Holland, 1748. Received a call from Lancaster, but was killed by the explosion of a gun which he was attempting to unload.

HENRY HOEGER, A Swiss minister who accompanied De Graffenried's Swiss colony which in 1710 founded Newberne, N. C. Subsequently resided in Virginia.

THEODORE L. HOFFEDITZ, D. D., b. Karlshaven, Hesse-Cassel, Ger., Dec. 16, 1783; d. Nazareth, Pa., Aug. 10, 1858. Came to America, 1807. Preceptor, Dr. S. Helffenstein. Lic., Syn. U. S., 1812; ord., 1815. Mt. Bethel ch., etc., 1812–'58. Commissioner to Germany, 1843–'44.

THEODORE C. W HOFFEDITZ, son of Dr. T. L., b. Upper, Mount Bethel, Northampton co., Pa., Dec. 26, 1818; d. Mercersburg, Pa., Feb. 3, 1859. Grad. M. Col.; 1840; Theol. Sem., Mercersburg, 1842. Past. Hamilton chg., 1842–'45. Subsequently without charge or account of impaired health.

EMANUEL H. HOFFHEINS, b. Dover tsp., York co., Pa., Sept. 18, 1815; d. Abbotstown, Pa., Mar. 28, 1863. Stud. Pennsylvania Col., Gettysburg; Theol. Sem., York, Pa. Lic. Zion's Cl., 1839; ord. Susquehanna Cl., 1839. Past., Beaver Dam ch., Snyder co., Pa., 1839–'40; Elizabethtown, 1840–'50; New Providence, 1850–'52; Abbotstown, 1852–'63.

ANDREW HOFFMAN, b. Bingen, Ger.,—; d. Upper Hanover, Montgomery co., Pa., —; Past. McKeansburg, Pa., 1832–'34; Falkener Swamp ch., 1834. Deposed, 1844.

DANIEL HOFFMAN, Lic. and ord., Syn. U. S., 1796.

HENRY HOFFMAN, b. Chester co., Pa., July 7, 1814; d. Monroeville, Clarion co., Pa., Nov. 27, 1879. Grad. Marshall Col,, 1842; Theol. Sem., 1843. Lic., Lebanon Cl., 1845; ord., Westmoreland Cl., 1846. Past. Beaver chg., Clarion co., Pa., 1846–'55; Shamokin chg., 1855–'58; Berwick Conyngham, 1858–'70; Shannondale chg., Clarion co., 1870–'75; Beaver chg., (2d time) 1875–'79.

JAMES HOFFMAN, brother of Daniel; b. Madison co., Va., 1760; d. Mansfield, O., Aug. 2, 1834. Lic. and ord.. Syn. U. S., 1796. Past. Woodstock, Va.; Chambersburg, Pa. (till 1818), and Shippensburg, etc., till ab. 1823. Removed to Ohio, 1826.

JOHN HENRY HOFFMEIER, b. Anhalt-Cöthen, Ger., Mar. 17, 1760. d. Lancaster, Pa., Mar. 18, 1 36. Stud. Univ of Halle.. Lic. in Bremen, Ger.; ord.

NECROLOGY. 399

Syn. U. S., 1794. Came to America 1793. Past. Lower Saucon, etc., Northampton co., Pa., 1794-1806; Lancaster, Pa., 1806-'31.

CHARLES FREDERICK HOFFMEIER, eldest son of Rev. John Henry; b. Hellertown, Pa., Sept. 24, 1803; d. Lancaster, Pa., Apr. 19, 1877. Preceptor, Rev. Dr. G. W. Glessner. Lic., Lebanon Cl., 1843; ord., Zion's Cl., 1843. Past. Newville chg., Pa., 1843; Bender's ch., Adams co., 1843-'47; Minersville and Pottsville, 1847-'49; Womelsdorf, Eng., 1849-'52; Palmyra chg., 1850-'52; Somerset, 1852-'56; Friend's Cove, 1856-'62; McConnelsburg, 1862-'65; Rebersburg, 1866-'68; New Berlin, 1868-'69; Armstrong Valley, 1869-'70; Liverpool chg., 1870-'72; Luthersburg chg., 1872-'75. Resided Duncannon, Pa., 1875, and in Lancaster.

JOHN WILLIAM HOFFMEIER, son of John Henry; b. Lancaster, Pa., Feb. 29, 1808; d. Manchester, Md., Aug. 30, 1873. Theol. Sem., York, Pa., 1833. Lic. and ord., Maryland Cl., 1833. Past. Glade chg., Md., 1833-'37; Boonsboro, 1837-'43; Woodstock, Va., 1843-'45; Orwigsburg, Pa., 1845-'56; Millersville, near Lancaster, 1856-'62; Manchester, Md., 1872-'73.

HENRY D. HOUTZ, stud. Heid. Col., 1865-'67; Theol. Sem., Tiffin, 1867-'69. Lic., 1869. Accepted a call to Boundary City chg., Ind., but died suddenly.

JOHN HOYMAN, h. Somerset co., Pa., Sept. 28, 1811; d. Delaware co., O., Aug. 16, 1867. Preceptor, Rev. Wm. Conrad. Lic., Westmoreland Cl., 1850; ord., 1852. Past. Shade ch., Pa., 1850-'56; Orangeville, Ill., 1856-'66; Second Marion ch., O., 1866-'67.

CHARLES W. HOYMAN, son of Rev. John; b. Wellersburg, Somerset co., Pa., Nov. 4, 1834; d. Somerset, O., Feb. 10, 1879. Grad. Heid. Col., 1857; Theol. Sem., Tiffin, O., 1858. Lic. and ord., 1858. Past. Somerset, O., 1858-'77. Without charge, from impaired health, 1877-'79.

F. HUNSCHE, d. Holmes co., O., 1874. Ord., 1860.

HERMAN GERHARD IBBEKEN, b. Rasteder, Oldenburg, Ger., Jan. 25, 1801; d. Somerset, Pa., Feb. 8, 1844. Stud. Giessen and Halle. Came to America, 1830. Lic. and ord., Syn. U. S., 1830. Past. Somerset, Bedford, Erie and Crawford cos., Pa., 1831-'44.

JOHN WILLIAM INGOLD, b. Ger.. Came to America, 1774. Past. Whitpain and Worcester; Boehm's ch.; Easton and Lower Saucon; Indianfield and Old Goshenhoppen, 1789; Amity, Berks co., 1791-'96.

JOHN M. INGOLD, son of Rev. John William'; d. Pittsburg, Pa., 1824. Lic. and ord., Syn. U. S., 1815. Past. of two congregations in or near Pittsburg.

MATTHEW IRVIN, b. Cumberland co., Pa., Dec. 22, 1817; d. Bedford, Pa., Apr. 21, 1857. Preceptor, Dr. A. H. Kremer. Lic. and ord., Mercersburg Cl., 1843. Past. Bedford co., Pa., 1843-'55.

JOSEPH H. JOHNSTON, b. Waynesboro, Pa., Aug. 30, 1832; d. Mount Pleasant, Pa., Aug. 26, 1863. Grad. F. and M. Col., 1859; Theol. Sem., 1861. Lic., Westmoreland Cl., 1861. Prof. Westmoreland Col.

JAMES W. JONES, lic., Syn. U. S., 1836. License revoked 1837. Resided in North Carolina.

GARDINER JONES, lic., 1841. Prof. in Marshall College.

WILLIAM KALS. An old minister who came from London, in 1756, with recommendations from Dr. Chandler. Sup. Phila., 1756-'57; Amwell N. J., 1757; German churches on the Raritan, 1758-'59; New York city, 1759-'60.

ABRAHAM KELLER, b. Hanover, Pa., Aug. 10, 1810; d. Bucyrus, O., Sept. 1

NECROLOGY.

1852. Theol. Sem., York, Pa. Lic. and ord., 1835. Past. Shanesville, O., 1835-'40 ; Osnaburg, 1840-'48 ; Bucyrus, 1848-'52.

CHRISTIAN KELLER, b. Schleitheim, Switz., Oct. 6, 1834 ; d. Bridesburg, Pa., Feb. 2, 1883. Ed. St. Crischona, near Basel, Switz. Ord. and sent as missionary to Chili, S. A. Labored 7 years and then returned to his native country. Came to North America, 1872. Past. Bridesburg, near Phila.

JACOB B. KELLER, b. Carlisle, Pa., Dec. 5, 1825; d. Carlisle, Pa., Dec. 28, 1858. Grad. Dickinson Col., 1846; Theol. Sem., Mercersburg, 1850. Lic. Zion's Cl., 1850; ord. Phila. Cl., 1850. Past. Boehm's ch , Montgomery co., Pa., 1850-'56 ; Sulphur Springs, near Carlisle, 1856.

JOHN KELLER, b. ab. 1800; d. Townline, Erie, co., N. Y., May 21, 1852. Preceptor, Rev. Geo. Weisz. Lic. and ord., Syn. O., 1827. Past. Townline, 1852.

DAVID W. KELLY, b. Wrightsville, Pa., Jan. 15, 1833; d. Manchester, Md., Feb. 3, 1877. Stud. Heid. Col.; Theol. Sem., Tiffin, O. Lic. and ord., 1858. Past. Bellevue, O., 1858-'60 ; Shelby chg., 1860-'63 ; New Bloomfield, Pa., 1863-'67; Bellefonte, 1867-'68 ; Turbotville, 1868-'70 ; Shamokin, 1870-'74 ; Manchester, Md., 1874-'76.

ADAM C. KENDIG, b. Conestoga Centre, Lancaster co., Pa., Jan. 8, 1828 ; d. Basil, O., Jan. 16, 1864. Grad. F. & M. Col., 1856 ; Theol. Sem., Mercersburg, Pa. Lic. and ord., Miami Cl., 1857. Syn. of O. Past. West Alexandria, 1858-'61 ; Basil ch., 1863-'64.

JOHN MICHAEL KERN, b. Ger., 1736 ; d. Rockhill township, Bucks co., Pa., Mar. 22, 1788. Ord. in Germany. Sent to America by consistory of Heidelberg, 1763. Past., Nassau street ch., New York City, 1763-'72 ; Montgomery, N. Y., 1772-'78. Loyalist. Resided in Halifax, 1772-'88. Returned, 1788, and accepted a call to Bucks co., Pa., but died the same year.

CHRISTIAN KESSLER, b. Schiers, Switzerland, Nov. 13, 1845; d. Lehighton, Pa., May 26, 1874. Came to America, with his parents, 1847. Grad. F. & M. Col., 1871 ; Theol. Sem., Mercersburg, 1872. Lic. 1871 ; ord., Lebanon Cl , 1872. Past. St. John's, Reading, Pa., 1872-'73 ; Lehighton, 1873-'74.

JOHN S. KESSLER, D. D., b. Schiers, Switzerland, Aug. 19, 1799 ; d. Allentown, Pa., Dec. 22, 1864. Univ. of Basel, 1821. Past. Davos, Switz., 1821-'40. Came to America, 1841. Past. near Woodstock, Va., 1841-'45 ; Asst. Past., Reading, Pa., 1845-'47 ; Fourth ch., Baltimore, Md., 1847-'54. Subsequently engaged in teaching, and preached to several congregations, near Allentown, Pa. Left in MS. " Bible Dictionary," unfinished.

CHRISTIAN RUDOLPH KESSLER, only son of Dr. John S., b. Davos, Switzerland, Feb. 20., 1823 ; d. Allentown, Pa., Mar. 4. 1855. Stud. Cantonal school, Chur ; Univ. of Leipsic. Came to America, 1841. Theol. Sem., Mercersburg, 1843. Lic. and ord., Va. Cl., 1843. Past. Pendleton co., Va., 1843-'44 ; Asst. Past., Salem's ch., Phila., 1844-'46. Founded the " Allentown Seminary," 1848.

S. NEVIN L. KESSLER, only son of Rev. C. R., b. Phila., April 7, 1846 ; d. Mulberry, Ind., April 15, 1879. Grad. Heidelberg Col., 1867 ; Theol. Sem., Tiffin, O., 1868. Lic. and ord., Tiffin Cl., 1868. Past. Liberty Centre chg., O., 1868-'69; Mulberry, Ind., 1869-'79.

NATHAN H. KEYES, b. Tollton N. H.: d. Princeton, Ills., Mar. 28, 1857. Grad. Dartmouth col., 1835 ; Theol. Sem., Andover, Mass. Missionary to Syria, 1840-'44. Entered Reformed ch., 1847. Past St. Paul's, Lancaster, Pa., 1847-'55. Congregational ch., Princeton. Ill , 1855-'57.

NECROLOGY. 401

RUDOHPH KITWEILER, (*Kidenweiler*) b. Switzerland, Jan. 1717; d. Great Swamp, Lehigh co., Pa., Oct. 2. 1764. Past. Long Swamp chg., 1756-'63; Great Swamp chg., 1763-64.

DANIEL J. H. KIEFFER, Lic. Syn. U. S., 1818; ord., 1819. Past. Somerset co., Pa., 1818-'36. Name erased, 1836.

EPHRAIM KIEFFER, b. near Mercersburg, Pa., Jan 17, 1812; d. Carlisle, Pa., May 11, 1871. Theol. Sem., York, Pa., 1836. Lic. and ord., Syn. U., S. 1836. Past. Bellefonte chg., Pa., 1836-'40; Mifflinburg, 1840-'57; Lykens Valley, 1857-'64; w. c., 1864-'66; Sulphur Springs, near Carlisle, 1866- 70.

HENRY KING, b. Rochingham co., Va., Oct. 23, 1802; d. Baltimore, O., Jan. 25, 1885. Preceptor, Rev. Geo. Weisz. Lic. and ord., Syn. O., 1825, Past. Tarlton etc., O., 1825-'49; Somerset chg., (supply); Union chg., 1857-'69. Supplied Stoutsville, etc.

JOHN GEORGE KISSEL, b. Apr. 11, 1798; d. South Whitley, Ind., Oct. 27, 1874. Lic. and ord., St. Joseph Cl., Syn. of Ohio, 1854. Miss. Colon, Mich. Past. Auburn, Ind.; South Whitley, Ind.

PHILIP KLEIN, lic., Phila. Cl., 1849. Name erased, 1850.

CHARLES KNAUS (*Knouse*), b. Montgomery co., Pa. (?) —; d. New York city, 1862 (?): Preceptor, Dr. S. Helffenstein. Ord., Syn. U. S., 1821. Past. Macungie, Pa., 1823; New York city, 1823-'27. Entered Ref. D. Ch. Past. Manhattan ch., N. Y. city, 1829-'33; w. c., 1862.

HENRY KNEPPER, b. Somerset co., Pa., Aug. 25, 1812; d. Orangeville, Ill., Aug. 2, 1879. Lic. and ord., 1841.

JESSE B. KNIPE, b. near North Wales, Pa., Sept. 12, 1804; d. Chester co., Pa., June 18, 1884. Preceptor, Rev. Geo. Wock. Lic. and ord., Syn. U. S., 1830. Past. Pikeland chg., 1830-'83.

HENRY HERMAN KNOEBEL, ord. in Germany. Conditionally received, Syn. U. S., 1820. Past. Schuylkill and Northumberland cos., Pa., 1822-'38. Deposed, 1839.

PHILIP KNOEPFEL, received by Syn. U. S., 1831. Miss. to Western N. Y. Returned to Germany.

HENRY KOCH, b. Northampton co., Pa., 1795; d. Rimersburg, Pa., Aug. 7, 1845. Grandson of Rev. John Egidius Hecker. Preceptor, Dr. C. L. Becker. Lic. and ord., Syn. U. S., 1819. Past. Clarion co., Pa., 1819-'45.

ROBERT KOEHLER, b. Ger., —; d. Meadville, Pa., Jan. 29, 1870. Stud. Univ. of Jena. Lic. and ord., Ref. Ministerium of Belgium ab., 1833. Came to America after 1838. Past. Mt. Eaton, O. (Ger. and French), 1846; Pittsburg, Pa., 1847-'49; Buffalo, N. Y.; Rochester, N. Y.; French ch., Mt. Eaton, O., 1853-'62; Akron, O., 1862-'64. Chaplain 108th Regt. Ohio Volunteers, 1863-'65. Miss. Titusville, Pa., 1866. Removed to Meadville, Pa., 1857, and became independent.

JOHN R. KOOKEN, b. Centre co., Pa., 1815; fell at the battle of Fredericksburg, Va., Dec. 13, 1862. Stud. High School, York, Pa.; Theol. Sem., Mercersburg, 1841. Lic. and ord., Susquehanna Cl., 1841. Past. Dauphin chg., 1841-'43; Grindstonehill, 1843-'44; Trappe, 1844-'47; Norristown, 1847-'52, where he founded the Elmwood Female Seminary; was Consul at Trinidad, Cuba; in 1862 he entered the Union army.

STEPHEN KIEFFER KREMER, son of Dr. A. H. Kremer; b. Shippensburg, Pa., Feb. 1, 1845; d. Greencastle, Pa., Aug. 16, 1876. Grad. F. and M. Col., 1865; Theol. Sem., Mercersburg, 1870. Lic., Lancaster Cl., Syn. U. S., 1870; ord., Virginia Cl., 1870. Past. Martinsburg, W. Va., 1870-'74; Greencastle, 1874-'76.

HENRY KROH, b. near Womelsdorf, Pa., June 17, 1799; d. Stockton, Cal., Dec. 15, 1869. Preceptor, Rev. Jonathan Helffenstein. Lic. and ord., Syn. U. S., 1824. Past. Newtown ch., Va., 1824- ab. 1827; Cavetown, Md., 1827-'29; Lebanon, Pa., 1829-'36; Mt. Carmel, ch., Ill., 1836; Evansville, Ind., 1842; Jonesboro, Ill., 1844; Cincinnati, O., 1845-'48, Removed to California, 1849.

H. KROLL, b. ab. 1780; d. Schuylkill co., Pa., 1845. Lic., Syn. U. S., 1810. License revoked, 1811. Preached irregularly in Schuylkill co., Pa.

EBERHARD KUELEN, b. —; d. Dahlgren, Minn., July 20, 1872.

CHARLES LANGE, past. Frederick, Glades, Taneytown, etc., Md., 1766-'68.

JOHN LANTZ, b. Lincoln co., N. C., May, 1811; d. Taneytown, Md., Jan. 26, 1873. Theol. Sem., York, Pa., 1837. Lic., Syn. U. S., 1837 ord., North Carolina Cl., 1838. Past. Rowan and adjacent cos., N. C., 1838-'68; Middlebrook chg., Va., 1863-'72; Taneytown, Md., 1872-'73.

JOHN JACOB LA ROSE, b. Macungie township, Lehigh co., Pa., Feb., 1755; d. Miamisburg, O.. Nov. 17, 1844. A soldier in the Revolutionary war. Lic., Presb. Ch., N. C., 1795; ord., Syn. U. S., 1821. Past. Guilford co., N. C., 1795-1804. Removed to Ohio, 1804. Montgomery co., O., 1805-'12; Highland co., 1812-'16; Montgomery co., 1816-'18; Eaton, 1818-'23. Engaged extensively in missionary labors, visiting and organizing churches in Ohio, Indiana, and Kentucky.

JOSEPH LA ROSE, b. Lehigh co., Pa., ab. 1800; d. Bloomsburg, Pa., —. Preceptor, Dr. J. C. Becker. Lic. and ord., Syn. U. S., 1823. Past. Hummelstown, Pa., 1823-'26; Bloomsburg, Pa., 1826- —.

F. LAUERER (*Launerer, Launer,* and *Lauer*), Admitted to "Free Synod" as an ordained minister, 1835. Appointed missionary in New Jersey.

ADAM M. LECHNER, preceptor, Rev. J. W. Dechant. Lic., Syn. U. S., 1829. Past. of congregations in Herkimer co., N. Y.

JACOB M. LE FEVRE, b. Warren co., O., Aug. 19, 1833; d. St. Paris, Champaign co., O., Apr. 2, 1882. Stud. Heid. Col. Lic., 1855; ord., 1856. Past. Carrollton chg., O., 1859-'64; Fairfield ch., 1864-'80.

JAMES LEIBERT, b. Forks twp., Northampton co., Pa., Dec. 14, 1836; d. Fremont, O., Nov. 13, 1870. Preceptors, Drs. E. W. Reinecke and Max Stern. Theol. Sem., Tiffin, O. Lic., Tiffin Cl., 1862; ord., Indiana Cl., 1863. Past. Dayton chg., Ind., 1863-'66; Galion, Eng., 1866-'68; Fremont ch., 1868-'70.

GEORGE LEIDY, b. Franconia twp., Montgomery co., Pa., Nov. 7, 1793; d. Norristown, May 30, 1879. Preceptor, Rev. Geo. Wack. Lic., Syn. U. S., 1818; ord., 1819. Miss. in Southern States, 1819-'20. Past. Woodstock, Va., 1820-'23; Westminster, Md., 1823-'31; Cumberland Valley, Pa., 1831-'36; Friend's Cove chg., 1836-'45. Agent for Church Periodicals.

THOMAS H. LEINBACH, b. Oley, Berks co., Pa., Jan. 18, 1802; d. Millersburg, Pa., March 31, 1864. Preceptor, Dr. F. L. Herman. Lic., "Free Synod," 1822; ord., 1823. Past. Millbach, etc., 1822; Tulpehocken chg., 1826-'64.

CHARLES H. LEINBACH, D. D., younger bro. of Thos. H.; b. Oley, Berks co., Pa., Nov. 7, 1815; d. Tulpehocken, Pa., July 15, 1883. Theol. Sem., Mercersburg, 1841. Lic. and ord., 1841. Past. Landisburg, Pa., 1842-'59; Lewisburg, 1859-'64; Tulpehocken, 1864-'83.

JOHN ADAM LEISS, b. Tulpehocken, Berks co., Pa., Feb. 8, 1807; d. near Wernersville, Pa., Oct. 28, 1877. Preceptors, Rev. Thos. Winters and Dr. David Winters. Lic. and ord., Syn. of O., 1835. Past. in Ohio, 1835-'36; Berks co., Pa., 1837-

NECROLOGY. 403

'38; York and Cumberland cos., 1838–'43; Lyken's Valley ch., 1843–'56; Ogle co., Ill., 1856–'57; Miamisburg, O., 1857–'67; w. c., 1867–'77.

SAMUEL B. LEITER, D. D., b. Leitersburg, Md., Apr. 19, 1809; d. Wadsworth, O., Mar. 31, 1883. Theol. Sem., York, Pa., 1835. Lic. and ord., Maryland Cl., 1835. Past. Mansfield, O., 1835–'44; Rome, Richland co., 1844–'49; Navarre, 1849–'68; Wadsworth, 1868–'83.

GEORGE A. LEOPOLD, —; d. Cal. Theol. Sem., York, Pa., 1832. Lic., Syn. U. S., 1832; ord., 1833. Past. Rockingham co., Va.; Winchester, Va. Suspended, 1842.

DANIEL B. LERCH, b. Pa., July 7, 1806; d. Cabarrus co., N. C., Mar. 18, 1834. Theol. Sem., York, Pa,, 1830. Past. Rowan co., N. C., 1830–'34.

JOHN W. LESCHER, b. near Easton, Pa., May 23, 1817; d. Millersburg, Pa., Jan. 27, 1875. Theol. Sem., Mercersburg, 1843. Lic. and ord., East Pa. Cl., 1844. Past. Wilkesbarre, Pa.; Bloomsburg; Selinsgrove; Lykens Valley.

JOHN PHILIP LEYDICH, b. Ger., April 28, 1715; d. Montgomery co., Pa., Jan. 4, 1784. Ord. in Germany. Sent to America, 1748, by Synod of South Holland. Past. Falkener Swamp, etc., Pa., 1748–'84.

JACOB LEYMEISTER (*Leymaster*); b. —; d. Orwisburg, Pa., July 12, 1833. Theol. Sem., Carlisle, Pa., 1830. Ord., Syn. U. S., 1831. Past. Zions and White Oak, Lancaster co., 1831–'33.

JOHN LEOPOLD LICHTENSTEIN, D. D., b. Hechingen, Ger., Apr. 10, 1813; d. Cincinnati, O., Nov. 4, 1882. Converted from Judaism to Christianity, 1834. Stud. at Erlangen and Berlin. Received the degree of Dr. of Theology from the University of Berlin, 1842. Ord. a Reformed minister, 1842. Came to America. 1845. Entered Presbyterian Church. Past. Ger. Presb. ch., Paterson, N. J., 1848–'51; New Albany, Ind., 1851–'54. Entered Ref. ch. Past. Buffalo, N. Y., 1854–'62; First Ref. ch., Cincinnati, O., 1862–'66. Returned to Presb. ch. Past. First Ger. Presb. ch., Cincinnati, 1866–82. A prolific author.

CHARLES LIENEKEMPER, b. Iserlohn, Westphalia, Ger., Aug. 10. 1822; d. Waukon, Iowa, Nov. 14. 1879. Stud. M. Col., and Theol. Sem., Mercersburg, Pa. Lic., 1854; ord., St. John's Cl., 1855. Past. Calcutta chg., O., 1855–'59; Medina, Wis., 1859–'65; Lowell, Wis., 1867–'73: Waukon, Ia., 1873-79.

JACOB LISCHY, b. Mülhausen, Switz.—; d York co., Pa., 1781. Ord. 1743. Preached in Lancaster, Berks, and York cos., Pa. Became a member of Coetus, 1748. Past., York, Pa., etc. Deposed ab. 1760. Published several pamphlets. See page 94.

ERICH F. LOEDERS, d. Lafayette, Ind., May 12, 1870, aged 58 years. Lic. and ord., Sandusky Cl., Syn. of O., 1854. Miss. Auglaize co., O., 1854. Past. Dayton, O., Second ch., 1857–'62.

DAVID LONG, b. Lebanon co., June 22, 1801; d. Somerset, O., June 19, 1833. Preceptor, Rev. Geo. Weiss. Lic. and ord., Syn. of O., 1826. Past. Somerset ch., O., 1826–'33.

GEORGE LONG, b. —, Jan. 6, 1814; d. Indianapolis, Ind., Dec. 26, 1879.

ANDREW LORETZ. Came to America, 1784 or 1785. Past. Tulpehocken, etc., 1785-'86. Returned to Switzerland.

ANDREW LORETZ, son of the preceding, b. Switzerland; d. near Lincolnton, N. C., 1812. Ord., Syn. U. S., 1789. Labored in North and South Carolina.

EDMUND A. LUDWIG, PH. D., b. Berne, Switzerland, —; d. Erie, Pa.,

1880. Educated in Europe. Prof. in Washington Col., Va. Lic., East Pa. Cl., 1868. Remained without charge.

LUDWIG LUPP, b. Europe, Jan. 7, 1733; d. Lebanon, Pa., June 28, 1798. Past Lebanon, Pa., 1786-'98. Also preached at Manheim, Maytown, and elsewhere.

JOHN B. MADOULET, d. Burlington, Ills., ab. 1855. Ord. 1848. Entered R. D. church, 1853.

WILLIAM H. MAERTENS, Lic., Syn. U. S., 1835; ord., Cl. of Md., 1836. Past. Washington city ch., 1836.

JOHN P. MAHNENSCHMIDT, b. Pennsylvania, 1783; d. Canfield, O., July 11, 1857. Lic., Syn. U. S., 1812; ord., 1817. Preached Westmoreland co., Pa., 1806-'11. Past. Columbiana and adjoining cos., O., 1812-'57.

JOHN MANN, Lic. and ord., Syn. U. S., 1792. Past. Lower Saucon and Springfield, Pa., 1792-'95. Removed to Mt. Bethel, Pa., and became a farmer, 1795. Name erased, 1802.

DAVID MARTZ, d. Shanesville, O., Feb. 19, 1849, aged 36. Lic. and ord., 1845. Past. Shanesville, O., etc , 1845-'49.

JACOB MAYER, b. Lykens Valley, Pa., Sept. 15, 1798; d. Lock Haven, Pa., Oct. 29, 1872. Preceptors, Rev. J. R. Reily and Dr. S. Helffenstein. Lic. and ord., Syn. U. S., 1822. Past. Woodstock, Va., 1822-'25; Shrewsbury, Pa., 1825-'33; Mercersburg and Greencastle, 1833-'36. Agent of Theol. Sem. for 8 years. Subsequently without charge.

LEWIS MAYER, D. D., b. Lancaster, Pa., Mar. 26, 1783; d. York, Pa., Aug. 25, 1849. Preceptor, Rev. Daniel Wagner. Lic., Syn. U. S., 1807; ord., 1808. Past. Shepherdstown, Va., 1808-'21; York, Pa., 1821-'25. First Prof. Theol. Sem., 1825-'37. Author of "Sin against the Holy Ghost;" "Lectures on Scriptural Subjects;" "History of German Ref. Church," vol. 1. See page 281.

PHILIP MAYER, b. Tulpehocken, Pa., May 12, 1783; d. Orwigsburg, Pa., July 10, 1870. Preceptor, Dr. C. L. Becker. Lic. and ord., Syn. U. S., 1809. Past. of churches in Berks and Schuylkilll cos., Pa., 1809-'57. W. c., 1857-'76.

VINCENT P. MAYERHOFFER, studied in Germany for R. C. priesthood. Ord., Syn. U. S., 1826. Past. Meadville, Pa., 1826-'28. Entered P. E. ch. and d. in Canada.

GREGORY H. MEIBOOM, b. Emden, East Friesland, Oct. 1, 1841; d. Milwaukee, Wis., July 18, 1876. Stud. Mission House, Sheboygan, Wis., 1869-'70. Lic. and ord., 1870. Asst. Past., Galion, O., 1870. Past. Ironton, O., 1870-'74; Jeffersonville, Ind., 1874-'76.

PHILIP JACOB MICHAEL, b. Ger. —; d. Lynn twp., Lehigh co., Pa., ab. 1770. Independent. Founder of " Ziegel" ch. Pastor at Maxatawny, etc.

JOHN JACOB MEYER. Rec'd, Synod U. S. 1848, from Switz.

ISAAC MIESE, b. Centre township, Berks co., Pa., Mar. 31, 1812; d. Bernville, Feb. 1, 1864. Past. Berks co., Pa. Declared himself independent, 1863.

SOLOMON S. MIDDLEKAUFF, b. Hagerstown, Md., 1818; d. Mineral Springs, N. C., May 21, 1845. Grad. Marshall Col., 1839; Theol. Sem., Mercersburg, 1842. Lic., Mercersburg Cl., 1842; ord., North Carolina Cl., 1842. Past. Lincolnton ch., N. C., 1842-'45.

PHILIP MILLEDOLER, D. D., b. Rinebeck, N. Y., Sept. 22, 1775; d. Staten Island, N. Y., Sept. 23, 1852. Grad. Columbia Col., N. Y., 1793. Preceptor, Dr. J. D. Gros. Lic. and ord., Syn. U. S., 1794. Past. Ger. Ref. ch., Nassau st., N. Y.,

NECROLOGY. 405

1794-1800; Pine st. (Presb.) ch., Phila., 1800-'05; Rutgers st. (Presb.) ch.. N. Y., 1805-'13; Collegiate (Ref. D.) ch., N. Y., 1813-'25. Elected Prof. of Theol., Ger. Ref. ch., 1820, but declined. Prof. of Theol. and Pres. of Rutgers Col., N. Y., 1825-'40.

HENRY MILLER, b. near Phœnixville, Pa., May 26, 1807; d. Waynesboro, Pa., May 29, 1883. Preceptor, Rev. Dr. S. Helffenstein. Lic., "Free Synod," 1831; ord., 1835. Past. London and St. Thomas, Pa., 1835-'38; Tarlton, O., 1838-'42. Subsequently without charge. Agent S. S. Union, etc.

JOHN C. MILLER, b. — Aug. 1826; d. Dayton, O., Oct. 5, 1851. Lic. and ord., Lancaster Cl., Syn. of O., 1850. Miss., Findlay and Bethlehem, O., 1850-'51.

JOHN PETER MILLER, b. Lautern, Palatinate, 1710; d. Ephrata, Pa., Sept. 23, 1796. Prior at Ephrata. See page 175.

SAMUEL MILLER, b. New Berlin, Pa., Mar. 23, 1815; d. Philada., Oct. 11, 1873. Lic., Lebanon Cl., 1842; ord., Susquehanna Cl., 1843. Past. Dauphin chg., Pa., 1843-'45; Harmony, 1845-'52; Grindstone Hill chg.; Pottsville, Pa., 1860. Supply, Meyerstown, Pa., 1858-'59. Wyoming, Del. Associate editor, "Messenger" and "Kirchenzeitung," 1852; sole editor of the latter, 1854-'58. Author of "Mercersburg and Modern Theology Compared," Phila., 1866.

GEORGE MILLS, b. Montgomery co., Pa., —; d. New York City. Preceptor, Dr. S. Helffenstein. Lic., Syn. U. S., 1822; ord., "Free Synod," 1829. Past. Forsyth st. ch., New York, 1829-'33. Dismissed to Presb. ch., 1834.

FREDERICK G. MOSCHOP. Lic., Syn. of O., 1835; ord., 1836. Past. Galion, etc., 1839. Name erased, 1842.

FREDERICK MOYER, b. Fairfield co., O., Mar. 22, 1844; d. Bremen, O., Jan. 24, 1869. Grad. Heid. Col. Lic., Tiffin Cl., 1868. Miss., Akron, O., 1868. Tutor in Heid. Col.

EMANUEL CHRISTOPHER MUELLER, b. Tübingen, Würtemberg, Aug. 14, 1845; d. Wheeling, W. Va., Oct. 22, 1875. Came to America, 1866. Stud. Miss. House, Sheboygan. Lic. and ord., Ind. Cl., 1868. Past. Crothersville, Ind., 1868-'69; Rising Sun, 1869-'72; Pittsburg, Pa., 1872-'73; Wheeling, W. Va., 1873-'75.

JOHN J. MUELLER (*Miller*). Past. Dagersheim, St. Gall, Switz. Came to America ab., 1835. Past. New Orleans, La., 1835-'39. Rec'd, Syn. of O., 1839.

THEODORE MUELLER, b. Stargard, Ger., Jan. 17, 1834; d. Canton, O., Dec. 29, 1870. Lic., St. John's Cl., Syn. of O.. 1869.

P. A. B. MEISTER. Rec'd, Maryland Cl., 1852. Past., Frederick City, Md., (German) 1853. Name erased, 1854.

DAVID MUCK, lic. and ord., Syn. of O., 1831. Past. Crawford, Venango, and Erie cos., Pa.

CHRISTOPHER MUNZ (*Mancius?*) In 1757 Coetus made a gift to his widow. Otherwise unknown.

BENJAMIN T. NEAL. Lic. and ord., "Free Synod," 1834. Miss. Troy, N. Y., 1836. Past. Clearspring, Md., 1841-'45. Dis. to Presb. ch., 1847.

FRANCIS NETSCHER, b. Hesse-Darmstadt, Ger., April 15, 1826; d. Millville, Clarion co., Pa., April 16, 1859. Came to America, 1838. Grad. F & M. Col., 1854. Theol. Sem., Mercersburg. Lic. and ord., 1856. Past., Benders chg., Adams co., Pa., 1856-'58; Redbank chg., Clarion co., 1858-'59.

JOHN W. G. NEVELLING, b. Westphalia, Ger., 1750; d. Philada., Jan. 18. 1844. Preceptors, Drs. Weyberg & Gros. Lic., Coetus, Pa., 1771; ord. 1772. Past.

Amwell, N. J., 1771-'82; Reading, Pa., 1883. Chaplain in the Revolutio.1. An invalid for sixty years.

J. A. NICOLAI, b. Hesse-Darmstadt, Ger., Aug. 7, 1821; d. Dickinson co., Kans., Nov. 20, 1882. Came to America, 1831.

JOHN JACOB OEHL (*Ehle—Eal.*) Past. West Camp, N. Y., 1710-'20 (?); Schoharie aud Valley of the Mohawk, 1720-'50 (?). Miss. to Mohawk Indians, 1720-7. Supplied Kinderhook, 1720-'27. Preached German and Dutch.

TRUMAN OSBORN. Received, 1838, from Presb. of Baltimore. Past., Germantown, Pa., 1838-'42. Dis. to Presb. ch., 1843.

WILLIAM OTTERBEIN, b. Dillenburg, Nassau, Ger., June 3, 1726; d. Baltimore, Md., Oct. 17, 1813. Stud. at Herborn, 1742. Lic., 1748; ord., 1749. Vicar at Ockersdorf, 1749. Came to America with Schlatter, 1752. Past., Lancaster, Pa., 1752-'58; Tulpehocken, 1758-'60; Frederick, Md., 1760-'65; York, Pa., 1765-'74; Second ch., Baltimore (Conway st.), 1774-1813. See page 214.

JACOB ORTH, b. Colony of Worms, Southern Russia, 1837; d. Yankton, Da., Nov. 3, 1883. Came to America ab., 1873. Lic. and ord., Sheboygan Cl., 1877. Missionary among his countrymen in Southern Dakota.

PHILIP REINHOLD PAULI, b. Magdeburg, Ger., June 22, 1742; d. Reading, Pa., Jan. 27, 1815. Stud. Univ. of Halle and Leipzig. Came to America, 1783. Teacher in Phila., 1783-'89. Lic. and ord., Coetus Pa., 1789. Past. Worcester and Whitpain, 1789-'93; Reading, Pa., 1793-1815.

WILLIAM PAULI, son of Philip R., b. Skippack twp., Montgomery co., Pa., March 9, 1792; d. Reading, Pa., May 20, 1855. Lic., Syn. U. S., 1812; ord., 1816. Past. Reading, Pa., 1816-'44. Subsequently independent.

CHARLES AUGUSTUS PAULI, son of Philip R., b. Reading, Pa., April 12, 1804; d. Reading, Pa., Oct. 5, 1871. Lic. and ord., Syn. U. S., 1825. Past. St. John's, Berks co , 1825-'26; Dauphin co., 1826-'33; Hain's etc., Berks co., 1834-'71. Independent after 1845.

CASPAR PLUESS, b. Aargau, Switzerland, Apr. 28, 1825; d. Crothersville, Ind., Feb. 28, 1878 Miss. Inst., Basel, Switz. Came to America, 1849. First missionary of the Synod of the Northwest. Past. Emmanuel's ch., Wis., 1849; Lawrence, Ind., Arnheim, O., 1859-'64; subsequently disabled and without charge.

FREDERICK W. PLASSMAN, b. 1816; d. Floral College, N. C., Sept. 30, 1848. Lic. and ord., 1844. Miss., China Grove, N .C., 1844. Past. Davidson co., N. C., 1846-'47.

PETER PAUL PERNISIUS, b. Graubünden, Switz. Came to America, 1784. Past. Allen, Lehigh and Moor township, Northampton co., Pa., 1784-91. Suspended.

NICHOLAS POMP, b. Manbüchel, near Zweibrücken, Ger., Jan. 20, 1734; d. Easton, Pa., Sept. 1, 1819. Stud. Marburg. Ord. at Cassel, Hesse. Sent to America by the Synods of Holland, 1765. Past., Falkener Swamp, 1765-'83; Baltimore, Md., 1783-'89; Goshenhoppen (supply) 1789-'91; Indianfield, etc., 1791- ab. 1800. Subsequently disabled and resided in Easton, Pa. Author of "Kurze Prüfungen etc.," Phila., 1774. See page 213.

THOMAS POMP, only son of the preceding, b. Skippack twp., Montgomery co., Pa., Feb. 4, 1773; d. Easton, Pa., Apr. 22, 1852. Lic., Syn. U. S., 1793; ord., 1795 Past. Montgomery co., 1793-'96; Easton, Pa., 1796-1852. Also pastor, at various times, of the Plainfield, Dryland, Lower Saucon, Upper Mt. Bethel, and other churches.

LOUIS R. PORTER, d. 1834. Lic. "Free Synod," 1831. Received by Syn. of O., 1834. Past. Mt. Vernon ch., Knox co., O., 1834-'35.

JOHN G. PFRIMMER (*Phriemer*), b. Alsace, 1762; d. near Corydon, Ind., 1825. Came to America, 1788. Irregularly ord. by a member of Coetus, probably by Gueting. Prominent among the founders of the "United Brethren in Christ."

JOSIAH J. PENNYPACKER, b. Philada., Pa., Dec. 13, 1835; d. London, Mercer co., Pa., Apr. 23, 1884. Grad. F. and M. Col., 1864; Theol. Sem., Lancaster, 1867. Past. Armstrong co., Pa., 1867–'72. Principal Reimersburg Collegiate Institute, 1872–'82; Mercer co. (mission), 1883–'84.

PITHAN (or *Bitthahn*). Past. Easton, Plainfield, Greenwich, and Dryland, 1769. Deposed 1771. Became an ecclesiastical vagabond, and preached a short time in many churches, from Pennsylvania to South Carolina.

JOHN PENCE, b. Rockingham co., Va., Dec. 13, 1799; d. Tremont city, O., Apr. 18, 1883. Preceptor, Dr. Thos. Winters. Lic. and ord., Ohio Cl., 1824. Past. of several charges in Ohio.

DANIEL RAHAUSER, d. Mifflin, O., Jan. 3, 1848. Lic. and ord., 1821. Past. Harmony, Pa., 1821; Columbiana co., O., etc., 1824; Ashland, O., ab. 1831.

JONATHAN RAHAUSER, b. York co., Pa., Dec. 14, 1764; d. Hagerstown, Md., Sept. 25, 1817. Preceptor, Dr. W. Hendel, Sr. Lic., Coetus Pa., 1789; ord., 1791. Past. Shamokin chg., 1789–'92; Hagerstown, Md., 1792–1817.

FREDERICK A. RAHAUSER, brother of Jonathan; b. York co., Pa. Mar., 1782; d. East Liberty, Pa., July 15, 1865. Preceptors, Rev. J. Rahauser and Daniel Wagner. Lic. and ord., Syn. U. S., 1808. Past. Emmittsburg, Md., 1808–'16; Harrisburg, Pa., 1819; Chambersburg, 1819–'36; Tiffin, O., 1836–'40; Sandusky and Seneca cos., 1840–'55.

WILLIAM C. RANKIN, b. North Carolina, —; d. Jasper, Ind., ab. 1839. Received from Presb. Ch., 1835. Miss. Mountain Creek, N. C., 1836; Jasper, Ind., 1838.

FRANCIS M. RASCHIG, b. Ger., Jan. 11, 1804; d. Cincinnati, O., Aug. 16, 1873. Theol. Sem., York, Pa. Lic. and ord., Syn. U. S., 1833. Dauphin co., 1833–'35; Cincinnati, O., 1835–'73. Independent after 1837.

HENRY RASSMAN, b. Ger., Apr. 20, 1753; d. Centre co., Pa., Dec. 23, 1832. Taught school in Lancaster and Centre cos. Lic., Syn. U. S., 1812; ord., 1818. Past. Boalsburg, Penns Creek, etc., 1812; Rebersburg, Aaronsburg, etc., 1813–'28.

CHRISTIAN HENRY RAUCH, b. Bernburg, Anhalt, Ger., July 5, 1718; d. Jamaica, West Indies, Nov. 11, 1763. Came to America, 1740. First Moravian missionary to the Indians. Ord. a minister of the Reformed branch of the "Congregation of God," ab. 1742. Preached at Heidelberg, Tulpehocken, and many other places in Lancaster, Berks, Lebanon, and York counties. Miss. among the negroes in the West Indies.

FREDERICK AUGUSTUS RAUCH, Ph. D., b. Kirchbracht, Hesse-Darmstadt, July 27, 1806; d. Mercersburg, Pa., March 2, 1841. Stud. Marburg, Giessen, and Heidelberg. Prof. extraordinary at Giessen. Came to America, 1831. Prof. of German, Lafayette Col., 1831–'32. Principal of High School at York, 1832–'35. Prof. in Theol. Sem., 1832–'41. President of Marshall Col., 1835–'41. See page 286.

JOHN REBAUGH, b. Abbottstown, Pa., Sept., 1802; d. Harrisburg, Pa., Feb. 1, 1871. Preceptor, Dr. Dashields. Served several years in the U. B. Church. Lic. and ord., Syn. U. S., 1830. Past. Shippensburg, Pa., 1830–'31; Boonsboro, Md., 1831–'37; Greencastle, Pa., 1837–'51, and Clearspring, Md., etc., till 1663. Subsequently disabled.

JOEL L. REBER, b. Heidelberg twp., Berks co., Pa., Nov. 8, 1816; d. York co., Pa., Aug. 15, 1856. Stud. Mercersburg, Pa., 1838–'42. Lic. and ord., Susquehanna

Cl., 1843. Past. Rebersburg, etc., 1843-'44; Jonestown, 1845-'51; Millersville, Lancaster co., 1852-'55; Codorus chg., 1855-56. Author of "Secten-Geist und Secten-Wesen," Chambersburg, 1850.

J. S. REGNIER, b. Switz., —; d. Bethlehem, O. Past. Berlin chg., Somerset co., Pa., 1834-'35; Bethlehem, O., 1835.

JOHN BARTHOLOMAUS RIEGER, c. Oberengelheim, Palatinate, Jan. 10, 1707; d. Lancaster, Pa., Mar. 11, 1769. Stud. Univ. of Heidelberg. Came to America, 1731. Preached in Lancaster, Pa., and vicinity. Also practiced medicine. One of the founders of the Coetus. See page 172.

CHARLES REIGHLEY, past. Frederick city, Md., 1833-'35. Deposed 1835.

JAMES ROSS REILY, b. Meyerstown, Pa., Oct., 31, 1788; d. York, Pa., Mar. 18, 1844. Preceptor, Dr. C. L. Becker. Lic., Syn. U. S., 1812; ord., 1817. Past. Lykens Valley, 1812-'18; Hagerstown, Md.; York, Pa., 1827-'31. Miss. to N. C., 1813. Agent in Europe for the Theol. Sem., 1825-'26. Withdrew from the active ministry, 1831, on account of ill health.

JOHN REINECKE, b. Helmarshausen, Hesse-Cassel, Aug. 11, 1789; d. Shrewsbury, Pa., Apr. 15, 1859. A soldier under Napoleon, and in the Prussian "army of liberation." Came to America, 1834. Lic. and ord., Cl. of Zion, 1837. Past. Shrewsbury chg., York co., Pa., 1837-'57.

JAMES REINHART, b. near Waynesburg, O., Apr. 16, 1839; d. Columbiana, O., Aug. 29, 1870. Stud. Heid. Col. Lic. St. John's Cl., 1860. Past. Springfield chg., 1860-'70.

WILLIAM REITER, b. Lancaster co., Pa., Sept. 30, 1799; d. Shanesville, O., May 16, 1826. Preceptor, Rev. H. Sonnedecker. Lic. and ord., Syn. U. S., 1823. Past. Shanesville, New Philadelphia, etc., O., 1823-'26.

SOLOMON REUTLINGER. d. Benita, West Africa, July 17, 1869.

HENRY L. RICE, b. 1795; d. Chambersburg, Pa., May 3, 1837. Lic. and ord., Ref. D. Ch., 1824. Miss., 1824-'26. Past. Spottswood, N. J., 1826-'34. Entered Ger. Ref. Ch., 1834. Past. Chambersburg, Pa., 1834-'37. Agent for institutions at Mercersburg, 1836-'37.

SIMON RIEGEL. Lic. and ord., 1821.

G. H. RIEMENSCHNEIDER. Lic. and ord., Free Syn., 1832. Dis., 1836.

J. J. RIEMENSCHNEIDER, brother of the preceding. Lic. and ord., Free Syn., 1832. Dis. 1836.

JACOB RIESS (*Reiss*), b. Ger., Apr. 10, 1706; d. Tohickon, Pa., Dec. 13, 1774. Past, Indianfield, 1749-'53; New Goshenhoppen, 1763-'66; Lower Saucon; Tohickon, 1774.

JOHN RIKE, b. Montgomery co., O., Feb. 11, 1826; d. Lancaster, O., Sept. 7, 1854. Theol. Sem., Columbus, O., 1848-49. Lic. and ord., Lancaster, O., 1849. West Alexandria, O., 1849-'54; Lancaster, O., 1854.

ABRAHAM ROSENKRANTZ, b. — d. ab., 1794. Past., Canajoharie, N. Y., 1758; Nassau st., ch., New York, 1758-'59; Schoharie, 1760-'65; Canajoharie and German Flats, 1765-'94.

FREDERICK ROTHENBUEHLER, b. Bern, Switzerland, July 29, 1726; d. Philadelphia, Aug. 7, 1766. Ord. in Europe, 1752. Past. Ger. Ref. Ch., London, Eng., 1759-'60. Came to America, 1760. Past. New York, 1761-'62; Race st. ch., Phila., 1762. Not received by Coetus on account of improper conduct. Organized an independent congregation, and built a church, which after his death was sold to

NECROLOGY. 409

the Methodists and is now known as "St. George's," the oldest Methodist church in Philadelphia.

JOHN CASPER RUBEL, b. Ger., — ; 1797. Came to America, with Schlatter, 1752. Pastor of 2d. congregation of Phila., ab., 1753-'55; Camp, Red Hook, and Rhinebeck, N. J., 1755-'59. Brooklyn, Flatlands, etc., 1759-'83. Deposed, 1784—.

JOHN RUDY, b. Switzerland, 1791; d. New York City, Feb. 8, 1842. Lic. and ord., Syn. U. S., 1821. Past., Guilford, N. C., 1821-'24; Germantown, N. Y., 1825-'35; Miss. to Germans, N. Y. City, 1835-'38. Ger. Ev. Mission, N. Y., 1838-'42. Entered Ref. D. church, 1840.

JOHN WILLIAM RUNKEL, b. Oberengelheim, Palatinate, Apr. 28, 1749; d. Gettysburg, Pa., Nov. 5, 1832. Came to America, 1764. Lic., Coetus Pa., 1777; ord., 1778. Past., Cumberland and adjoining counties, 1777-'81; Lebanon, etc., 1781-'84; Frederick, Md., etc., 1784-1802; Germantown, Pa., 1802-'05; Forsyth st. ch., N. Y., 1805-'12; Gettysburg, Pa., 1815-'22. W. c., 1822-'32. Performed much missionary labor, and preached for many churches in Pa., Md., and Va.

JOHN RUNKEL. Lic. and ord., Syn. U. S., 1808. Served in the ministry, 1808-'12, and then entered the medical profession.

CHRISTIAN C. RUSSELL, b. near Leitersburg, Md., Oct. 7, 1827; d. Camden, N. J., Nov. 17, 1871. Grad. F. & M. Col., 1853. Theol. Sem., Mercersburg, 1856. Lic. and ord., Mercersburg Cl., 1856. Past., Columbia, Pa., 1857; Latrobe, Pa., 1857-'71 ; Wyoming, Del., 1871.

WATSON RUSSELL. Lic., Lebanon Cl., 1853. Dis. to Presb. of Donegal, 1854.

J. B. RUHL, b. Ger., Dec. 14. 1821; d. Nappanee, O., Dec. 14, 1883. Came to America, 1836. Preceptor, Dr. P. Herbruck. Lic. and ord., Columbiana Cl., 1845. Past. Trumbull and Mahony cos., O., 1846-'63; Huntington, Ind.; St. John's cong., Elkhart co., Ind., 1865-'74; Spencerville, O., 1874-'76 ; Edgerton miss., 1876.

PAUL J. RUETENIK, b. New Lewin, Prussia, 1846; d. Clay City, Neb., Nov. 23, 1882. Mission House, Sheboygan, Wis., 1871. Lic. and ord., Sheboygan, Cl. Past., Washington co., Wis.: Gasconade co., Missouri.

ROBERT R. SALTERS, b. England, 1808; d. Joliet, Ill., Aug. 14, 1872. Preceptor, Rev. D. Winters. Lic. and ord., Cl. of Sandusky, 1843. Past. Evansport, etc., O.; Concord, Ind.; La Salle, Mich. Dism. to Presb. Ch., 1853.

JOHN L. SANDERS, b. 1809; d. Attica, Ind., Jan. 27, 1840. Lic. and ord., Cl. of Md., 1833. Past. Tiffin, O., 1834-'37; Attica, Ind., 1837-'40.

DANIEL B. SAUERS, stud. Mercersburg, Pa. Lic. and ord., Susq. Cl., 1845. Past. Blockhouse Settlement, Tioga co., Pa., 1845-'47. Name erased, 1847.

CONRAD SAURE, b. Darmstadt, Ger., Aug. 21, 1820; d. Cincinnati, O., May 21, 1873, Came to America, 1845. Preceptors, Drs. E. V. Gerhart and H. Rust. Lic., 1856; ord., 1858. Past. Salem's ch., Cincinnati, 1856-'73.

EUGENE SAUVAIN, b. 1831; d. Mt. Eaton, O., Feb. 11, 1872. Lic. and ord., 1856. Miss. in Brazil. Past. French ch., Mt. Eaton, 1868-'72.

ADAM SCHAEFER, d. Berks co., Pa., 1834. Lic , Free Syn. of Pa., 1828; ord., 1831. Past. Lebanon co., 1829; Weiss ch., Berks co., 1831.

HENRY B. SCHAFFNER, b. Apr. 5, 1784; d. Marietta, Pa., Apr. 9, 1852. Lic. and ord., Syn· U. S., 1808. Past. Marietta, Maytown, etc., Lancaster co., Pa. Susp., 1840.

MICHAEL SCHLATTER, b. St. Gall, Switz., July 14, 1716; d. near Philadelphia, Oct., 1790, and buried in the Reformed churchyard, now Franklin Square, Philadelphia. Founder of the Synod of the Reformed Church in the U. S. See page 196.

JESSE SCHLOSSER, b. Adams co., Pa., Mar. 18, 1812; d. Three Rivers, Mich., Jan. 13, 1875. Preceptors, Rev. A. Keller and Geo. Schlosser. Lic. and ord., 1844. Past. Jeromeville, O.; Reedsburg, Basil, Akron, and Fairfield. Entered Presb. Ch., but soon returned to Ref. Ch. Past. Three Rivers, Mich., 1873-'75.

F. SCHMECKENBECHER, preceptors, Rev. T. H. Leinbach and A. L. Herman. Lic. and ord.. Free Synod of Pa., 1835. Past. Peace ch., etc., Lycoming co., 1835-'39. Accidentally drowned.

BENJAMIN S. SCHNECK, D. D., b. near Reading, Pa., Mar. 14, 1806; d. Chambersburg, Pa,, Apr. 14, 1874. Preceptor, Dr. F. L. Herman. Lic. Free Synod, 1825; ord. 1826. Past. Centre co., Pa., 1825-'33; Gettysburg, 1834-'35; St. John's (Ger.) ch., Chambersburg, 1855-'74. First editor of the " Messenger," and " Kirchenzeitung." Commissioner to Germany, 1843. Prof. in Wilson Female Col., 1874. Author of " The Burning of Chambersburg," " Mercersburg Theology," etc.

BENJAMIN SCHNEIDER, D. D., b. New Hanover, Montgomery co., Pa., Jan. 18, 1807; d. Boston, Mass., Sept. 14, 1877. Grad. Amherst Col., 1830; Andover Theol. Sem., 1833. Entered Presb. Ch. Lic. and ord., New Castle Presbytery, 1833. Missionary of the American Board of Foreign Missions, Broosa, Asia Minor, 1834-'49; Aintab, Syria, 1849——. Returned to Broosa and labored there until 1875. Became connected with the Reformed Ch. in 1842, and was subsequently recognized as its foreign missionary. His wife wrote " Letters from Broosa," Chambersburg, 1846. See page 328.

JACOB SCHNEIDER (*Schneyder*), b. —; d. Leesport, Va., 1826, Lic. and ord., Coetus, Pa., 1785-'87. Came to Frederick, Md., 1787. Led the opposition to Rev. J. W. Runkel, and for some time held the church. Preached at Harpers Ferry, Lovettsville, and Woodstock, Va. Principal of an Academy at Leesburg, Va. Corwin ("Manual") calls him "George W. Schneyder."

CASPER LUDWIG SCHNORR. Independent. Past., Lancaster, Pa., 1744-'46; Germantown, N. Y., 1746-'49.

FREDERICK A. SCHOLL, b. Montgomery co., Pa., Sept. 3, 1787; d. Greencastle, Pa., May 13, 1865. Preceptors, Rev. A. Helffenstein and Dr. S. Helffenstein, Lic., Syn. U. S., 1814; ord., 1817. Past., York co., Pa., 1814-'18; Greencastle. Waynesboro, Mercersburg. etc., 1818– ab., 1852.

JACOB SCHOLL, b. Bucks co., Pa., Nov. 16, 1797; d. Perry co., Pa., Sept. 4, 1847. Preceptor, Dr. S. Helffenstein. Lic., Syn. U. S., 1818; ord. 1819. Miss. to Va. and N. C., 1819. Past. Sherman's Valley chg., 1819-'38; Landisburg, 1838-'40; New Bloomfield, 1840-'47.

GUSTAVUS W. M. SCHULZE, b. Breslau, Ger , Sept. 31, 1824; d. Newville, Ind.. July 31, 1863. Came to America ab., 1848. Theol. Sem., Mercersburg, 1857. Lic., Cl. of Md., 1858; ord., West Sus., Cl., 1858. Past. Adamsburg chg., Pa., 1858-'62; Newville, Ind., 1862-'63.

BENEDICT SCHWOB (*Schwope, Swope*, etc. Probably originally *Schwab*), b. Ger. ab., 1730; d. in Kentucky during the winter of 1809-'10. Ruling elder, St. Benjamin's ch., Md., 1763. Ord., Coetus, Pa., ab., 1771. Past., Second ch., Baltimore, Md., 1770-'73; Pipe Creek chg., Md., 1774-'76. Assisted Otterbein in organizing the conferences of " United Ministers," 1774-'1776. See page 216.

JACOB SECHLER, b. Turbut twp., Northumberland co., Pa., Mar. 18, 1806; d. Hanover, Pa., May 10, 1880. Theol. Sem., York, Pa., 1834; Gettysburg, 1835-'36.

Lic. and ord., Zion's Cl., 1837. Past., Hanover chg., Pa., 1837-'59; Littlestown, 1859-'66; Manheim chg., York co., 1866-'80.

SAMUEL SEIBERT, b. Dauphin co., Pa., Sept. 8, 1800; d. Greentown, O., July 8, 1863. Lic., Syn. U. S., 1824; ord., Free Synod, 1826. Past. Middletown, Pa., 1826; Selinsgrove, 1837; Boyertown chg., 1843-'50; Limerick and Keelers, 1850-'52; deposed, 1852; restored, 1858; Stark co., O., 1861.

JONAS SELLERS. Lic., Syn. U. S., 1831; ord., Free Synod ab., 1834. Miss. in Va., 1836.

JACOB SENN, b. Mar. 1775; d. Indianfield, Pa., Jan. 28, 1818. Stud. Univ. of Pa., Ord., Coetus Pa., 1795. Past., Newtown, etc., N. J., 1795-'1800; Tohickon, chg., Pa., 1800-'18.

JACOB B. SHADE, b. Upper Providence, Montgomery co., Pa., Apr. 25, 1817; d. Trappe, Pa., April 25, 1846. M. Col., 1841; Theol. Sem., Mercersburg, 1843. Lic. and ord., Mercersburg Cl., 1843. Past. McConnelsburg, Pa., 1843. Colporteur, Am. Tract. Soc., 1844.

GEORGE SHAFER. Lic. and ord., 1861. Resided at Nevins, O.

J. W. A. SHAEFFER. Licentiate of Sandusky Cl., Syn of O., 1852-'56. Resided at Burkittsville, Md., 1855.

HIRAM SHAULL, b. Jefferson co., Va., Mar. 14, 1819; d. Sidney, O., Apr. 23, 1883. Stud. M. Col. Lic. and ord., Va. Cl., 1844. Past., Mill Creek, Va., 1844-'45. Subsequently past. of various charges in Ohio.

DAVID SHEARER, b. Guilford co., N. C., Oct., 30, 1782; d. Huntingdon, Ind., Sept. 10, 1857. Removed to Ohio, 1804. Theol. Sem., Lancaster, O. Lic. and ord., 1822. Past, Highland co., O., 1823-'27; Shanesville, 1827-'39, w. c., 1839-'57.

EPHRAIM S. SHEIP, b. New Britain, Bucks co., Pa., May 7, 1836; d, Bellefonte, Pa., July 26, 1866. Theol. Sem., Mercersburg, 1863. Lic., Cl. of Goshenhoppen, 1864; ord., Cl. of West Susq., 1864. Pastor, Bellefonte, Pa., 1864-'66.

ISAAC SHELLHAMMER, b. Brier Creek, Northumberland co., Pa., Jan. 1, 1802; d. Conyngham, Pa., Feb. 22, 1873. Preceptors, Rev. John J. Benninger, Kessler, and La Rose. Lic., 1828; ord., 1829. Past., Black Creek, Conyngham, and other places in Luzerne and Columbia counties.

GEORGE A. SHOOK (*Schuck*), b., May 3, 1803; d. Redhook, N. Y., May 14, 1837. Grad. Union Col., Schenectady, N. Y., 1824. Theol. Sem., Carlisle, Pa., 1827. Ord., 1827; but in consequence of ill health remained without charge.

MORTIMER L. SHUFORD, b. Rutherford co., N. C., Jan., 24, 1818; d. Burkittsville, Md., Nov. 7, 1883. Grad. M.Col., 1843. Lic. and ord., Va. Cl. 1844. Past., Lovettsville, Va., 1845; Glade chg., Md., 1849-'57; Mt. Moriah, 1857-'63; Boonsboro', 1863-'67; Winchester, Va., 1867-'73; Burkittsville, Md., 1873-'83.

JOHN H. SMALTZ, b. Philada., Feb. 7, 1793; d. Phila., July 30, 1861. Theol. Sem., New Brunswick, N. J. Lic. and ord., Cl. of New Brunswick, Ref. (D.) Ch., 1819. Entered Ger. Ref. Ch., 1825. Past. Germantown, Pa., 1825-'29; Frederick co., Md., 1829-'34; Trenton Mission, N. J., 1834-'38; Harrisburg, Pa., 1838-'40; Reading, Pa., (Mission,) 1840. Dis. to Presb. ch., 1844.

WILLIAM SMIDMER. Lic., Free Synod of Pa., 1830. Preached in Huntingdon and Mifflin cos.

EDWARD D. SMITH. A noted impostor. In Virginia he was known as Dr. J W. Bond. His true name is believed to have been Elijah Bowen.

HENRY SNYDER. Preceptor, Rev. J. H. Fries. Lic., Syn. U. S., 1825. Ord. as a missionary 1825. Preached at Shepherdstown, Va., 1825.

HENRY SONNEDECKER, b. Washington co., Pa., June 11, 1792; d. North Lima, O., Oct. 16, 1851. Lic., Syn. U. S., 1818; ord., 1820. Past. Washington co., Pa., Wayne and Stark cos., O., 1820-'31; Columbiana co., 1831-'51.

WILLIAM SORBER, b. Flourtown, Pa., Oct. 4, 1826; d. near Brownback's ch., Chester co., Pa., Dec. 7, 1878. Preceptor, Dr. J. Helffenstein. Lic., Phila. Cl., 1852; ord., N. C. Cl., 1853. Past., Davidson chg., N, C., 1853-'55; Brownback's chg., Pa., 1855-'78.

CYRIACUS SPANGENBERG VON REIDEMEISTER, b. Hesse; d. 1795. A wicked impostor. Applied several times for licensure, but was refused. Preached independently, Shamokin, Selinsgrove, etc., 1784-'85; Franklin co., Pa., 1785-'90. When seeking to be settled in Berlin, Elder Glessner remonstrated, and Spangenberg stabbed him to the heart. He was convicted and executed.

CHARLES SPARRY. Received from Presbyterian Ch., 1840, but soon returned to that body.

WILLIAM T. SPROLE, D. D., b. ab., 1808; d. Detroit, Mich., June 9, 1883. Received from Presb. Ch., 1833. Past., Race st. Ref. Ch., Phila., 1832-'37. Returned to Presb. Ch. Chaplain at West Point.

GEORGE STAEGE. Lic. as a missionary, Syn. U. S., 1817.

SAMUEL STAEHR, b. Bucks co., Pa., Oct. 28, 1785; d. Springfield, Pa., Sept. 27, 1843. Preceptors, Rev. J. Senn, J. W. Dechant, and J. C. Becker, D. D. Lic., Syn. U. S., 1813; ord., 1816. Past., Springfield, Durham, etc., Bucks co., Pa., 1813-'43.

JOHN CHRISTIAN STAHLSCHMIDT, b. Nassau Siegen, Ger., Mar. 3, 1740; d. near Mülheim, Ger., about 1825. Came to America, 1770. Preceptor, Dr. C. Weyberg. Lic. and ord., Coetus Pa., 1777. Past., York, Pa., 1777-'79. Returned to Germany. Author of " Pilger-Reise zu Wasser und zu Land," Nuremberg, 1799.

STEPHEN STALEY.—d. Shenandoah co., Va., 1850. Lic., 1832; ord., 1833. Past., Lovettsville, Va., 1833; London, etc., 1836; Shenandoah co., Va., 1850.

CASPAR MICHAEL STAPEL. Past. Amwell, N. J., 1762-'63. Practiced medicine. See page 210.

JOHN CONRAD STEINER, b. Winterthur, Switz., Jan. 1, 1707; d. Philadelphia, July 6, 1762. Ord. in Europe. Past. Mettmenstetten; St. Peterzellen; St. Georgen—all in Switzerland. Came to America, 1749. Philada., 1751-'52; Germantown, Pa., 1751-56; Frederick, Md., 1756-'59; Philada., 1759-'62. See page 200.

JOHN CONRAD STEINER, JR., —; d. Allen township, Northampton co., Pa., 1782. Son of the preceding. Lic., Coetus Pa., 1771; ord., 1772. Past. Berks co. (Allemengel chg.,) 1771-'75; Allen township, Lehigh, etc., 1775-'82.

FRANKLIN D. STEM, b. 1829; d. Easton, Pa., Aug. 18, 1851. Grad. Lafayette Col., 1846; Theol. Sem., Mercersburg, 1849. Lic., East Pa., Cl., 1850; ord., 1851. Miss., Trenton, N. J., 1851.

MAXIMILIAN STERN, D. D., b. Altenkunstadt, Bavaria, Nov. 18, 1815, of Jewish parentage; d. Louisville, Ky., July 6, 1876. Came to America, 1839. Converted to Christianity. Theol. Sem., Mercersburg, 1845. Lic. and ord., Cl. of Goshenhoppen, 1845. Miss. New York City, 1845-'46. Past., Farmersville, etc., Northampton co., Pa., 1847-'52. Agent Am. Tract Soc., 1852. Past., Crawford ch., O., 1853; Galion, O., 1853-'62; Louisville, Ky., 1862-'70; Supt. of Missions, 1870- 71; Galion (2nd time,) 1871-'72; w. c. on account of ill health, 1872-'76.

NECROLOGY. 413

ISAAC F. STIELY, b. Berks co., Pa., May 12, 1800; d. Schuylkill co., Pa., Sept. 13, 1869. Preceptors, Dr. F. L. Herman and Thos. H. Leinbach. Lic., " Free Syn.," 1824; ord., 1827. Past. Schuylkill co., Pa., 1824–'69. In 1836 he united with the "Synod of the U. S.," but in 1841 withdrew and helped to organize the " Independent," or "Stiely," Synod. Subsequently independent until 1860, when he reunited with the regular synod.

PHILIP STIELY. Brother of the preceding. Independent. Columbia and adjacent counties, Penna.

PHILIP STOCK, b. Ger. —: d. Wooster, Ohio, —. Stud. at Duisburg. Came to America, 1789. Ord., " Coetus Pa.," 1791. Preached, York, 1739–'90. Past., Chambersburg, Shippensburg, and Scherer's, 1791.

JOHN STONEBERGER, b. Frankfort twp., Cumberland co., Pa., Feb. 15, 1820; d. Astoria, Ill., Dec. 8, 1865. Grad. Lane Theol. Sem., Cincinnati, O., 1848. Lic., Miami Cl., 1847; ord., 1848. Miss. Union co., Ill., 1848–'50; Patton, Mo., 1852–'59; Astoria, Ill., 1859–'65. Author of " Church Member's Manual," 1855.

JOHN S. STONER, b. Stark co., O., July 27, 1853; d. Wooster, O., Sept. 1, 1882. Grad. Heid. Col., 1875; Theol. Sem., Tiffin. O., 1877. Lic., Syn. of O., 1877; ord., 1879. Past., Navarre, O., 1879–'81; Wooster, O., 1881–'82.

WILLIAM STOY, b. Herborn, Ger., Mar. 14, 1726; d. Lebanon, Pa., Sept. 14, 1801. Studied in Germany. Came to America with Schlatter, 1752. Past. Tulpehocken, Pa., 1752–'55; Philadelphia, 1755–'56; Lancaster, 1758–'63; Lebanon, 1763–'72. Went to Leyden, Holland, ab., 1772, and studied medicine. Returned to America. Preached and practiced medicine, Berks and Lebanon counties, 1773–1801, Independent after 1770. Member Penna. Legislature, 1784. Discovered a supposed cure for hydrophobia, which bears his name.

JOHN ANDREW STRASSBURGER, b. Upper Milford, Lehigh co., Pa., Oct. 3, 1796; d. Sellersville, Pa., May 2, 1860. Preceptor, Dr. S. Helffenstein. Lic., Syn. U. S., 1818; ord., 1819. Past. Tohickon, Indianfield, and Charlestown, 1818–'54.

GEORGE STRICKLAND, b. Chester co., Pa., 1811; d. Circleville, O., 1844. Theol. Sem., Mercersburg, 1841. Lic., Syn. U. S., 1841; ord., 1842. Past. Circleville, O., 1842–'44.

ADAM STUMP, b. Richville, Stark co., O., Mar. 27, 1816; d. Port Jefferson, O., Oct. 2, 1856. Preceptors, Dr. Büttner and Geo. Schlosser. Lic. and ord., 1840. Past., Reedsburg, O., 1840–'45; Carrollton, 1845–'51; Rome chg., Richland co.; Port Jefferson, Shelby co.

FREDERICK R. STUMP, brother of the preceding, b. Stark co., O., Apr. 20, 1814; d. Port Jefferson, O., Nov. 11, 1850. Lic. and ord., 1843. Past. Fulton ch., 1843–45; Union ch.; Jefferson ch.

WILLIAM STUMP, brother of the preceding, b. Jan. 27, 1823; d. St. Paris, O., Nov. 4, 1851. Preceptors, Rev. J. Steiner and Geo. Schlosser. Lic. and ord., Miami Cl., 1849. Past., Union chg., 1849–'51.

SAMUEL SUTHER, b. Switzerland, May 18, 1722; d. Orangeburg, S. C., Sept. 28, 1788. Came to America, 1739. Teacher in Philadelphia, 1749. Past. Mecklenburg, N. C., 1768–'71; Guilford and Orange cos., N. C., 1771–'82 Mecklenburg (2nd time) 1782–86; Orangeburg District, S. C., 1786–'88.

PETER SWEIGERT, b. Franklin co., Pa., Mar. 23, 1815; d. Millersville, Pa., Oct. 22, 1846. Theol. Sem., Mercersburg, 1845; Lic. and ord., Lebanon Cl., 1845. Past., Millersville, Lancaster co., Pa., 1845–'46.

JOHN H. SYKES, b. Barnsley, Yorkshire, England, Nov. 5, 1834; d. Greencastle,

Pa., Nov. 10, 1880. Came to America, 1856. Stud. Allentown Sem. Lic., East Pa. Cl., 1863; ord., 1864. Past., South Easton, Pa., 1864-66; Somerset, 1866-'67; Martinsburg, 1868-'73; Woodcock Valley, 1873-'77; Greencastle, 1877-'80. Principal of Easton, Pa., High-School, 1863. Teacher in "Westmoreland College" and "Juniata Collegiate Institute."

J. R. TALLENTIRE. Received from Methodist Ch. Member of Sandusky Cl., Syn. of O., 1846-'49.

CONRAD TEMPELMAN, b. Ger., ab., 1687; d. near Lebanon, Pa., ab., 1761. Preached as a layman, 1727-'51. Ordained by direction of the Synod of North Holland, 1751. Pastor of churches in Lancaster and Lebanon cos., until ab., 1760. During the latter years of his ministry he was blind.

—THEUS (*Deiss.*) A native of Switzerland. Ord., 1739, by Presb. Synod. Pastor of churches on the Congaree, S. C., 1739-'75, and perhaps longer.

JOSEPH B. THOMPSON, b. Montgomery co., Pa., Aug. 9, 1820; d. Canaan, O., Oct 16, 1882. Stud.. Mercersburg, Pa. Lic. and ord., 1848. Past. Mansfield, O., 1848-'52; Tarlton, Delaware, Tremont, Sidney, Dayton; Red Bank, Clarion co., Pa., 1877-'82; Canaan, O., 1882. Supt. Butler Orphans' Home, ab., 1870-'77.

FREDERICK TOBERBILLER. A native of Switzerland. Settled at Purrysburg, S. C., ab., 1737, and labored in South Carolina and Georgia, 1737-'38—perhaps longer.

DANIEL S. TOBIAS, b. Berks co., Pa., Mar. 23, 1804; d. Rebersburg, Pa., Oct. 29, 1864. Preceptor, Rev. C. G. Herman. Lic. and ord., 1829. Past. Bloomsburg, Pa., 1829-'51; Rebersburg, 1851-'64.

PETER HENRY TORSCHIUS—*See Dorstius.*

EDWIN TOWN. Lic., Cl. of Phila., 1837. Entered Lutheran church. Received back by Cl. of Phila., and dismissed to Cl. of Md. Ord., 1844. Dismissed to Presb. Ch.

GEORGE F. TROEGER. Lic. and ord., Syn. U. S., 1822. Past. Chestnut Hill chg., Northampton co., Pa., 1822-'25.

GEORGE TROLDENIER, b. Anhalt Cöthen, Ger., 1754; d. Baltimore, Md., Dec. 12, 1800. Univ. of Halle. Sent to America, 1786, by Synods of Holland. Past. York, Pa., 1787-92; Gettysburg, 1790-91, (supply); Baltimore, 1st ch., 1791-1800.

—TWIFOOT. A candidate for the ministry in the Episcopal Church who was ordained by Coetus, in 1779, at the request of his congregations.

PETER TENDICK, b. Veldenz, Prussia, May 26, 1826; d. Attica, Seneca co., O., Apr. 1, 1883. Came to America, ab., 1851. Grad. Heidelberg Col., 1857. Lic. and ord., Tiffin Cl., 1858. Past. Seneca co., O., 1858-'64. Subsequently disabled.

JOHN J. UNGERER. Theol. Sem., Carlisle, 1826. Lic. and ord., Syn. U. S., 1827. Past., Northumberland and Columbia co., Pa; Lycoming co. Agent for S. S. Union Missionary, Washington, D. C., 1833.

FREDERICK WILLIAM VANDERSLOOT (*Van der Sloot,*) b. Germany —; d. Northampton co., Pa., 1803. Co-rector at Dessau. Came to America. Past., Montgomery co., Pa.; Dryland chg., Northampton co., 1802.

FREDERICK WILLIAM VANDERSLOOT (2d.,) b. Dessau. Ger., Nov. 11, 1773; d. York co., Pa., Dec. 14, 1831. Studied in Europe. Came to America, 1801. Lic. and ord., Syn. U. S., 1802. Past., Dryland ch., 1802-'11; Germantown, Pa., 1811-13; Goshenhoppen, 1813-'19; Salem ch., Philada., 1819-'24; Rockingham co., Va., 1824-'27; Paradise chg., York co., 1827-'31.

NECROLOGY.

FREDERICK WILLAM VANDERSLOOT (3d.,) son of F. W. (2d.,) b. Northampton co., Pa., Dec. 8, 1803; d. York, Pa., Sept. 11, 1878. Stud. Penna Col., Phila.; Theol. Sem., Carlisle, 1828. Lic. and ord., " Free Synod," 1830. Past., York co., Pa., 1830-'78.

J. SAMUEL VANDERSLOOT, b. Dillsburg, York co., Pa., Oct. 20, 1834; d. Philada., Pa., Dec. 6, 1882. Read law and admitted to the bar. Lic. by M. E. Ch., 1874. Received and ord., Phila. Cl., 1877. Past. St. John's Miss., West Phila., 1877-'81; Grace Miss., Phila., 1881-'82. Author of several popular religious works

HAMILTON VAN DYKE, b. 1807; d. Battzville, N. Y., 1836. Grad. Hamilton Col., 1826; Theol. Sem., York, Pa., 1828. Lic. and ord., Syn., U. S., 1832. Past., Chambersburg, Pa., 1832. Entered Ref. (D.) Ch. Battzville, N. Y., 1833-'36.

JACOB VAN LINGE, b. —; d. St. Catharine, Canada, 1845. Ord., 1841. Past., Delaware, O., 1842-'44; Buffalo, N. Y., 1844. St. Catharine, Ca., 1845.

LUDWIG FERDINAND VOCK. Came to America, Dec. 1749. Pastor in Lancaster, Pa., 1750.

HENRY ERNEST FRED. VOIGT, b. Leidenhausen, Lippe Detmold, Ger., Nov. 2, 1785; d. Mount Pleasant, Pa., Jan. 14, 1875. Univ. of Jena. Ass't Past. at Bega; Past. at Augustdorf. Came to America, ab., 1824. Past., Northampton co., Pa.; Eastern Ohio, 1829-'32; Somerset co., Pa.; Westmoreland co., Pa., 1833—ab., 72.

CASPAR WACK, b. Phila., Aug. 15, 1752; d. Trappe, Pa., July 19, 1839. Preceptor, Dr. C. D. Weyberg. Lic., Coetus Pa., 1770; ord., 1772. Past. Tohickon, etc., 1771-'82; German Valley etc., N. J., 1782-1809; Germantown and Whitemarsh, 1809-'21; Whitemarsh, 1821-'23.

JOHN JACOB WACK, bro. of the preceding, b. —; d. Fort Plain, N. Y., ab., 1851. Preceptor, Rev. Casper Wack. Ord., Syn. U. S., 1795. Past. Amwell, etc., N. J., 1795-1805; Mohawk Valley, N. J., 1805-'51. Chaplain in American army, 1812. Independent after 1816.

GEORGE WACK, eldest son of Rev. Casper Wack, b. Bucks co., Pa., Mar. 1, 1776; d. near Centre Square, Montgomery co., Feb. 17, 1856. Lic., Syn. U. S., 1801. Past. Boehm's Ch., Wentz's, Hilltown, etc., Pa., 1802-'46. Subsequently without charge.

CHARLES P. WACK, grandson of Rev. Casper Wack, b. —; d. 1866. Theol. Sem., New Brunswick, N. J., 18:9. Lic. and ord, " Free Synod," 1830. Past. Race st. ch., Phila., 1830-'31. Entered Ref. (Dutch) ch., 1831. Past. Carolina ch., N. J., 1831; Bellona, 1831-'35; Lebanon, 1835-'40; Trenton, 1st, 1841-'45. Returned to German Ref. Ch.,1845; w. c., 1845-'66. Resided in Easton, Pa.

DANIEL WAGNER, b. Eibelshausen, Nassau, Ger., Jan. 11, 1750; d. York, Pa., Dec. 17, 1810. Came to America with his parents, 1752. Preceptors, Drs. Gross and Hendel. Lic., Coetus Pa., 1771; ord., 1772. Past., Kreutz's Creek, York co., 1771-'74; York, Pa., 1774-'86; Tulpehocken, etc., 1786-'93; York, Pa., (2d time,) 1793-1802; Frederick, Md., 1802-'10.

HENRY WAGNER, b. Berks co., Pa., April 3, 1802; d. Lebanon, Pa., May 25, 1869. Theol. Sem., Carlisle, 1828. Lic. and Ord., Syn. U. S., 1828. Past., Milton, Paradise, Turbutville, etc., Pa., 1828-'35; Lebanon, etc., 1835-'51; McConnellsburg, 1851-'53; Mercersburg, 1853-'56; Orwigsburg, etc., 1856-'65.

FREDERICK WAHL, b. Wurtemberg, Ger., Mar. 21, 1821; d. Hallsville, O., 1881. Came to America, 1832. Minister of Evangelical Association, 1841-'45.

Entered Ref. Ch., 1845. Past, of charges in Ohio, Western Penna., Indiana, and Iowa, 1845-'78. Dis. to Presb. Ch., 1878.

FREDERICK H. WAHLERS, b. Hanover, Ger., Sept. 10, 1844; d. Crothersville, Ind., Mar. 18, 1868. Lic. and ord., Ind. Cl., 1867. Past. Crothersville, Ind., 1867-'68.

JOHN WALDSCHMIDT, b. Nassau, Ger., Aug. 6, 1724; d. Lancaster co., Pa., Sept. 14, 1786. Ord. in Holland. Came to America with Schlatter, 1752. Past., White Oak, etc., Lancaster co., 1752-'86. Sup. Tulpehocken and Heidelberg, Berks co., 1756-'58.

FREDERICK WALK, b. Franklin co., Pa., 1811; d. Phila., Pa., Oct. 24, 1880. Lic. and ord., Phila. Cl., 1874, Miss. to Germans in New Jersey.

GEORGE WALLAUER. Came to America, 1771. Past., Baltimore, Md., 1772-1776. Returned to Europe. Uncle of Rev. J. W. Dechant.

JACOB WEAVER, b. Middletown, Md, Jan. 28, 1810; d. Sidney, O., Dec. 28, 1882. Lic. and ord., Lancaster cl., Syn. of O., 1847. Past., Jerusalem ch., O., Port Jefferson, St. Paris, North Clayton, Sidney, etc.

WILLIAM C. WEBB, b. August 12, 1811; d. Cavetown, Md., Dec. 26, 1848. Lic., Md. Cl., 1839.

JESSE STROUD WEBER, b.—ab. 1832; d. Absecom, N. J., July 27, 1860. Lic., Phila. Cl., 1860.

JOHN WILLIAM WEBER, b., Witgenstein, Ger., March 5, 1735; d. Westmoreland co., Pa., July, 1816. Lic., Cœtus, Pa., 1771; ord. 1772. Past., Northampton co. (now Monroe co.), Pa., 1771-'82; Pittsburgh, Mt. Pleasant, Greensburg, etc., 1783-1816. First regular minister at Pittsburgh, Pa.

JOHN H. WEIKEL. Past., Boehm's ch., etc., Montgomery co., Pa., 1776-'81. See page 239.

CHRISTIAN WEILER, b. Baden, Ger., Jan. 28, 1804; d. Galion, O., Jan. 3, 1875. Preceptor, Dr. H. Bibighaus. Lic. and ord., Free Synod, 1836. Past., Orwigsburg, Pa., 1836; Reamstown, 1837-49; Crawford co., O., 1849-60.

HENRY WEIDER (*Weidner*), b. Switzerland; d. near Baltimore, Md., 1811. Class-leader in Second Ref. ch., Baltimore, 1774. Licensed by "United Ministers," 1776. Pastor of Bermudian ch., Adams co., 1790.

JACOB WEYMER (*Weimer*), b. Ger. ——; d. Hagerstown, Md., 1790. Past., Berks and Lehigh cos., Pa., 1770-71; Hagerstown, etc., Md., 1771-90. Organized churches at Chambersburg, Greencastle, and Grindstone Hill, Pa.

WILLIAM WEINEL, b. near Gelbhausen, Ger., Jan. 27, 1781; d. Leechburg, Pa., Jan. 28, 1865. Came to America, 1799. Preceptors, Drs. C. L. and J. C. Becker. Lic., Syn. U. S., 1815; ord. 1819. Past., Westmoreland and Armstrong cos., 1815-54.

DANIEL WEISER, D. D., b. Selinsgrove, Pa., Jan. 13, 1799; d. East Greenville, Pa., Dec. 2, 1875. Preceptors, Rev. J. R. Reily and Yost H. Fries. Lic., Syn. U. S., 1823; ord., 1824. Past., Selinsgrove, etc., 1823-'33; New Goshenhoppen and Great Swamp, 1833-'63. Translated and published Mead's "Almost a Christian," 1830.

GEORGE MICHAEL WEIS (*Weiss—Weitzius*), b. Stebbeck, Palatinate, Ger., ab. 1700; d. New Goshenhoppen, Pa., ab. 1763. Lic. and ord., Heidelberg, Ger., 1725. Came to America, 1727. Past., Phila. and Skippack, 1727-'29. Mission to Europe, 1729. Returned to America, 1731. Labored in New York (Burnetsfield,

NECROLOGY. 417

Rhinebeck, etc.), 1731-'46; New and Old Goshenhoppen, and Great Swamp, Pa., 1746-'63. Published several pamphlets. Earliest Reformed minister in Philada.

GEORGE WEISZ, b. Northumberland, Pa., June 21, 1793; d. Lancaster, O., Mar. 10, 1859. Rev. I. Gerhart and Dr S. Helffenstein. Lic., Syn. U S., 1817; ord. 1819. Labored in Fairfield, Perry, Pickaway, and Ross counties, O , 1817'56.

CASPER DIETRICH WEYBERG, D. D., b. Switzerland, ——; d. Phila., Sept. 26, 1790. Ord. in Europe. Came to America, ab. 1762. Past., Easton, Pa., 1763. First ch., Philada., 1763-90. See page 213.

SAMUEL WEYBERG (*Whybark*), son of the preceding, b. Phila., Sept. 19, 1773; d. Whitewater, Mo., June 18, 1833. Preceptors, Dr. F. L. Herman and C. Wack. Lic. and Ord., Syn. U. S., 1793. Made extensive missionary journeys. Past., North Carolina, ab. 1795-1803; Cape Girardeau, Missouri, 1803-'33. He is said to have preached the first Protestant sermon west of the Mississippi river, 1803.

DAVID H. WHITMORE, b. Augusta co., Va., April 24, 1843, d. near Martinsburg, W. Va., Mar. 3, 1883. Grad. Mercersburg col., 1872. Theol. Sem., Lancaster, Pa. Lic. and ord., Mercersburg cl., 1875. Past., Friends' Cove chg., Bedford co., Pa., 1875-'81.

ANDERSON J. WHITMORE, brother of the preceding, b. Augusta co., Va., June 20, 1846; d. —— January 16, 1883. Grad. Mercersburg col., 1875. Lic. and ord., Va. cl., 1876. Miss., Middlebrook, Va., 1876-79; Mint Spring, 1879-'81.

HENRY WIEGAND, b. Helmarshausen, Hesse, Ger., April 6, 1810; d. White Pigeon, Mich., Oct. 20, 1872. Lic. and ord., Cl. of Zion, 1841. Past., Lycoming co., Pa., 1841-'57; Michigan, 1857-'72.

CHARLES J. WIESER, b. Ger. ——; d. Abilene, Kansas, Feb. 22, 1877. Lic. and ord., Tiffin Cl., Syn. of O., 1874. Miss. Wathena, Kan., 1874-'75; Olney, Ill., 1875-'76; Turkey Creek, Kan., 1876-'77.

JACOB H. WIESTLING, b. near Harrisburg, Pa., 1793; d. Hanover, Penna., 1826. Lic., Syn., U. S., 1812; ord., 1822. Past. Hanover, etc., Pa., 1812-'26.

DIEDRICH WILLERS, D. D., b. Walle, near Bremen, Ger., Feb. 6, 1798; d. Varick, N. Y., May 13, 1883. Served as a soldier at the battle of Waterloo, 1815. Came to America, 1819. Preceptors, Rev. J. Geiger and J. C. Becker. Lic. and ord., Syn. U. S., 1821. Past. Bearytown, etc., Seneca co., N. Y. 1821-'82.

HENRY WILLIARD, b. Burkittsville. Md., Apr. 8, 1810; d. Lancaster, O., Nov. 29, 1875. Theol. Sem., York, Pa., 1837. Lic., Cl. of Md., 1837 ; ord., 1838. Miss. Plymouth, O., 1837. Past. Lancaster, O., 1838-'44; Xenia chg., 1844-'50; Lancaster, etc. (supply); Shelby chg., 1854-'57; Columbus, 1857-'65; Circleville, 1865-'69; Jerusalem and Mt. Zwingli, (supply) 1865-'73; Galion, (Eng.,) 1873-'75.

BERNHARD F. WILLY, b. Graubündem, Switz.—; d. Woodstock, Va., May 1810. Ord. in Europe. Sent to America by Synods of Holland 1784. Past. Reading, Pa., 1785-'86; Woodstock, Va., etc. Independent, 1786-1810.

JOHN C. WILMS, b. 1738; d. Lancaster co., Pa., Mar. 8, 1802.

ELIJAH B. WILSON, b. Milton,.Pa., Aug. 18, 1818; d. Adams co., Pa., May 17, 1868. Minister of "Evangelical Association." Lic., Zion Cl., 1863: ord., Mercersburg Cl., 1863. Past. Strasburg chg., 1863-'64; Grindstone Hill, 1864-'66: Orangeville, 1866-'68.

CHRISTIAN WEINBRENNER, b. Feb. 7, 1789; d. Woodbury, Pa., Feb. 12, 1858. Ord., " Free Synod," 1834. Past. Bedford and Huntingdon cos. Independent after 1846.

JOHN WEINBRENNER, b. Frederick co., Md., Mar. 25, 1797; d. Harrisburg,

Pa., Sept. 12, 1860. Preceptor, Rev. Dr. S. Helffenstein. Lic. and ord., Syn. U. S., 1820. Past. Harrisburg, Pa., etc., 1820——. Name erased 1828. Founder of "Church of God" or "Weinbrennerians." See page 278.

JOHN HERMAN WINKHAUS, b. Altena, Prussia, Nov. 26, 1758; d. Phila., Pa., Oct. 3, 1793. Stud. Univ. of Duisburg. Ord., 1780. Pastor at Berchum, 1780–'82. Came to America, 1784. Past. Worcester, Whitpain, and New Providence, 1784–'89. Supt. Lower Saucon, 1784–'87; Race st., Phila., 1790–'93. Died of yellow fever.

THOMAS WINTERS, b. Frederick co., Md., Dec. 18, 1777; d. West Alexandria, O., Oct. 2, 1863. Lic. by Otterbein and others, and served as missionary in Ohio, 1809–'15. Lic., Syn. U. S., 1815; ord., 1819. Past. for 20 years at Germantown, O. Founded many churches, and prepared young men for the ministry. His field of labor at one time extended over seven counties.

JOHN CONRAD WIRTZ (*Wuertz*), b. Zurich, Switz.; d. York, Pa., Sept. 21, 1763. Preached irregularly at Egypt, Lehigh co., Pa., 1742–'44; Saucon and Springfield, 1746(?)–'49; Rockaway and Valley, N. J., 1750–'61. Ord., Presbytery of New Brunswick, 1751; York, Pa., 1761–'63.

FREDERICK WISE, b. Madisonburg, Centre co., Pa., Oct. 11, 1818; d. South Bend, Armstrong co., June 30, 1876. Lic. and ord., Clarion Cl., 1852. Past. South Bend chg., 1852–'76.

JOHN JACOB WISSLER, b. Dillenberg, Nassau, —; d. Egypt, Lehigh co., Pa., 1755. Came to America with Schlatter, 1752. Past. Egypt chg., 1752–'55. In 1757 Coetus made a gift to his widow.

JOHN GEORGE WITNER, b. —; d. Dec. 25, 1779. Came to America before 1769. Past. Bethany chg., Lancaster co., 1766–'70; Upper Milford and Saltzburg, Lehigh co., 1771–'79.

WILLIAM WITZGALL, b. Voigtland, Saxony, 1820; d. Napoleon, O., June 22, 1870. Lic., Tiffin Cl., 1859; ord., 1860. Past. of churches near Napoleon.

BERNARD C. WOLFF, D. D., b. Martinsburg, W. Va., Dec. 11, 1794; d. Lancaster, Pa., Nov. 1, 1870. Theol. Sem., York, Pa.. Lic., Syn. U. S., 1832; ord., East Pa., Cl., 1833. Past. Easton, Pa., 1833–'44; Third ch., Baltimore, Md., 1844–'54. Prof. of Didactic and Practical Theol., Mercersburg, 1854–'64.

DAVID W. WOLFF, b. near Carlisle, Pa., Nov. 29, 1829; d. Carlisle, Mar. 16, 1876. Grad. F. & M. Col., 1854; Theol. Sem., Mercersburg, 1856. Lic. and ord., 1856. Past. Danville, Pa., 1856–'61; Schuylkill Haven, 1862; Mahanoy, 1865; Conowago chg., Adams co., 1866–'73; St. Petersburg chg., Clarion Cl., 1873–'76.

JOHN G. WOLFF, b. Martinsburg, W. Va., April 24, 1811; d. Lancaster, Pa., Jan. 22, 1878. Theol. Sem., York, Pa. Lic., Syn. U. S., 1836; ord., 1838. Past. Martinsburg, Pa., 1831; Taneytown, Md., 1841; — Va., 1851; McConnelsville, Pa., 1857; Alexandria; w. c., 1861–'78.

ANDREW S. YOUNG, b. Bucks co., Pa., 1811; d. Allentown, Pa., Feb. 15, 1848. Grad. M. Col., 1838; Theol. Sem. Mercersburg. Lic., Goshenhoppen Cl., and ord., Phila. Cl., 1843. Past., Trappe, Pa., 1843–'44; Mount Bethel, 1846. Founded Allentown Female Seminary ab. 1847.

DANIEL YOUNG, b. Goshen, N. Y., 1795; d. Augusta, Ga., Mar. 6, 1831. Grad. Union Col., 1819; Theol. Sem., Princeton, N. J. Lic., 1822; ord., Presbytery of Hudson, 1823. Entered Ref. Ch., 1829. Asst. Prof. of Theol., York, Pa., 1829–'31.

DANIEL ZACHARIAS, D. D., b. Washington co., Md., Jan. 14, 1805; d.

NECROLOGY. 419

Frederick City, Md., Mar. 31, 1873. Stud. Jefferson Col., Pa.; Theol. Sem., Carlisle, 1826-'28. Lic. and ord., Syn. U. S., 1828. Past., York co., Pa., 1828-'30; Harrisburg, 1830-'35; Frederick City, Md., 1835-'73.

AMOS F. ZARTMAN, b. Glenford, O., May 13, 1846; d. Tiffin, O., Apr. 29, 1875. Grad. Heidelberg Col., 1871; Theol. Sem., Tiffin, 1872. Lic. and ord., Syn. of O., 1872. Past., Wooster, O., 1872-'74.

JOHN NICHOLAS ZEISER, b. Europe ——; d. Luzerne co., Pa., 1840. Lic., Syn. U. S., 1821; ord. 1821. Past., Hanover, Conyngham, etc., Luzerne co., Pa., 1821-'40.

PHILIP ZEISER, son of the preceding, b. Schalbach, Ger., July 19, 1802; d. New Hamburg, Pa., Jan. 25, 1875. Came to America with his parents, 1819. Lic. and ord., " Free Synod," 1824. Past., Mercer and Crawford cos., Pa., 1825-'48. Subsequently physically disabled.

DANIEL ZELLER, b. Tulpehocken, Berks co., Pa., May 27, 1792, d. Allentown, Pa., April 12, 1868. Lic., Syn. U. S., 1815; ord. 1818. Past., Saucon chg., Lehigh co., Pa., 1815-57.

JONATHAN ZELLER, nephew of the preceding, b. near Lewisburg, Pa., Jan. 10, 1806; d. Lock Haven, Pa., Aug. 3, 1877. Stud. Dickinson Co.; Theol. Sem., York, Pa. Lic. and ord., Syn. U. S., 1830. Past., Huntington and Bedford cos., 1830-39. Subsequently physically disabled.

HENRY K. ZERBE, b. Berks co., Pa., July 21, 1813; d. Basil, July 28, 1846, Lic. and ord., 1845. Past., Basil chg., Fairfield co., O. 1845-'46.

DANIEL ZIEGLER, D. D., b. Reading, Pa., July 11, 1804; d. York, Pa., May 23, 1876. Theol. Sem., York, Pa. Lic. and ord., Syn. U. S., 1830. Kreutz Creek, etc., York co.; First church (German), York, Pa.

WILLIAM H. ZIMMERMAN, b. Frederick co., Md., Sept. 1, 1817; d. Frederick, Md., Nov. 22, 1873. Preceptor, Rev. Dr. D. Zacharias. Lic., Maryland Cl., 1839; ord. 1840. Past., Clearspring ch., 1840-'43. Subsequently physically disabled.

HENRY K. ZINK, b. Hamburg, Ger., June 15, 1817; d. Philipsburg, O., May 2, 1882. Came to America, 1848. Lic. and Ord., St. John's Cl., 1861. Past., Warren, O., 1861-'64; New Bedford chg., 1864-'65; Phillipsburg chg., 1865-'82. He was blind for many years, but faithfully attended to his pastoral duties.

JOHN JOACHIM ZUBLY, D. D. *(Zubley, Zübli,* and *Züblin),* b. St. Gall, Switz., Aug. 24, 1724; d. Savannah, Ga., July 23, 1781. See page 235.

JOHN ZUFALL. Past. Tulpehocken chg., Pa.. 1765-'69.

JOHN ZUILCH, b. Cassel, Ger., Apr. 3, 1796; d. Steinsville, Lehigh co., Pa., Feb. 2, 1875. Came to America with his parents, 1800. Preceptor, Dr. S. Helffenstein. Lic., Syn. U. S., 1816; ord., 1819. Past. Lehigh, Berks, Schuylkill, and Carbon, cos., (Jacob's, Ringold, Tamaqua, McKeansburg, etc.,) 1816-'75.

GERHARD HENRY ZUMPE, b. Tecklenburg, Ger., Jan. 12, 1803; d. Terre Haute, Ind., Aug. 7, 1883. Ed. Berlin Miss. School, for missionary work. Came to America, 1832. Ord. ab., 1834. Past. Wayne co., Ind., Clay co., Evansville, Poland, Clay co., Terre Haute.

CHARLES ZWISLER, b. Baltimore, Md., Nov. 30, 1803; d. Canfield, O., Sept. 19, 1874. Preceptor, Dr. C. L. Becker. Lic. and ord., Syn. U. S., 1825. Past. Washington, Fayette, and Westmoreland cos., Pa., 1825-'33; Wooster chg., O., 1833-'42; Findlay, 1842-'43; Summit co., 1843-'48; New Lisbon, 1848-'49; Canfield, 1849-'53; Congress chg., Wayne co.; Summit co., (2d time,) 1857-'58; Canfield (2d time,) 1858-'74.

ADDENDA.

J. BOSSARD, PH. D., b. Basel, Switz., July 25, 1815; d. Franklin, Wis., July 18, 1885. Came to America, 1847. Lic. and ord., 1848. Past. Ft. Wayne, Ind , and Sheboygan, Wis. Prof. in Missionary Institute for 25 years. '

ANDREW J. BOWERS, b. near Weyer's Cave, Va., Oct. 14, 1836; d. June 6, 1886. Grad. F. & M. col., 1864; Theol. Sem., 1867. Afterwards studied in Germany. Lic., Va. Cl., 1870. Prof. Ursinus col. Ord., 1875. Past. Mill Creek, Va., 1875-'76.

ISAAC G. BROWN, b. Union co., Pa., Aug. 14, 1828; d. Wichita, Kas., May 7, 1885. Grad. F. & M. C., 1855; Theol. Sem., 1857. Lic. and ord., Mercersb. Cl., 1857. Past. Mercersburg, Pa., 1857-'82; Wichita, Kas., 1883-'85.

HENRY I. COMFORT, b. Adams co., Pa., Aug. 19, 1830; d. Burkettsville, Md., Feb. 18, 1888. Past. Mechanicstown, Md.; Germantown, O., Grindstone Hill, Pa.; Burkittsville, Md., etc.

FREDERICK W. DECHANT, son of Rev. J. Wm., b. Macungie, Pa., Dec. 25, 1814; d. Reading, Pa., Feb. 17, 1888. Theol. Sem., 1846. Lic. and ord., 1847. Past. Somerset, O.; Bluffton, Ind.; Harmony, Pa.; Egg Harbor, N. J.

JOHN EICHEN, b. Baden, Ger., Dec. 15, 1821; d. Olney, Ill!., April 12, 1885. Lic. and ord., Tiffin Cl., 1857. Past. Crestline, O., Linton, Ind., Lanesville, Olney.

WILLIAM TRAUTMAN GERHARD, b. Tulpehocken, Pa., Dec. 10, 1809, d. Harrisburg, Pa., Aug. 17, 1886. Theol. Sem., York, 1834. Lic., " Free Synod," 1835; ord. 1836. Past. Berne ch., 1835-'38; Cherryville, etc., 1838-'44; Durham, 1844-'59; Bethany, etc., Lancaster co., 1859-'70; St John's (German) Lancaster, 1870-'75; Zwingli ch., Harrisburg.

JEREMIAH H. GOOD, D. D., b. Rebersburg, Pa., Nov. 22, 1822; d. Tiffin, O., Jan. 25, 1888. Grad. M. C., 1842; Theol. Sem., 1846. Lic. and ord., 1846. Past. Lancaster, O., 1846-'48. Prof. in Western Theol Sem., and Heidelberg College. Founded " Western Missionary," 1848. Author of several religious books.

JOHN GRING, b. Sinking Spring, Pa., March 15, 1801; d. Lebanon, Pa., Dec. 13, 1885. Preceptor, Rev. J. W. Dechant. Ord., 1824. Past. Fredericksburg, Pa., 1824-'81.

TILLMANN GROSSHUSCH, b. Rhine Prussia, 1818; d. Timothy Wis., March 30, 1887. Came to America, 1847. Theol. Sem., Tiffin, O. Lic. and ord., 1857. Past. Rochester, N. Y.; Ebenezer; Salem, Wis.; Zanesville, Ind.; Grand Prairie, Ill.; Linton; Salem, Wis.

JOSEPH HANNABERY, d. Ridgely, Md., Feb. 27, 1883, aged 58 years and 2 months. Grad. F. & M. Col., 1853. Lic. Phila. Cl., 1853, ord. Va. Cl., 1854. Past. Central ch., Va.; Strasburg, Pa.; Schellsburg; Sugar Grove, O.; New Providence, Pa.; Ridgely, Md.

DANIEL YOST HEISLER, D. D., b. Berks co., Pa., June 1, 1820; d. Easton,

Pa., Feb. 5, 1888. Studied at M. C., 1839; Theol. Sem., 1845. Lic. and ord., Mercersburg Cl., 1845. Past. Fannettsburg, Pa., 1845-'46; Columbia, 1846-'50; Hummelstown, 1853-'56; Lewisburg, 1856-'56; Sunbury. 1856-'58; Bethlehem, etc., 1858-'66; Mont Alto, 1869-'77; Grace chapel, Easton, 1877-'86. Superintendent of Orphan Home, 1866-'69. Author of " Wreathed Cross," etc. He succeeded Dr. Harbaugh as editor of the " Lives of the Fathers."

M. ZWINGLI HITTEL, b. Douglass twp., Montgomery co., Pa., Sept. 3, 1857; d. July 31, 1887. Theol. Sem., Tiffin, O., 1885. Past. Lima, O., 1886; Chambersburg, Pa., 1887.

THOMAS S. JOHNSTON, D. D., b. Phila., Pa., Aug. 4, 1818; d. Lebanon, Pa., June 11, 1887. Past. M. E. church, 10 years; Presbyterian ch., West Phila., 11 years. Entered Reformed ch., 1864. Past. St. John's ch., Lebanon, Pa., 1864-'85. Sec. of Board of Commissioners for Foreign Missions, 1885-'87.

HENRY KELLER, b. Boalsburg, Pa., Sept. 20, 1850; d. April 20, 1887. Grad. F. & M. col., 1874; Theol. Sem., 1877. Lic., 1877; ord., 1879. Past. Maquoketa, Iowa.

MOSES KIEFFER, D. D., b. Franklin co., Pa., May 5, 1814; d. Sioux City, Feb. 3, 1888. Grad. M. C., 1838. Lic. and ord., 1840. Past. Water Street ch., 1840-'44; Hagerstown, Md., 1844-'51; Reading, Pa., 2d ch., 1851-'55; Greencastle, 1871-'74; Gettysburg, 1871-80. Prof. of Theology and Pres. Heidelberg col., 1855-'68. See p. 337.

JOHN KLINGLER, b. Perry co., O., July 21, 1818; d. Upper Sandusky, O., Nov. 20, 1886. Past. Bedding, O.; Upper Sandusky, Stoutsville, etc.

GEORGE H. MARTIN, D. D., b. near Emmittsburg, Md., 1815; d. Timberville, Va., Sept. 19, 1887. Grad. M. C., 1838; Theol. Sem., 1841. Lic. 1841; ord. 1843. Pastor Lovettsville, etc., Va., 1843-'84; Burkittsville, Md.; Timberville, Va.

JOHN MECKLY, b. Hanover, Pa., Nov. 2, 1812; d. Petersburg, O., Apr. 16, 1886. Lic., by U. B. ch. Entered Ref. ch., 1869. Past. Berlin, O., 1870; Springfield, O., 1870-'82.

JONAS MICHAEL, b. Champaign co., O., May 24, 1819; d. Dec. 19, 1887. Past. Winamac, Ind.; Liberty Centre, O.

JOHN K. MILLETT, b Berks co., Pa., June 13, 1836; accidentally drowned near Watsontown, Pa., Sep. 9, 1885. Lic., 1860; ord., 1861. Past. Nittany ch., 1861-'73; Paradise ch., 1873-'85. A volume of his sermons has been published.

JOHN WILLIAMSON NEVIN, D. D., LL. D., d. June 6, 1886. See page 289.

JOHN RUHL, M. D., b. Iba, Hesse, May 4, 1821; d. Frostburg, Md., May 25, 1885. Came to America, 1836. Lic. and ord., Sandusky Cl., 1845. Past. Congress, O.; Akron, Defiance, Basil, Frostburg, Md., 1869-'85. Physically disabled, 1860-'69.

DAVID WINTERS, D. D., son of Rev. Thomas, b. Martinsburg, W. Va., Dec. 24, 1801; d. Dayton, O., May 9, 1885. Lic. and ord., Syn. of O., 1824. Past. Montgomery, Greene, and Miami co's, O.; Dayton, O., 1833-'50; Mt. Zion ch., 1850-'80.

JACOB D. ZEHRING, b. Lebanon co., Pa., July 25, 1817; d. Codorus, Pa., Feb. 5, 1887. Theol. Sem., Mercersburg. Lic. and ord., 1846. Past. Palmyra, Pa.; Petersburg; Hart; Emanuel, Jefferson, Pa. Subsequently lived in retirement.

MEETINGS OF SYNODS.

COETUS OF PENNSYLVANIA.[1]

Time	Place	Presidents	Time	Place	Presidents
1746	Philadelphia	(Prelim. Meeting)	1772	Lancaster	John T. Faber.
1747	"	M. Schlatter.	1773	Lancaster	C. L. Boehm.
1748	"	J. Philip Boehm.	1774	Philadelphia	A. Blumer.
1749	Lancaster	J. B. Rieger.	1775	Lebanon	F. Dalliker.
1750	Philadelphia	G. M. Weiss.	1776	Lancaster	J. C. Gobrecht.
1751		J. P. Leydich.	1777	Reading	J. H. Helfrich.
1752			1778	No Meeting.	
1753			1779	Lancaster	W. Hendel.
1754	Philadelphia		1780	No Meeting.	
1755	Lancaster	G. M. Weiss.	1781	Philadelphia	A. Helffenstein.
1756	Philadelphia	"	1782	Reading	C. D. Weyberg.
1757	Lancaster	W. Otterbein.	1783	Philadelphia	Nicholas Pomp.
1758	Philadelphia	J. C. Steiner.	1784	Lancaster.	
1759	Goshenhoppen	J. Waldschmidt.	1785	Reading	A. Blumer.
1760	Falkener Swamp	J. Philip Leydich.	1786	Philadelphia	J. H. Helfrich.
1761	Lancaster	J. G. Alsentz.	1787	Lancaster	F. Dalliker.
1762	Philadelphia	Jonathan Du Bois.	1788		
1763	Lancaster (?)	C. M. Stapel.	1789	Philadelphia	W. Hendel.
1764	Philadelphia	J. G. Alsentz.	1790	Falkener Swamp	F. Dalliker.
1765			1791	Lancaster	W. Hendel.
1766			1792	Philadelphia	D. Wagner.
1767					
1768				**Special Meetings.**	
1769	Germantown	Nicholas Pomp.	1755	Lancaster (?)	
1770	Philadelphia		1760	Germantown (?)	J. G. Alsentz.
1771	Reading	F. L. Henop.	1763	Philadelphia (?)	C. M. Stapel.

[1] The minutes of the years in which the place of meeting is not indicated are believed to be no longer in existence.

SYNOD OF THE UNITED STATES.

Time	Place	Presidents	Time	Place	Presidents
1793	Lancaster, Pa.	J. H. Winckhaus.	1807	New Holland, Pa.	L. Hinsch.
1794	Reading, Pa.	Casper Wack.	1808	Germantown, Pa.	J. T. Faber, Jr.
1795	Falkener Sw'p, Pa.	J. G. Troldenier.	1809	Hagerstown, Pa.	G. Geistweit.
1796	Philadelphia, Pa.	Fred. L. Herman.	1810	Harrisburg, Pa.	S. Helffenstein.
1797	York, Pa.	Wm. Hendel, Jr.	1811	Reading, Pa.	F. L. Herman
1798	Lancaster, Pa.	J. H. Helfrich.	1812	Philadelphia, Pa.	P. R. Pauli.
1799	Reading, Pa.	Daniel Wagner.	1813	Frederick, Md.	C. L. Becker.
1800	York, Pa.	P. R Pauli.	1814	Womelsdorf, Pa.	W. Hendel, Jr.
1801	Easton, Pa.	J. W. Runkel.	1815	Easton, Pa.	Thomas Pomp.
1802	Philadelphia, Pa.	W. Hendel, Jr.	1816	New Holland, Pa.	Caspar Wack.
1803	Lebanon, Pa.	J. H. Helfrich.	1817	York, Pa.	W. Hendel, Jr.
1804	Reading, Pa.	J. Rahauser.	1818	Carlisle, Pa.	J. H. Hoffmeier.
1805	Lancaster, Pa.	C. L. Becker.	1819	Lancaster, Pa.	Lewis Mayer.
1806	Baltimore, Md.	J. H. Hoffmeier.	1820	Hagerstown, Md.	S. Helffenstein.

MEETINGS OF SYNODS. 423

SYNOD OF THE UNITED STATES (*Continued*).

Time.	Place.	Presidents.	Time.	Place.	Presidents.
1821	Reading, Pa. . . .	L. L. Hinsch.	1857	Allentown, Pa . .	D. Gans.
1822	Harrisburg, Pa. .	F. W. Van der Sloot.	1858	Frederick, Md . .	J.H.A.Bomberger.
1823	Baltimore, Md . .	Thomas Pomp	1859	Harrisburg, Pa. . .	P. Schaff.
1824	Bedford, Pa . .	Wm. Hendel.	1860	Lebanon. Pa . . .	J. W. Nevin.
1825	Philadelphia, Pa .	A. Helffenstein, Sr.	1861	Easton, Pa. . . .	H. Harbaugh.
1826	Frederick, Md . .	Fred. Rahauser.	1862	Chambersburg, Pa.	E. V. Gerhart.
1827	York, Pa.	S. Helffenstein.	1863	Carlisle, Pa.	C. F. McCauley.
1828	Mifflinburg, Pa. .	T. L. Hoffeditz.	1864	Lancaster, Pa . .	B. Bausman.
1829	Lebanon, Pa. . .	Geo. Wack.	1865	Lewisburg, Pa . .	S. R. Fisher.
1830	Hagerstown, Md.	James R. Reily.	1866	York, Pa	John S. Foulk.
1831	Harrisburg, Pa. .	H. B. Schaffner.	1867	Baltimore, Md . .	S. N. Callender.
1832	Frederick, Md . .	J. W. Dechant.	1868	Hagerstown, Md .	Thomas G. Apple.
1833	Easton, Pa. . . .	D. Willers.	1869	Danville, Pa . .	J. W. Nevin.
1834	Pittsburg, Pa. . . .	S. Gutelius.	1870	Mechanicsb'rg, Pa.	A. H. Kremer.
1835	Chambersburg, Pa.	D. Zacharias.	1871	Pottstown, Pa . .	J. O. Miller.
1836	Baltimore, Md . .	T. L. Hoffeditz.	1872	Martinsburg,W.Va	M. A. Smith.
1837	Sunbury, Pa . . .	D. Willers.	1873	Bloomsburg, Pa .	C. H. Leinhach.
1838	Lancaster, Pa. . .	M. Bruner.	1874	Bethlehem, Pa . .	N. S. Strassburger.
1839	Philadelphia, Pa .	B. S. Schneck.	1875	Lancaster, Pa . .	I. E. Graeff.
1840	Greencastle, Pa. .	B. C. Wolff.	1876	Reading, Pa . . .	John Beck.
1841	Reading, Pa . . .	T. L. Hoffeditz.	1877	Allentown, Pa . .	G.W.Aughinbaugh
1842	Lewisburg, Pa . .	John Cares.	1878	Easton, Pa. . . .	J.H.A.Bomberger.
1843	Winchester, Va. .	J. F. Berg.	1879	Lebanon, Pa . . .	C. Z. Weiser.
1844	Allentown, Pa . .	H. Bibighaus.	1880	Meyerstown, Pa .	A. S. Leinbach.
1845	York, Pa	B. S. Schneck.	1881	Danville, Pa . . .	J. W. Steinmetz.
1846	Carlisle, Pa.	J. Casper Bucher.	1882	Bellefonte, Pa . .	Geo. H. Johnston.
1847	Lancaster, Pa. . .	S. Gutelius.	1883	Reading, Pa . . .	Thomas C. Porter.
1848	Hagerstown, Md .	Elias Heiner.	1884	Pottstown, Pa . .	Isaac K. Loos.
1849	Norristown, Pa. .	John Rehaugh.			
1850	Martinsburg, Va .	A. Helffenstein, Jr.		**Special Meetings.**	
1851	Lancaster, Pa. . .	M. Kieffer.			
1852	Baltimore, Md . .	J. F. Mesick.	1843	Lewisburg, Pa . .	John Cares.
1853	Philadelphia, Pa .	D. G. Bragonier.	1850	Harrisburg, Pa. .	John Rebaugh.
1854	Lewisburg, Pa . .	Robert Douglass.	1866	Philadelphia, Pa .	S. R. Fisher.
1855	Chambersburg, Pa.	Henry Harbaugh.	1868	Harrisburg, Pa. .	S. N. Callender.
1856	Reading, Pa . .	S. Helffenstein.	1873	Lancaster, Pa . .	M. A. Smith.

SYNOD OF PENNSYLVANIA AND ADJACENT STATES.

("FREE SYNOD.")

Time.	Place.	Presidents.	Time.	Place.	Presidents.
1822	Maxatawny . . .	(Prelim. Meeting.)	1830	Philadelphia . . .	F. L. Herman.
1822	Kutztown	F. L. Herman.	1831	Reamstown . . .	"
1823	"		1832	Mechanicsburg. .	"
1824	Colebrookdale . .	"	1833	Schaefferstown . .	H. Bibighaus.
1825	Philadelphia . . .	"	1834	Allentown	J. S. Dubbs.
1826	Reamstown . . .	"	1835	Orwigsburg . . .	C. G. Herman.
1827	Tulpehocken . . .	"	1836	Philadelphia . . .	T. H. Leinbach.
1828	Kutztown	"	1837	Pottstown	"
1829	Middletown . . .	"			

MEETINGS OF SYNODS.

SYNOD OF OHIO.

Time	Place	Presidents	Time	Place	Presidents
1824	N. Philadelphia, O.	J. P. Mahn'nschm't	1857	Carrollton, O.	M. Kieffer.
1825	Germantown, O.	Thomas Winters.	1858	Fort Wayne, O.	H. Rust.
1826	Lancaster, O.	George Weisz.	1859	Fairfield, O.	J. Heller.
1827	Germantown, O.	"	1860	Akron, O.	J. H. Good.
1828	Canton, O.	Thomas Winters.	1861	Delaware, O.	D. Winters.
1829	Adelphi, O.	George Weisz.	1862	Dayton, O.	G. B. Russell.
1830	Miamisburg, O.	H. Dieffenbach.	1863	Tiffin, O.	H. Rust.
1831	Uniontown, O.	J. W. Hamm.	1864	Canton, O.	J. Vogt.
1832	New Lancaster, O.	Thomas Winters.	1865	Miamisburg, O.	J. Riale.
1833	Xenia, O.	George Weisz.	1866	Galion, O.	J. H. Derr.
1834	Canton, O.	D. Winters.	1867	Fairfield, O.	S. B. Leiter.
1835	Tarlton, O.	"	1868	Shelby, O.	I. H. Reiter.
1836	Xenia, O.	John Pence.	1869	Delaware, O.	S. Mease.
1837	Osnaburgh, O.	L. L. Hinsch.	1870	Tiffin, O.	Reuben Good.
1838	Wooster, O.	George Weisz.	1871	Fairfield, O.	P. C. Prugh.
1839	Lancaster, O.	Thomas Winters.	1872	Canton, O.	H. Willard.
1840	District Synods.		1873	Shelbyville, Ills.	N. H. Loose.
1841	"		1874	Wooster, O.	David Winters.
1842	"		1875	Miamisburg, O.	H. M. Herman.
1842	Canton, O.	D. Winters.	1876	Canal Winchester.	L. H. Kefauver.
1843	Wooster, O.	George Weisz.	1877	Orrville, O.	S C. Goss.
1844	Greensburg, Pa.	D. Kemmerer.	1878	Xenia, O.	John M. Kendig.
1845	Xenia, O.	S. B. Leiter.	1879	Goshen, Ind.	John J. Leberman
1846	Columbus, O.	William Conrad.	1880	Columbiana, O.	Samuel B. Yockey.
1847	Carrollton, O.	Samuel Miller.	1881	Miamisburg, O.	Michael Loucks.
1848	Cincinnati, O.	A. P. Freeze.	1882	Akron, O.	John Vogt.
1849	Tiffin, O.	D. Winters.	1883	W. Alexandria, O.	William A. Hale.
1850	Navarre, O.	E. V. Gerhart.	1884	Delaware, O.	Austin Henry.
1851	Miamisburg.	Geo. W. Williard.		**Special Meetings.**	
1852	Wooster, O.	David Winters.	1850	Tarlton, O.	H. Shaull, *pro tem.*
1853	Neria, Mich.	George Long.	1850	Tiffin, O.	E. V. Gerhart.
1854	Greensburg, Pa.	N. P. Hacke.	1854	Delaware, O.	N. P. Hacke.
1855	Xenia, O.	W. K. Zieber.	1869	Dayton, O.	S. Mease.
1856	Tiffin, O.	L. D. Leberman.			

GERMAN (INDEPENDENT) SYNOD OF OHIO.

Time	Place	Presidents	Time	Place	Presidents
1846	New Lisbon, O.	S. K. Denius.	1850	North Jackson, O.	P. Herbruck.
1847	Mansfield, O.	J. W. Hamm.	1851	Marion, O.	S. K. Denius.
1848	Lancaster, N. Y.	J. Althaus.	1852	Delaware, O.	"
1849	Waynesburg, O.	J. W. Hamm.			

SYNOD OF THE NORTHWEST.

Time	Place	Presidents	Time	Place	Presidents
1867	Fort Wayne, Ind.	Max Stern.	1878	Fort Wayne, Ind.	H. J Ruetenik.
1868	Indianapolis, Ind.	"	1879	Galion, O.	John G. Zahner.
1869	Howard Grove, Wis	"	1880	Cleveland, O.	Charles T. Martin.
1870	Chicago, Ill	P. Greding.	1881	Chicago, Ill.	H. A. Muehlmeier.
1871	Cleveland, O.	J. H. Klein.	1882	Louisville, Ky.	Charles Schaaf.
1872	Galion, O.	"	1883	Milwaukee, Wis.	J. F. H. Dieckman
1873	Indianapolis, Ind.	H. A Muehlmeier.	1884	Fort Wayne, Ind.	M. G. I. Stern.
1874	Louisville, Ky.	J. F. H. Dieckman			
1875	Sandusky, O.	H A. Muehlmeier.		**Special Meeting.**	
1876	Terre Haute, Ind.	John H. Klein.			
1877	Sheboygan, Wis.	Peter J errris	1869	Crestline, O	Max Stern.

MEETINGS OF SYNODS.

PITTSBURG SYNOD.

Time	Place.	Presidents.	Time	Place.	Presidents.
1870	Pittsburg, Pa. (Preliminary.)		1877	Meadville, Pa . .	J. H. Apple.
1870	Buffalo, N. Y. . .	F. K. Levan.	1878	St. Petersburg, Pa.	J. M. Titzel.
1871	Greensburg, Pa .	D. Willers.	1879	Pittsburg, Pa . .	Albert E. Truxal.
1872	Greenville, Pa . .	J. G. Shoemaker.	1880	Centreville, Pa . .	D.S. Dieffenbacher
1873	Titusville, Pa . .	William Rupp.	1881	Greensburg, Pa .	John McConnell.
1874	Berlin, Pa.	John I. Swander.	1882	Red Bank, Pa . .	Frederick Pilgram.
1875	Kittanning, Pa . .	Thos. J. Barkley.	1883	Kittanning, Pa .	David B. Lady.
1876	Irwin, Pa	C.R.Dieffenbacher	1884	Mt. Pleasant, Pa .	C. U. Heilman.
		J. W. Love.			

SYNOD OF THE POTOMAC.

Time	Place.	Presidents.	Time	Place.	Presidents.
1873	Frederick, Md. (Preliminary.) .	J. O. Miller.	1878	Hagerstown, Md .	M. Kieffer.
1873	Chambersburg,Pa.	E. R. Eschbach.	1879	Frederick, Md . .	J. W. Santee.
1874	Hanover, Pa . . .	S. N. Callender.	1880	Woodstock, Va .	G. H. Martin.
1875	Winchester, Va .	P. S. Davis.	1881	Waynesboro, Pa .	I. G. Brown.
1876	York, Pa	D. Gans.	1882	Altoona, Pa . . .	N. H. Skyles.
1877	Baltimore, Md . .	J. A. Peters.	1883	Newton, N. C . .	G. W. Welker.
			1884	Hanover, Pa . .	W. C. Cremer.

GERMAN SYNOD OF THE EAST.

Time	Place.	Presidents.	Time	Place.	Presidents.
1875	Philadelphia, Pa .	John F. Busche.	1880	Buffalo, N. Y . .	John F. Busche.
1875	Buffalo, N. Y . .	Diedrich Willers.	1881	Baltimore, Md . .	Gustav Facius.
1876	Philadelphia, Pa .	Marcus Bachman.	1882	New York, N. Y .	John Roeck.
1877	Baltimore, Md . .	John Kuelling, DD	1883	Philadelphia, Pa .	John C. Hauser.
1878	New York, N. Y .	N. Gehr, D. D.	1884	Pittsburg, Pa. . .	W. C. A. Limberg.
1879	Philadelphia, Pa .	John B. Kniest.			

CENTRAL SYNOD.

Time	Place.	Presidents.	Time	Place.	President.
1881	Galion, O	H. J. Ruetenik.		Special Meeting.	
1882	Canton, O	John H. Klein.			
1883	Cincinnati, O. . .	Oswald J. Accola.			
1884	Crestline, O . . .	Frederick Forwick.	1884	Galion, O	Frederick Forwick.

GENERAL SYNOD OF THE REF. CH. IN THE U. S.

Time	Place.	Presidents.	Time	Place.	Presidents
1863	Pittsburg, Pa . .	J. W. Nevin.	1875	Fort Wayne, Ind .	Wm. K. Zieber.
1866	Dayton, O. . . .	D. Zacharias.	1878	Lancaster, Pa . .	D. Van Horne.
1869	Philadelphia, Pa .	E. V. Gerhart.	1881	Tiffin, O	J. H. Good.
1872	Cincinnati, O . .	J. H. Klein.	1884	Baltimore, Md . .	B. Bausman.

COMPARATIVE STATISTICS.

REFORMED CHURCHES HOLDING THE PRESBYTERIAN SYSTEM.

I. REFORMED CHURCHES.

THE Churches on the European Continent holding the Presbyterian System, and those in other parts of the world which are directly derived from them, are generally called "Reformed." The following statistics, which are in part derived from the Minutes of the "Reformed Alliance," recently convened at Belfast, Ireland, are very incomplete, but will serve to give the reader a general idea of the comparative numerical strength of the various branches of the Reformed Church throughout the world.

	Synods	Ministers	Congregations	Communicants	Adherents
1. Reformed Church in the Province of Austria	1	4	4	6,058	8,144
2. Reformed Church in the Province of Bohemia	1	53	53	44,924	68,386
3. Reformed Church in the Province of Moravia	1	24	26	23,780	39,680
4. Ref. Ch. of the Helvetic Confession, Hungary	5	1912	2003	*1,276,460	1,944,689
(The preceding four organizations compose the "General Synod of the Ref. Ch. in Austria.")					
5. Union of Evangelical churches, Belgium.					
6. Missionary Christian Ref. Ch., Belgium	1	14	27	3,923	*5,000
7. Walloon Ch., Belgium and Netherlands.					
8. Reformed Ch. of France	4	. .	. .	650,000	800,000
9. Free Reformed Church of France	.	. .	. .	150,000	*200,000
10. Old Reformed Church of Bentheim, Germany	1	7	9	2,400	4,000
11. Free (Dutch) Church, Elberfeld	.	5	3	440	*1,000
12. Reformed Church of the East Rhine	1	7	9	2,593	*5,000
13. Reformed Churches (Separatist), Ger.	.	. .	. .	*30,000	*40,000
14. Reformed Churches of Germany (in the Union).	.	. .	. .	*800,000	*1,000,000
15. Ref. Ch. of the Netherl'ds (incl. Dutch colonies).	10	1600	1349	2,091,432	*3,000,000
16. Christian Reformed Church, Netherlands	10	296	379	148,489	200,000
17. Reformed (Cantonal) Churches of Switzerland.	.	. .	. .	*1,200,000	1,667,100
18. Free Ref. Church of Geneva	1	4	4	400	600
19. Free Evangelical Reformed Ch. of Neufchâtel.	1	45	27	3,335	*5,000
20. Free Ev. Ref. Ch. of the Canton de Vaud	1	130	7	3,838	8,333
21. Waldensian Ev. Church	1	70	42	16,484	30,000
22. Free Christian Church of Italy	.	10	32	1,666	*2,000
23. Spanish Christian Church	.	15	27	3,000	10,000
24. Ref. Ch. in Russia (principally in Lithuania)	.	. .	. .	*150,000	*200,000
25. Separated Communities	1	. .	. .	*150,000	*150,000

* Estimated.

	Synods	Ministers	Congregations	Communicants	Adherents
26. Dutch Reformed Ch. in South Africa		143	140		*200,000
27. Dutch Reformed Ch., Orange Free State.					
28. Christian Reformed Ch. in South Africa		9			
29. Reformed Ch. in America (*Ref. Dutch Ch.*)	4	558	516	80,156	*240,468
30. True Reformed Dutch Church	1	10	13		
31. Christian Reformed Church in America	1	30	56	18,923	*56,769
32. **Reformed Ch. in the U. S.** (*Ger. Refor'd*).	7	780	1467	172,949	*518,847

* Estimated. The estimates of the numerical strength of the Reformed Churches of Germany are very unsatisfactory, and we feel assured that they ought to be much higher. They were, however, made by men supposed to be familiar with the subject, and have been left unchanged.

II. PRESBYTERIAN CHURCHES.

The Reformed Churches of Great Britain and Ireland, and those in other countries which are derived from them, are generally called "Presbyterian."

	Synods	Ministers	Congregations	Communicants	Adherents
1. Presbyterian Church of England	1	264	279	57,402	200,000
2. Church of Scotland, in England	1	17	20		
3. Presbyterian Church in Ireland	5	626	555	101,340	400,000
4. Reformed Presbyterian Church of Ireland	1	26	36	4,734	12,500
5. Eastern Reformed Presbyterian Church of Ireland	1		8		
6. Secession Church of Ireland	1	9	11	1,750	4,500
7. Presbyterian Church of Scotland	16	1480	1442	515,786	1,930,000
8. Free Church of Scotland	16	1091	1635	315,000	800,000
9. United Presbyterian Church of Scotland	1	600	557	176,299	500,000
10. Reformed Presbyterian Church of Scotland	1	7	9	1,120	2,844
11. United Original Secession Church of Scotland	1	32	39	5,500	15,000
12. Calvinistic Church in Wales	2	616	819	122,107	275,370
13. Presbyterian Church in the United States of America.	23	5218	5878	600,695	*1,802,085
14. Presbyterian Church in the United States (South)	13	1070	2040	127,017	*381,051
15. United Presbyterian Church of North America	9	730	644	85,443	*256,329
16. Associate Church of North America.					
17. Associate Reformed Church of the South	1	79	72	6,648	
18. Reformed Presbyterian Church in North America	1	37	48	6,700	7,500
19. Reformed Presbyterian Church of the U. S. or N. A.	1	112	124	10,625	
20. Welsh Presbyterian Church in the United States	6	84	175	9,563	
21. Reformed Presbyterian Presbytery of Philadelphia.					
22. Cumberland Presbyterian Church in America	27	1439	2591	130,000	650,000
23. Presbytery of Ceylon, Island of Ceylon		6	9	645	3,325
24. Presbyterian Church of East Australia, N. S. W.	1	12	11	273	3,150
25. Presbyterian Church of New South Wales	1	89	89	4,816	20,000
26. Presbyterian Church of Queensland	1	21	33	*10,000	25,000
27. Presbytery of South Australia		12	32	1,515	4,000
28. Presbyterian Church of Victoria	1	164	283	17,000	87,000
29. Presbytery of West Australia.					
30. Presbyterian Church of Tasmania		11			
31. Free Church of Tasmania.					
32. Presbyterian Church of New Zealand	1	70	162	15,000	30,000
33. Presbyterian Church of Otago and Southland	1	53	106	8,667	26,250
34. Presbyterian Church in Canada	4	693	1493	119,608	500,000
35. Presbyterian Church in Canada (Scotch)	1	15	24		
36. Church of Scotland in Nova Scotia, etc		12	12		
37. Presbyterian Church of Jamaica	1	31	31	8,405	

* Estimated.

SUMMARY.

	Synods.	Ministers.	Congregations.	Communicants.	Adherents.
Reformed Churches. . . .	53	5,726	6,233	7,031,310	10,405,025
Presbyterian Churches . .	139	14,726	18,667	2,333,658	7,905,904
Total of Reformed Churches holding the Presbyterian system.	192	20,452	24,900	9,364,968	18,310,929

These statistics are very incomplete. We have no reports from isolated congregations in non-Protestant countries, nor from the missionary stations in heathen lands, which now number many thousand adherents. The reports of some organizations are incomplete or entirely wanting, and we have not even an estimate of the number of ministers and congregations of the Reformed churches of France and of the established churches of Germany and Switzerland. The numbers given in the above summary are therefore far too small. In America it is almost impossible to form an accurate estimate of the number of adherents of the several churches, which should include not only children but all non-communicants, but in the case of the principal Reformed and Presbyterian churches, the column has been filled out with a number which is three times that of the reported communicants, and which is probably too low. In instances where the estimate was furnished by the authorities of the several churches, it has been allowed to stand unchanged.

PARTIAL ROLL OF THE REFORMED CHURCHES OF GERMANY.[1]

1. *Old Reformed Church of East Friesland and Bentheim.*
2. *United Reformed Church in the Province of Hanover.*—113 congregations with more than 50,000 adherents.
3. *Confederation of the Reformed Churches of Lower Saxony.*—Independent of the State. 7 congregations with 2,000 communicants.
4. *The Reformed Church of Bremen.*—Four large congregations in the city of Bremen, with several others in Bremerhaven, etc. Has 50,000 adherents.
5. *The Reformed Church of Lippe-Detmold.*—Has 50 congregations, 54 ministers, and 200,000 adherents.
6. *The Reformed Church of Lower Hesse.*—Has more than 200 congregations.
7. *The Reformed Church in Westphalia.*—Has 70 congregations with 150,000 adherents.

---

[1] Abridged from the Roll appended to the Minutes of the "Reformed Alliance."

8. *The Reformed Synod of Wesel.*—Four congregations of Dutch and French origin.

9. *The Reformed Church in the Rhine Provinces.*—Has 150 congregations with 500,000 adherents. These congregations, as well as those in Westphalia and Prussia, are in the Union, but have not been absorbed by it, and retain their Reformed Catechism, discipline, and order.

10. *The Reformed Church Confederation in the Province of Saxony.*—Has 10 congregations and 12 ministers.

11. *Reformed Church in Pomerania.*—Has 7 congregations with 7 ministers.

12. *The Reformed Churches in the Province of Silesia.*—Nine congregations with 11 ministers.

13. *The Free Reformed Churches of Silesia.*

14. *The Reformed Church in the Province of Prussia.*—Has 11 congregations and 11 ministers.

15. *The Reformed Church of the Province of Brandenburg.*—Has more than 20 congregations, among them the cathedral of Berlin, in which the emperor and his family worship.

16. *The Reformed Church of the French Colony in Brandenburg.*—Twelve congregations.

17. *The Reformed Churches of the Province of Posen.*—Five congregations and six ministers.

18. *The Reformed Churches of East Bavaria.*—Partly of French origin. Seven congregations and seven ministers.

19. *Two French Congregations in Hesse-Homburg, at Friedrichshof and East Homburg.*

20. *Single Congregations*, without any relation to other Reformed churches: the Reformed churches at Altona, at Hamburg (a German and a French one), at Accam in Oldenburg, at Frankfort-on-the-Main (a German and a French one), at Leipsic, at Dresden, at Hanau (a Dutch and a French one), at Elberfeld (Dutch), at Bützkow in Mecklenburg, at Stuttgart, and at Osnabruck.

21. *The Reformed Churches of Heidelberg and vicinity.*

22. *The Reformed Churches of the Bavarian Palatinate.*—Consisting of four-fifths of the Protestant churches of this territory.

23. *The Reformed Churches in Nassau.*

24. *The Reformed Churches in the Grand Duchy of Hesse-Darmstadt.*

25. *The Reformed Churches in the Duchy of Anhalt.*

26. *The Reformed Churches in the Grand Duchy of Saxe-Weimar.*

[The churches numbered 21 to 26 have been united with the Lutherans in one organization, and have thus been absorbed.]

COMPARATIVE SUMMARY OF THE REFORMED CHURCH IN THE UNITED STATES.

BEING A TRIENNIAL EXHIBIT FOR THE LAST TWENTY-ONE YEARS.

	1866	1869	1872	1875	1878	1881	1884	1887
Synods,	2	3	4	6	6	6	7	7
Classes,	29	31	35	44	45	48	52	54
Ministers,	485	526	586	631	710	762	783	802
Congregations,	1,144	1,179	1,312	1,342	1,369	1,403	1,465	1,481
Members,	109,925	117,910	130,299	142,872	147,788	161,002	169,530	183,980
Members Unconfirmed,	69,765	68,362	73,288	87,120	90,993	96,147	103,112	108,729
Baptisms, given year,	11,175	12,776	12,487	13,500	13,203	14,309	13,682	15,940
Baptisms, in 3 years,	33,638	36,117	38,605	41,272	40,943	43,750	41,825	46,553
Confirmed, given year,	6,845	7,068	7,462	8,766	8,456	9,113	9,233	10,733
Confirmed, in 3 years,	16,756	20,183	23,247	25,233	26,753	28,240	27,223	30,558
Certificate, given year,	2,421	3,592	3,369	3,733	3,716	4,113	5,043	5,582
Certificate, in 3 years,	6,205	8,779	9,889	10,912	11,184	12,263	14,046	16,472
Communed,	91,547	96,728	109,507	116,000	120,681	132,709	136,897	146,436
Dismissed, given year,	1,244	1,637	1,454	1,725	1,566	2,249	2,122	2,551
Dismissed, in 3 years,	2,975	4,459	4,762	5,000	5,185	5,791	5,819	7,250
Excommunicated or Erased, given year,	196	144	318	387	174	1,626	1,767	2,419
Excommunicated or Erased, in 3 years,	500	528	722	920	1,711	4,436	5,578	6,469
Deaths, given year,	4,207	3,773	4,425	4,494	4,887	4,591	4,787	4,638
Deaths, in 3 years,	13,486	11,186	12,594	12,000	14,102	14,492	15,292	14,207
Sunday-Schools,	939	1,020	1,021	1,220	1,237	1,346	1,378	1,422
Sunday-School Scholars,	34,000	49,000	63,038	75,868	89,982	103,511	114,720	122,695
Students for Ministry,			75	123	157	141	145	185
Beneficial Contributions, given year,	$60,977	$74,453	$86,650	$79,680	$61,727	$73,400	$101,148	$141,122
Beneficial Contributions, in 3 years,	202,718	228,818	247,387	253,766	207,417	194,869	327,899	382,493
Congregational Purposes, given year,				310,000	531,929	630,189	779,572	804,321
Congregational Purposes, in 3 years,				700,000	1,305,905	1,738,213	2,193,018	2,298,228

INDEX.

	PAGE		PAGE
Agricola	86	Bohemia	103
Alliance of Ref. Churches	375	Bomberger, Dr. J. H. A.	307, 364
Alva, Duke of	89	Bourbon, Charlotte de	120
Amwell	210	Brandenburg	70
Amyraldists	134	Brandenburg, Louise of	123, 142
Amyrault	161	Brandmiller, Rev. John	194
Anabaptists	22, 31, 34	Bregell	76
Anglican church	97	Bremen	69
Angrogna	75	Briconnet	36
Anhalt	70	Brill	91
Antes, Henry	190	Bucer	24, 52, 103
Antwerp	85	Bucher, Rev. J. Conrad	213, 231
Appel, Dr. Theodore	364	Buettner, Rev. J. G.	303
Apple, Dr. T. G.	296, 306, 364	Bullinger. 24, 27, 30, 34, 58, 99, 102,	
Arminius	130		130, 349
Arminian Controversy	37, 131	Burmann	133
Asbury, Rev. Francis	218		
Aughinbaugh, Dr. G. W.	307, 308	Calvin, John. 36, 47, 63, 87, 106, 129,	
Augsburg	66		347, 349
Augsburg Confession	52, 62, 64	Calvin College	309, 326
		California	319
Baden	70	Capito	17, 24
Bausman, Dr. B.	334, 335, 364	Cappei	23
Bartholomew, St.	80	Carranza	77
Bechtel, Rev. John	194	Cartesians	134
Becker, Dr. J. C.	277, 279, 287	Catawba College	307
Beecher, Rev. J. C.	283	Catechisms, American	256
Beggars, The	90	Catharine Belgica	121
Beissel, Conrad	181	Centennial	290
Belgic Confession	87	Chambersburg, Burning of.	338
Beneficiary Education	30, 329	Charity Schools	201
Bentheim, Gertrude von	122	Charles V.	74, 84, 88
Berleburg Bible	180	Charlotte de Bourbon	120
Berne, Synod of	29	"Christian World."	335
Bethman-Hollweg	295	Christman, Rev. Jacob	297
Beza, Theodore	45	Church under the Cross.	86
Bible, Swiss Translation	25	Cincinnati Society	233
Bisrampore	328	Clapp, Dr. J. C	307
Blaarer, Ambrosius	29	Classes, The	267, 353
Boehm, Rev. J. P.	161, 166, 194	Coccejus	133
Boehme, Jacob	178	Coetus	199, 243, 250
Boehringer, Rev. E.	343	Coligni	80
Boers, The	154	Comingoe, Rev. B. R.	208
Bogardus	157	Conflict of Languages	258

(431)

INDEX.

	PAGE
"Congregation of God."	188
Confirmation	348
Constitution	352
Correspondence	260
Cranmer	45, 99
Crevecoeur	243
Crypto-Calvinists	53
Cultus	354
D'Albret, Jeanne	119
De Bures, Idelette	118
Decline	205
Dechant, Rev. J. W	298
DeLasky, John	87, 102
De Witt, Dr. T	364
Dickinson College	280
Discipline	346
Doctrine	346
Dordrecht	105, 124, 131
Dorstius, Rev. P. H	173
Dubbs, Dr. J. S	276
Dunkers, The	177
Dutch Reformed Church,	87, 157, 251, 260, 369
Ebrard, Dr	364
Edict of Nantes	83
Edward VI	100
Einsiedlen	18
Elizabeth of England	70, 101
England	97
Ephrata	175
Erasmus	17, 86
Erastus	50
Esch, John	85
Evangelical Church	152
Fagius	105
Falkener Swamp	166
Farel, Wm.	36, 40, 42
Federalists	133
Female Education	310
Fisher, Dr. S. R.,	331, 332, 337, 352, 364
Foreign Missions	327
Flacius	53
Francis I., of France	79
Frederick I., of Prussia	125
Frederick II., of Prussia	70
Frederick William III., of Prussia	283
Frederick the Pious	49, 71

	PAGE
Franckenthal	4), 54
Franklin, Benjamin	241
Franklin College	241, 250
Franklin and Marshall College	305
Freeze, Rev. A. P.	303
Free Synod	272
Froschauer	25
Gansevoort	86
Gantenbein, Dr. J.	309
Gast, Dr. F. A.	296
Gebhard, Rev. J. G.	158, 209
Gehr, Dr. N.	335
General Synod	367
Geneva	11, 35, 79
Georgia	211, 235
Gerhart, Dr. E. V.	286, 295, 304, 306, 364
German Church in the West	321
German Ind. Synod	301
Gertrude von Bentheim	122
Goetschius, Rev. J. H.	304, 335
Gomarus	130
Good, Dr. J. H.	304, 335
Gordon, Gov.	164
Grey, Lady Jane	101
Gros, Dr. J. D.	209, 228, 240
Gruber, J. A.	190
Gualter, Rudolph	99
Guardian, The	335
Gueting, Rev. J. A.	221
Guldin, Dr. J. C.	335
Gustavus Adolphus	143
Hager, Rev. J. F.	162
Haller, Berthold	24
Hamilton, Patrick	108
Hanau	121
Harbaugh, Dr. H.	295, 362
Harbor Mission	320
"Hausfreund"	335
Heidelberg Catechism	54, 61, 72, 157, 347, 349, 365
Heidelberg, City	49, 148
Heidelberg College	306
Helffenstein, Rev. J. C. A.	232
Helffenstein, Dr. S.	236, 279, 314, 334
Helmuth, Dr.	240, 243, 265
Helvetic Confession	65
Hendel, Dr. W., *Senior*	213, 217, 252, 257

INDEX.

Hendel, Dr. W., *Junior* . 240, 298, 314
Henry IV, France 80
Henry VIII, England 97, 272
Hering, Archbishop 164
Herkimer, Gen. 226
Herman, Dr. F. L. . 233, 239, 259,
Herman V., Cologne 104
Herzog, Dr. . , ... 366
Hess, Rev. S. 256
Heshusius 53, 54, 62
Heusser, Meta 142
Higbee, Dr. E. E. 295
High School, York 284
Historical Society 366
Hochmann 180
Hoeger, Rev. Henry 163
Hoffeditz, Dr. F. L. . . . 291, 352
Holland Benefactions . . . 207, 251
Holland 84
Home Missions 315
Huguenots 70, 78
Hundeshagen, Dr. 364
Hooper, Bp. 100, 101
Hutchins, Rev. Jos. 245
Hymnologists 140
Hymn-books 256, 354
Ireland, Palatines in 151

Jackson, Maj. Wm. 233
Japan 329
Jesuits 77
Juda, Leo 16, 24, 26
Jung (Stilling), ... 141

Kern, Rev. J. M. 209, 234
Kieffer, Dr. M. . 304, 307, 337, 364
" Kirchenzeitung," 335
Klebitz 54
Klein, Dr J. H. 325
Knox, John 45, 106, 112
Krell, Dr. N. 45
Krummacher, F. A. 142
Krummacher, F. W. 290
Kunze, Dr. J. C. 240

Labadie, Jean de . . . 132, 136
Labadists 138
Lampe, F. A. 132, 142, 257
Larose, Rev. J. J. 297
Lasky, John de 87, 102

Leinbach, Rev. T. H. 275
Leyden, John of 33
Leyden, Siege of 93
Lippe 70
Lischy, Rev. J. 194
Literary Institutions 304
Liturgies 456
Livingston, Dr. J. H. 260
Lobwasser 141, 257
Lost Churches 207
Louis XIV 148
Loyalists 234
Loyala 77
Luther . . . 19, 26, 36, 51, 98, 348

Mack, Alexander 181
Maine 208
Maryland 214
Manheim, City 49, 148
Margaret of Navarre . . . 35, 38
Margaret of Parma 88
Mary of England 101
Mary of Scotland 110
Martyrs, The 73
Martyr Book 185
Martyr, Peter 88
Massacre of St. Bartholomew . 80
Mayer, Dr. Lewis .279, 281, 334, 358
Maximilian II 66
Medici, Catharine de 80
Marshall College 284
Melac 149
Melanchthon 51, 54
Melsheimer, Rev. F. V. . . . 247
Menken, G. 142
Mennonites 95, 165
Mercersburg College 308
Mercersburg Theology 293
" Messenger, The " 333
Michælius, Rev. Jonas 157
Miller, J. Peter 175
Miller, Rev. S. 334
Milledoler, Dr. P. . . 209, 240, 269
Minuit, Peter 158
Mission House 323
Missions, Home 315, 379
Missions, Foreign 327
M. Kieffer & Co. 337
Mohawk Valley 209
Montgomery, Gen. 232
Moravians 139, 262
Muhlenberg, Dr. H. E. 247

28

INDEX.

	PAGE		PAGE
Münster	33	Portugal	78
Münzer, Thomas	31	Presbyterian Church	114, 261
Myconius	15, 24	Printing Establishment	336
Mystics	139, 179	Provisional Liturgy	359
Muehlmeier, Dr. H. A.	321	Prussian Church Union	152
		Purrysbnrg	211
Nantes, Edict of	83		
Nassau	69	Rauch, Dr. F. A.	284
Navarre	119	Rauch, Rev. C. H.	194
Navarre, Henry of	80	Reformed Alliance	154
Netherlands	84, 91	Reformed Church	10, 11, 153
Nevin, Dr. J. W.	289, 306, 364	Reformed Church in America—	
New Berne	211	See " Dutch Ref. Church."	
New Jersey	210	Reformed Ch. Pub. Board	339
New York	158	Reformed Publishing Co.	335, 339
North Carolina	211, 307	Reformed Publishing House.	325, 339
Nova Scotia	208	Reformed Name	9
		Reichenbach, Prof.	247
Ochino	76, 105	Reiff, Jacob	169
Oecolampadius	24	Reily, Rev. J. R.	282, 315
Ohio, Synod of	297	Reinhard, Anna	116
Olevianus	55	Revolutionary War	225
Oley	191	Richelieu	83, 144
Oregon	319	Rieger, Rev. J. B.	172, 184, 200
Orange, Wm. of	92	Rochelle	79
" Order of Worship"	360	Ross, Prof. James	247
Organization	349	Ruetenik, Dr. H. J.	321
Orphan Homes	343	Rupert, Abbot	86
Otterbein, Rev. W.	201, 207, 214-224	Russell, Dr. G. B	334, 364
		Rush, Dr. B.	245
Palatinate	11, 48	Rust, Dr. H.	203
" Invasion	148		
Palatinate, Electors of—		Saint Bartholomew	80
Otto Heinrich	49	Samson, B.	19
Frederick III.	49, 54, 71	Saur, Christopher	203
Louis	60, 62, 72	Schaff, Dr. P.	291, 356, 362
John Casimir	60, 58, 72	Schinner, Cardinal	17
Palatinate Liturgy	357	Schlatter, Rev. M.	196, 207, 231
Palatines	150	Schlatter, Anna	142
Palatinate College	308	Schneck, Dr. B. S.,	291, 334, 337, 364
Pastorius, F. D.	165		
Patriotic Ministers	229	Schneider, Dr. B.	328
Parochial Schools	340	Scholastics	132
Peace Commission	360, 370	Schoharie	209
Penn, William	161	Schotel, Dr	364
Philadelphia	166	Schwenkfeld	32
Philipism	51	Schwenkfelders	328
Philip II.	77, 88	Schwarzenau	181
Pietists	139	Schwob, Rev. Benedict	216
Poland	103	Scotland	106
Pomp. Rev. N.	215, 252	Servetus	44
Porter, Dr. T. C.	364	Seymour, Jane	99

INDEX. 435

	PAGE		PAGE
Skippack Church.	166, 170	Virginia	210
Smith, Dr. William.	232	Vitringa	133
South America	319	Vœtius	132
South Carolina.	212	Voes, Henry	65
Spain.	77		
Spangenberg	191	Wack, Rev. C.	213, 259, 314
Spener	140	Wack, Rev. J. J.	209
Stapel, Rev. C. M	210	Waldenses	11, 74
Steiner, Rev. J. C	200, 206	Wallauer, Rev. G.	217
Steiner, Dr. L. H.	364, 366	Washington, Geo.	233
Stern, Dr. M	321	Weber, Rev. J. W.	239
Stilling.	141	Weikel, Rev. J. H.	230
Steuben.	226	Weinbrenner, Rev. J.	278
Switzerland	12	Weis, Rev. G. M.	161, 168
Swedes in America.	158	Wesel, John de	86
Sunday-schools.	342	Wesel, City of	79, 89
Synods.	253, 353	Wessel, John	86
"Synodalordnung".	252, 352	Western Theol. Seminary	303
		Westminster Confession.	113
Tercentenary	362	Westphal	53
Tersteegen	138, 141	Westphalia, Treaty	143
Theologians.	128	Weyberg, Dr. C. D	213, 230
Theological Seminary.	269, 296	Whitemarsh Church	165
Thirty Years' War	135, 143	Whitfield, Rev. G.	192
Title, Change of	368	Widows' Fund	313
Tremellius	105	William of Orange	92
Trent, Council of.	61	Williard, Dr. G. W.	72, 307
Triennial Convention	368	Witgenstein	179
Triglot Catechism	365	Winnebago Indians	329
Tri-Synodic Union.	319	Wolfians	134
Troldenier, Rev. Geo	239	Wolff, Dr. B. C.	295, 314, 364
Tulpehocken	176	Wolmar, Melchior	38
		Women of the Ref. Church	511
Ullmann, Dr. C	364	Wycliffe	98
Unionistic Tendencies	264	Wyttenbach	16
"United Brethren".	221		
"United Ministers"	219	Young, Rev. D.	16
Untereyck.	140		
Ursinus.	57	Zacharias, Dr. D.	334
Ursinus' Commentary	72	Zinzendorf	192
Ursinus College.	308	Zollikofer	141, 257
Ursinus Union	319	Zubly, Dr. J. J.	211, 235
		Zurich	22, 25
Van Lodenstein	138	Zurich Consensus	45, 53
Van Vleck, Rev. P.	165	Zwingli, Ulric	14-23, 63, 116
Viretus	47	Zwingli Festivals	375

www.ingramcontent.com/pod-product-compliance
Lightning Source LLC
Chambersburg PA
CBHW020534300426
44111CB00008B/662